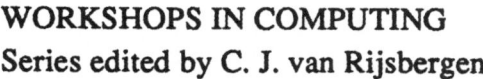

WORKSHOPS IN COMPUTING
Series edited by C. J. van Rijsbergen

Also in this series

Women into Computing: Selected Papers 1988–1990
Gillian Lovegrove and Barbara Segal (Eds.)

3rd Refinement Workshop (organised by BCS-FACS, and sponsored by IBM UK Laboratories, Hursley Park and the Programming Research Group, University of Oxford), Hursley Park, 9–11 January 1990
Carroll Morgan and J. C. P. Woodcock (Eds.)

Designing Correct Circuits, Workshop jointly organised by the Universities of Oxford and Glasgow, Oxford, 26–28 September 1990
Geraint Jones and Mary Sheeran (Eds.)

Functional Programming, Glasgow 1990, Proceedings of the 1990 Glasgow Workshop on Functional Programming, Ullapool, Scotland, 13–15 August 1990
Simon L. Peyton Jones, Graham Hutton and Carsten Kehler Holst (Eds.)

4th Refinement Workshop, Proceedings of the 4th Refinement Workshop, organised by BCS-FACS, Cambridge, 9–11 January 1991
Joseph M. Morris and Roger C. Shaw (Eds.)

AI and Cognitive Science '90, University of Ulster at Jordanstown, 20–21 September 1990
Michael F. McTear and Norman Creaney (Eds.)

Software Re-use, Utrecht 1989, Proceedings of the Software Re-use Workshop, Utrecht, The Netherlands, 23–24 November 1989
Liesbeth Dusink and Patrick Hall (Eds.)

Z User Workshop, 1990, Proceedings of the Fifth Annual Z User Meeting, Oxford, 17–18 December 1990
J.E. Nicholls (Ed.)

IV Higher Order Workshop, Banff 1990
Proceedings of the IV Higher Order Workshop, Banff, Alberta, Canada, 10–14 September 1990
Graham Birtwistle (Ed.)

ALPUK91 Proceedings of the 3rd UK Annual Conference on Logic Programming, Edinburgh, 10–12 April 1991
Geraint A.Wiggins, Chris Mellish and Tim Duncan (Eds.)

Specifications of Database Systems, 1st International Workshop on Specifications of Database Systems, Glasgow, 3–5 July 1991
David J. Harper and Moira C. Norrie (Eds.)

7th UK Computer and Telecommunications Performance Engineering Workshop, Edinburgh, 22–23 July 1991
J. Hillston, P.J.B. King and R.J. Pooley (Eds.)

Logic Program Synthesis and Transformation, Proceedings of LOPSTR 91, International Workshop on Logic Program Synthesis and Transformation, University of Manchester, 4–5 July 1991
T.P. Clement and K.-K. Lau (Eds.)

Building Interactive Systems: Architectures and Tools,
Philip Gray and Roger Took (Eds.)

continued on back page...

John Darlington and Roland Dietrich (Eds.)

Declarative Programming, Sasbachwalden 1991

PHOENIX Seminar and Workshop on Declarative Programming, Sasbachwalden, Black Forest, Germany, 18–22 November 1991

Springer-Verlag London Ltd.

John Darlington, BSc (Hons), PhD
Department of Computing
Imperial College of Science, Technology and Medicine
180 Queen's Gate
London SW7 2BZ, UK

Roland Dietrich, Dr. rer. nat.
GMD Forschungsstelle an der Universität Karlsruhe
Vincenz-Prießnitz-Straße 1
D-7500 Karlsruhe 1
Germany

ISBN 978-3-540-19735-5

British Library Cataloguing in Publication Data
Darlington, John, *1947–*
    Phoenix seminar and workshop on declarative programming
    I. Title   II. Dietrich, Roland, *1958–*
005.13
ISBN 978-3-540-19735-5   ISBN 978-1-4471-3794-8 (eBook)
DOI 10.1007/978-1-4471-3794-8
Library of Congress Data available

34/3830-543210 Printed on acid-free paper

Preface

Declarative programming languages have many advantages for software development due to their sound mathematical foundations. These advantages include powerful descriptive capabilities, the availability of program analysis techniques and formal manipulation and transformation rules, and the potential for parallel execution. Declarative programming paradigms which have been deeply investigated include logic, functional, equational, and constraint programming.

In November 1991, the ESPRIT Basic Research Action PHOENIX, in collaboration with the ESPRIT Basic Research Action Integration, organized a Seminar and Workshop on Declarative Programming at Sasbachwalden in the Black Forest, Germany. These Basic Research Actions have been investigating the foundations of Declarative Programming, exploring the integration of the various language paradigms and developing many aspects of this technology including implementation techniques, program analysis and transformation, parallelism and concurrency, and programming in the large.

The aim of this Seminar and Workshop has been to present state of the art results arising from the Basic Research Actions together with contributions from other research workers in this field. The programme consisted of invited talks from leading members of the Research Actions together with submitted and refereed papers. In order to enable information exchange and discussions within a wide scientific community, participation in the workshop was open to everybody interested in the field.

The submitted papers were reviewed and the program was assembled by a programme committee consisting of the following members of the Basic Research Actions:

John Darlington	(Imperial College London, co-chair)
Roland Dietrich	(GMD Karlsruhe, co-chair, local organiser)
Sophia Drossopoulou	(Imperial College London)
Stefan Jähnichen	(GMD Karlsruhe)
Kees Koster	(University of Nijmegen)
Erik Meijer	(University of Nijmegen)
Antonio Porto	(University of Lisbon)

We would like to acknowledge all those who contributed to the successful execution of the workshop, especially Mrs Christine Harms and the

German National Research Centre for Computer Science (GMD) for professional assistance in the organization. Part of the work reported in these proceedings has been supported by the EC under ESPRIT BRA 3147 (PHOENIX) and 3020 (Integration).

November 1991   John Darlington
                                                 Imperial College London

                                                      Roland Dietrich
                                                       GMD Karlsruhe

Contents

Languages and Semantics

A Design Space for Integrating Declarative Languages

John Darlington   Yike Guo   Helen Pull

Department of Computing

Imperial College

180 Queen's Gate London SW7 2BZ U.K.

August 12, 1991

Abstract

We present a survey of the Phoenix Design Space (PDS) and its applications. The PDS is a conceptual framework for studying declarative programming languages based on assertional programming as a uniform presentation of declarative language semantics, and a constraint abstract machine as a general computational model for declarative programming. The PDS provides a methodology for systematically integrating functional and logic programming languages. We present a simple classification of existing integrated functional and logic programming systems and show how the design space induces a powerful new programming paradigm, constraint functional logic programming, and provides insights into other aspects of declarative programming such as concurrency and program transformation.

1 INTRODUCTION

The **Phoenix Design Space (PDS)** was developed to provide a comprehensive framework for studying declarative languages and a useful design space for integrating different language paradigms. The structure of the PDS was motivated by our extensive classification of integrated functional and logic languages [9]. It takes a uniform view of declarative programming by using **assertional programming** as the presentation of declarative programming language semantics, by developing a **constraint abstract machine** as a general computational model for declarative programming and by taking **general constraint programming** as the methodology for integrating functional and logic languages.

Assertional programming is a uniform framework which characterises the common semantic features of declarative programming languages. Programming in a declarative language is viewed as simply making assertions. These assertions are axioms that the programmer believes to be true in a well-understood mathematical system which provides the underlying semantic logic of the language. Computation is viewed as satisfying the semantic properties of the program by using the program assertions as premises of a deductive inference system which is applied to a submitted problem (or goal). Declarative programming systems are identified, therefore, by the mathematical semantic foundations on which their programming assertions are based. For the computational model of the assertional programming world, we develop a very general scheme by extending the traditional "computation = deduction" approach to "deduction as constraint solving". We develop a general constraint abstract machine, to show how the idea of "computation as approximation" provides a model for studying the computational behaviours of declarative languages. The overall structure of the PDS is reviewed in section 2.

We show in section 3 that the PDS is not only a space for the analysis of various integrated declarative programming systems but also a space which provides significant insights for developing new ones. We survey a classification of existing integrated functional and logic programming languages using the PDS. The development of a new combined programming paradigm, constraint functional logic programming, is presented to show how the PDS has been used to explore new programming languages. In section 4 we discuss the potential of the PDS for investigating other aspects of declarative programming.

2   THE PHOENIX DESIGN SPACE

In this section, we review the PDS which provides a uniform perspective of declarative programming languages using Meseguer's presentation of *general logics* [25] (section 2.1) as a high level meta language to characterise the semantics of *assertional programming systems* (section 2.2). The fundamental concepts of the assertional programming formalism unify the model-theoretic semantic structure and proof-theoretic semantic structure of declarative programmming systems, permitting languages to be studied systematically by investigating their semantic models. We present a constraint abstract machine as the uniform PDS computational model in section 2.3. In section 2.4 we show Horn clause logic programming and functional programming as concrete representations of the PDS.

2.1   GENERAL LOGICS

The framework of general logics is a metalanguage used to define the semantics of assertional programming systems. The syntax of a logic is a set of *sentences*. The meaning of these sentences can be established either by the *satisfaction relation* between models and sentences or by the *entailment relation* between sentences. The former, model-theoretic approach, is similar to defining the declarative semantics of a logic programming system, where the model is given by an interpretation of the symbols in a program over a mathematical structure. The latter, proof-theoretic approach, asserts the provability of a sentence with respect to a set of sentences and is traditional in mathematical logic where entailment systems, such as the proof theories of Tarski and Hertz-Gentzen, provide an abstraction towards symbolic deduction. The two semantic systems are connected by the *soundness axiom*, which states that a sentence φ is entailed by a set of sentence Γ only when all models of Γ satisfy φ. We axiomatise our presentation of general logics below before discussing these concepts in detail.

Definition 2.1 *A logic is a tuple* $\mathcal{L} = (\Sigma, Sen(\Sigma), Mod, \vdash, \models)$ *such that:*

1. $(\Sigma, Sen(\Sigma), \vdash)$ *is an entailment system*

2. $(\Sigma, Sen(\Sigma), Mod, \models)$ *is an institution*

3. *If* $(\Sigma, Sen(\Sigma), \models^{\bullet})$ *is the entailment system associated with the institution, then the following soundness condition holds:*

$$\forall \Gamma \subset Sen(\Sigma).\Gamma \vdash \varphi \Longrightarrow \Gamma \models^{\bullet} \varphi$$

A logic is complete if

$$\forall \Gamma \subset Sen(\Sigma).\Gamma \vdash \varphi \Longleftarrow \Gamma \models^{\bullet} \varphi$$

Entailment Systems. Entailment systems originate from first order logic, in which a signature Σ consists of ranked alphabets of function and predicate symbols. Sentences are defined with respect to a signature. The entailment relation:

$$\Gamma \vdash \varphi$$

holds between a set of sentences Γ and a sentence φ when φ is derivable from Γ. The sentences Γ can be seen as *assumptions*, *premises* or *axioms*, and φ as the *conclusion*. The entailment relation $\vdash$ can be abstracted from any inference system. It plays a central role in the proof theoretic semantics of a logic system, since it is independent of any particular inference (or deduction) system. Therefore, we can define an entailment system as a triple $\mathcal{E} = (\Sigma, Sen(\Sigma), \vdash)$ where Σ is the signature, $Sen(\Sigma)$ is the set of all Σ-sentences and $\vdash$ is the entailment relation over $Sen(\Sigma)$. An entailment system satisfies the following properties:

Reflexivity: $\forall \phi \in Sen(\Sigma).\{\phi\} \vdash \phi$

Monotonicity: $\forall \Gamma, \Gamma' \subset Sen(\Sigma).$ If $\Gamma \vdash \phi$ and $\Gamma \subseteq \Gamma'$ then $\Gamma' \vdash \phi$

Transitivity: $\forall \Gamma \subset Sen(\Sigma).$ If $\Gamma \vdash \phi$ and $\Gamma \cup \{\phi\} \vdash \varphi$ then $\Gamma \vdash \varphi$

The entailment relation should be "stable under translation", i.e. provability should be independent of representation. As we will see, these ideas extend to higher order logics where the traditional set-theoretic structure is no long adequate.

Model Classes. Given a signature Σ, a finite set of Σ-sentences, Γ, forms the axioms of a *theory* consisting of all its conclusions (or consequences). Therefore, a theory can be represented as a pair $T = (\Sigma, \Gamma^*)$ where Γ^* is the closure of Γ under the entailment relation. Γ itself is a finite presentation of the theory. Consider first order logic again; given a signature Σ, we can associate with it a class of Σ-models. A Σ-model consists of a domain together with a Σ-interpretation of each n-ary function symbol as an n-ary function and each n-ary predicate symbol as an n-ary relation. The satisfaction relation of a Σ-model M and a Σ-sentence φ is denoted as $M \models \varphi$. As with entailment systems, the model-theoretic semantics of a logic should be independent of its representation, expressed as the *satisfaction condition axiom.* Goguen and Burstall established the theory of institutions in [14] as a categorical treatment of the the model class of a logic which satisfies this axiom. Informally, we can define an institution as a quadruple $\mathcal{I} = (\Sigma, Sen(\Sigma), Mod, \models)$ where Mod stands for the model class and $\models$ is the satisfaction relation between models and Σ-sentences such that the satisfaction condition axiom always holds. The logics which underlie declarative programming systems such as first order logic, equational logic, order sorted logic and typed λ-calculus are all institutions. Given a set of Σ-sentences Γ, in an institution, we denote as $Mod(\Sigma, \Gamma)$ the subclass of Mod satisfying all the sentences in Γ, i.e. the set of M such that $M \models \varphi$ for each $\varphi \in \Gamma$. We can show that the relation $\models^*$ between sets of sentences and sentences which is defined as

$$\Gamma \models^* \varphi \Longleftrightarrow M \models \varphi \qquad \forall M \in Mod(\Sigma, \Gamma)$$

is an entailment relation. Therefore, any institution $\mathcal{I} = (\Sigma, \Gamma, Mod, \models)$ yields an entailment system $\mathcal{I}^* = (\Sigma, Sen(\Sigma), \models^*)$. Since this entailment system is defined by all conceivable models of Γ, it is obviously impossible to find a deduction system to generate it. However, in any complete logic such as first order logic, completeness ensures that this model-theoretic entailment relation coincides with the proof-theoretic entailment system defined above. Thus, it can be generated from a variety of deduction calculi. Therefore, in a complete logic, we can always use the model-theoretic entailment relation $\models^*$ to define logical consequence.

2.2 Assertional Programming

Given a logic $\mathcal{L}$, a program Γ in an $\mathcal{L}$-assertional programming system is a set of sentences. There exists a semantic model M_Γ which gives the intended meaning of the program. A special class of $\mathcal{L}$-sentences called goals is used to ask if certain properties hold in M_Γ. Therefore, computation in assertional programming is an attempt to justify the satisfaction relation between the intended model M_Γ and a goal φ. Computation is performed by a *deduction calculus* over Γ. If φ is a deducible consequence of Γ, then deduction will return a set of answers to justify the satisfaction of φ in M_Γ. Each answer corresponds to a particular computation path of φ. If φ is not deducible from Γ then the computation will either stop to report "failure" or run forever.

We axiomatise our definition of the assertional programming framework as follows.

Definition 2.2 *An assertional programming system $\mathcal{AP}$ is a tuple $(\mathcal{L}, \mathcal{P}, \mathcal{Q})$:*

1. *$\mathcal{L} = (\Sigma, Sen(\Sigma), Mod, \vdash, \models)$ is a logic .*

2. *$\mathcal{P} \subset Sen(\Sigma)$ is the set of assertions which represent programs in $\mathcal{AP}$*

3. *$\mathcal{Q}$ is the set of assertions which represent goals in $\mathcal{AP}$*

where for any assertional program, $(\Gamma \subset \mathcal{P}, \varphi \subset \mathcal{Q})$ in $\mathcal{AP}$, there is an associated intended model, $M_\Gamma \in Mod$, and the following property holds:

Completeness Condition:
$$\Gamma \vdash \varphi \Longleftrightarrow M_\Gamma \models \varphi$$

The distinguishing feature of the assertional programming framework is that the semantics of a declarative program is characterised by its intended model. Surprisingly, although it emphasises only the intended model, the assertional programming approach is a broader notion than logic programming in which the intended model is a proof-theoretic structure. The purpose of emphasising the intended model is to ensure that assertional programming is powerful enough to model higher order functional programming and constraint programming which are all based on well-understood mathematical domains. Functional programming systems may be expressed in the assertional programming framework using categorical logic [25]. This presentation regards a functional program as a higher order equational theory. Such a theory has an associated free category generated by the program as its "abstract theory". The initial element of this category is the intended model. Since the model is generated following the rules of the logic, the reduction calculus which is the operational model of the logic becomes the realisation of the intended model. Therefore, its completeness condition can easily be verified for goals of the form: $\exists x.e = x$ where e is a ground expression.

2.3 COMPUTATION IN THE PHOENIX DESIGN SPACE

The task of programming is simply constructing objects. For example, functional programming constructs values of expressions; logic programming constructs logical theories.

Essential to declarative programming is the fact that a programmer should never be concerned with the way in which an object is actually constructed in the machine; rather programming is the formal specification of the object to be computed. The specification must be computable, i.e. it must be possible for a machine to use it to construct the desired object. Computation may be viewed as an approximation procedure, therefore a programmer using declarative languages should not have in mind an instructable CPU and memory pair, but an engine for approximation. To have a better understanding of the computational behaviour of declarative programs, a precise description of this conceptual computational engine is necessary.

In the PDS, such a computing system is modelled by a **constraint abstract machine** (**CAM**) which consists of a set of *agents* P and a global store M. The information stored in M is a set of constraints. At any stage of a computation only partial information about the object to be computed may be available. That is, constraints provide a finite representation of a possibly infinite set of valuations. An agent behaves as a computing station which communicates with the store by either adding constraints to the store (i.e. write or tell constraints), probing the information in the store (i.e. read or ask constraints) or decomposing itself into a set of new agents running in parallel.

Computation proceeds by imposing new constraints onto the store to refine the object being computed. Imposing constraints does not change the value of a variable but rules out certain values that were possible previously. It is essential that this approximation procedure is monotonic. This monotonic refinement can be modelled by a transition function f which transforms each constraint in the store to the next stage of computation. When the computation starts with the store c, the refinment will go through the sequence:
$$c, fc, f(f(c)), \ldots, f^n c, f^{n+1} c, \ldots,$$

If at any stage, further applications of f leave the current store unchanged the computation quiesces having upgraded the store to its refined configuration. All such stable stores in the CAM are the fixed points of the function f. To specify the approximation precisely, we impose a partial order over stores which shows how close two stores are to stability, i.e. $c_1 \leq c_2$ means c_2 contains more information than c_1 (c_2 is closer to stability than c_1). This ordering is defined by a compact entailment relation over constraints (since we can only deal with finite sets of constraints during computing). So stores can be arranged as an algebraic lattice where the elements are sets of constraints closed under the entailment relation and the partial ordering is set inclusion. Over this lattice, all transition functions modelling the operations of agents should be closure operators, that is, functions which are increasing ($\forall x, x \leq fx$), i.e. computation can refine the store by adding more information to it; monotonic ($\forall x, y \, x \leq y \iff fx \leq fy$), i.e. the more information in the store the closer the approximation to the result; and idempotent $(f(fx) = fx)$, i.e. all observable components of the store are dealt with. Moreover, to deal with an infinite approximation procedure, the transition function is required to be continuous.

Thus, the CAM provides a uniform view of the computational model of declarative programming languages which permits the data space of any declarative programming system to be organised as a constraint system. This **general constraint programming** view of declarative programming is the computational counterpart of the semantic-orientated assertional programming framework.

2.4 Programming Languages in the Phoenix Design Space

To provide concrete instantiations of the PDS we discuss Horn logic programming and functional programming in this framework. This reveals the fundamental differences between these two paradigms and lays the groundwork for their integration.

Logic Programming. Given a logic $\mathcal{L}$, a logic programming system can be based on proof systems of $\mathcal{L}$. A logic program Γ of an $\mathcal{L}$-logic programming system is a finite set of sentences of $\mathcal{L}$ which form the axioms of a $\mathcal{L}$-theory. A special class of $\mathcal{L}$-sentences called *queries* are used for asking questions about a program. Computation is performed by a deduction calculus to establish if the query is a logical consequence of the program theory. This view of logic programming regards a logic programming system as a theorem prover. Actually, this is not enough. As specified in the assertional programming framework, an additional requirement is imposed on logic programming languages: every program should be interpreted as its intended model. To be consistent with the theorem proving approach, the intended model should possess initiality which can be characterized by the property that only what is provable is true, and everything else is false. Initiality of the intended model of a logic program provides a foundation for the database, i.e. "closed world", semantics of the program. Therefore, when a program Γ is loaded, we can imagine that the program itself is responsible for approximating this "closed world". Queries then become constraints which add more information to the closed world to approximate the results. Whenever a query is imposed on the store, the set of valuations describing the resultant store is the intersection of the set of valuations describing the "closed world" and those describing the query constraints. In the case of pure Horn clause logic programming , the "closed world" of a program is defined as its least Herbrand model. Moreover, as we will present in section 3.2, this "closed world" can generally be modelled by a constraint system as in constraint logic programming.

Functional Programming. From the assertional programming point of view, a functional program can be regarded as a higher order equational theory. To verify the goal $\exists x.e = x$, the ground expression e is evaluated to its canonical form. That is, the goal is proved constructively by computing the value of e. It is essential for functional programming that functions are basic data objects. The appoximation view of computing functional objects is central to the theory of computable functions. For example, Scott's information system [35] provides an explicit way to define the procedure to approximate computable functions. However, it is not natural to perform this approximation procedure in terms of intersecting constraints, as in the constraint-based computation model of the CAM. The reduction model of functional languages computes the value of expressions directly by unfolding rules defining functions. It is well known that this procedure is typically an approximation procedure and can also be modelled by closure operators [36]. With respect to the CAM model, functional computation is somehow orthogonal to logic computation in the sense that it never writes any constraints to the store to enrich its information; rather it maps a store to a more informative form. This observation motivates a very interesting approach to integrating functional and logic languages in terms of constraints (section 3.2).

3 LANGUAGE INTEGRATION IN THE PHOENIX DESIGN SPACE

In this section, we illustrate the systematic integration of functional and logic programming systems to form more powerful declarative programming systems using concepts from the PDS. Following the discussion of the PDS, it seems that two methodologies are possible: integrating semantic logics or integrating constraint computational models.

3.1 INTEGRATING LOGICS

This approach integrating language paradigms by integrating their semantic logics, i.e. integrating the entailment systems and the institutions of the component logics. The integrated logic forms a new logic which is taken as the semantic base for the resulting integrated system [25]. Two logics may be integrated by constructing a new logic which subsumes them, or by mapping one logic to the other.

For example, many existing systems which integrate Prolog-like logic programming with functional languages are based on the combination of Horn clause logic with equational logic taking equational logic as the semantic logic for (first order) functional programming. This gives Horn clause logic with equality as the semantic foundation of the new languages. We call this the $H + E$ paradigm, in which languages have a similar syntax to Horn clause programming except that atomic formulas may contain equality predicates. As proposed by J. Goguen and J. Meseguer [17], the mathematical semantics of a $H + E$ program P is given by its initial model. Suppose the signature of the system is $\Sigma = (F, \Pi)$ where F, Π contain ranked function and predicate symbols respectively. The initial model has a functional part consisting of the quotient algebra $T_F/\equiv_E$ where the congruence relation $\equiv$ over ground terms T_F is defined by the entailment relation of the underlying logic system. That is,

$$t \equiv t' \Longleftrightarrow P \vdash t = t'$$

The relational part of the model which assigns denotations to every predicate in P is defined by:

$$([t_1], \ldots, [t_n]) \in [\![p]\!] \Longleftrightarrow P \vdash p(t_1, \ldots, t_n)$$

where $[t_1]$ denotes the congruence class of t_1.

This initial model is an "intended" E-model with respect to J. Robinson's E- interpretation for clausal logic with equality [30] by partitioning the Herbrand space by the congruence relation defined by all ground equations logically implied by the program. We classify $H + E$ languages into three further categories:

$H \oplus E$: where E is integrated into Horn clause logic by a separated consistent equational theory. That is, the equational theory is defined without involving any predicates other than equality. Therefore, the quotient $T_F/\equiv_E$ is independent of any Horn clause program, and E is always intended to specify a certain predetermined algebra on which a Horn clause program is superimposed. This semantics has been studied by Jaffar et. al. [19] as a *Logic Programming Scheme*. Each $H \oplus E$ language is an instance of the scheme by supplying equational theories for the scheme's parameter.

$E \subseteq H$ where equality is "included" in the Horn clause logic by treating it as a normal predicate axiomatised by a set of clauses [11] EQ. Therefore, equations and non-equational atoms have the same status syntactically. The semantics of a program is given in terms of traditional Herbrand interpretations. Therefore, for a program P in the framework, the semantic equivalence between the $E-$model of P and the Herbrand model of $P \cup EQ$ must be established. In [11], van Emden and Yukawa proved the bijective mapping between the $E-$interpretation and that subset of the Herbrand base of P which forms a congruence closure. This result establishs the correctness of transforming equational logic to the Horn clauses EQ.

$H \subseteq E'$ where equational logic is used as the unique foundation for integrating the two logics. Horn clause logic is simulated by transforming it into its equational form. Predicates are defined by boolean valued functions, hence Horn clauses and atoms are transformed to conditional rewrite rules and equations respectively [12]. The declarative semantics of these equational programs can be given following traditional equational logic, e.g. [29] and [21].

A further, novel approach combines functional and logic programming following this logic oriented approach by taking a computable higher order logic as the uniform semantic base for integration. Since λ-calculus is a common language to functional programming, and higher order unification in typed λ-calculus is semi-decidable, this brave approach seems to be computationally feasable. Nadathur's and Miller's λ-Prolog system [24] pioneered this direction.

3.2 INTEGRATING CONSTRAINT SYSTEMS

Under this approach all integrated systems are constraint programming systems which combine the computational behaviours in the CAM of the component paradigms. The result should be a constraint programming system where functions, relations and constraints are integrated as a uniform approximation procedure. There are three schools following this approach: constraint logic programming, which is discussed in section 3.2, constraint functional programming which is covered in section 3.2, and the new paradigm of constraint functional logic programming, section 3.3, which subsumes both of these paradigms.

Constraint Logic Programming (CLP). As presented in section 2.4, Horn clause logic programming is a simple constraint programming system with the Herbrand term space as its underlying constraint system. A program defines relations as closure operators that upgrade stores. Computation progresses by imposing more and more constraints onto the store to approximate the answers to a query, which is itself regarded naturally as a set of constraints. This constraint semantics of deduction still works if the underlying constraint system is replaced by a more sophisticated one since the closure operators are independent of the underlying constraint system. This is the idea of constraint logic programming.

CLP languages perform logic programming over some intended constraint systems and have a similar syntax to Horn clause languages except that constraints are allowed as atomic formulas. (A general denotational semantics of these languages is presented in [18].) That is, the data space of logic programming is extended to various distinguished data structures instead of only the monoform of finite trees. When the underlying constraint system possesses some built-in operators (such as arithmetic and logical functions), some functional computation is introduced.

From our general treatment of constraint programming we see that the constraint approach to language integration subsumes CLP. For example, for any $H \oplus E$ language, the E part of a program can be regarded as a constraint system which consists of all congruence classes of the Herbrand terms defined by the equational theory. The H part is a CLP program taking equality of terms modulo E as basic constraints. Alternatively, constraints in CLP can be regarded as a statement of the intended model of the program theory. Goguen takes this view when introducing constraints into the theory of institutions [14]. Goguen and Meseguer presented the semantics of CLP languages following this approach in [26] which regards a CLP language as an assertional programming system.

Constraint Functional Programming (CFP). Constraint functional programming enhances the expressive power of functional programming languages by adding constraint programming facilities to functional languages via the capability to solve equations over expressions. We consider two approaches.

The first one concerns work on "functional programming with logic variables" which we identify as "functions as passive constraints". The variables in CAM are logical variables. A logical variable enables the incremental construction of data structures by the intersection of constraints. In a functional language this feature can be introduced by adding logic variables as "place holders". A functional language augmented in this way maintains its reduction model; there is no multiple use of function definitions. If an expression whose logic variables are not sufficiently instantiated to continue reduction, e.g. the information in the current store about a variable is not enough to match a definition of the function in question, the expression is left untouched until the variable becomes sufficiently instantiated by other computation. This approach of introducing logical variables is quite consistent the CAM model. It is easy to show that a first order sublanguage in this framework is a constraint language where functions are closure operators. Moreover, a higher order langauge is also a constraint language system where functions are modelled extensionally as graphs of closure operators [33]. Many languages have been proposed which introduce logical variables into functional langauges in this way. Among them, Arind proposed the I-structure to support updatable arrays [2], Lindstrom designed the FGL+LV system in which logic variables are first class citizens in a lazy functional language [22], and Ait-Kaci proposed the language Le Fun as one dimension of his language trinity LIFE in which logic variables act as a communication channels between alternative dimensions. All these languages can be modelled systematically in the CAM by regarding functions as passive constraints.

The second class represents a more radical approach following the work of *absolute set abstraction* by Darlington et. al. [4] which we characterise as "functions as active constraints". In this approach a solving capability is superimposed on top of a functional language and functional programs can be used both to evaluate expressions and to solve constraints. Solving constraints is computing an environment in which the query constraint evaluates to true. Various language constructions, such as the **absolute set abstraction** have been proposed to collect the solutions of constraint solving. Languages which take this approach are also called functional logic languages by Reddy [31] which means "functional syntax, logical semantics". A constraint solver for a general functional logic system is presented in [5] by generalising the narrowing based equation solver to incorporate general constraints. With in this framework, there is no way to define anything via constraints; constraints appear only as computation goals. The importance of this approach is that by exploring the constraint solving ability of functional programs, we reveal how constraints form the interface of the two paradigms of CLP and CFP to form *constraint functional logic programming* as the complete integration of functional and logic languages.

3.3 DEVELOPING CONSTRAINT FUNCTIONAL LOGIC PROGRAMMING

In section 3.1 we discussed how Horn clause logic with equality may be used as the semantic logic for integrated logic and functional programming systems. In these $H \oplus E$ languages, (first order) functional programming is mapped onto purely symbolic logic. Then, in section 3.2 the CLP paradigm was disscussed, which permits logic programming over distinguished data domains. We saw that $H \oplus E$ languages are specific CLP languages in which the equational theory is represented as a constraint system. This motivates us to integrate functional and logic programming using the CLP framework, by taking the functional component of the integrated system as the underlying constraint system of a CLP language in place of equational logic. Moreover, constraint programming over a functional language has been well studied, as reviewed in section 3.2. This route is attractive because the functional component of the integrated languages need not be interpreted as some other logic, but may take its standard denotational semantics. We have called this language paradigm **constraint functional logic programming (CFLP)**.

The development of CFLP is discussed in [5]. With a purely functional language subsystem, CFLP inherits the desirable features of functional programming, including lazy evaluation and the efficiency of functional computation. The paradigm represents a generalisation of the constraint system of CLP to admit user-defined functions, and a generalisation of CFP to admit user-defined constraints (i.e. relations). The distinguishing features of CFLP languages are the ability to use constraints over expressions in a functional language when defining relations, and the ability to pass functions as arguments to relations.

We claim that CFLP represents a smooth and cohesive integration of constraint, logic and functional programming. Moreover, it provides an integrated functional and logic system in which functional programming is totally uncorrupted. This new and powerful framework is a direct result of our systematic and rigorous analysis of declarative programming languages as formalised by the PDS.

4 FUTURE RESEARCH

Further research will be devoted to consolidating the space in a uniform and general way. Also, we would like to use the PDS to study new declarative programming systems and the theory of program development. Current research includes work on concurrent programming, object orientated programming and program transformation.

In keeping with the PDS, two formalisms for concurrent programming are being considered. On the assertional programming side we are interested in two recently developed logics, Girard's **linear logic** [13] and Meseguer's **rewrite logic**[27] which have the capacity to specify concurrent activities naturally. Both have been axiomatised within the general logics framework. We are studying and comparing these logics with reference to the PDS. Within the constraint programming framework there are similarities between the CAM and many concurrent computational models based on shard memory. The distinguishing feature of the CAM is that it exhibits clearly the natural link between approximational computation and concurrency. When there are more than one agents running in parallel a concurrent language may be used to specify the behaviours of the closure functions which represent the agents. Many concurrent systems such as UNITY [3] and the concurrent constraint programming system of [34] follow this line. We are currently investigating concurrent computation in terms of the CAM model and the relationship between the model and other similar models for concurrency such as Hoare's conjunction model [6].

The introduction of object oriented programming facilities in to declarative programming is a recent subject of research. For example, McCabe has incorporated object oriented programming into Horn clause logic programming [23]. Objects are defined by a logical theory and the relations defined by the axiom rules of the theory are the means to manipulate objects. Deduction corresponds to message passing among objects and inheritance between objects is established by introducing a hierarchy of theories. Also, Goguen and Meseguer proposed an integrated object oriented functional logic programming system based on order-sorted equational logic following a similar approach [16]. In the theoretical foundation a logic is regarded abstractly as an institution. The PDS provides the possibility to study these proposals systematically since logic theories (i.e. objects) are first class citizens in the assertional programming framework, while the constraint-based computational model of theory objects exhibits the inheritance property.

Because declarative programming systems have mathematically-based semantics, whenever a declarative programming system is designed, an associated transformation approach immediately becomes available. This leads us to believe that there must be some general principles for developing program transformation systems for declarative programming languages. By using assertional programming as a uniform framework of declarative programming systems, it becomes clear that a common underlying logical structure of program transformation exists. We have establised that program transformation is closely related to the inductive proving procedure over programs. Instead of proving an assertion to be an inductive consequence of a program, the task of program transformation is to produce a program for which a given specification become its inductive consequences. We hope that this treatment of program transformation helps us to explore the logical structure of transformation systems in general.

5 CONCLUSIONS

We have presented an informal survey of the Phoenix Design Space, a conceptual framework for studying declarative programming languages and their integration. We have illustrated its power by some successful applications of the PDS in analysing and developing declarative programming systems. We believe that the scope of the PDS extends beyond studying the semantics and computational models of declarative languages, to other aspects of declarative programming technology such as program transformation, analysis and implementation. We claim that this very broad application is a direct benefit of taking a very wide perspective of the essential characteristics of declarative languages, particularly, the use of general logics to formulate declarative language semantics, and the adoption of general constraint programming as the model of computation. Further research will be devoted to consolidating the space in a uniform and general way. Particularly, we would like to use the PDS further to study concurrent programming, object orientated programming and the theory of program development.

6 ACKNOWLEDGEMENTS

We are indebted first and foremost to Dr. Sophia Drossopoulou and Dr. Ross Paterson, our two collegues in the Phoenix project at Imperial college, for many valuable discussions. We thank Mr. Hendrick Lock, and all other members of the Phoenix project and also Prof. J-L Lassez, Prof. J. Goguen, Dr. Meseguer, Dr. J. Jaffer and Dr. U. Reddy for their encouragement and help on this research. We would like to thank all the people in the Functional Programming Section at Imperial college who contribute to a stimulating working environment. This work was carried out under the European Community ESPRIT funded Basic Research Action 3147 (Phoenix).

REFERENCES

[1] Hassan Ait-Kaci. LIFE: A natuaral language for natural lanaguage. MCC Tech. Report ACA-

ST-074-88. Microelectronics and Computer Technology Corp, Austin, TX., Feb. 1988.

[2] Arvind, R. Nikhil and K. Pingali *I-structure: Data Structures for Parallel Computing* ACM Transactions on Programming Languages and Systems,11, Oct 1989.

[3] M. Chandy and J. Misra *Parallel Program Design - A foundation.* Addison Wesley, 1988.

[4] J. Darlington, A.J. Field and H. Pull, *The Unification of Functional and Logic Languages* in *Logic Programming: Relation, Function and Equation* P.37–P70. Prentice-Hall, Englewood Cliffs, New Jersey. 1986.

[5] J. Darlington, Y. Guo and H. Pull *Introducing Constraint Functional Logic Programming* Tech. Report, Dept of Computing, Imperial College, Aug.1991.(In this proceedings)

[6] C.A. R. Hoare *A Theory of Conjunction and Concurrency* Oxford PRG, May 1989

[7] N. Dershowitz and M. Okada *Conditional Equational Programming and the Theory of Conditional Term Rewriting* Proceedings of the FGCS'84, 1984

[8] N. Dershowitz and D.A. Plaisted, *Equational Programming* in Machine Intelligence , 1986.

[9] Y. Guo and H. Lock. *A classification for the integration of functional and logic languages* Technical report, Dept. of Computing, Imperial College and GMD Forschungsstelle an der Universität Karlsruhe, March 1990. Deliverable, ESPRIT BRA 3147.

[10] N. Dershowitz and J.P. Jouannaud. *Rewrite systems* in Van Leuven, editor, *Handbook of Theoretical Computer Science* North Holland, 1990

[11] M.H. van Emden and K. Yukawa *Logic Programming with Equations* Journal of Logic Programming, Vol4. Number 4, 1987.

[12] Laurent Fribourg. SLOG: *A logic programming language interpreter based on clausal superposition and rewriting* In *Proceeding of the 2nd IEEE Symposium on Logic Programming, Boston,* 1985.

[13] J. Y. Girard *Linear Logic* Theoretical Computer Science, 50:1-102, 1987.

[14] J. Goguen and R.Burstall *INSTITUTIONS: Abstract Model Theory for Specification and Programming* TR CSLI-85-30 SRI, 1985.

[15] J. Goguen *Types as Theories* PRG, Oxford University, Feb. 1990.

[16] J. Goguen and J, Meseguer *Unifying Functional, Object-oriented and Logic Programming with Logical Semantics* Technical Report CSLI-87-93, CSLI, Stanford University, March 1987.

[17] J. Goguen and J. Meseguer *Equality, Types, Modules, and (why not?) Generics for Logic Programming* Journal of Logic Programminglp,Vol 2, 1984.

[18] Y. Guo *General Constraint Programming: A Paradigm for Integrating Functional and Logic Languages* Forthcoming Ph.D thesis, Dept. of Computing, Imperial College, 1991.

18

[19] Joxan Jaffar and Jean-Louis Lassez. Logical programming scheme. In D. DeGroot and G. Lindstrom, editors, *Logic Programming*, pages 441–467. Prentice-Hall, Englewood Cliffs, New Jersey, 1986.

[20] J. Jaffer , J. Lassez and M. Maher *Constraint Logic Programming* Proc. of 14th ACM Symp. POPL, 1987

[21] S.Kaplan *Conditional Rewrite Rules* Theoretical Computer Science Vol.33,

[22] A. G. Lindstrom *Implementing Logical Variables on a Graph Reduction Machines* Proc. of a Workshop on Graph Reduction, Santa Fe,New Mexico , Springer LNCS 279, 1987 pp175-193, 1984.

[23] F. McCabe *Logic and Objects* Tech. Report, Dept. of Computing,Imperial College, 1986.

[24] Dale Miller and Gopalan Nadathur. *A logic programming approach to manipulating formulas and progams* In *Poceedings of the 4th Symposium on Logic Programming, San Francisco*, pages 379–399, 1987.

[25] J. Meseguer *General Logics* SRI-I-CSL-89-5 Mar,1989.

[26] J. Goguen and J. Meseguer *Models and Equality for Logic Programming* Proceedings TAPSOFT 87, LNCS 250, 1987.

[27] J. Meseguer *Rewriting as a Unified Model of Concurrency* SRI–CSL-90-02R Feb,1990.

[28] N. Marti-Oliet and J. Meseguer *An Algebraic Axiomatization of Linear Logic Models* Technical Report SRI-CSL-89-11, SRI International, Computer Science Lab, December 1989.

[29] N. Dershowitz and M. Okada. *Conditional equational programming and the theory of conditional term rewriting* In *Proc. of the FGCS' 84*, 1988.

[30] J. Robinson and L. Wos *Paramodulation and Theorem Proving in First Order Theories with Equality* Machine Intelligence, Vol.4, 1972.

[31] U.S.Reddy *Functional Logic Programming Part I* Proc. of a Workshop on Graph Reduction, Santa Fe, New Mexico , Springer LNCS 279, 1987

[32] Y. Guo, J. Darlington, and H. Lock. *Deloping phoenix design space: A uniform framework for investigating declarative programming languages* Technical report, Dept. of Computing, Imperial College and GMD Forschungsstelle an der Universiät Karlsruhe, April 1990.

[33] R. Jagadeesan and K. Pingali *Abstract Semantics for Higher Order Functional Language with Logic Variables* TR91-1220 Dept. of Computer Science, Cornell Univ.Ithaca, July 1991.

[34] V. Saraswat, M. Rinard and P. Panangaden *Semantic Foundations of Concurrent Constraint Programming* Proceedings of POPL, 1991

[35] D.Scott *Domains for Denotational Semantics* In Proceedings of ICALP, 1982.

[36] D.Scott *Data Types as Lattice* SIAM, 5(3):522-587, 1976.

[37] G.Smolka *Logic Programming over Polymorphically Order-Sorted Types* Ph.D Thesis Universitat Kaiserslautern 1989.

Introducing Constraint Functional Logic Programming

John Darlington   Yike Guo   Helen Pull

Department of Computing

Imperial College, University of London

180 Queen's Gate London SW7 2BZ U.K.

E-mail: jd, yg, hmp@doc.ic.ac.uk

August 5, 1991

Abstract

A new declarative programming paradigm, constraint functional logic programming (CFLP) is presented, which unifies systematically all features of constraint, functional and logic programming. CFLP extends constraint functional programming (CFP), which supports equation solving over a functional program, to general constraint programming permitting the use of constraints for programming as well as for posing queries. It also generalises constraint logic programming (CLP), by admitting user-defined functions as a purely functional subsystem of a CLP language. This paper presents the motivation for designing CFLP and its semantics. Programming examples are given in the concrete CFLP language Falcon.

1 INTRODUCTION

In recent years many systems which integrate functional and logic programming languges have been developed with varying degrees of semantic rigorousness. The following examples are taken from the classification of [10].

Guarded Functional Programming which takes a pragmatic approach by permitting logical formulas, defined by a separate logic programming system, as guards in guarded functional definitions. The semantics for the functional component is a special form of equational logic defined over the domain containing all constructor terms; predicate logic over this domain serves as the semantics for the logic programming component. Therefore computation is performed over a symbolic domain. Example languages are K-Leaf [8], Guarded Term ML [17] and the language of Kieburtz [14].

Although the logic programming component may have little impact on the language features or implementation of the functional part, the semantics of the integrated systems is unclear.

Constraint Functional Programming (CFP) which extends the expressive power of functional languages by supporting equation solving over over a functional program. Equations are defined in terms of the continuous equality function which may be viewed as a particular constraint system. Examples of this work include [20] [21], [5], [1] and [16]. Equations are restricted to computational queries and may not be used in program definitions.

Equational Logic Programming which takes Horn clause logic with equality as the semantic base for integrated functional and logic systems, following the example of EqLog [9]. This paradigm provides a rigorous semantic foundation but captures first order computation only. Many important functional programming features, for example, lazy programming are hard to model in this logic.

Constraint Programming which was introduced by Steel [23] and is becoming increasing pertinent to the design of declarative programming languages. Constraint Logic Programming (CLP) [13] involves logic programming over a predefined domain of discourse which is represented by a specific constraint system; different logic languages are obtained by using different underlying constraint systems. Examples include Prolog II and Prolog III I[2] [3], CLP(R)[13] and general typed logic programming as proposed by Smolka [22].

Higher Order Logic Programming which takes a higher order logic, λ-calculus, as the uniform semantic base for integrating functional and logic programming, as in, for example, λ-Prolog [18]. However, we believe that this formalism is more powerful than is required for practical programming. Also, whether higher order unification works reasonably in general polymorphic λ-calculus is an open question [12].

All of these approaches are interesting but all have deficiencies. In this paper we introduce a new declarative programming paradigm, Constraint Functional Logic Programming (CFLP), which brings together first order logic programming and higher order functional programming. CFLP inherits the desirable features of functional programming, including typed programming, lazy evaluation and efficiency of functional computation, while retaining a rigorous mathematical semantics. Functional programming is combined with the constraint logic programming framework, rather than with the conventional Prolog system. Thus, the CFLP paradigm represents a generalisation of the constraint system of CLP to admit user-defined functions, and a generalisation of CFP to admit user-defined constraints (i.e. relations). We claim that this route provides a smooth integration of functional, constraint and logic programming.

A detailed discussion of the theoretical foundation, design and operational model of the CFLP scheme is given in [6]. In section 2 the formal framework for a CFLP scheme is presented. In section 3, a concrete CFLP language, Falcon, is defined. Falcon programming examples are given in section 4, and concluding remarks in section 5.

2 THE CONSTRAINT FUNCTIONAL LOGIC PROGRAMMING SCHEME

In this section we develop a scheme for constructing CFLP languages. We establish the general concept of constraint programming, since any declarative programming language can be viewed as a constraint system. Two important examples, constraint functional programming (CFP) and constraint logic programming (CLP) are presented as constraint systems. Constraint functional logic programming is constructed from CFP and CLP to form a powerful and cohesive integrated declarative language paradigm.

2.1 CONSTRAINT SYSTEMS

Constraint systems were motivated by the desire to perform computation over some well studied domains such as boolean algebra, integers, rational numbers, lists. Such a computational domain together with its operators can be regarded as an algebra. The logical formulas of the algebra are abstractly regarded as *constraints*. Constraints provide a way of defining objects implicitly by stating their logical relations.

Definition 2.1 (Constraint System) *Given a computational domain $\mathcal{A}$, equipped with a set of primitive operators $\mathcal{F}$, and a set of variables $\mathcal{V}$, $\mathcal{A}$-expressions are constructed by applying operators to the objects in $\mathcal{A}$ and variables in $\mathcal{V}$. We define a constraint system C, formally as a tuple: $< \mathcal{A}, \mathcal{F}, \mathcal{V}, \Phi, \mathcal{I} >$ where Φ is a decidable set of constraints over $\mathcal{A}$-expressions. $\mathcal{I}$ is a solution-mapping $[\![ ]\!]^{\mathcal{I}}$ which maps every constraint $\phi(\vec{x}) \in \Phi$ to $[\![\phi(\vec{x})]\!]^{\mathcal{I}}$, a set of $\mathcal{A}$-valuations, α, which are the solutions of $\phi(\vec{x})$, for solution variables $\vec{x}$, such that: $\forall \alpha \in [\![\phi(\vec{x})]\!]^{\mathcal{I}}, A \models \phi(\alpha\vec{x})$. Let Val_A be the set of all $\mathcal{A}$-valuations. A constraint is satisfiable in C iff its solution set is non-empty. A constraint ϕ is valid in I iff $[\![\phi]\!]^{I} = Val_A$. For a set of constraints Φ, I is a model of Φ if all the constraints in Φ are valid in I.*

In this paper we assume that all constraint systems are closed under the logical connectives $\wedge, \vee, :-$ and $\exists$, and contain equality constraints. Constraints which do not contain logical connectives are *atomic constraints*.

We require that a constraint system comes with a set of *solved forms* such that every constraint in solved form is satisfiable. For every satisfiable constraint G, there exists a complete set of solved forms Sol_G such that the disjunction of all constraints in the set is equivalent to G. That is, for all $G_i' \in Sol_G$ and $G' = \bigvee_{i=1}^n G_i'$, $[\![G]\!]^I = [\![G']\!]^I = \bigcup_{i=1}^n [\![G_i']\!]^I$. A procedure which computes solved forms in a constraint system is called *constraint solver*. We use $\longrightarrow_c$ to denote the derivation relation of a constraint solver C.

Definition 2.2 (Soundness and Completeness) *Let* $< \mathcal{A}, \mathcal{F}, \mathcal{V}, \Phi, \mathcal{I} >$ *be a constraint system and C a constraint solver of the system.*

Soundness: *C is sound iff for any constraint G: $G \longrightarrow_c G' \Longrightarrow [\![G']\!]^I \subseteq [\![G]\!]^I$*

Completeness: *C is complete iff for any constraint G, $\forall \alpha \in [\![G]\!]^I$, there exists a constraint G' which is in solved form such that: $G \longrightarrow_c G'$ and $\alpha \in [\![G']\!]^I$.*

We present an example of a constraint system over the real number computational domain.

Example 2.2.1 The Constraint System $\mathcal{S}_{Real}$: **Linear Equations over Real Numbers.** *Let $\mathcal{R}$ be the real number domain equipped with the arithmetic operations $F :< +, -, * >$ and Φ_R be the set of linear equations. $\mathcal{S}_{Real} =< \mathcal{R}, \mathcal{F}, \mathcal{V}, \Phi_R, \mathcal{I}_R >$ is a constraint system over real numbers where the interpretation $\mathcal{I}_R$ maps each linear equation to the (possibly infinite) set of its solutions. A set (or conjunction) of linear equations:*

$$y_1 \quad = \quad a_{1,1} x_1 + \ldots + a_{1,n} x_n + c_1$$
$$\ldots$$
$$y_m \quad = \quad a_{m,1} x_1 + \ldots + a_{m,n} x_n + c_m$$

is in solved form if the variables $y_1, \ldots, y_m$ and $x_1, \ldots, x_n$ are all distinct. Algorithms for solving linear equations, such as Gaussian elimination, are sound and complete constraint solvers for the system. Linear arithmetic constraints have been studied extensively by Lassez and Jaffer el.al. and used as the predefined component of a constraint logic programming system[15] [13].

Constraint programming may, at first, appear rather limited because it is always restricted to a specific computational domain. However, as shown in [6], for any program in a integrated functional and logic programming language there exists a corresponding constraint system. The functional subset of a program contributes to the functional component $\mathcal{F}$, and the relational subset contributes to the constraint component Φ. This is the basic concept underlying the design of CFLP.

2.2 CONSTRAINT FUNCTIONAL PROGRAMMING (CFP)

We characterise constraint functional programming as functional programming enhanced with the capability to solve equations over expressions in the language [5][7].

We define a kernel functional language in terms of sugared λ-calculus. We assume variables ranged over by x, constants ranged over by a, data terms ranged over by t, functional variables ranged over by f and expressions ranged by e. The following abstract syntax of expressions is adopted:

$$Exp \quad := \quad x \mid a \mid f \mid (e_1, \ldots, e_n) \mid \lambda x.e \mid e_1 e_2 \mid \mathbf{fix}\, f.e$$

A functional program is a set of function definitions of the form: $f = e$. A semantic domain A is constructed by taking D as the domain containing all basic types (e.g. real numbers, booleans values, characters), and taking the minimal solution of the equation:

$$A = D_\perp + A^n + A \to A$$

We distinguish the subdomain $\tilde{A} = D_\perp + \tilde{A}^n$ as the domain of data objects, which in a typed functional language, denotes the class of expressions which can be typed by the first order subset of the type system.

The semantics of a program is given by the function which maps function definitions to the environment which associates each function name with its denotation. Denotations are given by a semantic function $\mathcal{E}[\![\,]\!] : Exp \to (Var \to A) \to A$ which maps an expression together with an environment $\eta : Var \to A$ (a A-valuation) to an element of A.

$$
\begin{aligned}
\mathcal{E}[\![x]\!]\eta &= \eta x \\
\mathcal{E}[\![a]\!]\eta &= a \\
\mathcal{E}[\![f]\!]\eta &= \eta f \\
\mathcal{E}[\![(e_1, \ldots, e_n)]\!]\eta &= (\mathcal{E}[\![e_1]\!]\eta, \mathcal{E}[\![e_2]\!]\eta, \ldots \mathcal{E}[\![e_n]\!]\eta) \\
\mathcal{E}[\![\lambda x.e]\!]\eta &= \lambda v.\mathcal{E}[\![e]\!]\eta.\{x \leftarrow v\} \\
\mathcal{E}[\![\mathbf{fix}\, f.e]\!]\eta &= Y(\lambda v.\mathcal{E}[\![e]\!]\eta.\{f \leftarrow v\}) \\
\mathcal{E}[\![e_1 e_2]\!]\eta &= \begin{cases} \mathcal{E}[\![e_1]\!]\eta\, \mathcal{E}[\![e_2]\!]\eta & \text{if } \mathcal{E}[\![e_1]\!]\eta \in D \to D \\ \perp & \text{otherwise} \end{cases}
\end{aligned}
$$

Constraint functional programming is defined by superimposing a solving capability onto the functional programming model. Let $C :< \tilde{A}, \mathcal{F}, \mathcal{V}, \Phi_C, I_C >$ be an abstract constraint system associated with the data domain $\tilde{A}$, with V a set of variables over $\tilde{A}$, $\mathcal{F}$ contains all primitive functions over $\tilde{A}$ and Φ_C is a set of constraints containing equality predicates. Each atomic constraint in Φ_C is of the form $p(e_1, \ldots, e_n)$ for a relation p and e_i as an expression over $\tilde{A}, \mathcal{F}$ and $\mathcal{V}$.

C may be extended by a functional program Γ, to give a new constraint system $F(C) :< \tilde{A}, \mathcal{F} \cup \mathcal{F}', \mathcal{V}, \Phi_C, I_C >$ where $\mathcal{F}'$ contains the denotations of all functions defined by Γ. In this way constraints may be defined over general expressions involving user-defined functions. The semantic function for a constraint $\phi : p(e_1, \ldots, e_n) \in \Phi_C$ becomes:

$$\llbracket \phi \rrbracket^{I_C} = \{\eta \mid \tilde{\mathcal{A}} \models p(\mathcal{E}\llbracket e_1 \rrbracket(\eta_0 \cup \eta), \ldots, \mathcal{E}\llbracket e_n \rrbracket(\eta_0 \cup \eta))\}$$

where η_0 is the environment which maps function symbols to elements of $\mathcal{F}'$. The solved form of $F(C)$ is that of C, with some extension to deal with lazy evaluation (see [19]).

This semantics reveals constraint programming in the CFP paradigm as "computing environments" which satisfy constraints in $\tilde{\mathcal{A}}$; however, there is no facility to use constraints as programming constructs.

2.3 Constraint Logic Programming (CLP)

We focus here on the constraint Horn clause logic programming paradigm. Let $C :< \mathcal{A}, \mathcal{F}, \mathcal{V}, \Phi_C, I_C >$ be a constraint system with Φ_C as a set of primitive constraints over $\mathcal{A}$. A constraint (Horn clause) logic program Γ over C is a set of rules of the form:

$$p(x_1, \ldots, x_n) :- c_1, \ldots, c_k, B_1, \ldots, B_m$$

where $p(x_1, \ldots, x_n)$ and the B_i are atoms, i.e. p is an n-ary user-defined predicate and the $c_i \in \Phi_C$. An interpretation I of Γ over C is defined by a function interpreting a predicate symbol p as a relation over $\mathcal{A}$. A model of Γ over C is an interpretation which satisfies all rules of Γ. Models of a CLP program can be ordered in terms of the set inclusion ordering. The minimal model M_Γ of Γ over C may be constructed as the least fixed point of the traditional "bottom-up" iteration which computes ground relations entailed by a program[22]. That is, M_Γ is the limit $\bigcup_{i \geq 0} M_\Gamma^i$ of the sequence of interpretations:

$$p(x_1, \ldots, x_n)^{M_\Gamma^0} = \emptyset$$
$$p(x_1, \ldots, x_n)^{M_\Gamma^{i+1}} = \{\alpha \mid \alpha \in \bigcap_{i=1}^j \llbracket c_i \rrbracket^{I_C} \cap \bigcap_{i=1}^m \llbracket B_i \rrbracket^{M_\Gamma^i}\}$$

where $p(x_1, \ldots, x_n) :- c_1, \ldots, c_j, B_1, \ldots, B_m \in \Gamma$

Therefore a CLP extends its underlying constraint system C, by defining new relational constraints, and may be represented by the new constraint system:

$$\Pi(C) :< \mathcal{A}, \mathcal{F}, \mathcal{V}, \Phi_C \cup \Phi_\Pi, I_C \cup I_\Pi >$$

Φ_Π contains all atoms of the form $p(x_1, \ldots, x_n)$ where p is an $n-$ary predicate symbol and each user-defined predicate symbol is interpreted by I_Π which maps the predicate to a relation over $\mathcal{A}$ defined by the minimal model of Γ over C.

2.4 Constraint Functional Logic Programming

The preceding sections demonstrated two routes for extending a constraint system $C :< \mathcal{A}, \mathcal{F}, \mathcal{V}, \Phi_C, I_C >$: constraint logic programming which permits **user-defined constraints**, (i.e. relations over $\mathcal{A}$); and constraint functional programming which permits **user-defined functions**, which provide richer $\mathcal{A}$- expressions. These two approaches are combined in the CFLP paradigm which is represented by the constraint system:

$$\Pi F(C) :< \mathcal{A}, \mathcal{F} \cup \mathcal{F}', \mathcal{V}, \Phi_C \cup \Phi_\Pi, I_C \cup I_\Pi >$$

with respect to a constraint logic program and a functional program with common computational domain $\mathcal{A}$.

The computational domain $\mathcal{A}$ contains continuous functions: $\mathcal{A} \to \mathcal{A}$, i.e. higher order objects exist in the relational world; however, their use is restricted. In section 1 we stated that a higher order solving capability is beyond the requirements of practical programming languages. We therefore restrict elements of Φ_C to constraint first order objects only, eliminating the need for higher order unification. While relations may take functions as arguments, function-typed solution variables will never arise. Relations may apply function arguments to objects, but no solving or extensional relations over the function space are supported. $\bar{A}$ may contain some total finite objects which are regarded in the relational world as special constants, representing function names. We assume a primitive function *apply*, in the relational component of the language, which is responsible for the application of such pseudo functions to arguments. This simulation of functions in a relational world is similar to that of other functional logic systems, for example [24,8].

When constructing the model of a CFLP program, the semantics for its functional component is traditional functional language semantics. The minimal model of the relational component is constructed using the "bottom up" iterative procedure presented in [22] and taking the functionally enhanced constraint system as the underlying constraint system. To ensure that the model is recursively enumerable we require that constraint satisfaction in the functionally enhanced constraint system is computable. Compared with other functional logic systems, this general notion of constraint satisfaction permits us, not only to define equational constraints over finite data terms, but also to introduce more general domain specific constraints, and constraints over partial terms. Therefore, partial objects as defined by lazy functional programming may exist in the relational world. This gives uniform support for laziness in a fully integrated functional logic programming system. Some programming examples are given in section 4.

3 FALCON: A CFLP LANGUAGE

We introduce a small concrete CFLP language, a subset of the language Falcon (Functional And Logic language with CONstraints). The full definition of Falcon appears in [11].

A program in Falcon is a collection of declarations. Declarations include type, data, function and relation declarations, plus function and relation definitions.

$$\begin{aligned}
\textit{program} \quad &\longrightarrow \quad \textit{decl}_1; \ldots; \textit{decl}_n \\
\textit{decl} \quad &\longrightarrow \quad \textit{typedecl} \mid \textit{datadecl} \mid \textit{functiondecls} \mid \textit{relationdecls} \\
&\quad\mid \quad \textit{functiondefn} \mid \textit{relationdefn} \\
\textit{functiondecls} \quad &\longrightarrow \quad \textbf{functions } \textit{dcl}_1, \ldots, \textit{dcl}_n \\
\textit{relationdecls} \quad &\longrightarrow \quad \textbf{relations } \textit{dcl}_1, \ldots, \textit{dcl}_n \\
\textit{dcl} \quad &\longrightarrow \quad \textit{vars}_1, \ldots, \textit{var}_n :: \textit{type}
\end{aligned}$$

The following name spaces of variables are used: *var*, user-defined functions and relations, and formal parameters; *tycon*, type constructors; *tyvar*, type variables; *con*, constructors. Patterns, which appear as pat_i, are constructed from formal parameter variables and constructors only.

A polymorphic type system and traditional algebraic free data types, as found in most functional languages, are assumed. A type is one of, a function type, a constructed type, a tuple type, a list type or a parenthesised type. A syntax similar to that of HASKELL[4] is used:

$$\begin{aligned}
\textit{typedecl} \quad &\longrightarrow \quad \textbf{type } \textit{type} \\
\textit{type} \quad &\longrightarrow \quad \textit{tyvar} \mid \textit{tycon} \mid \textit{type}_1 \longrightarrow \textit{type}_2 \mid \textit{tycon } \textit{type}_1, \ldots, \textit{type}_n \\
&\quad\mid \quad (\textit{type}_1, \ldots, \textit{type}_n) \mid [\textit{type}] \mid (\textit{type}) \\
\textit{datadecl} \quad &\longrightarrow \quad \textbf{data } \textit{tycon } \textit{tyvar}_1, \ldots, \textit{tyvar}_k = \textit{constr}_1 \mid \ldots \mid \textit{constr}_n \\
\textit{constr} \quad &\longrightarrow \quad \textit{con } \textit{type}_1 \ldots \textit{type}_n
\end{aligned}$$

Functions are curried and are defined as follows:

$$\textit{functiondefn} \quad \longrightarrow \quad \textit{var } \textit{pat}_1, \ldots, \textit{pat}_n[\mid \textit{gd}] = \textit{exp}$$

where the optional guard, *gd*, is a boolean-valued expression (the usual functional programming language restrictions of left linearity and nonambiguity of left hand sides apply).

Expressions include variables, constructors, literals, tuples, lists, application, parenthesised expressions and may introduce local declarations:

$$\begin{aligned}
\textit{exp} \quad &\longrightarrow \quad \textit{var} \mid \textit{con} \mid \textit{literal} \mid (\textit{exp}_1, \ldots, \textit{exp}_n) \mid [\textit{exp}_1, \ldots, \textit{exp}_n] \\
&\quad\mid \quad \textit{exp}_1 \textit{exp}_2 \mid (\textit{exp}) \mid \textit{exp } \textbf{where } \textit{wheredecls } \textbf{end} \\
\textit{wheredecls} \quad &\longrightarrow \quad \textit{wheredecl}[, \textit{wheredecls}] \\
\textit{wheredecl} \quad &\longrightarrow \quad \textit{functiondefn} \\
&\quad\mid \quad \textit{pat}_1, \ldots, \textit{pat}_n[\textit{gd}] = \textit{exp}
\end{aligned}$$

Relations over expressions may be defined:

$$\begin{aligned}
\textit{relationdefn} \quad &\longrightarrow \quad \textit{atom } \textbf{when } \textit{constraint}_1, \ldots, \textit{constraint}_n \\
\textit{atom} \quad &\longrightarrow \quad \textit{var } \textit{exp}_1, \ldots, \textit{exp}_m \\
\textit{constraint} \quad &\longrightarrow \quad \textit{atom} \\
&\quad\mid \quad \textit{exp}
\end{aligned}$$

A relation may be defined in terms of other relations (including itself). or boolean valued expressions. The relational definition $r\ exp_1,\ \ldots,\ exp_m$ **when** $c_1,\ \ldots,\ c_n$ should be read as: $exp_1,\ \ldots,\ exp_n$ belong to the relation r, whenever the constraints $c_1,\ \ldots,\ c_n$ are satisfied. Equality predicates associated with the basic domains are assumed to be predefined.

A query in Falcon takes one of two forms: exp or $[<\ x_1,\ \ldots,\ x_m\ >].c_1,\ \ldots,\ c_n$. These correspond to evaluating the ground functional expression exp, or finding solutions for variables $x_1,\ \ldots,\ x_m$ which satisfy constraints $c_1,\ \ldots,\ c_n$ respectively. $<\ x_1,\ \ldots,\ x_m\ >$ is optional, any $y \in Var(c_1,\ \ldots,\ c_n)$ not listed here existentially quantified in $c_1,\ \ldots,\ c_n$.

, The above definitions provide a simple basis for constraint functional logic programming. This language may be regarded as a scheme into which more sophisticated programming constructs may be incorporated. We now use Falcon in some concrete programming examples.

4 PROGRAMMING WITH FUNCTIONS, RELATIONS AND CONSTRAINTS

In this section we present some programming examples using Falcon to illustrate the style of programming and the expressive power of the language. We show that CFLP subsumes all of functional programming, logic programming, constraint programming and their combinations.

4.1 FUNCTIONAL PROGRAMMING

The CFLP paradigm provides an integration of functional and logic programming in which the functional programming component is totally uncorrupted. The functional subset of Falcon is polymorphically typed, curried, higher order, lazy and permits user-defined, algebraic free data types. The following program is self-explanatory.

```
data    [alpha] = [] | alpha : [alpha]
functions
        ++ :: [alpha] — [alpha] — [alpha]
        member :: alpha — [alpha] → Bool
        front :: Int — [alpha] — [alpha]
        ints :: Int — [Int]

[] ++ z = z
(x : y) ++ z = x : (y ++ z)

member x [] = False
member x (y : l) | (x = y) = True
member x (y : l) | (x ≠ y) = member x l
```

front 0 *y* = []

front *n* (*x* : *y*) | (*n* > 0) = *x* : (*front* (*n* - 1) *y*)

ints *n* = *n* : (*ints* (*n* + 1))

The expression:

member 15 (*front* 10 (*ints* 5))

asks whether 15 appears in the first ten integers succeeding 5. Computation is lazy and reduces ground expressions to weak head normal form.

4.2 Typed Logic Programming

As a fully integrated functional and relational programming system, functions and relations in Falcon share a computational domain. Therefore the Hindley-Milner type system is imposed over relations. Relations naturally are not curried, however in Falcon to provide an elegant uniform syntax, curried notation (i.e. no brackets around or commas between arguments) is used. (The full definition of Falcon includes some, optional, syntactic sugar which permits the definition and use of relations with a functional programming like syntax.)

Logic programming gives a greater expressive capability than functional programming by providing a solving capability. Logical variables also increase the expressive power of these languages, as demonstrated by the following version of *append* for difference lists.

data *Diff-list* *alpha* = [*alpha*] / [*alpha*]
relations
     append :: (*Diff-list* *alpha*, *Diff-list* *alpha*, *Diff-list* *alpha*)

append (*x* / *y*) (*y* / *z*) (*x* / *z*)

The relational programming capability of Falcon is greatly enhanced by the functional programming subsystem as shown in the following example of quicksort, which uses difference lists, and in which the partitioning of the input list is represented naturally as a function. This use of functions in relation definitions is regarded as constraint solving.

functions

    $partition :: Int \rightarrow [Int] \rightarrow ([Int],[Int])$

relations

    $qsort :: ([Int], \textit{Diff-list } Int)$

$partition \; n \; (m : l) \mid (m \leq n)$

    $= (m : l_1, l_2) \;$ **where** $(l_1, l_2) = partition \; n \; l \;$ **end**

$partition \; n \; (m : l) \mid (m > n)$

    $= (l_1, m : l_2) \;$ **where** $(l_1, l_2) = partition \; n \; l \;$ **end**

$partition \; n \; [] = ([], [])$

$qsort \; (n : l) \; (x \; / \; y) \;$ **when**

    $partition \; n \; l = (l_1, l_2), qsort \; l_1 \; (x \; / \; (n : z)), qsort \; l_2 \; (z \; / \; y)$

$qsort \; [] \; (x \; / \; x)$

Not only does the functional component of Falcon enhance relational programming, but also relations increase the expressiveness of functions. For example, we can express *front* more declaratively than in the previous section in terms of the functions $++$ and *length*, as follows:

functions $length :: [alpha] \rightarrow Int$

$length \; [] = 0$

$length \; (x : l) = 1 + (length \; l)$

relations $front :: (num. [alpha], [alpha])$

$front \; n \; l \; l_1 \;$ **when** $\; l_1 {+}{+} \; l_2 = l, length \; l_1 = n$

4.3   CONSTRAINT LOGIC PROGRAMMING

In Falcon CLP is fully supported as a subsystem by defining relations using constraints over the underlying primitive domains (i.e. without incorporating any user-defined functions). An example of this programming style, exploiting a real number constraint solver appears below.

relations $capital\text{-}instalments :: (Real, [Real])$

$capital\text{-}instalments \; c \; (r : (capital\text{-}instalments \; (1.1(c - r))))$

$capital\text{-}instalments \; c \; [c]$

The first clause for *capital_instalments* says that capital of c may be repaid in instalments, the first of which is r, and the remainder of which are calculated recursively by subtracting r from c and multiplying by 1.1 to represeñt 10% interest. This examples is due to [3]. The query:

$<i>.capital\text{-}instalments\ 1000\ [i, 2i, 3i]$

asks for a real number i, such that \$1000 may be repaid in instalments of $i, 2i, 3i$. Its solved form is the constraint $i = 207 + 413/641$.

Falcon extends CLP further by permitting constrained relations to employ user-defined functions. An example appears in section 4.5.

4.4 CONSTRAINT FUNCTIONAL PROGRAMMING

As discussed in section 2.2, we characterise constraint functional programming (CFP) as providing a constraint solving ability over a functional program. For example, using the functional program in section 4.1 we can pose the queries:

$Q1:\quad < l_1, l_2 >.(l_1 ++ l_2) = [1, 2, 3]$

$Q2:\quad < l_1 >.(l_1 ++ l_2) = (ints\ 1),\ length\ l_1 = 10$

Q1 splits the list $[1, 2, 3]$, Q2 computes the first integers. Note that in these examples, equality is interpreted as the identity relation on lists, and is inductively defined over the structure of lists, so it is not, in general, computable. However in Falcon we support only a computable subset of this relation. Other CFP languages restrict equality to finite data terms[8] and in doing so make sacrifices in the support for lazy evaluation and infinite structures. In Falcon, by using a more general notion of the constraint satisfaction relation, we provide support for constraint solving over recursively defined data types. Research is currently underway to define the appropriate subset of the constraint satisfaction relation and to establish the completeness of its solver [6].

CFP represents a powerful enhancement of functional programming. However, it lacks the ability to define functions via equations, in contrast with CLP, in which relations may be defined using constraints. The Falcon universe provides more than the sum of its component language paradigms.

4.5 CONSTRAINT FUNCTIONAL LOGIC PROGRAMMING

The previous sections have provided many CFLP examples, viewed as various other language paradigms. In the CFLP framework, all these paradigms are brought together in a single universe. This universe consists of a constraint system, enhanced functionally via a functional program, and extended relationally via a constraint logic program. In this way CFLP is a general constraint programming system. The previous examples have already demonstrated the expressiveness and flexibility of this integration.

The distinguishing features of CFLP languages are the ability to use constraints over expressions in a functional language when defining relations, and the ability to pass functions as arguments to relations. All these features are demonstrated by the following definition of quicksort in which the polymorphically typed relation *quicksort* uses difference lists for sorting and takes the appropriate ordering function as an argument. and which incorporates constraint solving over the user-defined function *partition*.

functions

$$partition :: (alpha \rightarrow alpha \rightarrow Bool) \rightarrow alpha \rightarrow [alpha] \rightarrow$$
$$([alpha],[alpha])$$

relations

$$quicksort :: ((alpha \rightarrow alpha \rightarrow Bool), [alpha], \textit{Diff-list } alpha)$$

$partition\ f\ n\ (m\ :\ l)\ |\ f\ m\ n$
$\quad = (m\ :\ l_1,\ l_2)\ \textbf{where}\ (l_1,\ l_2) = partition\ f\ n\ l\ \textbf{end}$
$partition\ f\ n\ (m\ :\ l)\ |\ not\ (f\ m\ n)$
$\quad = (l_1,\ m\ :\ l_2)\ \textbf{where}\ (l_1,\ l_2) = partition\ f\ n\ l\ \textbf{end}$
$partition\ f\ n\ [] = ([],\ [])$

$quicksort\ f\ (n\ :\ l)\ (x\ /\ y)\ \textbf{when}$
$\quad partition\ f\ n\ l = (l_1,\ l_2),$
$\quad quicksort\ f\ l_1\ (x\ /\ (n\ :\ z)),\ quicksort\ f\ l_2\ (z\ /\ y)$
$quicksort\ f\ []\ (x\ /\ x)$

One further Falcon program is given. The relation *perm_map*, defined below, applies a given function to each element of all permutations of a list.

relations $\quad perm\text{-}map :: ((alpha \rightarrow beta), [alpha], [beta])$
$perm\text{-}map\ f\ (a\ :\ l)\ (l_1\ ++\ (f\ a\ :\ l_2))\ \textbf{when}\ perm\text{-}map\ f\ l\ (l_1\ ++\ l_2)$
$perm\text{-}map\ f\ []\ []$

5 CONCLUSION

This paper has presented a new way to integrate the functional and logic programming paradigms, constraint functional logic programming, which provides a uniform framework to perform declarative programming in terms of functions, relations and constraints. This integration is made by exploiting their inherent semantic links and combining them consistently instead of by an ad hoc amalgamation. Functional programming and logic programming are inherited as subsystems of the framework. Moreover, functional and logic programming now are tightly and systematically interleaved to form a consistent and powerful declarative programming framework with a succinct and rigorous semantic foundation. This was achieved by taking constraint programming as the basis for unifying functional and logic programming. Work remains on both the semantics, for example, the roles of lazy evaluation and negation in the new framework, and on the implementation, for example the interaction of the various constraint computational models and with traditional functional and logic computation. We hope that the paradigm will be widely used and evolve into a practical declarative programming system.

6 Acknowledgements

We are indebted first and foremost to Dr. Sophia Drossopoulou and Dr. Ross Paterson, our two collegues in the Phoenix project at Imperial college, for many valuable discussions. We thank Prof. J-L Lassez, Prof. J. Goguen, Dr. Meseguer, Dr. J. Jaffer and Dr.U. Reddy for their encouragement and help on this research. We also thank Mr. H. Lock for his enlightening discussions. We would like to thank all the people in the Functional Programming Section at Imperial college who contribute to a stimulating working environment. This work was carried out under the European Community ESPRIT funded Basic Research Action 3147 (Phoenix)

References

[1] H. Ait-Kaci and R. Nasr. Integrating logic and functional programming. *Lisp and Symbolic Computation*, 2(1), February 1989.

[2] A. Colmerauer. Prolog and infinite trees. In K.L. Clark and S.A. Tarnlund, editors, *Logic Programming*. Academic Press, New Yok, 1982.

[3] A. Colmerauer. Opening the Prolog III universe. *Byte, July*, 1987.

[4] Haskell Committee. Haskell: A non-strict, purely functional language. Technical report, Dept. of Computer Science, Yale University, April 1990.

[5] J. Darlington and Y. Guo. Constraint equational deduction. Technical report, Dept. of Computing, Imperial College, March 1990. will be presented in CTRS' 90.

[6] J. Darlington, Y.K. Guo, and H. Pull. The design of constraint functional logic programming. Technical report, Dept. of Computing, Imperial College, March 1991. Deliverable for the ESPRIT Basic Research Action No.3147.

[7] John Darlington and Yike Guo. Constraint functional programming. Technical report, Imperial College, November 1989.

[8] C. Moiso E. Giovannetti, G. Levi and C. Palmidessi. "kernel leaf: An" experimental logic plus functional language - its syntax, semantics and computational model. ESPRIT Project 415, Second Year Report, 1986.

[9] Joseph A. Goguen and Jose Meseguer. Equality, types, modules, and (why not?) generics for logic programming. *Journal of Logic Programming*, 2:179–210, 1984.

34

[10] Y. Guo, H. Lock, J. Darlington, and R. Dietrich. A classification for the integration of functional and logic languages. Technical report, Dept. of Computing, Imperial College and GMD Forchungsstelle an der Universitat Karlsruhe, March 1990. Deliverable for the ESPRIT Basic Research Action No.3147.

[11] Y.K. Guo and H. Pull. Falcon: Functional And Logic language with CONonstraints–language definition. Technical report, Dept. of Computing, Imperial College, February 1991.

[12] G. Huet. *Constrained Resolution: A Complete Method for Higher-Order Logic.* PhD thesis, Case Western Reserve University, 1972.

[13] Joxan Jaffar and Jean-Louis Lassez. Constraint logic programming. In *Prod. of POPL 87,* pages 111–119, 1987.

[14] Richard B. Kieburtz. Functional+ logic in theory and practice. Technical report, Oregon Graduate Center, Beaverton, Oregon 97006 U.S.A., February 1987.

[15] J-L. Lassez and K. McAloon. A constraint sequent calculus. Technical report, IBM T.J. Watson Research Center, 1989.

[16] William Leler. *Specification and Generation of Constraint Satisfaction Systems.* PhD thesis, The University of North Carolina at Chapel Hill, February 1987.

[17] Hendrik C.R. Lock. Guarded Term ML. In *Workshop on Implementations of Lazy Functional Languages,* Aspenas,Sweden, Sept. 1988.

[18] Gopalan Nadathur and Dale Miller. An overview of λ-Prolog. Technical report, Computer and Information Science Department, Univ. of Pennsylvania, March 1988.

[19] Helen M. Pull. *Equation Solving in Lazy Functional Languages.* PhD thesis, Submitted to Dept. of Computing, Imperial College, University of London, November 1990.

[20] Uday S. Reddy. Functional Logic Languages, Part 1. In J.H. Fasel and R.M. Keller, editors, *Poceedings of a Workshop on Graph Reduction, Santa Fee,* number 279 in Lecture Notes in Computer Science, Springer Verlag, pages 401–425, 1986.

[21] Frank S. K. Silbermann and B. Jayazraman. Set abstraction in functional and logic programming. In *Proc. of FPCA 89',* 1989.

[22] Gert Smolka. *Logic Programming over Polymorphically Order-Sorted Types.* PhD thesis, Vom Fachbereich Informatik der Universitat Kaiserlautern, May 1989.

[23] G.L. Steele. *The Definition and Implementation of a Computer Programming Language Based on Constraints.* PhD thesis, M.I.T. AI-TR 595, 1980.

[24] D.H.D. Warren. Higher-order extension to Prolog: are they needed? In *Machine Intelligence 10.* Ellis Horwood Ltd., 1982.

How to Use Guarded Functional Programming

Roland Dietrich

GMD Research Laboratory Karlsruhe

Vincenz-Prießnitz-Straße 1, D 7500 Karlsruhe

e-mail: *dietrich@karlsruhe.gmd.dbp.de*

Abstract

Guarded functional programming (GFP) has been proposed as an approach to integrate functional programming, represented by equations and rewriting, and logic programming, represented by Horn clauses and SLD resolution. The basic programming constructs are guarded equations, i.e. equations conditioned by guards which are Horn logic goals. When an equation is applied to rewrite an expression, its guard must be solved first. If a guard has more than one solutions, only one is considered (committed choice). In an extension of GFP, list comprehensions can be used to collect all solutions of a goal (GFP*). This paper presents a systematic approach how to use GFP* with respect to a classification of functions and relations regarding non-determinism properties. A sample problem is described whereof a taxonomy of functions and relations is derived. It is shown how the programming constructs of GFP* reflect this taxonomy and a systematic solution of the sample problem is outlined.

1 Introduction

Declarative programming languages like functional languages (ML, Hope) or logic languages (Prolog) have a great potential for software productivity: As high level specification languages they can serve to produce running specifications of software systems which is important since testing is still necessary and formal verification is far from being as available as needed in practice. They are amenable to formal manipulation rules for program analysis and transformation. Moreover, since advanced and parallel hardware architectures are evolving and declarative languages are well suited to run on parallel hardware, these languages will get increased importance also as production languages.

Research activities in this area have evolved a great number of declarative programming languages which can roughly be classified into logic, equational, functional and constraint languages. Many attempts have been made to integrate different instances of these language classes (See [GL90] for an overview). The question arises, for which problems which language class is appropriate and, for integrated languages, how the different language features support different kinds of problem structures. In this paper, we try to answer this question for a pragmatic approach to integrate functional and logic programming: Guarded Functional Programming (GFP, [DL91]). The basic programming feature of GFP are guarded equations: an equation can be applied to reduce an expression if its guard which is a Horn logic query, succeeds. This gives rise to non-deterministic executions if guards have more than one possible solution. An extension to GFP allows to collect all solutions of queries in so called stream comprehensions (GFP*).

To approach our goals, we study a sample problem (an interpreter for inference systems, Section 2) and try to identify basic problem structures. This results into a taxonomy of functions and relations, where non-determinism plays a crucial rôle (Section 3). Then we present a solution to the sample problem using GFP* and show which programming features of GFP* correspond to which elements of the taxonomy (Section 4). We summarize our results and give some concluding remarks in Section 5.

2   A Sample Problem

The example problem we have chosen is the implementation of a simple interpreter for inference systems. Inference systems as a problem solving paradigm replace the deterministic execution of algorithms by non-deterministic searching: Problems and solutions are well defined elements of a state space, and in order to solve a problem one has to try to infer a solution state from a problem state by successive application of inference rules on states. The set of all possible inferences comprise a search space. A control strategy defines in which way inferences are generated, i.e. it controls the searching process. Expert systems and theorem provers can be seen as special instances of this paradigm.

Inference Systems.   In [Die90], a formal and application independent framework is presented, which allows the standardized description and comparative analysis of inference systems. According to this framework, an *inference system* consists of four components $I = \langle S, R, P, F \rangle$ where

1. S is a decidable set, the set of *states*.

2. $R \subseteq 2^{S \times S}$ is a finite set of decidable binary relations, the *inference rules* or, for short, the *rules*. For every $s \in S$ and $r \in R$ the set $\{s' | r(s, s')\}$ must be finite.

3. $P \subseteq S$ and $F \subseteq S$ are decidable subsets of the states, the *problem states* and the *solution* or *final* states.

If $x, y \in S$ and $r(x, y)$ for some $r \in R$, we say that r is *applicable* in x and y is a (direct) *successor* of x. Solving a problem by means of an inference system means, given a problem state x_0, finding a sequence of states $x_1, \ldots, x_n$ such that x_i is a successor of x_{i-1} for $i = 1, \ldots, n$ and x_n is a solution state. It is the task of a control strategy to find such a sequence (see below).

As an example, consider Robinson's resolution calculus [Rob65], which can be (informally) defined as an inference system $Res = \langle S_{Res}, R_{Res}, P_{Res}, F_{Res} \rangle$ where

1. The states $s \in S_{Res}$ are sets of clauses.

2. R_{Res} contains two relations describing the resolution rule and the factorization rule, that is $R_{Res} = \{res, factor\}$ where $res, factor \in S_{Res} \times S_{Res}$ and

   - $res(s_1, s_2)$ iff there is a resolvent c of two clauses in s_1 and $s_2 = s_1 \cup c$,
   - $factor(s_1, s_2)$ iff there is a factor c of a clause in s_1 and $s_2 = s_1 \cup c$.

3. All states are problem states: $P_{Res} = S_{Res}$.

4. Final states contain the empty clause: $F_{Res} = \{s \in S_{Res} | \Box \in s\}$.

Rule Schemes. The computation of state transitions w.r.t. an inference rule can be defined in a more fine grained way. Applying an inference rule often means (1) to *select* a possible application occurrence (a *redex*) within a state, (2) to *test* whether the inference rule is really applicable at this redex, and (if yes) (3) to *construct* the successor state. The test for applicability of a rule at a redex can yield some parameters which can be used together with the redex to construct the successor state[1]. This structure of computing a state transitions is modeled by *rule schemes* $\langle RX^r, TP^r, sel^r, tst^r, cns^r \rangle$ for every inference rule r of an inference system where

1. RX^r and TP^r are decidable sets, the *redex domain* and the *transition parameter domain*,

2. $sel^r \subseteq S \times RX^r$ is a decidable relation, the *selection relation*, such that for every $s \in S$ the set $\{x | sel^r(s, x)\}$ is finite,

3. $tst^r : S \times RX^r \longrightarrow TP^r \cup \{F\}$ is a computable function, the *test function*,

---

[1]One might argue that selecting a *possible* redex and testing whether a rule is *really* applicable should be considered as *one* logical step when computing a state transition. But often the search for a redex is done in an iterative manner as described here, and one has to perform many unsuccessful application tests before a real redex is found, and we prefer to make this explicit in our model.

```
df-search(s;s'):
  INPUT: a problem state s;
  OUTPUT: a solution state s' which is inferable from s or failure;
  VARIABLES: x,y: states.

  x := s;
  WHILE x ≠ fail AND NOT solution(x) DO
      successor(x,y);
      x := y
  ENDLOOP
END df-search.
```

Figure 1: Depth-first search.

4. $cns^r : S \times RX^r \times TP^r \longrightarrow S$ is a computable function, the *construction function*,

5. for all $s, s' \in S$ the following holds:

$$r(s, s') \Longleftrightarrow \exists x \in RX^r \exists y \in TP^r : sel^r(s, x) \wedge tst^r(s, x) = y \wedge cns^r(s, x, y) = s'.$$

For example, a rule scheme for the resolution rule of the inference system *Res* (see Example 2) can be defined informally as follows:

1. The redex domain RX^{res} consists of quadruples (c_1, c_2, l_1, l_2) such that c_1, c_2 are clauses, and l_1, l_2 are literals.

2. The transition parameter domain consists of all substitutions.

3. $sel^{res}(s; c_1, c_2, l_1, l_2)$ holds, iff c_1, c_2 are clauses of s, l_1 is a positive literal of c_1, and l_2 is a negative literal of c_2.

4. $tst^{res}(s; c_1, c_2, l_1, l_2) = \sigma$ iff σ is the most general unifier of $\neg l_1$ and l_2. If $\neg l_1$ and l_2 are not unifiable, then $tst^{res}(s; c_1, c_2, l_1, l_2) = F$.

5. $cns^{res}(s; c_1, c_2, l_1, l_2; \sigma) = s \cup \{\sigma((c_1 - l_1) \cup (c_2 - l_2))\}$.

A similar rule scheme can be defined for the factorization rule. In this case the redex domain contains triples of one clause and two literals.

Control Strategies. An interpreter for inference systems takes a problem state as input and successively applies inference rules to infer new states until a solution state is reached. I.e. an interpreter realizes a control strategy for inference systems.

There are many control strategies for inference systems, an overview of which is given in [Nil82]. Two of them, namely depth-first search and depth-first search with backtracking are described in Figure 1 and Figure 2, respectively. We assume that procedures successor(s,s') and all_successors(s,S) compute one successor s' and and the list S of all successors of a state s. These procedures can be defined using the

```
dfb-search(s;s'):
   INPUT: a problem state s;
   OUTPUT: a solution state s' which is inferable from s or failure;
   VARIABLES: L,S: list of states; x: state.

   L := [s];
   WHILE L ≠ [] AND "no solution in L" DO
       x := head(L); L := tail(L);
       all_successors(x,S);
       L := S & L
   ENDLOOP;

   IF "there is a solution x in L"   THEN s' := x
                                     ELSE s' := fail

   ENDIF
END dfb-search.
```

Figure 2: Depth-first search with backtracking.

elementary functions tst^r, sel^r, and cns^r of the rule schemes for every inference rule r. "&" denotes list concatenation.

Depth-first search stops whenever a state has no successor. Depth-first search with backtracking continues in this case with a previously generated state considering alternative successors of that state. For that purpose, a set of alternatives must be kept during the search (the list L in dfb-search).

Breadth-first search differs from depth-first search in the order of considering alternatives. Instead of considering alternatives only upon need, it always considers all alternatives first. The only difference in the algorithm is, that new generated successors are appended at the tail of the current alternative list L within the WHILE-loop in the algorithm of Figure 2.

In summary, the sample problem which we investigate consists in programming control algorithms which assume an inference system being defined by means of rule schemes. A subproblem thereof is to define functions which compute one or all successors of a state.

3   A Taxonomy of Functions and Relations

Declarative programming, as represented by functional and logic programming, provides syntactical means to specify mathematical objects, as functions and relations over some domains, and these specifications are executable such that the functions and relations can be computed over some syntactical representations of the domains (types or the term universe). In this section, we investigate which mathematical objects have to be specified to get a solution for our sample problem and present a classification of different objects. The classification evolved from a pure Prolog solution for the sample problem [Die91, DP91] by investigating whether Prolog predicates, i.e. relations, are used in its full generality or in some restricted way.[2]

Pure Relations   The characteristic of a relation, e.g. if specified as a Prolog predicate, is to use it with varying arguments as input or output (different I/O-modes). For example, to solve the sample problem an unary relation is-rule will be useful which allows (1) to test whether a certain object denotes an inference rule and (2) to generate the rules of an inference system. In the second case, another characteristic of pure relations is non-determinism: for a query is-rule(X) it is not determined which rule is generated first. (Although, in most of the Prolog interpreters there is a fixed search strategy, the result is non-deterministic from a declarative semantic point of view.) Because we cannot distinguish input and output, the signature of a pure relation r is denoted by

$$r \subseteq D_1 \times \cdots \times D_n$$

where D_i are the types of the arguments.

Pure Functions   In many (if not in most) cases, Prolog predicates are used in a unique, well determined way: (1) it is fixed which arguments are input and which are output, and (2) the result is unique with respect to a certain input. That is, functions are modeled as relations. For example, the construction function of a rule scheme is of this kind. The signature of a pure function is denoted by

$$f : I_1 \times \cdots \times I_k \longrightarrow O_1 \times \cdots \times O_m$$

where I_i and O_j are the type(s) of the input and output arguments, respectively.

Non-deterministic Functions   There is a specific case in-between pure relations and pure functions, namely relations which are used with a fixed I/O -mode, but can have more than one result with respect to a certain input. An example is the selection function of a rule scheme, which has a rule and a state as input and can have different redexes as outputs. Another example is a function which computes one out of many successors of a state. A non-deterministic function even can have no result for a specific input (the call fails), e.g. if there is no redex or no successor for a given state. We denote the signature of a non-deterministic function by

$$f : I_1 \times \cdots \times I_k \Longrightarrow O_1 \times \cdots \times O_m.$$

---

[2]It has been shown in [Dra87] that the relational language Prolog is seldom used to program true relations and often to simulate functions.

type	signature	properties
relation	$r \subseteq D_1 \times \cdots \times D_n$	multiple modes multiple results
function	$f : I \longrightarrow O$	single mode single result
non-deterministic function	$f : I \Longrightarrow O$	single mode multiple results
set valued function	$f : I \longrightarrow \{O\}$	single mode single set result

Figure 3: A taxonomy of functions and relations. I and O, the domain or type of input and output arguments may be tuples $I_1 \times \cdots \times I_k$ or $O_1 \times \cdots \times O_m$, respectively.

Set Valued Functions It has been proven useful to have not only one, but all results of a non-deterministic function available for computation. In Prolog, for example, the meta-predicate set_of is commonly used. In the sample problem, we need a function which provides *all* successors of a state (cf. the algorithms for control strategies, Figure 1 and Figure 2). Such a function has just to collect all the possible results of a non-deterministic function which computes one successor. The signature of set valued functions is denoted by

$$f : I_1 \times \cdots \times I_k \longrightarrow \{O_1 \times \cdots \times O_m\}.$$

Note that the result value of a call of a set valued function is unique. If the non-deterministic function call fails, the corresponding set-valued function delivers the empty set. Thus, set valued functions can be considered as a special case of deterministic functions. The non-determinism inherent in the underlying non-deterministic functions is hidden by the fact that the elements of a set are not ordered.

Figure 3 summarizes the taxonomy of functions and relations.

4 A Solution with GFP*

In this section we outline a solution to our sample problem, i.e. a program which realizes an interpreter for inference systems according to the model presented in Section 2 by means of the guarded functional programming paradigm with lazy stream comprehensions (GFP*, [DL91]). At first, we give a systematic view on the sample problem using the taxonomy of Section 3 to specify which functions and relations have to be realized, and secondly we give a brief introduction into the basic concepts of GFP*.

type state.	the states
type rule.	the rule identifiers
type redex.	possible redexes of states
type trans-par.	possible transition parameters
is-rule ⊆rule.	determines rule identifiers
final ⊆states.	determines final states
select: rule × state ⟹ redex.	selection relation
test: rule × state × redex ⟶ trans-par ∪ {F}.	test function
cons: rule × state × redex × trans-par ⟶ state.	construction function

Figure 4: Representation of inference systems.

The Sample Problem Revisited

In order to implement an interpreter, i.e. control strategies, for inference systems one has to specify how inference systems are expected to be represented. According to the model presented in Section 2, we assume that there is a type **state** representing states and a type **rule** representing rule identifiers (a collection of identifiers). For each rule, we assume that there is a rule scheme defining this rule. That is, there is a type **redex** and a type **transition-par** which represents redexes and transition parameters, and there are a non-deterministic function **select** which has a rule and a state as input and produces a redex, a pure function **test** which has a rule, a state, and a redex as input and produces a transition parameter of the value F, and the construction function **cons**, which (deterministically) computes a successor of a state with respect to a rule, a redex, and a transition parameter. In addition, there are two relations, **is-rule** and **final** which determine the rules and the final states of an inference system. The latter can also be modeled as a deterministic boolean function, whereas the former can be used to determine whether a certain identifier denotes a rule or to generate all the rules of an inference system and, hence, is a true relation. Figure 4 summarizes the representation of inference systems.

As a subproblem, we have identified the task of computing successors of a state. There are 4 variants of this task which can be used in an interpreter for inference systems: computing one successor of a state with respect to a specific rule, computing an arbitrary successor of a state, computing all successors of a state with respect to a specific rule and computing all successors of a state. The former two are non-deterministic functions, the latter two are set valued functions, as summarized in Figure 5.

Finally, we will implement three different control strategies which are non-

r-succ: rule × state $\Longrightarrow$ state.	one successor of a state w.r.t. a rule
succ: state $\Longrightarrow$ state.	one successor of a state
all-r-succs: rule × state $\longrightarrow$ {state}.	all successors of a state w.r.t. a rule
all-succs: state $\longrightarrow$ {state}.	all successors of a state

Figure 5: Successor functions.

df-search: state $\Longrightarrow$ state.	depth-first search
dfb-search: state $\Longrightarrow$ state.	depth-first search with backtracking
bf-search: state $\Longrightarrow$ state.	breadth-first search

Figure 6: Control strategies.

deterministic functions: depth-first search, depth-first search with backtracking, and breadth-first search.

Guarded Functional Programming

Basically, there are four syntactic constructs to define functions and relations in GFP*:

1. $A_0 \leftarrow A_1, \ldots, A_n$ (*Horn clauses*)
2. $f(t_1, \ldots, t_m) = e$ (*equations*)
3. $f(t_1, \ldots, t_m) \, [\!] \, G = e$ (*guarded equations*)
4. $f(t_1, \ldots, t_m) = < e \, \| \, G >$ (*stream producers*)

where t_i are patterns (terms composed only of constructors and variables), e is a functional expression, G is a Horn logic goal, A_i are atoms of the form $p(t_1, \ldots, t_n)$ (p is a predicate symbol and t_i are patterns). That is, function symbols and constructor symbols are distinguished, left-hand sides of equations have only constructor terms as arguments, and the term universe in the Horn clause part of GFP* is restricted to constructor terms (data terms). In addition, GFP* has a polymorphic type system in the Milner style and some other common features of functional languages like *if-then-else* and *let*-constructs. A GFP* program is a set of Horn clauses, equations, guarded equations, and stream producers.

The semantics of guarded equations $l \, [\!] \, G = r$ is informally that l equals r iff G is satisfiable. Operationally, any expression e which matches l with a substitution τ evaluates to $\sigma\tau r$ iff τG can be proven by SLD-resolution w.r.t. the Horn clauses of the program, and the answer substitution of τG is σ.

If the left-hand side of a stream producer $l = < e \, \| \, G >$ matches a term with a substitution τ, this term evaluates to the stream of all expressions $< \sigma_1 \tau e, \sigma_2 \tau e, \ldots >$

where σ_i are all answer substitutions which satisfy the goal τG w.r.t. the Horn clauses of the program. The right-hand side of a stream producer is called *stream comprehension*. The stream data structure is principally the same as the list data structure. We write $<>$ for the empty stream and $< e|S >$ for a stream with first element e and rest stream S. Streams can be infinite (a goal can have infinitely many solutions), and lazy evaluation is used to deal with them. There is a built-in polymorphic type $stream(T)$ which denotes streams with elements of type T.

As Horn clauses in Prolog, (guarded) equations and stream producers are tried in textual order. If a guard of an equation fails, the next equation is tried. If the goal of a stream comprehension fails, the comprehension evaluates to the empty stream. If a guard has more than one solution, only one is considered and the rest of the solutions are committed ("committed choice"). As we will see in the following, any of the four syntactic categories of GFP* programs corresponds to one of the semantic categories identified in Section 3.

A derivate of GFP, GuardedTermML [Loc88] has been implemented based on an abstract machine [MMTC91] and is currently being extended by stream comprehensions. A prototype implementation supporting finite streams on top of Prolog is already available [Cha91].

Solving the Sample Problem with GFP*

Guards as a Logic Programming Interface. One of the more pragmatic aspects of GFP* is that one can use guards as an interface from a functional language to Horn logic programs.[3] In our case study, we make use of this as follows: we assume that the specification of inference systems, i.e. the selection, test, and construction function of rules schemes (cf Figure 4), are completely defined as Horn logic predicates, and we re-implement only successor functions and control algorithms in GFP*.

For example, for any inference system and any inference rule we assume that the constructor function of a rule scheme is defined as a Horn logic predicate, i.e. a relation,

cons $\subseteq$ rule $\times$ state $\times$ redex $\times$ trans-par $\times$ state.

In fact, cons is considered to be a function

cons: rule $\times$ state $\times$ redex $\times$ trans-par $\longrightarrow$ state.

This function can be defined as a GFP* function using guards as an interface to the predicate. To distinguish both kinds of objects, we add a prefix rs- to the Prolog

---

[3]We consider a Horn logic program as a collection of Horn clauses where queries or goals are executed by means of SLD-resolution. We avoid the term "Prolog", because the Prolog programming language contains a lot of additional features. But in principle, any GFP* implementation can have full Prolog as its logic part.

predicates, which define the elementary functions of rule schemes. The GFP* function select, test and cons can now be defined by

```
select(R,S)     []  rs-select(R,S,RX) = RX.
test(R,S,RX)    []  rs-test(R,S,RX,TP) = TP.
cons(R,S,RX,TP) []  rs-cons(R,S,RX,TP,SS) = SS.
```

The latter two are considered to be deterministic functions, but their determinacy can only be ensured if the predicates rs-test and rs-cons have a deterministic behaviour, i.e. if the corresponding calls yield a unique result. The select function is non-deterministic, and the non-deterministic predicate rs-select is used to introduce non-determinism into the definition of the function via the guard.

Pure Relations. Since Horn clause logic is completely integrated in GFP*, it is obvious that pure relations are just defined with Horn clauses, without use of any functional features of GFP*. For example the relations is-rule and final of an inference system specification are considered to be defined by Horn clauses.

Pure Functions. We have already seen, how deterministic functions can be defined by means of deterministic predicates through guards as an interface to Horn logic programs. But, of course, GFP* can be used as a pure functional programming language, if one uses only (non-guarded) equations. For example, a function for appending two streams can be defined as follows:

```
s-append: stream(T) ×stream(T) ⟶stream(T).

s-append( <  > ,S) = S.
s-append( < E::S > ,SS) = < E::s-append(S,SS) > .
```

Non-Deterministic Functions. In guarded equations, the guard not necessarily has a unique answer substitution as expected for the predicate rs-cons in the definition of the function cons above. In general, guards can have more than one solution. This fact can be used to program non-deterministic functions in GFP*. For example, this has been done to specify the non-deterministic function select based on the predicate rs-select. It can be used together with the other elementary functions of rule schemes to define a function r-succ, which computes the successor of a state with respect to an inference rule:

```
r-succ: rule ×state ⟹state.

r-succ(R,S) =   let RX = select(R,S)
                in let test(R,S,RX) = TP
                   in if TP ≠ F
                         then cons(R,S,RX,TP).
```

r-succ is a non-deterministic function, because the right-hand side expression is based on select which is non-deterministic. In particular, r-succ may fail (because TP = F), and if it has a result, it is not uniquely determined.

This definition of the r-succ function has one problem: for any state, only *one* redex is produced by the non-deterministic select function. If the test fails for this redex, r-succ fails as well although there might be other redexes where the test succeeds. The intention of r-succ is different: if there is a redex where the test succeeds, r-succ must deliver a successor. To solve this problem, one must be able to investigate *all* possible redexes of a state. This can be expressed by using a stream valued function which produces a stream of redexes. In this stream, a "right" redex can be looked for.

Set-Valued Functions. The stream valued functions mentioned above can be considered as a realization of the set-valued functions of the taxonomy presented in Section 3. For example, a stream valued function selects which produces the stream of all redexes of a state can be defined in GFP* as follows

selects: rule ×state —→stream(redex).

selects(R,S) = < RX ‖ rs-select(R,S,RX) > .

The equation defining selects is a *stream producer* which uses the predicate rs-select as a goal in a stream comprehension, whereas in the definition of select it is used as a guard. In the former application, the goal produces *all* solutions, whereas in the latter only the first solution is considered (committed choice).

With that, a correct version of the function r-succ can be realized by means of a help function r-s, which takes a stream of redexes as input, and looks for the first one, where a test succeeds. This input stream of redexes has to be initialized by the one produced by selects as defined above:

r-succ: rule ×state ⟹state.

r-succ(R,S) = r-s(R,S,selects(R,S)).

r-s: rule ×state ×stream(redex) ⟹state.

$$r\text{-}s(R,S, < \; RX{::}RXS > \;) = \quad \text{let test}(R,S,RX) = TP$$
$$\text{in} \;\; \text{if } TP \neq F$$
$$\text{then cons}(R,S,RX,TP)$$
$$\text{else r-s}(R,S,RXS).$$

In a similar way, we can define a stream- (set-) valued function all-r-succ which computes all successors of a state with respect to a certain rule. This time, a function all-r-s is introduced, which investigates a stream of redexes and produces the stream of all states which can be inferred form these redexes.

all-r-succs: rule ×state ⟶stream(state).

all-r-succs(R,S) = all-r-s(R,S,selects(R,S)).

all-r-s: rule ×state ×stream(redex) ⟶stream(state).

all-r-s(R,S, < >) = < > .
all-r-s(R,S, < RX::RXS >) = let test(R,S,RX) = TP
                       in if TP ≠ F
                             then < cons(R,S,RX,TP)::all-r-s(R,S,RXS) >
                             else all-r-s(R,S,RXS).

Finally, a stream-valued function computing all successors of a state (with respect to all possible rules), can be defined by taking the stream of all rules of an inference system, and successively appending the corresponding streams of successors computed by all-r-succ.

all-succs: state ⟶stream(state).

all-succs(S) = s(S, < R ‖ is-rule(R) >).

s: state ×stream(rule) ⟶stream(state).

s(S, < >) = < > .
s(S, < R::RS >) = s-append(all-r-succs(S,R),s(S,RS)).

Note that the predicate is-rule specifies which rule belongs to an inference system (cf. Figure 4).

Since the functions for basic state transitions are now defined, we are ready to program control strategies in GFP*. We start with depth-first search.

df-search: state ⟹state.

df-search(S) ⟦ final(S) = S.
df-search(S) = if < SS::_ > = all-succ(S)
                 then df-search(SS)
                 else "dead-end".

The interesting point in this definition is that only the first element of the stream produced by all-succ is used. That is, the non-deterministic function succ computing *one* successor of a state (cf. Figure 5) is superfluous, or it can be simply defined by

succ: state ⟹state.

succ(S) = let < SS::_ > = all-succ(S) in SS.

This shows a way to use a stream-valued function as a non-deterministic function, because the order in which values occur in a stream is not determined. Lazy evaluation of stream comprehensions can guarantee that no useless computations are done.

As second control strategy, we define breadth-first search as a stream valued function producing every solution for a problem state:

bf-search: state $\longrightarrow$ stream(state).

bf-search(S) = bfs(< S >).

bfs: stream(state) $\longrightarrow$ stream(state).

bfs(< >) = < > .
bfs(< S::SS >) [] final(S) = < S::bfs(SS) > .
bfs(< S::SS >) = bfs(s-append(SS,all-succ(S))).

bfs takes a stream of states (states which have not yet been considered for applying rules), outputs final states and updates the list with successors of those states already contained in the list. bf-search initializes the state list with the problem state. If an expression bf-search(S) with some concrete state S is evaluated lazily, it does not care whether a state has infinitely many solutions. For example, if one only needs one solution, the expression

let < S::_ > = bf-search(S) in S.

will do. In this case, the stream argument of bfs realizes some kind of explicit "back-tracking stack" in functional computations. Lazy evaluation ensures that only as much information is explicitly stored as is necessary. All true backtrack points which are needed to fill the argument stream are kept in the logic world and addressed through stream comprehensions.

5 Conclusions

Guarded Functional Programming with lazy stream comprehensions (GFP*) is a pragmatic combination of functional and logic programming. We have shown a systematic way how to use (GFP*) to solve a practical problem, the implementation of an interpreter for inference systems. The problem has been structured by means of a taxonomy of functions and relations which distinguishes pure (deterministic) functions (fixed I/O mode, unique result), non-deterministic functions (fixed I/O-mode, multiple results including failure), set-valued functions (fixed I/O-mode, a unique set of results), and relations (multiple I/O-modes, multiple results including failure).

Orthogonally to this taxonomy, GFP* provides four basic programming constructs: Pure equations apply to an expression if pattern matching with the left-hand side

type of function/relation	GFP* programming constructs
pure (deterministic) function	equations with deterministic rhs
non-deterministic function	guarded equations equations with non-determinstic rhs selecting one element of a stream
set-valued function	stream comprehensions equation with stream-valued rhs
relation	Horn clauses

Figure 7: The taxonomy of functions and relations vs. basic GFP* programming constructs.

succeeds. Guarded equations apply if pattern matching succeeds and, in addition, the guard which is a Horn logic query can be solved with respect to a Horn logic program. Stream comprehensions are based on a Horn logic query as well, and they evaluate to a (possibly infinite) stream of expressions determined by the solutions of the query. Finally, Horn clauses can be used to define pure relational programs. Figure 7 summarizes different ways to use the programming constructs of GFP* in order to program the different kinds of functions and relations of the taxonomy.

As to functions and relations, the taxonomy can be applied to expressions, e.g. the right-hand sides of equations in Figure 7: a deterministic expression reduces to a unique result, a non-deterministic expression can reduce to different results and a set-valued expression reduces to a (unique) set of values. A relational expression is a query. Besides the systematic use of GFP*-concepts shown in Figure 7 there is also some kind of unproper use of concepts, for example one can use a guarded equation to program functions, if the guard is deterministic (as shown for the specification of the functions of rule schemes in Section 4).

GFP* strictly separates the functional and logic programming world. In principle, only relational programming gives rise to non-determinism and multiple solutions of expressions. Guards and stream comprehensions are used to customize the non-determinism introduced by relational or logic programming to be exploited in functional expressions. Lazy evaluation of streams enables to deal with infinite solutions and avoids superfluous computations (cf. [DL91]).

Although the strict separation of functional and logic (or deterministic and non-deterministic) computations has certain benefits for implementations, it restricts the expressive power. Future extensions of GFP* will allow strict functional expressions as arguments of guards and simple equations on non-deterministic expressions as guards. Also, the logic part of GFP* is conceptually not restricted to Horn logic programming. Any other non-deterministic and relational formalism is appropriate, e.g. relational data base queries.

Acknowledgements. This work has been done in the context of the ESPRIT Basic Research Action No. 3147 (PHOENIX) and was partially funded by the CEC. We are grateful for many discussions and the stimulating environment created by the members of this project. Special thanks to Manuel Chakravarty, Birgit Heinz, Hendrik Lock and Nick Graham who contributed either directly or through critical reviews to the development of the concepts of Guarded Functional Programming.

References

[Cha91]   M. M. T. Chakravarty. Die funktional logische Programmiersprache Guarded termml: Sprachdefinition. Technical report, GMD Research Laboratory Karlsruhe, May 1991.

[Die90]   R. Dietrich. *Vergleichende Analyse von Inferenzsystemen*. GMD-Bericht Nr. 188. R. Oldenbourg Verlag, 1990.

[Die91]   R. Dietrich. The PHOENIX case study: EXIS - an environment for experimenting with inference systems. GMD-Studie Nr. 190, April 1991.

[DL91]   R. Dietrich and H. C. R. Lock. Exploiting non-determinism through laziness in guarded functional languages. In *TAPSOFT'91, Colloquium on Combining Paradigms for Software Development*, Brighton, England, April 1991.

[DP91]   R. Dietrich and H. Pull. Case studies in declarative programming. GMD Forschungsstelle Karlsruhe and Imperial College, London, PHOENIX-Deliverable A.2.1, March 1991.

[Dra87]   W. Drabent. Do logic programs resemble conventional programs. In *4th IEEE Symposium on Logic Programming, San Francisco*, pages 389–397, 1987.

[GL90]   Yi-Ke Guo and H. C. R. Lock. A Classification Scheme for Declarative Programming Languages. - Syntax, Semantics, and Operational Models. GMD-Studien Nr. 182, August 1990.

[Loc88]   Hendrik C.R. Lock. Guarded Term ML. In *Workshop on Implementations of Lazy Functional Languages*, Aspenas, Sept. 1988. Report 53, PMG, Univ. of Goteborg, Sweden.

[MMTC91] H. C. R. Lock M. M. T. Chackravarty. The Implementation of Lazy Narrowing. In *Programming Language Implementation and Logic Programming (PLILP'91), Passau*, August 1991. Springer LNCS (to appear).

[Nil82]   N. J. Nilsson. *Principles of Artificial Intelligence*. Springer, 1982.

[Rob65]   J. A. Robinson. A machine oriented logic based on the resolution principle. *JACM*, 12, No.1:23–41, January 1965.

Enriching Prolog with S-Unification

Andreas Kågedal
Feliks Kluźniak*
Dept. of Computer and Information Science
Linköping University†

Abstract

The concept of S-unification provides a semantically clean way of combining logic programs with functions written in other languages. This paper shows how to implement a logic programming language with S-unification by transforming it to a Prolog program. The scheme is reasonably efficient if Prolog supports efficient coroutining.

1 Introduction

In the past decade, a number of attempts have been made to integrate logic and functional programming. The resulting languages can be classified roughly into two groups:

- Those that integrate a logic programming language with an existing functional language. Examples: LOGLISP [RS82], QLOG [Kom82], POPLOG [MH84] and APPLOG [Coh86].

- Completely new languages that allow definitions of both functions and relations. Examples: EQLOG [GM86], LEAF [BBLM86], FUNLOG [SY86], Le Fun [AKLN87] and Aflog [SNHM87].

The major drawback of the first approach is that unrestricted access to features of the underlying language often makes it hard to give a declarative reading to the programs. The second approach uses equational systems to implement functions, and requires equational unification, which—in its full generality—creates computational problems.

In both kinds of approaches the aim was to obtain a single language in which one could specify both the logical and the functional part of the program. In practice it may often be more convenient to develop an application that uses some existing library procedures written in another language (e.g. the math library for C). These procedures would be the functional part of the program. Some Prolog

---

*(on leave from the Institute of Informatics, Warsaw University)
†S-581 83 Linköping, Sweden. email: andka@ida.liu.se

systems allow this, but it is difficult to assign a logical meaning to the combined programs. A more rigorous approach to amalgamating a logic language with external procedures was presented in [Bon89, BM88]. The approach has the following properties:

- The functional component of the language is not fixed. In principle, functions can be written in any language.

- The declarative semantics of the logic programming language is clean.

- The operational semantics is based on an incomplete equational unification, called S-unification (as in Structure-oriented).

The advantage of the approach is that it is possible to (re-)use external software and still have an amalgamated program with clean declarative semantics (as long as the external software has no side effects).

The concept of S-unification could be viewed as an extension to ordinary syntactic (Robinson) unification in which functional terms (i.e. terms that corresponds to invocations of external functions) are treated differently. This paper shows how to implement a logic programming language that uses S-unification. The language is called GAPLog (General Amalgamated Programming with Logic). Programs written in GAPLog are compiled into Prolog by exploiting the resemblance of S-unification to syntactic unification. For this approach to work, the Prolog system must have some sort of foreign language interface (e.g. like Quintus or SICStus Prolog).

The rest of the paper is organized as follows: Section 2 introduces the concept of S-unification and defines basic terminology. Section 3 outlines an augmented resolution mechanism for GAPLog. In section 4 the S-unification algorithm is modified to fit in the framework of a scheme that transforms GAPLog programs to Prolog. Sections 5–8 contain a step-by-step development of the transformation scheme. A small example is presented in section 9, and the paper ends with the conclusions in section 10.

2 Preliminaries

The alphabet of function symbols is partitioned into two parts: the set of *constructors* and the set of *defined symbols*. Terms built solely from constructors and variables are called *pure terms*. A term whose principal functor is defined is called a *functional term*. A *functional call* is a term of the form $f(s_1, \ldots s_n)$ where f is a defined symbol and $s_1, \ldots s_n$ are pure terms. Each defined symbol has an associated external procedure. A ground functional call $f(s_1, \ldots s_n)$ represents a ground pure term which can be obtained by applying the associated external procedure to $s_1, \ldots s_n$. This pure term is denoted by $f(s_1, \ldots s_n)\!\downarrow$.

The general strategy of Bonnier's S-unification algorithm is to transform the set of equations to be unified, E, into a *normal form* N. An equation is an expression of the form $u \doteq t$, where u and t are arbitrary terms. In the following definition, "u occurs in N" means "u is a (sub)term on the left hand or right hand side of some equation in N":

Definition 2.1 Let N be a finite set of equations. N is in *normal form* iff:

- $N = \{x_1 \doteq s_1, \ldots x_n \doteq s_n, r_1 \doteq d_1, \ldots r_m \doteq d_m\}$, where $n, m \geq 0$,

- each x_i is a variable which occurs only once in N,

- each d_i is a nonground functional call which occurs only once in N,

- all s_i and r_j are pure terms.

If, in addition, $r_1, \ldots r_m$ are all distinct variables and there exists a permutation π on $\{1, \ldots m\}$ such that $1 \leq i \leq j \leq m$ implies that $r_{\pi i}$ does not occur in $d_{\pi j}$, then N is in *solved form*. In this case the substitution $\mathsf{sol}(N)$ is defined by:

$$\mathsf{sol}(N) = \{x_1/s_1, \ldots x_n/s_n\}\{r_{\pi 1}/d_{\pi 1}\} \cdots \{r_{\pi m}/d_{\pi m}\} \qquad \square$$

Example 2.1 Let s and 0 be constructors and let f be a defined symbol. Then the sets:

$$N_1 = \{x \doteq s(y), y \doteq f(y), 0 \doteq f(s(y))\}$$
$$N_2 = \{x \doteq s(y), y \doteq f(s(w)), w \doteq f(z)\}$$

are both in normal form. In addition, N_2 is in solved form, and:

$$\mathsf{sol}(N_2) = \{x/s(f(s(f(z)))), y/f(s(f(z))), w/f(z)\} \qquad \square$$

An algorithm which attempts to transform a finite set E of equations into normal form can be described as the following Normal Form Procedure (this is the algorithm given in [Bon89]):

NFP:
Initially, let $E_0 = E$ and $i = 0$. Repeatedly do the following: Select any equation $u \doteq t$ in E_i such that one of the rules 1 to 9 applies. If no such equation exists then stop with E_i as result. Otherwise perform the corresponding action, i.e. stop with failure or construct E_{i+1} from E_i and increment i by 1.

1. u and t are identical. Remove $u \doteq t$.

2. u is a variable which has at least two occurrences in E_i and t is a pure term distinct from u. If u occurs in t then stop with failure, otherwise replace all other occurrences of u by t (i.e. leave $u \doteq t$ unchanged).

3. u is a nonvariable and t is a variable. Replace $u \doteq t$ by $t \doteq u$.

4. $u = c_1(u_1, \ldots u_{n_1})$ and $t = c_2(t_1, \ldots t_{n_2})$ where c_1 and c_2 are constructors. If $c_1 \neq c_2$ or $n_1 \neq n_2$ then stop with failure, otherwise replace $u \doteq t$ by $u_1 \doteq t_1, \ldots u_{n_1} \doteq t_{n_1}$.

5. u and t are both functional calls. Let z be a variable not in $var(E_i) \cup var(E)$. Replace $u \doteq t$ by the two equations $z \doteq u$ and $z \doteq t$.

6. u or t has a functional call d as a proper subterm. Let z be a variable not in $var(E_i) \cup var(E)$. Replace all occurrences of d in E_i by z, then add the equation $z \doteq d$.

7. u is a functional call and t is a pure term. Replace $u \doteq t$ by $t \doteq u$.

8. u is a pure term and t is a functional call which occurs elsewhere in E_i. Replace all other occurrences of t by u (i.e. leave $u \doteq t$ unchanged).

9. t is a ground functional call. Replace $u \doteq t$ by $u \doteq t{\downarrow}$. □

Now an algorithm that S-unifies two terms t_1 and t_2 can be outlined:

S-Unify1:
Apply NFP to $\{t_1 \doteq t_2\}$. Then carry out one of the alternatives 1 to 3 below, depending on the result:

1. If the result is failure, then terminate and output *fail*.

2. If the result is a set N in solved form, then terminate and output sol(N).

3. If the result is a set in normal form which is not in solved form, then terminate and output "don't know". □

3 Augmenting resolution with lazy cancellation

The purpose of S-unification is to replace ordinary unification in the resolution mechanism of a logic programming language. But if a resolution mechanism uses S-unification, then an attempt to unify a goal literal g with the head h of a clause might yield "don't know" as an answer. What is the mechanism to do then? There are two obvious possibilities:

- Terminate the search for a solution right away and report that it is not known whether this goal has a solution or not. This will be called *eager cancellation*.

- Continue to search for solutions to the goal in the hope that g and h are unifiable. As the refutation progresses and more variables are bound it might become possible to determine whether g and h are unifiable. If the end of the refutation is reached and it is still not known whether g and h can be unified, then the resolution mechanism must give a don't know message. This will be called *lazy cancellation*[1].

The eager approach decreases the likelihood that the program will not terminate. It is also easier to check statically whether a program could give a "don't know" answer. The lazy approach may find solutions where eager cancellation would give a "don't know" answer: it is thus "less incomplete". This paper will describe how to implement a logic programming language that uses S-unification and lazy cancellation.

---

[1]The notion of S-SLD resolution, very similar to lazy cancellation, has been independently investigated by Johan Boye. A formal treatment is given in [Boy91].

When the S-unification algorithm signals "don't know", it is because NFP was only able to transform the set of equations into a set N that is in normal but not solved form. This means that there are some equations in N for which S-unification could not determine their solvability. They might become solvable (or unsolvable) as more variables become instantiated. For the present they play a role somewhat similar (though more restricted) to the constraints of Constraint Logic Programming languages [JL87, Hen89, DHS+88].

Definition 3.1 A *constraint* is an equation $r \doteq d$ where r is a pure term and d is a nonground functional call. □

Definition 3.2 Let $N = \{x_1 \doteq s_1, \ldots x_n \doteq s_n, r_1 \doteq d_1, \ldots r_m \doteq d_m\}$ (where $n, m \geq 0$) be a set in normal form. Define:

$$\text{unif}(N) = \{x_1/s_1, \ldots x_n/s_n\}$$

$$\text{constr}(N) = \{r_1 \doteq d_1, \ldots r_m \doteq d_m\}$$

□

It follows from the definition of *solved form* that the only equations in N that might affect whether N is in solved form or not are those in $\text{constr}(N)$.

Suppose that S-unification of two literals resulted in the set N which is in normal but not solved form. Since it is not in solved form, N cannot be represented as a substitution. $\text{unif}(N)$ is a substitution that can be applied to the remaining goal, but $\text{constr}(N)$ must be explicitly passed on in the resolution process. To cater for this, the S-unification algorithm and the resolution mechanism must be modified somewhat.

The new version of the S-unification algorithm which unifies the terms t_1 and t_2 and also takes a set C of constraints as an argument, would be as follows:

S-Unify2:
Apply NFP to $\{t_1 \doteq t_2\} \cup C$. If the result is failure, then terminate and output *fail*. Otherwise the result is a set N in normal form, so terminate and output the pair $\langle \text{unif}(N), \text{constr}(N) \rangle$. □

S-Unify2 thus either fails or returns a pair $\langle \sigma, C' \rangle$ where σ is a substitution and C' is a new set of constraints.

Augmented Resolution Scheme:
Let G be the goal to be proved. Let $G_0 = G$, $C_0 = \emptyset$ and $i = 0$. Repeatedly do the following until G_i is the empty goal or no further progress is possible:

G_i has the form $g_1, \ldots g_n$. Select a goal literal g_k from G_i and find (if possible) a renamed version of a program clause $h :- b_1, \ldots b_m$ such that S-unification does not fail when applied to g and h together with C_i. S-unification thus returns a pair $\langle \sigma, C \rangle$. Let $C_{i+1} = C$ and $G_{i+1} = (g_1, \ldots g_{k-1}, b_1, \ldots b_m, g_{k+1}, \ldots g_n)\sigma$ and increment i.

If G_i is the empty goal and C_i is in solved form then $G_0, \ldots G_i$ is a refutation, but if C_i is not in solved form then it might not be a refutation: output a "don't know" message or show the remaining constraints. □

4 Using syntactic unification

It would not be difficult to implement a GAPLog interpreter using the augmented resolution scheme and S-Unify2. Such an interpreter, however, would be much less efficient than a good implementation of Prolog. Extending WAM to accommodate S-unification and writing a new compiler might be a viable solution, but it turns out there is a much easier way to construct a reasonably efficient implementation.

A closer investigation of NFP reveals obvious similarities with ordinary syntactic unification. Rules 1–4 are essentially syntactic unification, and rules 5–9 deal with functional terms. Note that the S-unification algorithm reduces to syntactic unification if the terms being unified are both pure. In principle, the efficiency of a GAPLog program without functional terms should not be worse than the efficiency of an equivalent Prolog program.

This suggests that a GAPLog program could be transformed into an equivalent Prolog program where the S-unification and calls to external procedures are explicit. The S-unification algorithm must be modified to exploit the syntactic unification of the underlying Prolog system. This is accomplished by first applying rule 6 of NFP to lift all functional calls out of the two terms being unified. The new terms can then be unified with syntactic unification. Algorithm S-Unify2 could now be rewritten to:

S-Unify3:

1. Repeatedly apply rule 6 of NFP to $\{t_1 \doteq t_2\}$ until this is no longer possible. This yields a set $\{t'_1 \doteq t'_2, z_1 \doteq d_1, \ldots z_n \doteq d_n\}$, where $n \geq 0$, $z_1, \ldots z_n$ are new variables, $d_1, \ldots d_n$ are functional calls and t'_1 and t'_2 look like t_1 and t_2 except that all functional subterms have been replaced with variables from the set $\{z_1, \ldots z_n\}$.

2. Then try to unify t'_1 and t'_2 using syntactic unification. If this fails then terminate and return *fail*, otherwise let σ_1 be the unifier.

3. Then apply σ_1 to all terms of the set $\{z_1 \doteq d_1, \ldots z_n \doteq d_n\} \cup C$ and give the new set to NFP. If this fails then return *fail*, otherwise a set N in normal form is obtained. Let $\sigma_2 = \mathrm{unif}(N)$ and return $\langle \sigma_1 \sigma_2, \mathrm{constr}(N) \rangle$. □

Now, since both $\{z_1 \doteq d_1, \ldots z_n \doteq d_n\}$ and C are sets of constraints, S-Unify3 only applies the full NFP to a set of constraints. It is therefore easy to see that rules 5–7 will never be used, and hence can be removed from the algorithm. Rules 5 and 7 can be removed because, after step 2 of S-Unify3, every equation will have a pure term as its left side (and there is no rule that replaces a pure term with a functional call or adds a new equation with a functional call as its left side). Rule 6 has already been applied wherever possible, and there is no way any new functional calls could later be introduced as subterms in the equations.

A useful observation is that since no substitution of the form v/d, where d is a functional term, will be applied to to the program, rule 6 can be applied statically, i.e. at compile time. The augmented resolution scheme will use only steps 2 and 3 of S-Unify3, i.e. a slightly modified syntactic unification algorithm.

5 A Transformation Scheme

It is now possible to give a scheme that transforms a GAPLog program into a Prolog program where the S-unification is explicit. This is done in three steps. First rule 6 of NFP is applied to the program, giving an equivalent GAPLog program where the constraints are visible, then constraints are made explicit by "threading" them through the program clauses, and finally code is added for "normalizing" the constraints. This transformation scheme will be called *Transformation-1*.

5.1 Applying rule 6 statically

As has been noted rule 6 of NFP can be applied statically. Applying rule 6 yields a set of constraints that are added to the program as "constraint literals".

In the first step of the transformation, every clause $h : -B$ is transformed as follows:

> For each atom b of B, construct $\{v \doteq b\}$, where v is a new variable. Apply rule 6 to this set, as many times as possible. This yields $\{v \doteq b', z_1 \doteq d_1, \ldots z_n \doteq d_n\}$. Replace b with the atoms $z_1 \doteq d_1, \ldots z_n \doteq d_n, b'$. Let B' be the new body.

> Then apply rule 6 as many times as possible to $\{v \doteq h\}$, where v is a new variable. This yields $\{v \doteq h', z_1 \doteq d_1, \ldots z_n \doteq d_n\}$.

> The transformed clause will be $h' : - z_1 \doteq d_1, \ldots z_n \doteq d_n, B'$.

Example 5.1 Let f and g be defined symbols. The clause:

```
q(f(X),X)  :- p(g(X,X)).
```

is translated to:

```
q(Z1,X)  :- Z1 ≐ f(X),  Z2 ≐ g(X,X),  p(Z2).
```

□

5.2 Augmenting resolution by constraint threading

The purpose of the next transformation step is to make it possible to utilize the execution mechanism of Prolog for simulating the augmented resolution algorithm of section 3. This is achieved by "constraint threading". Each literal is extended with two additional arguments. At runtime one of them will be instantiated to the set of constraints accumulated before resolution with the literal, and the other to the modified set of constraints obtained after the literal has been reduced.[2] In effect, the propagation of constraints is made implicit w.r.t. the resolution mechanism by making it explicit in the text of the program.

Let CS be the clause schema:

---

[2]The scheme is very similar to that normally used for transforming DCG rules into Prolog clauses, where variables representing the string of terminal symbols are "threaded" through the literals that represent the nonterminals.

$$h(Arglist_h) :- C_h,$$
$$C_1, b_1(Arglist_1),$$
$$\vdots$$
$$C_{m-1}, b_{m-1}(Arglist_{m-1}),$$
$$C_m, b_m(Arglist_m).$$

(where C_h and $C_1, \ldots C_m$ represent sequences of constraint literals)
  Threading a constraint set through CS will result in:

$$h(Arglist_h, E_{old}, E_{new}) :-$$
$$b_1(Arglist_1, [C_h, C_1|E_{old}], E_1),$$
$$\vdots$$
$$b_{m-1}(Arglist_{m-1}, [C_{m-1}|E_{m-2}], E_{m-1}),$$
$$b_m(Arglist_m, [C_m|E_{m-1}], E_{new}).$$

5.3 Explicit normalization of constraints

Now steps 1 and 2 of S-Unify3 have been compiled into the program, but the actual "normalization" of the constraint sets has not. In S-Unify3 the normalization occurs just after the modified goal literal has unified with the modified head literal of a clause c. This implies that an explicit call to NFP should be placed first in the body of c.

The constraint set that is normalized in step 3 of S-Unify3 consists of the new constraints from the goal literal and the head literal, and the old constraints from earlier S-unifications. The constraints from the head literal are already present in the beginning of the clause body (C_h), and the constraints from the goal literal are passed to the clause (together with the old constraints) through an argument (E_{old}) in the head.

Let `normalize/2` be a predicate that applies NFP to its first argument and unifies the resulting set in normal form with its second argument. If NFP fails then `normalize/2` fails.

The fully transformed version of CS would be:

$$h(Arglist_h, E_{old}, E_{new}) :-$$
$$\texttt{normalize}([C_h|E_{old}], E_{norm}),$$
$$b_1(Arglist_1, [C_1|E_{norm}], E_1),$$
$$\vdots$$
$$b_{m-1}(Arglist_{m-1}, [C_{m-1}|E_{m-2}], E_{m-1}),$$
$$b_m(Arglist_m, [C_m|E_{m-1}], E_{new}).$$

A transformed program can now run in a Prolog system if the predicate `normalize/2` is provided. The overhead generated by the calls to `normalize/2` could still be prohibitive.

6 Specializing the Normal Form Procedure

In Transformation-1 NFP (`normalize/2`) is only applied to constraints. As noted in section 4, this means that there is no need for rules 5–7. There is also room for other improvements.

When NFP is applied to a set of constraints it can initially use only rules 8 and 9. But all equations generated or changed by rule 8 or 9 can only be processed by rules 1–4, i.e. they will be subject to syntactic unification. Syntactic unification can be incorporated directly into rules 8 and 9, giving a Specialized Normal Form Procedure, whose starting point is a set of constraints C:

> *SNFP:*
> Initially, let $C_0 = C$, $\theta_0 = \varepsilon$ and $i = 0$. Repeatedly do the following: Select any constraint $u \doteq t$ in C_i such that one of the rules 8 or 9 applies. If no such equation exists then stop with C_i and θ_i as result. Otherwise perform the corresponding action, i.e. stop with failure or construct C_{i+1} and θ_{i+1} and then increment i by 1.

1.–7. Not needed.

8. t is a functional call which occurs elsewhere in C_i. Let $u_1 \doteq t, \ldots u_n \doteq t$ be the other constraints where t occurs. Try to syntactically unify $u, u_1, \ldots u_n$. If this fails then stop with failure. Otherwise the syntactic unification yielded a substitution σ. Let $C_{i+1} = (C_i - \{u_1 \doteq t_1, \ldots u_n \doteq t_n\})\sigma$ and $\theta_{i+1} = \theta_i\sigma$. (Note that the original constraint $u \doteq t$ is not removed.)

9. t is a ground functional call. Try to syntactically unify u and $t{\downarrow}$ (i.e. the value returned by the call). If this fails then stop with failure. Otherwise the syntactic unification yielded a substitution σ. Let $C_{i+1} = (C_i - \{u \doteq t\})\sigma$ and $\theta_{i+1} = \theta_i\sigma$.

$\square$

7 An improved transformation scheme

Suppose that the Prolog system that is used to run the transformed GAPLog programs implements the coroutining predicate `gfreeze/2`, which delays calling its second argument until its first argument is ground.[3] Then rule 9 of SNFP can be implemented in an alternative way. Let $s \doteq d$ be a constraint and `funcall/2` be a predicate that takes a ground function call as its first argument and unifies its second argument with the result of making this function call. A literal of the form `gfreeze(d, funcall(d, s))` would thus wait until d is ground and then syntactically unify $d{\downarrow}$ and s. This is exactly what rule 9 does.

To exploit this in the transformation scheme, static application of rule 6 should produce `gfreeze/2` literals instead of $\doteq$/2 literals (see section 5.1). The constraints must of course still be threaded through the clauses, but `normalize/2` is now simpler: it only applies rule 8.

The transformation of CS would now result in:

$$h(Arglist_h, E_{old}, E_{new}) \;:\text{--} \; W_h,$$
$$\texttt{normalize}([C_h|E_{old}], E_{norm}),$$

---

[3] `gfreeze/2` is similar to `freeze/2` of Prolog II [Col82], but `freeze/2` only waits until the first argument is instantiated. The first is trivial to implement in terms of the latter.

$$W_1, b_1(Arglist_1, [C_1|E_{norm}], E_1),$$
$$\vdots$$
$$W_{m-1}, b_{m-1}(Arglist_{m-1}, [C_{m-1}|E_{m-2}], E_{m-1}),$$
$$W_m, b_m(Arglist_m, [C_m|E_{m-1}], E_{new}).$$

Where, for each sequence C_i of the form $z_1 \doteq d_1, \ldots z_n \doteq d_n$, W_i represents the sequence gfreeze$(d_1,$ funcall$(d_1, z_1))$,$\ldots$gfreeze$(d_n,$ funcall$(d_n, z_n))$.

The potentially costly calls to normalize/2 are now needed only to implement rule 8. But, is rule 8 really necessary?

This is an open question. Application of rule 8 avoids some redundant calls to external functions (by removing duplicate functional calls). But the main reason for introducing this rule was to obtain a certain completeness result which says that S-unification will produce a "don't know answer" only if there is really not enough information to determine whether it should succeed or fail [Bon91]. Although examples for which rule 8 is essential have been constructed [Bon89], they are contrived and very atypical of what one would expect in a logic program. It is therefore very likely that S-unification without rule 8 would be quite satisfactory for all practical purposes.

If rule 8 is discarded from SNFP then normalize/2 does not have any rules to apply to the sets of constraints, and thus both the threaded constraints and the normalize/2 literals can be removed from the transformed program.

Transforming CS using the simplified transformation scheme would yield:

$$h(Arglist_h) :- W_h,$$
$$W_1, b_1(Arglist_1),$$
$$\vdots$$
$$W_{m-1}, b_{m-1}(Arglist_{m-1}),$$
$$W_m, b_m(Arglist_m).$$

where W_i is defined as above.

It is easy to see that this transformation scheme introduces no overhead if the GAPLog program does not contain any functional terms. W_h and $W_1, \ldots W_m$ would then be empty sequences. For programs that do contain functional terms, the overhead is that associated with the coroutining mechanism—and this can be implemented efficiently [Car87].

The above transformation scheme will be referred to as *Transformation-2*.

8 Bringing rule 8 back

It may turn out that even in practice it is desirable to keep rule 8 in the normal form procedure. In that case Transformation-1 would do the job, but it is possible to find a better transformation scheme, *Transformation-3*, that uses some of the ideas of Transformation-2. In this scheme normalize/2 literals will not be inserted into every clause. Instead—informally speaking—"every constraint will take care of its own normalization".

Let 'F'/3 be a predicate that applies SNFP to a constraint together with a set of old constraints, and let static application of rule 6 produce 'F'/3 literals instead of the gfreeze/2 literals of Transformation-2. The constraints must be threaded through the clauses again.

Transformation-3 would convert CS to:

$$h(Arglist_h, E_{old}, E_{new}) :-$$
$$\text{'F'}\,(C_{h1}, E_{old}, E_{h1}),\ \ldots \text{'F'}\,(C_{hn_h}, E_{h(n_h-1)}, E_{hn_h}),$$
$$\text{'F'}\,(C_{11}, E_{hn_h}, E_{11}),\ \ldots b_1(Arglist_1, E_{old}, E_1),$$
$$\vdots$$
$$\text{'F'}\,(C_{(m-1)1}, E_{(m-2)n_{m-2}}, E_{(m-1)1}),\ \ldots b_{m-1}(Arglist_{m-1}, E_{m-2}, E_{m-1}),$$
$$\text{'F'}\,(C_{m1}, E_{(m-1)n_{m-1}}, E_{m1}),\ \ldots b_m(Arglist_m, E_{m-1}, E_{new}).$$

where $C_{i1}, \ldots C_{in_i}$ is the sequence C_i of constraints.

What is the function of 'F'/3? The idea is to use coroutining also to implement rule 8. Informally, every constraint will be "responsible" for finding the other constraints with an identical functional call as their right side. This can be accomplished by using a coroutining predicate vfreeze/2 that delays calling its second argument if its first argument is a variable. The second argument is called when the variable becomes bound in any way, e.g. to another variable.[4]

The function of 'F' ($s \doteq d$, OldConstraints, NewConstraints) is to search the set of old constraints for constraints where the functional call is identical to d. For every constraint $s' \doteq d$ it finds, it should (syntactically) unify s with s'. This is however not enough. As execution proceeds and more variables become bound, more functional calls may become identical to d. So whenever a variable occurring in d is bound, the set of constraints must be searched again. This is easily accomplished by "vfreezing" on all variables of d after the the search.

The scheme is correct only if the search is made over the full set of "current" constraints, including constraints that were introduced after the activation of the literal where this constraint occurred. This is achieved by representing the set of constraints as a difference list. The new constraint is just added to the end of the list:

```
'F'(S≐F, E-[S≐F | End], E-End) :-
      rule_eight(S≐F, E),
      gfreeze(F, funcall(F, S))).

rule_eight(C, E) :-
      find_identical_and_unify(C,E),
      vfreeze_on_all_vars_or_succeed_if_none(C,E).
```

A minor problem so far is that rule_eight/2 does not actually remove the duplicate constraints from the threaded set of constraints. This can be fixed by associating the constraint with a flag that, if instantiated, signals that this constraint is removed. The same flag can also be used by rule 9 (the gfreeze/2 literal) to avoid making the function call more than once.

Transformation-3 clearly has the same property as Transformation-2: if the source program does not contain any functional terms, it will generate an ordinary

---

[4]This is different from freeze/2 which will not call its second argument until the first argument is bound to a nonvariable. vfreeze/2 can be found e.g. in the "internals" of SICStus Prolog

Prolog program with no overhead for S-unification. But for programs that do contain functional terms the overhead is still significantly larger. It could be decreased e.g. by replacing the list of constraints with a more appropriate data structure.

9 An Example

In this section a small GAPLog program is subject to the various transformation schemes presented above. The program computes the length of a given list. +/2 is assumed to be a defined symbol with the obvious meaning:

```
length([], 0).
length([X | List], Length + 1) :-
    length(List, Length).
```

Transformation-1 would yield:

```
length([], 0, Ein, Eout) :-
    normalize(Ein, Eout).
length([X | List], Z, Ein, Eout) :-
    normalize([Z ≐ Length + 1 | Ein], E1),
    length(List, Length, E1, Eout).
```

Transformation-2 (which does not implement rule 8) would yield:

```
length([], 0).
length([X | List], Z) :-
    gfreeze(Length + 1, funcall(Length + 1, Z)),
    length(List, Length).
```

And Transformation-3 would yield:

```
length([],0,E,E).
length([X | List], Z, Ein, Eout) :-
    'F'(Z ≐ Length + 1, Ein, E1),
    length(List, Length, E1, Eout).
```

A query is transformed as a clause body except that the constraint set given to the first goal atom in the query is empty, and that an extra "don't know check" is added at the end.

9.1 Timings

To give a rough idea of the efficiency of the transformed program, the query length([_,_,...], Length) is timed for lists containing 50, 100, 500 and 1000 items. There were five versions of length/2:

v1. the result of Transformation-2 as given above.

v2. the result of Transformation-3 as given above.

v3. a straightforward Prolog formulation (with is/2).

v4. a tail recursive Prolog formulation.

v5. the straightforward Prolog formulation with a redundant call to gfreeze/2 (the object is to measure the overhead of gfreeze/2 when its first argument is ground).

The times are given in CPU milliseconds as reported by SICStus Prolog running on a Sun SPARC station SLC. (+ was implemented in terms of is/2.)

Compiled

Length:	50	100	500	1000
v1.	20	40	200	450
v2.	479	1849	44630	179200
v3.	0	9	9	30
v4.	0	0	0	10
v5.	9	30	139	279

Interpreted

Length:	50	100	500	1000
v1.	29	69	330	679
v2.	500	1879	45550	181569
v3.	9	29	109	210
v4.	9	19	109	210
v5.	29	70	300	570

As expected, Transformation-3 does not produce an efficient program. This may be due to the fact that a list is not the best way to represent the constraints.

The result of Transformation-2 is reasonably efficient, especially in comparison with interpreted Prolog. Comparison with the last row of each table shows that more than half of the cost is that of decomposing terms (gfreeze/2 is implemented in terms of freeze/2 and =../2).

It must be stressed that length/2 is a "worst case" example: there is a function call for every resolution step. The overhead would be much less noticeable in a larger and more realistic program, so Transformation-2 (i.e. v1.) seems to give satisfactory results.

10 Conclusions

The syntactic unification mechanism of Prolog is extended to S-unification [Bon89, BM88] yielding a system called GAPLog. The contributions of this paper are:

- An informal presentation of an augmented resolution scheme that makes S-unification useful in practice.

- A demonstration that logic programs using augmented resolution scheme with S-unification can be implemented by transforming them to Prolog.

- A stepwise development of the appropriate transformation schemes.

More specifically three transformation schemes are presented.

Transformation-1 is a simple scheme, but it generates Prolog code with significant overhead: calls to normalize/2 are added to every clause.

Transformation-2 uses coroutining. It produces reasonably efficient programs, but at the cost of some functionality of S-unification. Rule 8 of the Normal Form Procedure is omitted. This is believed not to be a problem, since it is hard to find programs which utilize rule 8. Omitting rule 8 can be compared to omitting the occur-check in Prolog. Some theoretical results are lost, but in practice it does not matter. Moreover omitting rule 8 does not affect the soundness of S-unification, only its completeness.

Transformation-3 is a scheme that also uses coroutining, but does not omit rule 8. The overhead is substantial, but can probably be reduced by using a better data structure for the constraint sets. This will be investigated in the near future.

GAPLog is a language that can use external functions in a declaratively clean way. It has been shown that it can be implemented simply and reasonably efficiently.

11 Acknowledgments

We are very grateful to Staffan Bonnier for explaining to us the mysteries of S-Unification, and to Jan Małuszyński for his support and encouragement. This work is a contribution to ESPRIT Project BRA 3020 and was partially supported by the Swedish Natural Science Research Council (NFR).

References

[AKLN87] H. Aït-Kaci, P. Lincoln, and R. Nasr. Le Fun: Logic, Equations and Functions. In *Proc. Symposium on Logic Programming* [IEE87].

[BBLM86] R. Barbuti, M. Bellia, G. Levi, and M. Martelli. LEAF: a Language which integrates Logic, Equations and Functions. In DeGroot and Lindstrom [DL86].

[BM88]   S. Bonnier and J. Małuszyński. Towards a Clean Amalgamation of Logic Programs with External Procedures. In Robert A. Kowalski and Kenneth A. Bowen, editors, *Logic Programming, Proc. of the fifth International Conference and Symposium*, Seatle, 1988. ALP, IEEE, MIT Press.

[Bon89]   Staffan Bonnier. *Horn Clause Logic with External Procedures: Towards a Theoretical Framework*. Licentiate thesis, Linköping University, Dep. of Computer and Information Science, S-581 83 Linköping, Sweden, 1989.

[Bon91]   Staffan Bonnier, 1991. Personal communication.

[Boy91]   Johan Boye. Operational completeness of logic programs with external procedures. Master's thesis, Linköping University, Dep. of Computer and Information Science, S-581 83 Linköping, Sweden, 1991. Report no: LiTH-IDA-Ex-9104.

[Car87]   Mats Carlsson. Freeze, indexing, and other implementation issues in the WAM. In Jean-Louis Lassez, editor, *Logic Programming, Proc. of the Fourth International Conference*, pages 40–58, Melbourne, 1987. MIT Press.

[Coh86]   S. Cohen. The APPLOG Language. In DeGroot and Lindstrom [DL86].

[Col82]   Alain Colmerauer. Prolog II – manuel de référence et modèle
            théoretique. Technical report, Groupe d'Intelligence Artificielle, Uni-
            versité d'Aix-Marseille II, 1982.

[DHS+88]   M. Dincbas, P. Van Hentenryck, H. Simonis, A. Aggoun, T. Graf, and
            F. Berthier. The constraint logic programming language chip. In *Proc.
            of the International Conference on Fifth Generation Computer Systems*,
            pages 693–702, Tokyo, 1988. Institute for New Generation Computer
            Technology, Ohmsha, Ltd.

[DL86]   D. DeGroot and G. Lindstrom, editors. *Logic programming, functions,
            relations and equations*. Prentice-Hall, 1986.

[GM86]   J. Goguen and J. Meseguer. EQLOG: Equality, Types and Generic
            Modules for Logic Programming. In DeGroot and Lindstrom [DL86].

[Hen89]   P. V. Hentenryck. *Constraint Satisfaction in Logic Programming*. MIT
            Press, 1989.

[IEE87]   IEEE. *Proc. Symposium on Logic Programming*, San Francisco, 1987.
            Computer Society Press.

[JL87]   J. Jaffar and J.L. Lassez. Constraint Logic Programming. In *14th ACM
            POPL Conf.* ACM, 1987.

[Kom82]   J. Komorowski. QLOG – The Programming Environment for Prolog
            in LISP. In K.L. Clark and S.-Å. Tärnlund, editors, *Logic Programming*.
            Prentice-Hall, 1982.

[MH84]   C. Mellish and S. Hardy. Integrating Prolog in the Poplog Environ-
            ment. In J. Campbell, editor, *Implementations of Prolog*. Ellis Horwood,
            1984.

[RS82]   J. Robinson and E. Sibert. LOGLISP: Motivation, Design and Imple-
            mentation. In K. Clark and S.-Å. Tärnlund, editors, *Logic Programming*.
            Prentice-Hall, 1982.

[SNHM87]   D.W. Shin, J.H. Nang, S. Han, and S.R. Maeng. A Functional Logic
            Language based on Canonical Unification. In *Proc. Symposium on Logic
            Programming* [IEE87], pages 328–333.

[SY86]   P. Subrahmanyam and J-H. You. Funlog: A computational model
            integrating logic programming and functional programming. In De-
            Groot and Lindstrom [DL86].

A Tiny Functional Language with Logical Features

Ross Paterson*

Abstract

The non-deterministic lambda-calculus is a tiny core language in terms of which all the declaratively understood constructs of constraint functional languages may be defined. This paper describes a denotational semantics based on lower powerdomains, and a polymorphic type system. The calculus has a confluent operational semantics, which may be formulated in several ways—an extension of de Bruijn's calculus is used here.

More useful language constructs may be defined in terms of the core language. The aim of this translation is not to give an implementation—higher-level languages will typically provide efficient implementations of the specific features they provide. Rather the translation to the core language gives a semantics for the higher-level constructs, and provides a standard against which their implementations may be judged. Similarly, transformations at the higher-level may be justified by translating them to transformations proved correct for the core.

Many languages have been proposed as integrations of functional and logic programming. The present study, rather than proposing yet another full-blown language, seeks to isolate the essential features of integrated languages in a minimal core language. We do not claim to cover all such integrations, as we start with the plan of extending a minimal functional language (the λ-calculus) to comprehend logical features. This bias arises from our intended application of these languages to program transformation. We view integrated languages as wide-spectrum languages, allowing solutions to be easily, if inefficiently, expressed. We want the language to have a subset which is efficiently implementable, so that inefficient specifications may be transformed into equivalent (or possibly more specific) implementations in the subset. Further, we choose as this subset the deterministic programs, *i.e.* a functional programming language. Also, we would like the integrated language to preserve as far as possible the advantages of functional programming, *e.g.* compact notation and equational reasoning.

In fact, very little need be added to the λ-calculus to obtain such a language. Choice constructs have been added to λ-calculi before, in connexion with studies of concurrency

---

*This work was supported by Esprit Basic Research Action 3147: PHŒNIX.

and "don't care" non-determinism[2, 5, 7]. However, logical features correspond to "don't know" non-determinism; we are interested in all the choices. The analyses from that work are still relevant here, but not all the alternatives are useful.

We also need to add failure (an easy concept to implement), and an object representing all possible values, and thus having the effect of a logical variable. The related work of Silbermann on a semantics of relative set abstraction[14, 15] provides some inspiration for our definitions.

In the next section we define the syntax of our little language. In section 2, we give a denotational semantics using powerdomains. In section 3, we show how more useful features may be defined in terms of our core language. Of course, a real language would provide direct implementations of subsets of these constructs, but the translation to a core language with a simple denotational semantics provides a standard against which the correctness of implementations may be measured. In section 4, we consider how a Hindley-Milner-style type system may be defined for our little language. Finally, we consider operational models.

1 THE LANGUAGE

The language defined here is an extension (adding pattern matching and a universal value) of the non-deterministic λ-calculus considered by Hennessy[5].

We assume a set $\mathcal{V}$ of variables, a set $\mathcal{F}$ of function symbols and an indexed family $(\mathcal{C}_n)_{n \in \omega}$ of constructor symbols. Expressions have the syntax

$$x \mid \lambda p.e \mid e_1 e_2 \mid f \mid c \mid \Omega \mid \mho \mid e_1 \, [\!] \, e_2$$

where each p is a pattern, with syntax

$$x \mid c p_1 \ldots p_n$$

where $c \in \mathcal{C}_n$, such that no variable occurs twice in a pattern. As usual, in the expression $\lambda p.e$ any free occurrences in e of the variables of p are bound by the λ.

The intended semantics of these expressions is that they denote non-empty sets of values. The new constructs and their intended meanings are:

Ω	the set comprising only $\perp$,
$\mho$	the set of all values (so that an argument bound to $\mho$ behaves like a logical variable), and
$e_1 \, [\!] \, e_2$	the union of the sets denoted by e_1 and e_2.

This will be made more precise later.

2   DENOTATIONAL SEMANTICS

In considering the meaning of a non-deterministic λ-calculus, we face an array of options. Not all properties of the plain λ-calculus can be retained. We shall attempt to retain those most useful for transformation of programs. As mentioned above, many of these options have been considered before as models for don't-care non-determinism [2, 6, 7, 5]. The most desirable semantics for don't-know determinism turns out to be simpler—in particular there is no need for a special treatment of higher-order values.

The new constructs require that the semantics of an expression be a mapping from environments to sets of some kind. The first question is whether variables in an environment represent sets of values or single values. The former choice corresponds to a call-by-name operational semantics, while the latter corresponds to call-by-value and call-by-need evaluations[5]. We choose the latter, because it permits local algebraic reasoning. For example, the expression

$$(\lambda x.x + x)(2 \| 3)$$

is equivalent to

$$(\lambda x.2 * x)(2 \| 3)$$

only when each instance of x represents one value at a time. This choice also permits conventional implementation techniques.

To represent these sets, we shall require a powerdomain construction (see [10] for more details). For any cpo D, the lower powerdomain $\mathcal{P}D$ is the free continuous algebra generated by D with a binary operation $\cup$ satisfying the following axioms:

$$x \cup x = x$$
$$x \cup y = y \cup x$$
$$x \cup (y \cup z) = (x \cup y) \cup z$$
$$x \sqsubseteq x \cup y$$

That $\mathcal{P}D$ is free implies that there is a continuous function $\{\cdot\} : D \to \mathcal{P}D$ with a unique extension property: for any continuous algebra A satisfying the above axioms and continuous function $f : D \to A$ there is a unique continuous $\cup$-preserving function $f^\dagger : \mathcal{P}D \to A$ such that $f^\dagger(\{x\}) = f(x)$. Given these functions, we can continue to use set notation, but with the understanding that it refers to lower powerdomains.

This is the simplest of the powerdomains: the sets in $\mathcal{P}D$ are non-empty, inductive, downward-closed subsets of D, ordered by inclusion. In the special case of a flat cpo $S_\perp$, $\mathcal{P}(S_\perp)$ is equivalent to the ordinary powerset of S. An example is the usual Herbrand (partial correctness) semantics of logic programs, which uses the powerset of the set of ground terms. But when we wish to deal with lazy evaluation and infinite objects, like functions, we require a non-flat universe, and the generality of lower powerdomains.

Other powerdomains have been defined[13, 16], but the lower powerdomain is most suitable for our purposes because:

- It provides an analogue of the empty set (to represent failure); if we define $\phi = \{\perp\}$, then $\phi \cup x = x \cup \phi = x$. Note, however, that functions need not preserve ϕ.

- It provides the correct relationships for transformations of programs. Initially one specifies a program as a non-deterministic expression, and successively transforms it to a more deterministic and presumably more efficient program. Many useful transformations, e.g the fold-unfold methodology[4], guarantee only that their result is smaller than the original, and a separate termination proof is required when transformation is complete. In the case of the lower powerdomain, these two orders coincide.

Besides the powerdomain, we shall also the using the standard domain constructions $D_\perp$, $D + D'$ (coalesced sum), $D \times D'$ and $D \to D'$.

The semantics of expressions will thus be given as elements of the lower powerdomain of a cpo D, to be defined shortly. Since expressions denote sets of values, while variables denote single values, functions denote elements of $D \to \mathcal{P}D$. The semantics domain D also contains values built with the constructors. Thus, our domain D must satisfy

$$D \cong (D \to \mathcal{P}D) + \sum_{n,c \in C_n} (D^n)_\perp$$

It is a standard result of domain theory that such definitions always have a minimal solution. Thus D exists, and there are injections

$$i_F : (D \to \mathcal{P}D) \to D$$
$$i_c : D^n \to D$$

for each $c \in C_n$. Let $c_D \in D$ denote the curried and fully non-deterministic counterpart of i_c:

$$c_D = i_F(\lambda v_1 \ldots \{i_F(\lambda v_n.\{i_c(v_1,\ldots,v_n)\})\} \ldots)$$

We also assume for each function symbol f a denotation $f_D \in D$.

For each expression e, the rules of figure 1 define a denotation $\mathcal{E}[e] : (\mathcal{V} \to D) \to \mathcal{P}D$. In each case η is a map from variables to elements of D.

The rule for $e_1 e_2$ relies on the fact that the elements of the powerdomain are never empty (they always contain $\perp$). For example, with this semantics, we have

$$\mathcal{E}[(\lambda x.\lambda y.x)e_1 e_2]\eta = \mathcal{E}[e_1]\eta$$

$$
\begin{aligned}
\mathcal{E}[x]\eta &= \{\eta(x)\} \\
\mathcal{E}[\lambda p.e]\eta &= \{i_{\mathbb{F}}(f)\}, \text{where } f(v) = \begin{cases} \mathcal{E}[e]\eta\xi & \text{for the } \xi \text{ such that } \mathcal{E}[p]\xi = \{v\} \\ \phi & \text{if there is no such } \xi \end{cases} \\
\mathcal{E}[e_1 e_2]\eta &= \bigcup\{f(v) : i_{\mathbb{F}}(f) \in \mathcal{E}[e_1]\eta, v \in \mathcal{E}[e_2]\eta\} \\
\mathcal{E}[f]\eta &= \{f_D\} \\
\mathcal{E}[c]\eta &= \{c_D\} \\
\mathcal{E}[\Omega]\eta &= \phi \\
\mathcal{E}[\mho]\eta &= D \\
\mathcal{E}[e_1 \| e_2]\eta &= \mathcal{E}[e_1]\eta \cup \mathcal{E}[e_2]\eta
\end{aligned}
$$

Figure 1: Semantic equations

even if e_2 is Ω, or loops indefinitely.

We have defined $\mho$ as representing the full domain D. This amounts to a generalization of the Herbrand semantics of logic programs, in which logical variables are treated as schemes of ground values. Since D is ω-algebraic (by standard domain theory) it is possible to implement $\mho$ by simply listing the finite elements of D. In practice, it is preferable to allow the result of a computation to include $\mho$, providing a more concise answer. This corresponds to the Prolog style of permitting logical variables in answers, making the answers generic. In this we follow Silbermann[14, 15], who has defined a semantics of relative set abstraction using lower powerdomains. He also demonstrated that the unification rules give a correct implementation of guards involving the usual equality function.

3 DERIVED FORMS

In this section we seek to demonstrate that most of the declarative features of constraint functional languages may be defined in terms of the above raw calculus. This gives them a (partial correctness) denotational semantics, as well as an implementation (see section 5), though this is sometimes very inefficient. A typical language would provide restricted forms of these constructs in place of the raw language. The restrictions will often make possible more efficient implementations, whose partial correctness may still be justified in terms of the above semantics.

To represent Boolean values, assume that C_0 contains the constants true and false.

3.1 PATTERN MATCHING

We define

$$\lambda p_1.e_1 \mid \cdots \mid p_n.e_n \triangleq \lambda x.((\lambda p_1.e_1)x \parallel \cdots \parallel (\lambda p_n.e_n)x)$$

The above semantics gives:

$$\mathcal{E}[\lambda p_1.e_1 \mid \cdots \mid p_n.e_n]\eta = \{i_F(f)\}, \text{where } f(v) = \bigcup\{\mathcal{E}[e_i]\eta\xi_i : \mathcal{E}[p_i]\xi_i = \{v\}\}$$

We could also define an extended form

$$\lambda p_{11}\ldots p_{m1}.e_1 \mid \cdots \mid p_{1n}\ldots p_{mn}.e_n$$

Typical functional languages correspond to the deterministic subset of the language, which uses the generalized form of λ-expressions, with the patterns required to be non-overlapping, and omits the Ω, $\mho$ and $\parallel$ forms.

3.2 LOGICAL VARIABLES

If we define

$$\text{any } x.e \triangleq (\lambda x.e)\mho$$

then its meaning is:

$$\mathcal{E}[\text{any } x.e]\eta = \bigcup_{v \in D} \mathcal{E}[e]\eta[x \mapsto v]$$

That is, logical variables may stand for anything. They will be restricted (*i.e.* assigned values) by patterns that are applied to them. However, care is required. For example, if a and b are constants, the expression

$$\text{any } z.(z, (\lambda a.b)z)$$

should be equivalent to

$$(a, b) \parallel (\mho, \Omega)$$

and thus the expression

$$(\lambda(x, y).x)(\text{any } z.(z, (\lambda a.b)z))$$

should be equivalent to $\mho$.

3.3 GUARDS

Assuming that the expression b is Boolean-valued, we define

$$e :- b \triangleq (\lambda \text{true}.e)b$$

The above semantics gives:

$$\mathcal{E}[e :- b]\eta = \begin{cases} \mathcal{E}[e]\eta & \text{if } i_{\text{true}} \in \mathcal{E}[b]\eta \\ \phi & \text{otherwise} \end{cases}$$

A typical language might further restrict the form of guards, and use a constraint solver in this special case.

3.4 UNIFICATION

For example, we might restrict guards to equations. The equality is just the usual binary function returning a Boolean value, returning true if its arguments are non-functional, finite, completely defined, and equal. Equal but infinite (or partial) arguments cause an infinite loop. The function could even be defined by an enormous case analysis over all possible pairs of constructors.

In certain contexts it is possible to provide more useful implementations. We define

$$equable \triangleq \lambda x. x = x$$

$$any_{eq} \, x.e \triangleq any \, x.e :- equable(x)$$

In the context of the quantifier any_{eq} some short-cuts are also available without departing from the above semantics:

- $e :- x = x$ can be rewritten to e, if x is constrained to be equable.

- $any_{eq} \, x.(e :- x = y)$ can be rewritten to $[y/x]e$, provided y is equable.

- $any_{eq} \, x.(e :- x = ce_1 \dots e_n)$, where $n \in C_n$, can be rewritten to

$$any_{eq} \, x_1, \dots, x_n.([cx_1 \dots x_n/x]e :- x_1 = e_1 \wedge \cdots \wedge x_n = e_n)$$

- $e :- x = t$ can be rewritten to Ω, if t contains x, with only constructors applied to it.

These rules can be recognized as a slightly restricted form of the usual unification algorithm with the occurs check. The main differences are the equability constraints, and the care required about the scope of the any quantifier.

Instantiation to reducible terms is forbidden because this would amount to allowing the guard to succeed when evaluation of the equality function might not terminate. For example, the expression

$$any_{eq} \, x.(1 :- x = \Omega)$$

should be equivalent to Ω, not 1.

Unification differs from pattern matching in that it works only for fully-defined first-order objects, while pattern matching may assign any value to a variable. Thus is not possible to define λ-abstraction in terms of unification.

$$\frac{A, A_{vars(p)} \vdash p : t \qquad A \vdash e_1 : t \to t'}{A, x : t \vdash x : t \qquad \frac{A, A_{vars(p)} \vdash e : t' \qquad A \vdash e_2 : t}{A \vdash \lambda p.e : t \to t' \qquad A \vdash e_1 e_2 : t'}}$$

$$A \vdash \Omega : t \qquad A \vdash \mho_t : t \qquad \frac{\begin{array}{c} A \vdash e_1 : t \\ A \vdash e_2 : t \end{array}}{A \vdash e_1 \, \| \, e_2 : t}$$

Figure 2: Type rules

4 A POLYMORPHIC TYPE SYSTEM

Here we consider a Hindley-Milner-style polymorphic type system on our little language. For the most part this is straight-forward enough—the only problem is $\mho$. We choose to replace $\mho$ by a family of terms $\mho_t$ for each monotype t. That is, $\mho$ may be viewed as having type $\exists \alpha.\alpha$.

We define the new symbols $\mho_t$ in terms of existing expressions for all t by induction. We may define $\mho_t$ for function types by

$$\mho_{t \to t'} \triangleq \lambda x.\mho_{t'}$$

We assume that the other type constructors, and the constructor symbols, are introduced by algebraic data type definitions like

$$\tau \alpha_1 \ldots \alpha_n \triangleq c_1 t_{11} \ldots t_{1n_1} \oplus \cdots \oplus c_m t_{m1} \ldots t_{mn_m}$$

where each $c_j \in C_{n_j}$. If we set $t'_{ij} = [t_1/\alpha_1, \ldots, t_n/\alpha_n] t_{ij}$, then we can define

$$\mho_{\tau t_1 \ldots t_n} \triangleq c_1 \mho_{t'_{11}} \ldots \mho_{t'_{1n_1}} \, \| \, \cdots \, \| \, c_m \mho_{t'_{m1}} \ldots \mho_{t'_{mn_m}}$$

For example, the following expression means "all lists of elements of type t":

$$\mho_{\text{list } t} = \text{nil} \, \| \, \text{cons} \, \mho_t \, \mho_{\text{list } t}$$

The type rules are given in figure 2. Each t in the rules is understood to be a monotype. The rules of the top row are the normal type rules for the λ-calculus, extended to the pattern-matching lambda. We also assume that each function symbol f is supplied with a type scheme (polymorphic type), and we add an axiom scheme assigning f each instance of that type scheme. Similarly, each constructor symbol is supplied with an axiom scheme derived from the algebraic data type definition in which it was introduced.

The rules thus assign to an expression a set of monotypes. However, since only one rule is applicable to any kind of expression it follows that any expression either has no type or its types are exactly the instances of some type scheme, or polymorphic type, containing variables standing for types[11]. In fact, interpreting the rules as a Prolog program yields an algorithm to check and infer types.

We will be left with subexpressions $\mho_t$, where t is in general a polymorphic type. As long as these $\mho$s are only instantiated by narrowing or unification (see section 3), we will discover no new type information at runtime[1]. Thus the subscript t may be ignored.

For a semantics for these type assertions, we rehearse the definitions of [9], with the obvious extension to powerdomains. We inductively define an ideal D_t for each monotype t as follows:

$$D_{t \to t'} \triangleq \{i_F(f) : \forall x \in D_t \; f(x) \subseteq D_{t'}\}$$

$$D_{\tau t_1 \ldots t_n} \triangleq \bigcup i_{c_j}(D_{t'_{j_1}} \times \ldots \times D_{t'_{j_{n_j}}}) \cup \{\bot\}$$

The meaning of the type assertion $x_1 : t_1, \ldots, x_n : t_n \vdash e : t$ is

$$\forall \eta \; \eta(x_1) \in D_{t_1} \wedge \cdots \wedge \eta(x_n) \in D_{t_n} \Rightarrow \mathcal{E}[e]\eta \subseteq D_t$$

It can be shown that the type rules of figure 2 are sound with respect to this interpretation.

5 OPERATIONAL SEMANTICS OF CHOICE

We consider here an operational semantics for a subset of the language with choice and β-reduction.

Because we are interested in all the answers supplied by an expressions, the state will be a set of expressions. Our criterion for reduction rules will be confluence, in the sense that different computation paths produce the same *set* of answers. We propose to use a version of the β-rule of the λ-calculus and the following **forking rule**:

Select an expression in the set having a subexpression $e_1 \| e_2$ not inside a λ-binding, and replace it with with two copies, in which the subexpression is replaced with e_1 and e_2 respectively.

We do not promote a choice operator inside a λ-binding; each application of the function may make an independent choice. For example, the expression

$$(\lambda f.f \; 1 + f \; 4)(\lambda x.x + (2 \| 3))$$

---

[1]Run-time types might however be useful in the case of small enumerated types, when $\mho$ could be profitably enumerated.

should yield four answers.

The first thing we notice is that expressions resuling from β-reduction must be represented as graphs. For example, in a β-reduction of

$$(\lambda x.x + x)(2 \| 3)$$

we cannot duplicate the sub-expression $2 \| 3$, for that would yield more answers than if β-reduction follows forking.

The body of a λ-expression should be copied during β-reduction; other examples show that this copying must preserve its graph structure. However, previously substituted actual parameters should still be shared: the expression

$$(\lambda y.(\lambda f.f\ 1 + f\ 4)(\lambda x.x + y))(2 \| 3)$$

should yield two answers. The essential point for confluence is to avoid duplicating function arguments, even when they have been substituted into other function bodies. That is, the implementation must preserve not only the graph structure of the expression being evaluated, but also its combinator structure.

The first formulation of a confluent rewriting system for a non-deterministic λ-calculus involved an explicit treatment of unevaluated substitutions[2]. It is essentially an abstract description of an environment machine. Another equivalent formulation would be to decompose the expression to be translated into combinators[8], and proceed using the usual graph-reduction steps[12]. Note, however, that the full-laziness transformation is *not* always correct—the transformed program might produce fewer answers.

The following treatment is less closely associated with existing implementation techniques. Our method will be to recast the λ-calculus, by an extension of de Bruijn's notation, and by treating expressions as graphs. Then we add the choice construct, claiming the resulting system is confluent.

5.1 An Extension of de Bruijn Notation

In de Bruijn's notation, a variable is replaced by a number n, indicating the variable bound by the nth enclosing λ, counting from zero. Thus the syntax of λ-expressions becomes:

$$n \mid e_1 e_2 \mid \lambda e$$

The β-reduction rule then requires renumbering of variables in the substituted argument, so that they still refer to the same λ.

The extension we propose involves firstly a unary representation of variable numbers:

$$0, S0, SS0, \ldots$$

Then we permit the S term constructor to be applied to any term, obtaining the syntax:

$$0 \mid Se \mid e_1 e_2 \mid \lambda e$$

A term of the λ-calculus is translated into this language by first translating it into de Bruijn form, and giving variable numbers their unary representation. In the course of reduction the more general forms will appear.

The β-rule is now reformulated as:

$$(S^n \lambda e)e' \Rightarrow [e'{_0^n}]e$$

with substitution defined by:

$$
\begin{aligned}
[e'{_0^n}]0 &= e' \\
[e'{_{m+1}^n}]0 &= 0 \\
[e'{_0^n}]Se &= S^n e \\
[e'{_{m+1}^n}]Se &= S[e'{_m^n}]e \\
[e'{_m^n}](e_1 e_2) &= ([e'{_m^n}]e_1)([e'{_m^n}]e_2) \\
[e'{_m^n}]\lambda e &= \lambda[e'{_{m+1}^n}]e
\end{aligned}
$$

The advantage of this scheme is that actual parameters need never be copied.

There are some similarities to the $\lambda\sigma$-calculus [1], in which unevaluated substitutions are treated explicitly. Our expressions Sa are written there as $a[\uparrow]$, while the substitution $[b_m^n]a$ is equivalent to

$$[0 \cdot \ldots \cdot 0[\uparrow^{m-1}] \cdot b[\uparrow^m] \cdot \uparrow^{m+n}]$$

The principal difference is that we consider Sa to be irreducible. This gives a simpler expression structure, but the β-rule is more complicated, as seen above.

5.2 GRAPHS

As noted above, substituted actual parameters must be shared, so expressions must be rooted, directed, labelled graphs. The graphs may also be cyclic, to represent recursive definitions. Sub-expressions are now considered as nodes, and the grammar of expressions is re-interpreted as describing the labels and out-degrees of various kinds of node. To make substitution meaningful, graphs are required to satisfy the following condition:

> On each path through the graph from node e to node e', the number of λs minus the number of Ss on the path, excluding the last node, is the same.

We use the notation $m(e, e')$ for this number. We also define the *body* of a λ-node e to be all those nodes e' such that $m(e, e') > 0$, and $m(e, e'') > 0$ for each intermediate node e''. The *boundary* of the body comprises nodes e' labelled 0 or S such that $m(e, e') = 1$.

We must re-interpret the above rewriting rules as acting over graphs. The β-rule becomes

Replace all references to a node $(S^n \lambda e)e'$ by references to the node $[e'^n_0]e$.

The above definition of $[e'^n_0]e$ is re-interpreted as creating new copies of each node in the body of the λ-node of the redex, except the boundary, with corresponding out-edges. References to boundary nodes are replaced as follows

- references to boundary nodes labelled 0 are replaced by references to the argument.

- references to boundary nodes Se are replaced by references to $S^n e$.

Note that if the body was 0 or Se, the copy will be empty. Thus, for example, $[e'^n_0]0$ is e', a node already existing in the graph.

A modification of the proof for the ordinary λ-calculus[3] yields:

Theorem 1 *The β-reduction relation on graphs is confluent.*

5.3 CHOICE

Now we are ready to add the choice operator. The definition of substitution given above is extended by (the graph equivalent of):

$$[e'^n_m](e_1 \parallel e_2) = ([e'^n_m]e_1) \parallel ([e'^n_m]e_2)$$

The reduction rules are the β-rule and the forking rule, revised as follows:

Select an expression in the set having a node $e_1 \parallel e_2$ at level 0, and replace it with with two copies, in which references to the node are replaced with references to e_1 and e_2 respectively.

Under the new definition, β-reduction will never duplicate such a node. Thus forking commutes with simultaneous β-reductions on independent expressions in the solution set. Since β-reduction is confluent (Theorem 1), we have:

Theorem 2 *The reduction relation $\Rightarrow$ defined above is confluent.*

In later work, we plan to extend the semantics of section 2 to this graphical calculus. We expect that these rewriting rules may then be shown preserve the semantics of graphs.

REFERENCES

[1] M. Abdali, L. Cardelli, P.-L. Curien, and J.-J. Lévy. Explicit substitutions. In *17th Annual ACM Symposium on Principles of Programming Languages*, pages 31–46, 1990.

[2] E. Astesiano and G. Costa. Sharing in nondeterminism. In *6th International Conference on Automata, Languages and Programming*, volume 71 of *Lecture Notes in Computer Science*, 1979.

[3] H. P. Barendregt. *The Lambda Calculus – its Syntax and Semantics*. North Holland, 2nd edition, 1984.

[4] Rod M. Burstall and John Darlington. A transformation system for developing recursive programs. *Journal of the ACM*, 24(1):44–67, 1977.

[5] M. C. B. Hennessy. The semantics of call-by-value and call-by-name in a nondeterministic environment. *SIAM Journal on Computing*, 9(1):67–84, 1980.

[6] M. C. B. Hennessy and E. A. Ashcroft. Parameter passing mechanisms and nondeterminism. In *9th Annual ACM Symposium on Theory of Computing*, pages 306–311, 1977.

[7] M. C. B. Hennessy and E. A. Ashcroft. A mathematical semantics for a nondeterministic typed λ-calculus. *Theoretical Computer Science*, 11:227–245, 1980.

[8] John Hughes. Supercombinators – a new implementation technique for applicative languages. In *Proceedings of the 1982 ACM Symposium on LISP and Functional Programming*, pages 1–10, Pittsburgh, 1982.

[9] David MacQueen, Gordon D. Plotkin, and Ravi Sethi. An ideal model for recursive polymorphic types. *Information and Computation*, 71:95–130, 1986.

[10] Michael G. Main. A powerdomain primer. *Bulletin of the EATCS*, 33:115–147, October 1987.

[11] Robin Milner. A theory of type polymorphism in programming. *Journal of Computer and System Sciences*, 17(3):348–375, 1978.

[12] Simon L. Peyton Jones. *The Implementation of Functional Programming Languages*. Prentice Hall, Englewood Cliffs, NJ, 1987.

[13] Gordon D. Plotkin. A powerdomain construction. *SIAM Journal on Computing*, 1976.

[14] Frank S. K. Silbermann. *A Denotational Semantics Approach to Functional and Logic Programming*. PhD thesis, Tulane University, 1989.

[15] Frank S. K. Silbermann and Bharat Jayaraman. Set abstraction in functional and logic programming. In *Conference on Functional Programming Languages and Computer Architecture*, London, 1989. ACM.

[16] Mike B. Smyth. Powerdomains. *Journal of Computer and System Sciences*, 16:23–36, 1978.

Parallelism and Concurrency

Temporal Constraint Functional Programming:
A Declarative Framework For Concurrency and Interaction

T.C. Nicholas Graham

GMD Forschungsstelle an der Universität Karlsruhe
Vincenz-Prießnitz-Str. 1
D-7500 Karlsruhe 1, Germany
E-Mail: graham@karlsruhe.gmd.de

Abstract

This paper introduces Temporal Constraint Functional Programming (TCFP), a declarative paradigm suitable for concurrent programming. The paper defines an example TCFP language, a method for specifying the semantics of TCFP languages, and the basis of a transformation methodology for TCFP programs. The main advantages of TCFP are:

- Functional programs are free of control flow, allowing process bodies to be programmed without explicit reference to time or sequencing;

- Through temporal constraints, I/O, communication and time are explicitly recognized in a declarative way, and are formalized as a natural extension to the semantics of the underlying functional language;

- The temporal logic provides a natural abstraction for global and persistent state, long a problem in functional programming in the large;

- The framework gives support for transformation of concurrent programs, the correctness of which can be demonstrated via proofs in temporal logic.

1 Introduction

This paper introduces Temporal Constraint Functional Programming (TCFP), a declarative paradigm suitable for concurrent programming. The paper defines an example TCFP language, a method for specifying the semantics of TCFP languages, and the basis of a transformation methodology for TCFP programs.

TCFP introduces the concepts of parallelism, communication and synchronization to functional programming. A TCFP program is organized as a set of processes that communicate via asynchronous communication channels (or streams). Each process (or component) is a purely functional program which takes a set of streams as input, and gives a set of streams as output. (Streams can be thought of as lazy lists.) The communication structure of programs is expressed via constraints in a temporal logic, called stream logic. Constraints can specify how components are connected, how the communication between components is synchronized, and monitor-style sharing of global state.

Since the temporal logic in which the constraints are expressed cannot be implemented in full generality, we take the approach of providing predefined constructs with associated temporal constraints (in the style of [1]). These predefined constructs can then be combined to provide the temporal behaviour desired in the program. The temporal logic therefore forms a *semantic framework* for reasoning about the temporal properties of programs, and for proving the correctness of program tranformations. Since the semantic framework is applicable to a wide class of concrete languages, we refer to TCFP as a paradigm.

The paper is organized as follows. The following section introduces *Clock*, the concrete language to be used in the paper. Section 3 provides an overview of the TCFP semantic framework. Section 4 introduces *stream logic*, the constraint language. Sections 5 and 6 describe the semantics and transformation methodology for functional programs.

2 The *Clock* Language

Clock is a language based on Guarded Term ML [10], extended to provide constructs for interaction and concurrency. The philosophy behind *Clock* is that functional programming is successful for tasks in programming in the small. However, for programming in the large, one requires the ability to talk about persistent state (such as file systems), to communicate in an asynchronous manner with a variety of input and output devices, and to split the program on the basis of abstract data types, objects, or some other form of module system. We are experimenting with temporal logic as a formalism for expressing these sorts of programming-in-the-large features. In *Clock*, temporal logic constraints are used as a meta-programming feature, where constraints guide the evaluation of a set of pure-functional computations. Programming in the small is on the level of the process. A process is a pure functional computation, whose value always consists of a request to the I/O system, and a follow-up process to be forked once the request has been fulfilled. Temporal constraints sequence and synchronize these I/O requests and the concurrent creation and execution of processes.

This approach is in essence the same as the continuation passing style of functional programming (first introduced in the Nebula project [9]) and also builds on experience with a parallel extension to Guarded Term ML [11]. The novel contribution of TCFP is the the use of temporal logic to describe process creation, communication, and synchronization in a declarative way, and the construction of a semantic model where I/O and concurrency are explicitly recognized.

Clock is an extension of the Guarded Term ML (GTML) language [10]. GTML is a pure-functional variant of ML [13] based on the term universe, and featuring laziness, pattern matching, higher-order functions, static typing, modules, and access to logical computation [3]. *Clock* provides I/O constructs based on Perry's result continuations [16] and constructs for non-determinism similar to those in Gordon's PFL+ [5]. Non-determinism is required in a concurrent environment to reflect the many possible ways in which the I/O of two processes may be interleaved. Constraints can be written over these non-deterministically generated I/O traces,

The following I/O requests are predefined:

```
type ioRequest ::=
        read(inputStream,failCont,retCont)
    ++ write(outputStream,A,failCont,successCont)
    ++ all([process])
    ++ any([process])
    ++ error(errorMessage)
    ++ done.
```

where

```
type streamId      ==    string.
type inputStream   ==    streamId.
type outputStream  ==    streamId.
type errorMessage  ==    string.
type failCont      ::    errorMessage => ioRequest.
type successCont   ==    ioRequest.
type retCont       ::    A => ioRequest.
type process       ::    [inputStream] # ioRequest # [outputStream].
```

The error continuation is defined as:

```
fun errorC -> fn Message => error(Message).
```

Figure 1: *Continuation-Based Input/Output in* Clock

thus introducing a form of synchronization. In *Clock*, a set of predefined operators provide implicit temporal constraints, in the style of Burton [1].

The type of a *Clock* program is always *ioReqest*, a request to the I/O system together with a process fork directive. After a process executes to termination, the resulting I/O request is served, then the new process is forked. The fork request consists of a function that is to be applied to the result of the I/O operation; such a function is usually called a *continuation function* [8,16]. For example, a request to read a value and then perform some computation based on it looks like:

```
read (stdIn, errorC, fn X => f X)
```

Here the continuation function fn X => f X is applied to the result of the read from stream *stdIn*. (The function *errorC* is also a continuation function, to be applied in the case that the read fails.) This method introduces implicit sequentialization: here the read request must be served before any I/O activity resulting from the application of the continuation function.

Figure 1 shows the I/O requests supported by *Clock*. As well as the usual *read* and *write* operations, there is the *any* I/O request, which takes a list of processes as parameters, and non-deterministically chooses one of them to be executed, and the *all* I/O request, which executes all of a list of processes in parallel.

The following example shows a very simple *Clock* program, and how the program can be combined with temporal constraints. The constraints are expressed in *stream logic*, as described in section 4. More sophisticated examples of *Clock* programs are given in another report [6].

Example 2.1 (Fifo Merge) Consider we wish to construct a process whose job it is to merge two infinite streams and produce a third stream with the merged values. We would write this as a function with type:

```
type merge :: inputStream # inputStream # outputStream => ioRequest.
```

That is, a process that takes two input streams and an output stream, and executes indefinitely. In fact, the program describes an infinite sequence of processes, each of which performs one step of the merge, then forks another instance of itself.

```
fun merge (In1, In2, Out) ->
    let mergeStep = any(In1!copy(In1,Out,errorC, mergeStep)!Out
                     || In2!copy(In2,Out,errorC, mergeStep)!Out)
    in mergeStep.

type copy :: inputStream # outputStream
             # failCont # successCont -> ioRequest.
fun copy (In, Out, ErrC, SuccC) ->
    read(In, ErrC,
        fn ValToBeCopied => write(Out, ErrC, SuccC)).
```

Here, the *any* construct non-deterministically chooses between a copy of one element from the input stream *In1* onto the output stream *Out*, and a copy from *In2* onto *Out*. The recursive definition of *mergeStep* carries on this copying indefinitely. The arguments to *any* are processes, i.e. functional expressions to be evaluated. The notation

```
In1!copy(In1,Out,errorC, mergeStep)!Out
```

indicates that the *copy* function is to be called, and declares that the stream *In1* is to be used as an input stream, and that *Out* is to be used as an output stream. Consider that we wish to merge the inputs from two devices (say a mouse and keyboard) in the order that the user generated them. We can use the *merge* process supplemented by a temporal constraint that states that items are to be merged in the order in which the items were generated (i.e., *fifo*). If the streams involved are called *m* for the mouse inputs, *k* for keyboard inputs and *mk* for the result of the merge, the call to *merge* would be:

```
merge (m, k, mk)
```

with the attached constraint:

$$fifo(m,k) \land fifo(k,m)$$

where

$$fifo(s_1,s_2) \stackrel{\text{def}}{=} older(s_1,s_2) \supset (exit(s_1) \ll exit(s_2))$$

The definition of *fifo* can be (informally) read as: if the first element on stream s_1 arrived before the first element on stream s_2, then the first element on s_1 must be processed before the first element on s_2. (The symbol "$\ll$" is read as "precedes".) Within the temporal logic, streams are treated as queues – if we model a keyboard buffer as a stream, keystrokes are enqueued as the user types them, and dequeued as the program reads them in. (This constraint is an example of *stream logic*, as defined in section 4.)

This example shows our strategy in combining logical constraints with functional programs. The function *merge* specifies all possible I/O behaviours a merge may take on. The *fifo* constraint then restricts the set of possible behaviours to those in which we are interested, in particular the fifo ones. The interface between the functional and constraint world is on the level of input/output events: we say that if the system is in a particular state (e.g., a keyboard input occured before a mouse input), then a particular input/output event should happen next (e.g. the keyboard input should be processed first.) This is reflected in the *merge* function by constraining the (non-deterministic) decision as to which branch of the *any* construct should be followed. This merge and its associated constraint are provided as a predefined construct built into the language.

The remainder of this paper is concerned with the semantic framework that facilitates the definition of and reasoning about TCFP languages.

3   Overview of the Semantic Framework

The long range goal of our formalization of TCFP is to provide a basis for program transformation of concurrent and interactive functional programs. The goal, as is usual with program transformation, is to allow a programmer to write a program at as high and simple a level as possible, and through semantic-preserving transformations to then move to a more efficient form. We are primarily interested in architectural transformations, which attempt to reorganize the program on the level of its parallelism and communications structure. Examples would be the optimization of communication routes, the transformation of asynchronous to synchronous communication, and the introduction of coarse-grain parallelism. These new transformation techniques should then be integrated with existing transformation methodologies for functional languages.

The basis of this method is a separation between a pure semantics and an interaction semantics; the pure semantics is the traditional semantics of functional programs, while the interaction semantics specifies how the results of programs in this language are presented to a user. The interaction semantics of a program is simply the set of all possible I/O behaviours the program may produce. As shown in figure 2, the addition of temporal constraints to specify sequencing and synchronization is defined as a restriction (or subset) of the interaction semantics of the program.

Our approach is to define the pure and interaction semantics in some appropriate formalism, such as denotational semantics. The semantics of the temporal constraints are expressed model theoretically. The restricted interaction semantics is then the set of behaviours permitted by the temporal constraints, intersected with the program's interaction semantics. This approach differs from more traditional formalisms for describing the semantics of concurrency (such as CSP [7] or CCS [14]) in that it is declarative rather than operational. More recent formalisms also provide a two-level semantics of the sort proposed here, such as the π-calculus [12], which combines the λ-calculus with CCS style operators.

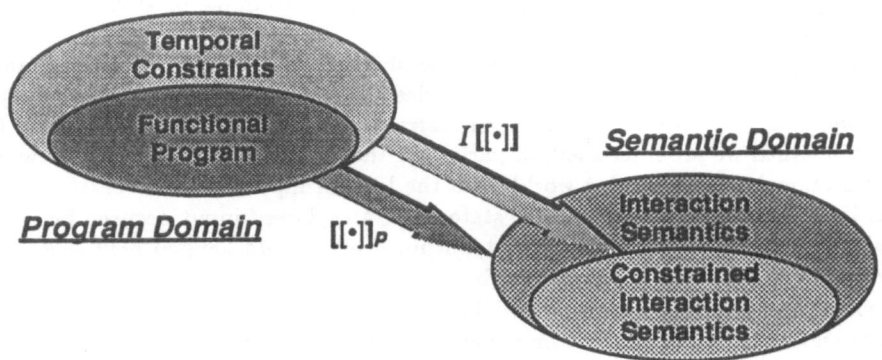

Figure 2: *The TCFP Semantic Framework: the interaction semantics captures the semantics of the functional language, mapping a functional program to a set of possible behaviours. The restricted semantics takes into account the temporal constraints that restrict the possible behaviour of the program.*

Informally, we can view a programming language as a pair of semantic functions $\langle [\![\,\cdot\,]\!]_p, [\![\,\cdot\,]\!]_c \rangle$ defined over functional programs and sets of temporal constraints respectively:

$$[\![\,\cdot\,]\!]_p : program \to streamAssignments$$
$$[\![\,\cdot\,]\!]_c : constraints \to streamAssignments$$

where

$$streamAssignments \stackrel{\text{def}}{=} \mathcal{P}(streamId \to stream)$$

where a *streamId* refers to an input/output channel used in the program, and a stream is a recording of all activity over a particular channel throughout the execution of the program. Since programs may be non-deterministic, stream assignments are a set of possible I/O activities. This allows the definition of the restricted interaction semantics function:

$$\mathcal{I}[\![\,\cdot\,]\!] : program \times constraints \to streamAssignments$$

Definition 3.1 (Restricted Interaction Semantics) *The restricted interaction semantics of a program* $\langle p, c \rangle$ *consisting of a functional program* p *and a set of well-formed formulae in stream logic* c *is:*

$$\mathcal{I}[\![\langle p, c \rangle]\!] \stackrel{\text{def}}{=} [\![p]\!]_p \cap [\![c]\!]_c$$

□

That is, the restricted interaction semantics of a program is the program semantics restricted by the temporal constraints.

We can then describe transformations as follows:

Definition 3.2 (Semantic Preserving Transformation) *A transformation*

$$t : program \times constraints \rightarrow program \times constraints$$

is called semantic preserving *iff for all programs p and sets of constraints c,*

$$\mathcal{I}[\![t(\langle p, c \rangle)]\!] \subseteq \mathcal{I}[\![\langle p, c \rangle]\!]$$

and

$$\mathcal{I}[\![t(\langle p, c \rangle)]\!] \neq \emptyset \; if \; \mathcal{I}[\![\langle p, c \rangle]\!] \neq \emptyset$$

$\square$

That is, the transformed program must allow at least some of the possible behaviours of the original program.

The following two sections introduce the two components in our semantics, corresponding the two functions $[\![\cdot]\!]_p$ and $[\![\cdot]\!]_c$. Section 4 introduces the stream logic used to express constraints over the execution of functional programs, and section 5 gives an overview of the interaction semantics of functional programs. The combined semantics is formalized in section 6.

4 A Stream Logic

The functional description of a concurrent program provides no restrictions on the order in which communication events take place. To express these constraints, a second level of description is used. Here, assertions are written in a temporal logic about the events that occur on the I/O streams. These streams are treated as queues: values arrive at some time, and are processed, either immediately, or at some arbitrarily later time. (For example, if the stream is being fed by a keyboard, values may be processed as soon as they are typed, or may be buffered arbitrarily until the program processes them.) Streams thus model asynchronous communication channels.

If at a particular time, a value is buffered on a stream s, we say $pending(s)$ is true at that time. If a value v is *output to* a stream s at a particular time, we say that at that time $enter(s, v)$ is true. If a value v is *input from* a stream s, then we say that at the time of the input, $exit(s, v)$ is true. If the next available value on stream s_1 has been pending for longer than the next value on stream s_2, then $older(s_1, s_2)$ is true. These primitive predicates over streams form the basis of this constraint language.

As well as the usual logical connectives, two temporal operators are provided. $\Diamond p$ (*sometime* p) is true if at some time in the future p will become true. $p \ll q$ (*p precedes q*) is true if q is never true in the intervening time between now and the next time p becomes true. The following section gives a formal definition of the constraint language. This definition is structured very similarly to Gabbay's definition of his USF logic [4].

4.1 Syntax

Atomic formulae are built from terms and stream formulae. Assume we have an alphabet of symbols *variableName* to denote variables, a family of alphabets *functionSymbol$_n$* to denote functions of arity $n \in I\!N$ and *predicateSymbol$_m$*, to denote predicates of arity $m \in I\!N$, and the alphabet *streamId* to denote streams. We define terms and atomic formulae as follows:

Definition 4.1 (Term)

- *All variables $v \in$ variableName are terms;*
- *If $f \in$ functionSymbol$_n$ and $t_1, ..., t_n$ are terms, then $f(t_1, ..., t_n)$ is a term.* □

Definition 4.2 (Atomic Formula)

- *If $s, s_1, s_2 \in$ streamId and v is a term, then the following are atomic formulae:*

$pending(s)$	*(item available on stream s)*
$enter(s, v)$	*(item enqueued on stream s)*
$exit(s, v)$	*(item dequeued from stream s)*
$older(s_1, s_2)$	*(first item on s_1 arrived later than first item on s_2)*

- *If $p \in$ predicateSymbol$_m$ and $t_1, ..., t_m$ are terms, then $p(t_1, ..., t_m)$ is an atomic formula.* □

The well-formed formulae (*wffs*) are built from the atomic formulae using the traditional propositional connectives and first-order quantifiers. In addition, two temporal operators are provided:

Definition 4.3 (Well-Formed Formula)

- *All atomic formulae are well-formed formulae.*
- *Given p, q wffs and $x \in$ variableName, the following are wffs:*
  $\neg p$ *(negation)*
  $p \wedge q$ *(conjunction)*
  $\forall x.p$ *(universal quantification)*
  $\Diamond p$ *(sometime) p*
  $p \ll q$ *(p precedes q)*

□

The remaining standard operators of classical logic (disjunction, implication, and existential quantification) can be defined in terms of those from definition 4.3 in the usual way.

4.2 Semantics of Stream Logic

Our eventual goal when executing functional programs restricted by temporal constraints will be to attempt to maintain every constraint at every point of the programs execution. The *interpretation* of a constraint (or *wff* of stream logic) will be defined to be the set of times at which the constraint is true. (We use discrete totally-ordered time, as represented by the natural numbers.) A *model* for a set of constraints is then an interpretation which makes every constraint true for all of time.

An interpretation consists of a universe of values and an interpretation function which maps well-formed formulae to the set of times over which they hold. This interpretation function is built, in part, from a stream assignment function, which assigns an input/output trace to each stream identifier. An I/O trace records all the activity over a stream over the entire execution of a program: when a value entered a stream (i.e., was output by some process), and when it exited the stream (i.e. was input by some other process) .

Definition 4.4 (Stream) *A stream s over a universe of values U is a set of tuples $\langle t_\alpha, v, t_\beta \rangle$, where $v \in U$, and $t_\alpha, t_\beta \in I\!\!N$ are time points, where $t_\alpha \leq t_\beta$. The set must be totally ordered by $<_s$, where $\langle t_{\alpha_1}, v_1, t_{\beta_1} \rangle <_s \langle t_{\alpha_2}, v_2, t_{\beta_2} \rangle$ iff $t_{\alpha_1} < t_{\alpha_2}$ and $t_{\beta_1} < t_{\beta_2}$.*
□

Intuitively, each tuple is an input/output event on the stream. v is a value being sent/received, t_α is the time the value is first received on the stream and t_β is the time the value was accepted from the stream for processing. If a stream were representing a keyboard buffer, t_α would represent the time the user typed a key, and t_β the time the program read in the input.

Definition 4.5 (Interpretation) *An interpretation $\mathcal{I}$ for a system of formulae $\mathcal{F}$ consists of the four-tuple $\langle U, \mathcal{S}, \mathcal{T}_0, \mathcal{T}[\cdot] \rangle$, where U is a universe of values, time $= I\!\!N$ is the universe of time points, $\mathcal{T}_0$ is a family of functions:*

$$\mathcal{V}[\cdot] \; : \; variableName \to time \to U$$
$$\mathcal{F}[\cdot] \; : \; functionSymbol_n \to time \to U^n \to \mathcal{P}(time)$$
$$\mathcal{P}[\cdot] \; : \; predicateSymbol_m \to U^m \to \mathcal{P}(time)$$

and $\mathcal{S}$ is a stream interpretation function:

$$\mathcal{S}[\cdot] \; : \; streamId \to stream$$

and where the interpretation function

$$\mathcal{T}[\cdot] \; : \; wffs \to \mathcal{P}(time)$$

is constructed from $\mathcal{T}_0$ in the following way; given $x \in variableName$, $f \in functionSymbol$, $p \in predicateSymbol$, $s, s_1, s_2 \in streamId$, and $p, q \in \mathcal{F}$, then the term interpretation function

$$\mathcal{VAL}[\cdot] \; : \; term \to time \to U$$

is defined as:

$$\mathcal{VAL}[x] \stackrel{\text{def}}{=} \mathcal{V}[x]$$
$$\mathcal{VAL}[f(t_1, \ldots, t_n)] \, t \stackrel{\text{def}}{=} \mathcal{F}[f] \langle \mathcal{VAL}[t_1] t, \ldots, \mathcal{VAL}[t_n] t \rangle$$

and the interpretation function $T[\cdot]$ *is defined as:*

$$T[p(t_1,\ldots,t_m)] \stackrel{\text{def}}{=} \{t \mid t \in P[p]\langle \mathcal{VAL}[t_1]t,\ldots,\mathcal{VAL}[t_n]t\rangle\}$$

$$T[pending(s)] \stackrel{\text{def}}{=} \{t \mid \exists\langle t_\alpha, v, t_\beta\rangle \in S[s] \text{ s.t. } (t_\alpha \le t \le t_\beta)$$

$$T[enter(s)] \stackrel{\text{def}}{=} \{t_\alpha \mid \exists t_\beta \text{ s.t. } \langle t_\alpha, v, t_\beta\rangle \in S[s]\}$$

$$T[exit(s)] \stackrel{\text{def}}{=} \{t_\beta \mid \exists t_\alpha \text{ s.t. } \langle t_\alpha, v, t_\beta\rangle \in S[s]\}$$

$$T[older(s_1, s_2)] \stackrel{\text{def}}{=} \{t \mid \exists\langle t_{\alpha_2}, v_2, t_{\beta_2}\rangle \in S[s_2] \text{ s.t. } ((t_{\alpha_2} \le t \wedge t_{\beta_2} > t)$$
$$\wedge \not\exists\langle t_{\alpha_1}, v_1, t_{\beta_1}\rangle \in S[s_1] \text{ s.t. } (t_{\alpha_1} \le t_{\alpha_2} \le t \wedge t_{\beta_1} > t))\}$$

$$T[\neg p] \stackrel{\text{def}}{=} time - T[p]$$

$$T[p \wedge q] \stackrel{\text{def}}{=} T[p] \cap T[q]$$

$$T[\forall x.p] \stackrel{\text{def}}{=} \{t \mid \forall d \in D . (T[x \mapsto d])[p]\}$$

$$T[\Diamond p] \stackrel{\text{def}}{=} \{t \mid \exists t' > t \text{ s.t. } (t' \in T[p])\}$$

$$T[p \ll q] \stackrel{\text{def}}{=} \{t \mid \exists t' \in T[p] \text{ s.t. } (t' \ge t \wedge \not\exists t'' \in T[q] \text{ s.t. } (t' \le t'' \le t'))\}$$

□

A model can then be defined as an interpretation for which all formulae hold at all times.

Definition 4.6 (Model) *An interpretation* $M = \langle U, S, T_0, T[\cdot]\rangle$ *is a model for a set of formulae* $\mathcal{F}$ $(M \models \mathcal{F})$ *iff for all* $f \in \mathcal{F}$, $T[f] = \mathbb{N}$. □

5 Semantics of I/O Constructs

The following presents the skeleton of a denotational semantics for *Clock* with the continuation-based I/O constructs presented in section 2. This semantics can be combined with the semantics of stream logic (section 4) to produce the restricted interaction semantics (section 6).

The structure of the semantics models the style of interaction provided by the continuation passing style of I/O. A *cps* program has as type *ioRequest*, meaning that when a program executes, an I/O request is given as the result, and the program terminates. This level of execution we call the *pure semantics*. When an I/O request is obtained, the external environment (or *operating system*) evaluates the request, and applies the continuation function, thereby commencing a new functional computation. This level, where the interaction between a sequence of functional computations and the external environment is made explicit, we term the *interaction semantics*.

The pure semantics are given through the semantic function:

$$\mathcal{E}[\cdot] : expr \rightarrow env \rightarrow val$$

The *val* domain is the usual domain of denotable values, extended to include a domain *ioReq* which is used to model requests to the I/O system. In this pure semantics, a program of type *ioRequest* will have as its denotation a value from the domain *ioReq*. This models the notion that a program executes to the first I/O request and then terminates.

The interaction semantics of a functional program are then expressed through the function

$$\mathcal{IO}[\![\cdot]\!] : ioReq \rightarrow time \rightarrow ioTrace \rightarrow ioTraces$$

which maps programs containing I/O requests to a set of possible I/O traces. Each I/O trace captures when I/O events occur over each of the active streams in the program; interaction semantics therefore capture an explicit notion of time, absent from pure semantics. Because execution is non-deterministic, a set of possible I/O traces is returned.

The semantics described here is based on the standard Scott-Strachey approach, where semantic domains are complete partial orders [18].

5.1 Pure Semantics

The pure semantics of the functional language presented is simply an extension of the usual pure semantics of Guarded Term ML [2]. Here we have, as usual, a semantic function

$$\mathcal{D}[\![\cdot]\!] : decl \rightarrow env \rightarrow env$$

to collect declarations and record then in an environment, and

$$\mathcal{E}[\![\cdot]\!] : expr \rightarrow env \rightarrow val$$

to evaluate expressions to the domain of denotable values *val*. In order to handle I/O requests, *val* is extended to include the new domain *ioReq*.

5.1.1 Semantic Domains for Pure Semantics

The denotable values are built in the usual way from basic values, with the inclusion of I/O requests:

$$val \stackrel{\text{def}}{=} basicValue + value \times value + value \rightarrow value + ioReq$$

This domain must be accompanied by the appropriate projection and injection functions; these are left implicit where their use is clear.

Environments provide an interpretation for identifiers:

$$env \stackrel{\text{def}}{=} ident \rightarrow val$$

Stream requests are simply tuples representing a request and its arguments:

$$strId \stackrel{\text{def}}{=} id$$
$$ioReq \stackrel{\text{def}}{=} \{\texttt{write}\} \times strId \times val \times ioReq$$
$$+ \quad \{\texttt{read}\} \times strId \times (val \rightarrow ioReq)$$
$$+ \quad \{\texttt{all}\} \times ioReqList$$
$$+ \quad \{\texttt{any}\} \times ioReqList$$
$$+ \quad \{\texttt{done}\}$$

5.2 Semantic Equations in Pure Semantics

The expression function is extended with the following equations:

$$\mathcal{E}[\![\texttt{read}(s,c)]\!]\mu \stackrel{\text{def}}{=} \langle \texttt{read}, \mathcal{E}[\![s]\!]\mu, \mathcal{E}[\![c]\!]\mu\rangle$$

$$\mathcal{E}[\![\texttt{write}(s,v,c)]\!]\mu \stackrel{\text{def}}{=} \langle \texttt{write}, \mathcal{E}[\![s]\!]\mu, \mathcal{E}[\![v]\!]\mu, \mathcal{E}[\![c]\!]\mu\rangle$$

$$\mathcal{E}[\![\texttt{all}([(i_1,a_1,o_1),...,(i_n,a_n,o_n)])]\!]\mu \stackrel{\text{def}}{=} \langle \texttt{all}, [\mathcal{PR}[\![(i_1,a_1,o_1)]\!]\mu, ..., \mathcal{PR}[\![(i_n,a_n,o_n)]\!]\mu]\rangle$$

$$\mathcal{E}[\![\texttt{any}([(i_1,a_1,o_1),...,(i_n,a_n,o_n)])]\!]\mu \stackrel{\text{def}}{=} \langle \texttt{any}, [\mathcal{PR}[\![(i_1,a_1,o_1)]\!]\mu, ..., \mathcal{PR}[\![(i_n,a_n,o_n)]\!]\mu]\rangle$$

$$\mathcal{E}[\![\texttt{done}]\!] \stackrel{\text{def}}{=} \texttt{done}$$

A helper function gives meanings to processes:

$$\mathcal{PR}[\![\cdot]\!] : process \rightarrow val$$

A process is also an I/O request, with a list of declarations of which streams the process uses for input ($[i_1, ..., i_m]$) and for output ($[o_1, ..., o_n]$). The semantics of a process is then the value of its I/O request, under the environment where the streams used by the process are defined. Stream identifiers are simply defined as themselves.

$$\mathcal{PR}[\![([i_1,...,i_m], a, [o_1,...,o_n])]\!]\mu \stackrel{\text{def}}{=} \mathcal{E}[\![a]\!]\mu'$$
$$\text{where } \mu' = \mu[i_1 \mapsto i_1, ..., i_m \mapsto i_m,$$
$$o_1 \mapsto o_1, ..., o_n \mapsto o_n]$$

5.3 Interaction Semantics

The interaction semantics of a program are built up from the pure semantics by evaluating the I/O requests, and assigning times to I/O events as they occur. The value of a program is then the (possibly infinite) trace of inputs and outputs performed during the program's execution. Since the I/O constructs introduce non-determinism, a program is mapped to a set of such I/O traces. A correct implementation of the program would be expected to produce any one of these traces.

5.3.1 Semantic Domains in Interaction Semantics

Streams are represented as lists of events. Since streams model asynchronous communication channels, at any time instant a stream can be viewed as being a buffer: events are enqueued (through the write I/O request), and later dequeued (through the read I/O request). Events over a particular stream are then modelled as a three-tuple, consisting of a value, the time at which the value was enqueued on the stream, and the time the value was dequeued from the stream:

$$time \stackrel{\text{def}}{=} \mathbb{N}_\perp$$
$$tag \stackrel{\text{def}}{=} val$$
$$event \stackrel{\text{def}}{=} val \times tag$$
$$streamEvent \stackrel{\text{def}}{=} time \times event \times time$$

A stream is a list of such events:

$$stream \stackrel{\text{def}}{=} [streamEvent]$$

The value of a program is the trace of its I/O activity, that is, the value of all the streams that the program uses. A non-deterministic program will have a set of such possible traces as its semantics:

$$ioTrace \overset{\text{def}}{=} streamId \to stream$$
$$ioTraces \overset{\text{def}}{=} \mathcal{P}(ioTrace)$$

The domain constructor $\mathcal{P}(\cdot)$ is the usual mathematical power set. Note that for all domains D, $\mathcal{P}(D)$ forms a complete partial order (in fact, a lattice) with the empty set $\emptyset$ as bottom element, and D as top element. The requirement of a more complicated power domain construction (as summarized by Paterson [15]) is avoided, since the domain $ioTraces$ is not reflexive.

The list domain constructor ($[\cdot]$) is defined as follows: for any domain D,

$$[D] \overset{\text{def}}{=} (Nil + D \times [D])_\perp$$

This defines the domain of finite and infinite lists over D. The domain Nil contains the single element nil, and is used to represent the null list. Given D a domain, $d, e \in D$ and $ds \in [D]$, we define the $cons$ constructor as a syntactic abbreviation:

$$d\ cons\ ds \overset{\text{def}}{=} \langle d, ds \rangle$$

Another useful constructor is

$$snoc : [D] \times D \to [D]$$

which is used to append an element to the end of a list:

$$nil\ snoc\ d \overset{\text{def}}{=} d\ cons\ nil$$
$$(d\ cons\ ds)\ snoc\ e \overset{\text{def}}{=} d\ cons\ (ds\ snoc\ e)$$

It follows that $snoccing$ onto an infinite list is the identity function, since $\perp\ snoc\ d = \perp$. We introduce traditional list notation as syntactic sugar: for $d_1, \ldots, d_n \in D$,

$$[d_1, d_2, \ldots, d_n] \overset{\text{def}}{=} d_1\ cons\ d_2\ cons\ \ldots\ cons\ d_n\ cons\ nil$$

5.3.2 Semantic Functions for Interaction Semantics

The interaction semantics of programs are defined through the function:

$$\mathcal{IO}[\cdot] : ioReq \to time \to ioTrace \to ioTraces$$

This function takes as arguments an I/O request, the current time, and the current I/O history, and gives as result the set of possible resulting I/O traces.

In defining $\mathcal{IO}[\cdot]$, we first define three helper functions:

$$enqueue\ :\ stream \times time \times streamEvent \to stream$$
$$dequeue\ :\ stream \times time \to stream$$
$$firstEvent\ :\ stream \to event$$

The $enqueue$ function appends a new event onto a stream following a write, dequeue finds the first event on the stream that has not been removed, and records the time of its removal, and *firstEvent* finds the first event on the queue that has not been removed.

$$enqueue(s, t, v) \stackrel{\text{def}}{=} s \ snoc \ \langle t, v, \perp \rangle$$

$$dequeue(\langle t_\alpha, v, \perp \rangle \ cons \ es, t_\beta) \stackrel{\text{def}}{=} \langle t_\alpha, v, t_\beta \rangle \ cons \ es$$
$$dequeue(\langle t_\alpha, v, t \rangle \ cons \ es, t_\beta) \stackrel{\text{def}}{=} \langle t_\alpha, v, t_\beta \rangle \ cons \ dequeue(es, t_\beta)$$
$$\text{for } t \neq \perp$$

$$firstEvent(\langle t_\alpha, v, \perp \rangle \ cons \ es) \stackrel{\text{def}}{=} v$$
$$firstEvent(\langle t_\alpha, v, t_\beta \rangle \ cons \ es) \stackrel{\text{def}}{=} firstEvent(es)$$
$$\text{for } t_\beta \neq \perp$$

A **write** request of value v to stream s may potentially be serviced any time (τ') following the current time (τ). The request is modelled by enqueuing a new stream event to the stream s and executing the continuation function:

$$\mathcal{IO}[\![(\text{write}, s, v, c)]\!]\tau\sigma \stackrel{\text{def}}{=} \bigcup_{\tau' > \tau} \mathcal{IO}[\![c]\!]\tau'\sigma'$$
$$\text{where } \sigma' = \sigma s \mapsto enqueue(\sigma s, \tau', v)]$$

A **read** request from stream s with continuation function c may potentially be serviced at any time (τ') following the current time (τ). The request is modelled by dequeuing the first event from s, and applying c to this first event:

$$\mathcal{IO}[\![\langle \text{read}, s, c \rangle]\!]\tau\sigma \stackrel{\text{def}}{=} \bigcup_{\tau' > \tau} \mathcal{IO}[\![c \ v]\!]\tau'\sigma'$$
$$\text{where } v = firstEvent(\sigma s)$$
$$\text{and } \sigma' = \sigma[s \mapsto dequeue(\sigma s, \tau')]$$

Our approach to defining the *all* I/O request can be informally motivated by the following example. Consider a simple (and not so useful) program:

```
fun p1 ->
    let p1cont = read(twos, fn X => write(ones, X-1, p1cont)) in
        write(ones, 1, p1cont).

fun p2 -> read(ones, fn X => write(twos, X+1, p2cont)).
```

The effect of this program is that process p_1 executes indefinitely, producing an infinite stream of 1's, while p_2 produces an infinite stream of 2's. The processes are mutually dependent, in that p_2 consumes the *ones* stream produced by p_1, while p_1 consumes the *twos* stream produced by p_2. We are therefore obliged to construct the semantics of the all request as the least upper bound of a chain of sets of approximations to the I/O trace of the set of processes. Ignoring non-determinism and time-stamping for the time-being, the chain σ_i of approximations looks like this:

$$
\begin{aligned}
&\sigma_0 : && ones \mapsto nil && twos \mapsto nil \\
&\sigma_1 : && ones \mapsto 1\ cons\ nil && twos \mapsto nil \\
&\sigma_2 : && ones \mapsto 1\ cons\ nil && twos \mapsto 2\ cons\ nil \\
&\sigma_3 : && ones \mapsto 1\ cons\ 1\ cons\ nil && twos \mapsto 2\ cons\ nil \\
&\cdots && \cdots && \cdots \\
&\sigma_\infty : && ones \mapsto 1\ cons\ 1\ cons\ 1\ cons \cdots && twos \mapsto 2\ cons\ 2\ cons\ 2\ cons \cdots
\end{aligned}
$$

The I/O trace σ_{i+1} is created by evaluating each process under σ_i, and then combining the resulting new traces. Each process contributes the values for its output streams to the combination. We shall use the standard fixed-point theorem to show that σ_∞ exists. To handle non-determinism, the chain of approximations is in fact over a set of I/O traces.

Formally, this is achieved as follows. To obtain the next set of approximations from a particular I/O trace, we define the helper function

$$
\mathcal{IO}_{1-Step}[\![\,\cdot\,]\!] : ioReq \to time \to ioTrace \to ioTraces
$$

This function evaluates a set of processes under the current approximation to the I/O trace, and combines the results to give a new set of approximations. The combination is guided by the process declarations, which indicate which streams each process uses as output streams. A combined I/O trace is built from the original I/O trace, supplemented by the new events contributed by each process. The cross-product of all I/O traces generated by each process is used to give the set of new approximations. For $i_1, o_1, \ldots, i_n, o_n : [id]$ and $a_1, \ldots, a_n : ioReq$:

$$
\mathcal{IO}_{1-Step}[\![\langle \texttt{all}, [\langle i_1, a_1, o_1 \rangle, \ldots, \langle i_n, a_n, o_n \rangle] \rangle]\!]\tau\sigma
$$
$$
\stackrel{\text{def}}{=} \{\sigma[\sigma_1/o_1, \ldots, \sigma_n/o_n] \mid \sigma_1 \in \mathcal{IO}[\![a_1]\!]\tau\sigma, \ldots, \sigma_n \in \mathcal{IO}[\![a_n]\!]\tau\sigma\}
$$

The new approximations (the σ_i) are combined using the notational abbreviation that for $\sigma, \sigma' \in ioTrace$ and $s_1, \ldots, s_k : strId$,

$$
\sigma[\sigma'/\{s_1, \ldots, s_k\}] \stackrel{\text{def}}{=} \sigma[s_1 \mapsto \sigma's_1, \ldots, s_k \mapsto \sigma's_k]
$$

We can finally define the semantics of all constructs to be the fixed point of a function of type $ioTraces \to ioTraces$, defined in terms of $\mathcal{IO}_{1-Step}[\![\,\cdot\,]\!]$. The function combines the initial I/O trace with the best set of approximations generated so far to produce a better set of approximations.

$$
\mathcal{IO}[\![\langle \texttt{all}, rs \rangle \tau\sigma_0 \stackrel{\text{def}}{=} FIX\ \lambda\Sigma. \bigcup_{\sigma' \in \Sigma} \mathcal{IO}_{1-Step}[\![\langle \texttt{all}, rs \rangle]\!]\tau\sigma'
$$
$$
\text{where } \Sigma' = \{\sigma_0[\sigma/\{o_i \mid 1 \le i \le n\}] \mid \sigma \in \Sigma\}
$$
$$
\text{and } rs = [\langle i_1, a_1, o_1 \rangle, \ldots, \langle i_1, a_1, o_1 \rangle]
$$

The **any** I/O request follows one of the list of possible paths; the semantics is then simply the union of all the possibilities.

$$
\mathcal{IO}[\![\langle \texttt{any}, [\langle i_1, a_1, o_1 \rangle, \ldots, \langle i_n, a_n, o_n \rangle] \rangle]\!]\tau\sigma
$$
$$
\stackrel{\text{def}}{=} \mathcal{IO}[\![a_1]\!]\tau\sigma \bigcup \cdots \bigcup \mathcal{IO}[\![a_n]\!]\tau\sigma
$$

Finally, the **done** request terminates a program:

$$
\mathcal{IO}[\![\texttt{done}]\!]\tau\sigma \stackrel{\text{def}}{=} \sigma
$$

6 Combined Semantics

We are now in a position to formalize the combined semantics and transformation methodology first presented in section 3.

The interface between the stream logic semantics of section 4 and the semantics of the functional language of section 5 is on two levels:

- the data domain of the functional languages is also the data universe over which atomic formulae in stream logic are constructed;

- the *ioTrace* domain in the functional semantics is equated to the stream assignments of stream logic.

Recall that we wish to define the semantics of a programming language in terms of two semantic functions:

$$[\cdot]_p \; : \; program \to streamAssignments$$
$$[\cdot]_c \; : \; constraints \to streamAssignments$$

where

$$streamAssignments \stackrel{\text{def}}{=} \mathcal{P}(streamId \to stream)$$

and where *stream* is as defined for stream logic (definition 4.4), over the domain of denotable values *val*, as defined in section 5.1.1. We first define the program function for *Clock*:

Definition 6.1 ($[\cdot]_p$) *Assume we have a function*

$$unpack : ioTraces \to streamAssignments$$

which maps elements from the cpo-structured ioTraces domain to simple sets of functions from identifiers to streams. Then for all Clock programs p:

$$[p]_p \stackrel{\text{def}}{=} unpack(\mathcal{IO}[\mathcal{E}[p]\mu_{init}] \, 0 \, \sigma_{init})$$
$$where \; \mu_{init} \stackrel{\text{def}}{=} \bot_{env}$$
$$and \; \sigma_{init} \stackrel{\text{def}}{=} \bot_{ioTraces}$$

□

I.e., we take first the pure semantics of the program (through $\mathcal{E}[\cdot]$), then the interaction semantics (through $\mathcal{IO}[\cdot]$) starting at time 0. The result is then cast from an element of the cpo-structured domain *ioTraces* to a member of the simple set *streamAssignments*.

The restriction function, tailored to *Clock*, is:

Definition 6.2 ($[\cdot]_c$) *For all sets c of well-formed formulae of stream logic, we define:*

$$[\cdot]_c \stackrel{\text{def}}{=} \{S \mid \exists \mathcal{T}_0, \mathcal{T}[\cdot] \; s.t. \; \langle val, S, \mathcal{T}_0, \mathcal{T}[\cdot] \rangle \models c\}$$

□

I.e., the restriction function gives all possible stream valuations over *val* that form part of a model for the given set of temporal constraints *c*.

Then the definitions for a combined semantics (definition 3.1) and for semantic-preserving transformations (definition 3.2) hold.

7 Conclusions

The work described in this paper is really just a beginning. Further work will continue in three directions.

Firstly, we have defined *Clock*, a simple extension to Gurded Term ML that allows I/O, process creation and communication, and non-determinism. Building from the simple primitives in this language, it will be interesting to define more useful combinators that provide higher level abstractions for concurrency. These abstractions can be domain specific, reflecting the range of software architectures one might wish to exploit: for example, the combinators suitable to building concurrent user interfaces might be different from those suitable for programming distributed systems. Properties of these combinators could be derived by reasoning about the temporal aspects of their constituent components.

Secondly, the question of concrete transforms has not yet been addressed. Transforms in the general framework of the simple language should be investigated, as well as transforms over domain-specific combinators. The stream-logic may well have to be extended: there is as yet no real provision for dynamic reconfiguration of systems, which will probably require moving to a sorted logic.

Thirdly, we have claimed that constraints form a natural abstraction for persistent state. It would be interesting to exploit this to allow the inclusion of external software, described as the "black-box" implementation of a solver for some set of constraints. An example might be to try to describe some aspects of the X Window System [17] in terms of constraints.

Acknowledgements

The work described in this paper was partially supported by ESPRIT Basic Research Action 3147, the Phoenix Project. Joachim Schullerer implemented the theorem prover for a subset of stream logic. I would like to thank the members of the Phoenix group, in particular Hendrik Lock and Andrew Martin for many discussions related to this work, and Manuel Chakravarty for his help with the GTML compiler. Particular thanks are due to Nigel Perry for his willingness to share his great knowledge and experience in this area, and to Gerd Kock for his aid with the denotational semantics.

References

[1] F. Warren Burton. Non-determinism with referential transparency in functional programming languages. *The Computer Journal*, 31(3):243–247, 1988.

[2] Roland Dietrich, Birgit Heinz, and Hendrik C.R. Lock. Guarded functional programming and lazy streams. ESPRIT Basic Research Action 3147, the Phoenix project, Deliverable B.2.2(ii), 1991.

[3] Roland Dietrich and Hendrik C.R. Lock. Exploiting Non-Determinism through Laziness in Guarded Functional Languages. In *TAPSOFT*, 1991.

[4] Dov Gabbay. The declarative past and imperative future. In *Temporal Logic in Specification*, volume LNCS 398, pages 409–448. Springer Verlag, 1987.

[5] Andrew Gordon. PFL+: A kernel scheme for functional I/O. Technical report, University of Cambridge Computer Laboratory, March 1989.

[6] T.C. Nicholas Graham. Temporal constraint functional programming: A semantic framework. ESPRIT Basic Research Action 3147, the Phoenix project, Deliverable B6.1, 1991.

[7] C.A.R. Hoare. *Communicating Sequential Processes*. Prentice-Hall, London, 1985.

[8] Paul Hudak, Philip Wadler, Arvind, Brian Boutel, Jon Fairburn, Joe Fasel, John Hughes, Thomas Johnsson, Dick Kieburtz, Simon Peyton Jones, Rishiyur Nikhil, Mike Reeve, David Wise, and Jonathon Young. Report on the functional programming language Haskell. Technical report, Yale University, December 1988.

[9] Kent Karlsson. Nebula – a functional operating system. Technical report, Chalmers University, 1981.

[10] Hendrik C.R. Lock. An amalgamation of functional and logic programming languages. Technical Report 408, GMD, September 1989.

[11] Hendrik C.R. Lock and Stefan Jänichen. Linda meets functional programming. In *Proceedings of the Second IEEE Workshop of Future Trends of Distributed Computing Systems*, 1990.

[12] R. Milner, J. Parrow, and D. Walker. A calculus of mobile processes. Technical Report ECS-LFCS-89-85, Laboratory for Foundations of Computer Science, University of Edinburgh, 1989.

[13] Robin Milner. The Standard ML Core Language. *Polymorphism*, 2(2):1–28, October 1985.

[14] Robin Milner. *Communication and Concurrency*. Prentice-Hall, Hemel Hempstead, 1986.

[15] Ross Paterson. Non-deterministic λ-calculus: a core for integrated languages. Technical Report IC/FPG/Phoenix/7, Imperial College, University of London, January 1991.

[16] Nigel Perry. I/O and inter-language calling for functional languages. In *Proceedings of the Ninth International Conference of the Chilean Computer Science Society and Fifteenth Latin American Conference on Informatics*, July 1989.

[17] Robert W. Scheifler and Jim Gettys. The X window system. *ACM Transactions on Graphics*, 5(2):79–109, 1986.

[18] David A. Schmidt. *Denotational Semantics: A Methodology for Language Development*. Wm. C. Brown Publishers, Dubuque, Iowa, 1986.

Eight queens divided:
an experience in parallel functional programming

K.G. Langendoen   W.G. Vree

University of Amsterdam,

Kruislaan 403, 1098 SJ Amsterdam, The Netherlands

e-mail: koen@fwi.uva.nl

Abstract

The eight queens puzzle is a popular benchmark program used by many implementors of parallel functional languages to show the performance of their systems. Straightforward parallelisation of the classical algorithm with a fork-join annotation, however, results in poor parallel behaviour because of the strict synchronisation between the adjacent stages in the pipeline of recursive invocations. This paper analyses the performance bottleneck and provides a transformation that results in an efficient divide&conquer algorithm with minimal synchronisation between parallel tasks. An additional advantage is that the grain size of the parallel tasks can be easily controlled in the transformed divide&conquer program, whereas the original algorithm provides no obvious handle to do so. Usage of the *inside-out* transformation is not restricted to the eight queens puzzle, it can be applied to all applications with a comparable recursive iteration pattern.

1   Introduction

Parallel functional programming is still in its infancy; only a few prototype parallel graph-reduction machines have become available for experimentation. The immaturity shows in the benchmark programs used to determine the performance of those machines: most popular is the nfib program, which is ideally suited for parallel execution since it has a straightforward decomposition into large threads. The solution of the eight queens puzzle is another favourite, but it is far more interesting than nfib because of its greater complexity and frequent usage of shared data. Although the program has been used extensively to demonstrate the parallel performance of various machine designs with success, it performs poorly when executed under our FRATS parallel reduction strategy [Langendoen91].

The FRATS parallel reduction strategy aims at the efficient implementation of lazy functional languages on a shared memory multiprocessor equipped with caches. It is based on the usage of an explicit annotation to denote fork-join parallelism and is well suited for divide&conquer programs. FRATS successfully exploits the resulting tree task structure by equipping the leaf tasks with private heaps; this facilitates local garbage collection and obviates the usage of expensive cache coherency protocols.

To study the feasibility of the FRATS design a set of parallel-performance analysis tools have been developed. The analysis starts by handing an explicitly annotated program to an interpreter that records task-specific information like the size and execution time in a trace file. The trace file is fed to a simulation program which models the execution according to FRATS on an ideal parallel machine that has an unlimited number of processors, zero communication delay, and no scheduling overhead. Because of these simplifications the model's output won't be achieved in practice, but it provides an upper bound of the application's inherent parallelism. Besides measures like speed-up and the number of tasks, the simulator also computes a parallel profile of the application: the number of active tasks at each time step.

FRATS's analysis tools expose the eight-queens performance bottleneck and motivate the transformation to a divide&conquer style algorithm.

2   The eight queens puzzle

The "eight queens puzzle" asks how to place eight queens on a chessboard so that no two queens hold each other in check (i.e. no two queens are in the same row, column, or diagonal). The classical solution, as outlined in many textbooks [Abelson87, Bird88], is to design a function that works across the board, placing a queen in each column. Placing n queens consists of a recursive call to determine all legal placements of n-1 queens in the first n-1 columns of the board, followed by the extension of those partial solutions with a queen in column n if possible. This algorithm is presented in Figure 1 as a program written in Miranda [Turner85].

```
main = queens 8

queens 0 = [[]]
queens n = [q:sub | sub <- queens (n-1); q <- [1..8]; safe 1 q sub]

safe d q []     = True
safe d q (x:xs) = q ~= x  &  abs(q-x) ~= d  &  safe (d+1) q xs
```

Figure 1: Classical algorithm to solve the eight queens puzzle.

The definition of "queens" uses list comprehension [Bird88] to iterate over all partial solutions ("queens (n-1)") and row positions of the nth queen ("[1..8]"), while filtering all legal positions with the (recursive) function "safe". List comprehension, also known as set abstraction [Turner81], is the functional language equivalent of the mathematical set notation, except that it specifies an ordered list instead of an unordered set.

2.1   Performance

The eight queens program as defined in Figure 1 contains a lot of potential parallelism since the iterations in the list comprehension are independent of each other; an invocation of "queens n" expands into #"queens (n-1)"*8 independent "safe 1 q sub" calls to determine the legal board positions. Since FRATS is based on program annotations we have to transform the original program to make the parallelism explicit. Note that the usage of explicit annotations is common practice despite the compiler-derived parallelism approach of most parallel functional language implementation projects. See, for example, the codes listed in [Hammond90] and [Augustsson89].

To facilitate the insertion of parallelism annotations we transform the high-level "sub <- queens(n-1)" iteration inside the list comprehension into a low-level loop process:

```
queens 0 = [[]]
queens n = loop (queens (n-1))

loop []        = []
loop (sub:1st) = append (extend sub) (loop 1st)

extend sub = [q:sub | q <- [1..8]; safe 1 q sub]
```

The inner iteration ("q <- [1..8]") is rewritten analogously, but for simplicity one can consider the "extend sub" calls as the basic units of work. Insertion of the *sandwich* annotation [Vree90] in the loop makes the parallel tasks visible to the analysis tools.

```
loop []        = []
loop (sub:1st) = sandwich append (extend sub) (loop 1st)
```

In general the sandwich annotation can be put in front of any function application and has the following syntax:

```
sandwich F arg1 arg2 ...
```

Whenever the value of a sandwich annotated expression is needed the current thread of control is suspended and function F's arguments (arg1 arg2 ...) are handed to the runtime support system for parallel evaluation. When all arguments have been evaluated completely to normal forms, the suspended thread is awakened and execution continues with the application of F to its arguments. Thus a task (= thread) reduces some sandwich argument; during its execution a task may itself invoke a sandwich, and on termination the task will return the normalised argument to its parent.

Now the eight queens program can be processed by the parallel-performance analysis tools, which yields the parallel profile listed in Figure 2.

A surprising result: the eight queens program performs poorly and makes only a speed-up of 4.5 on an ideal machine. The remarkable dips to one active thread provide the clue to the cause of this poor parallel behaviour. Apparently there is some strict synchronisation between the (recursive) invocations of the "queens" function. Recall that parent processes are suspended during the execution of their children; the profile of all tasks (active + suspended) versus execution time is given in Figure 3 and shows a sawtooth pattern in phase with the active-tasks dips.

Both parallel profiles can be explained by a close look at the code that generates the parallel tasks (the "queens" and "loop" definitions). The program expands into an 8 deep pipeline of "loop" invocations connected by means of result lists; the program starts by calling "queens 8", which unfolds into "loop (queens 7)". This triggers the evaluation of "queens 7", which expands into "loop (queens 6)" etc. until the recursion stops at "queens 0". As soon as the results come available, each "loop" invocation will spark a set of "extend sub" processes, which results in the schematic parallel profile shown in Figure 4.

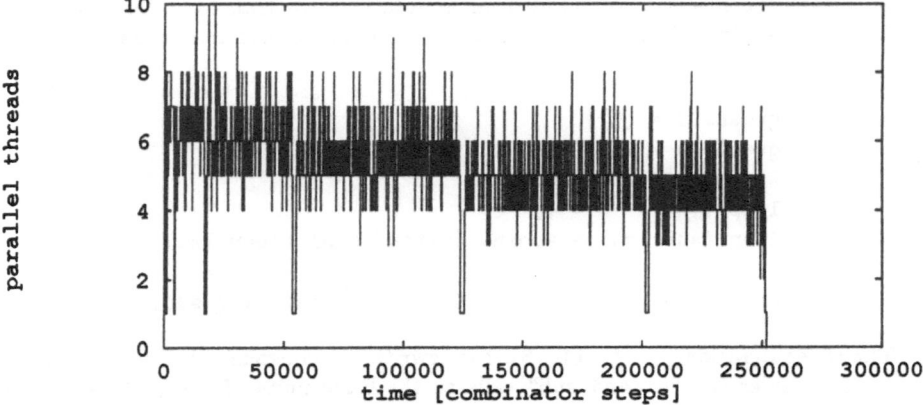

Figure 2: profile of fork-join parallelism
speed-up = 4.49; number of tasks = 53056

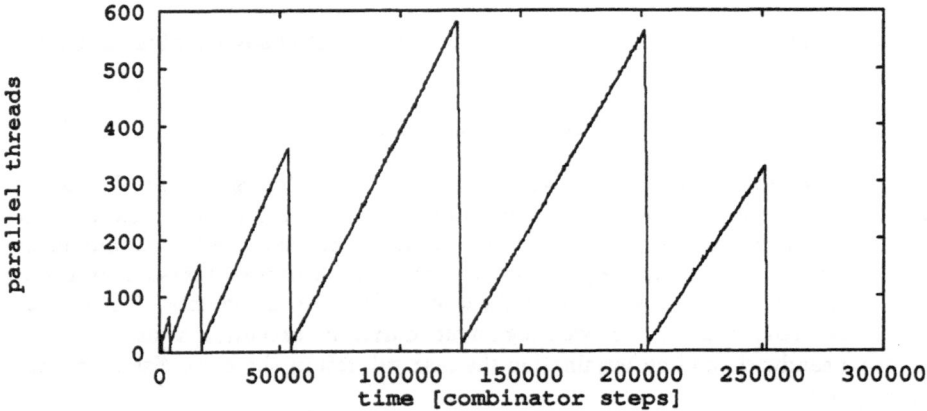

Figure 3: profile of total (active + suspended) threads

Sparking of the parallel "extend sub" tasks, however, is not done in one step but tasks are created one after another while loop "walks down" its list argument. Since parent processes are suspended during the execution of their children, this results in a chain of processes waiting for the last one to terminate, hence, the sawtooth profile. As soon as the last task has finished all parent tasks will be awakened one after another to perform the append operation to glue the results together. This causes the sequential dips in the active parallel profile.

The "flat" profiles between the synchronisation dips in Figure 2 are caused by the linear sparking of tasks by "loop" as well: as soon as the first "extend sub" task finishes the system enters an equilibrium where new tasks will be generated at the same rate as old ones die. This effect is visualised in Figure 5. The small variations in the number of active threads occur because the run lengths of all "extend sub" worker tasks are not precisely equal ("safe" stops as soon as it finds an offending

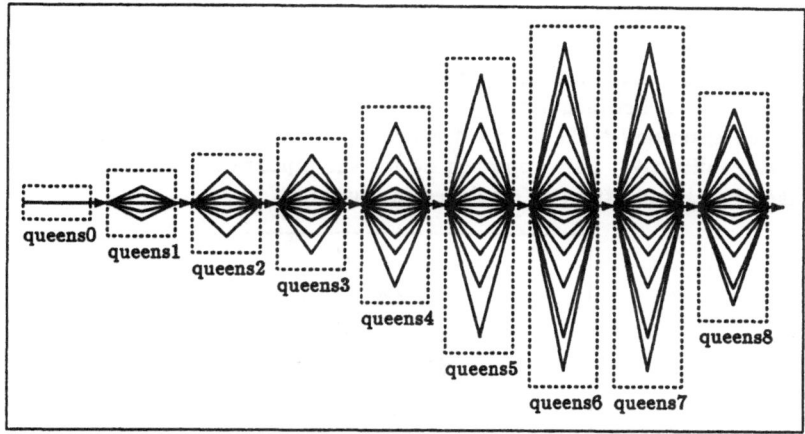

Figure 4: pipeline process structure

queen).

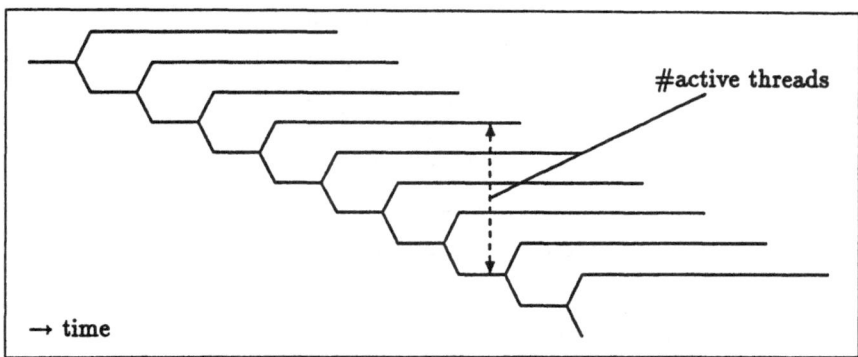

Figure 5: loop process structure

Usage of the term pipeline in the previous paragraphs is somewhat misleading because the data is shifted from one stage to another in its entirety, which excludes the possibility of concurrent processing in different pipeline stages. This limitation is a direct consequence of the fork-join semantics of the sandwich annotation. The usage of a "real" pipeline of processes interconnected through lazy streams can be expected to improve the parallel performance of the eight queens program because the sparking of tasks in various stages can be overlapped. For example the "queens 5" can start as soon as "queens 4" has produced its first legal board with 4 queens, instead of waiting until the complete list of all boards of 4 queens has been computed. Lazy streams cannot be specified with fork-join annotations, therefore we pursue this possibility with another annotation in section 4.

3 Transformations

As shown above, performance of the parallel eight queens program is limited by the strict synchronisation between recursive invocations of the "queens" function. Each invocation starts by unwrapping the list of partial solutions produced by the recursion, sparks parallel processes to extend these boards with another queen, and finally packs the process results into a single result list. These wrapping/unwrapping actions at each interaction between two recursive calls (pipeline stages) are wasted: why not have the extension tasks themselves spark the associated tasks in the following pipeline stage directly? This approach avoids the pipeline bottleneck and results in a tree like process structure, as displayed in Figure 6.

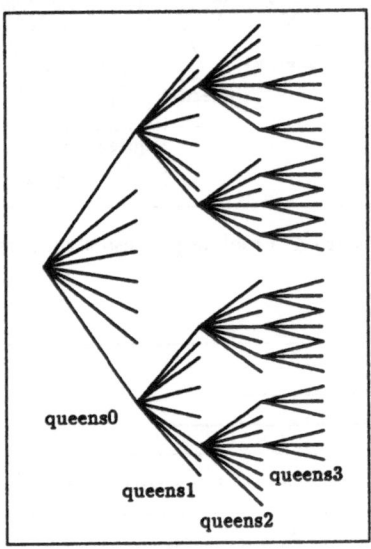

Figure 6: tree process structure

The advantages of this tree structure are obvious: task creation occurs in parallel and unnecessary synchronisation between tasks of the same generation is avoided. In order to achieve such a divide&conquer style program the control flow in the classical eight queens algorithm has to be reversed: instead of "queens 8" calling "queens 7" ... calling "queens 0", the computation should start with "queens 0" calling "queens 1", etc. This can be accomplished by applying a standard transformation that transforms a linear recursive function into a tail recursive one. Applying the *partial inversion* transformation described in [Partsch90] to the original definition of the eight queens algorithm in Figure 1 yields the following code:

```
main = queens 0 [[]]
```

```
queens 8 sub = sub
queens n sub = queens (n+1) [q:b | b<-sub; q<-[1..8]; safe 1 q b]
```

Now the algorithm starts out with a set that just contains an empty board. Each invocation of "queens" extends the partial solutions in its accumulating parameter "sub" with another queen, and passes the result on to the next recursive "queens" call. The recursion stops when 8 queens have been put on the board and the "queens" function simply returns the solutions listed in its accumulating argument.

Although the control flow now has the correct direction ("main" calls "queens 0"), the transformation has not changed the pipeline process structure: each "queens" call passes on the extended solutions in one single list to the next one. Another transformation is needed to derive a divide&conquer style algorithm.

Observe that the "queens" function operates on the individual elements of its accumulating argument and never needs to inspect that set in its entirety. Therefore it should be possible to separately call "queens (n+1)" as soon as a legal board has been found in the list comprehension instead of accumulating all boards into one set. Applying an ad hoc program transformation based on this observation to the code above results in the following program:

```
main = queens 0 [[]]

queens 8 sub = sub
queens n sub = concat[queens (n+1) [q:b]|b<-sub;q<-[1..8];safe 1 q b]
```

The "concat" function is needed to glue all result lists of the various "queens" calls together into one single list. The square brackets around the "q:sub" expression are needed to convert a legal board into a single item list to conform to the type of queens's second input parameter. A correctness proof of this last transformation is given in appendix A.

The efficiency of the last eight queens program can be improved somewhat by observing that "queens" is always called with a list as second argument that contains a single element: "[]" or "q:b". A small cosmetic transformation that removes the list notation yields the final program in Figure 7.

```
main = queens 0 []

queens 8 sub = [sub]
queens n sub = concat [queens (n+1) (q:sub)| q<-[1..8]; safe 1 q sub]

safe d q []     = True
safe d q (x:xs) = q ~= x  &  abs(q-x) ~= d  &  safe (d+1) q xs
```

Figure 7: code for the eight queens puzzle; divide&conquer approach.

The previous sequence of small transformation steps can be packed into a single transformation. This *inside-out* transformation can be applied to all functions that have a recursive iteration pattern that is comparable to the one of the eight queens puzzle. In general the inside-out transformation rewrites a pipeline function with the following recursion pattern:

```
main  =  F X₀

F Xₙ  =  [Valₙ]
F x   =  [Val i j | i <- F (f x); j <- J; Pred i j ]
```

into a tree version:

```
main    =  F Xₙ Valₙ

F X₀ i  =  [i]
F x i   =  concat [F (f⁻¹ x) (Val i j) | j <- J; Pred i j]
```

provided that there exists an inverse function of f such that $f^{-1}(f(x)) = x$.

108

In principle the *inside-out* transformation can be automagically performed by a smart compiler, but it is more likely that the programmer will have to apply the transformation himself since often the program will have to be adapted to fit the required format of the recursive function F. For example, if the listcomprehension uses a third iterator (say k <- K) then we simply put the last two iterators into one tuple (t <- [(j,k) | j<-J; k<-K]) to enforce the format of the inside-out transformation.

3.1 Performance

The transformation of the classical eight queens algorithm has resulted in the typical divide&conquer style program of Figure 7: each recursive invocation of "queens" specifies 8 independent sub-tasks to compute part of the solution. Straightforward parallelisation of the "q<-[1..8]" iteration yields the desired parallel program; like before, we rewrite the high-level list comprehension into a low-level loop process to explicitly insert parallelism annotations:

```
queens 8 sub = [sub]
queens n sub = loop n sub [1..8]

loop n sub []      = []
loop n sub (q:lst) = sandwich append (extend n sub q) (loop n sub lst)

extend n sub q = queens (n+1) (q:sub),    safe 1 q sub
                 [],                       otherwise
```

Note that the "concat" function in the "queens" definition has been unfolded into the "append" operator in the loop code. Running this code through the performance analysis tools produces a parallel profile as depicted in Figure 8.

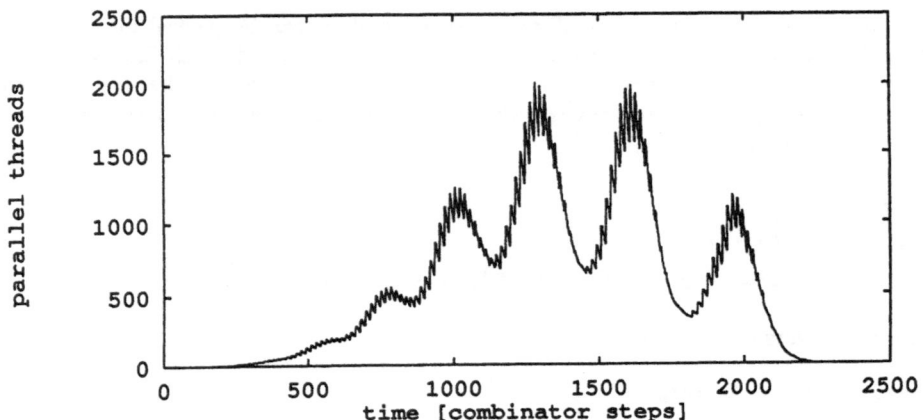

Figure 8: profile of fork-join parallelism; divide&conquer algorithm
speed-up = 482; number of tasks = 46161

The inside-out transformation has been extremely effective: more than a hundred fold increase in speed-up (from 4.5 to 482). As we expected, the synchronisation dips to one active thread of the classical profile have disappeared. Still we can easily recognise various "queens" generations by the peaks in the profile. Note that the relative height of these peaks highly correlates with the sawtooth profile of all threads in Figure 3. The ragged edge of the profile is caused by the immediate rejection of most partial solutions by the "safe" condition in the "extend" code, hence many tasks only execute one "safe" call and die immediately. The generation of these "null" tasks can be prevented by moving the "safe" test into the "loop" and only spark parallel tasks with a legal partial board. Unfortunately this halves performance on the ideal parallel machine because of the sequential execution of the 8 "safe" calls. On a real machine with non negligible task creation times, however, it is probably an advantageous modification.

4 Spark&wait

The strict fork-join synchronisation of the sandwich annotation, which clashed with the pipeline nature of the classical eight queens algorithm, can be dealt with through the transformation to a divide&conquer style algorithm. An interesting question remains about the performance of the classical approach with a more powerful annotation that is capable of generating a real pipeline of processes interconnected through lazy lists. The familiar spark&wait strategy [PeytonJones87] has the useful property that the parent task directly continues execution after sparking child processes and only waits when it needs the result of a child that has not finished yet. When using spark&wait semantics instead of fork-join semantics, we expect the classical algorithm to perform much better because the next pipeline stage (a parent process) can proceed as soon as the first partial solution has been computed by a child process.

The performance analysis tools have the option to execute sandwich annotations with spark&wait semantics instead of the fork-join default. Thus "sandwich F x y" will spark two child tasks to evaluate "x" and "y", and immediately continues execution with calling "F". Running the parallel version of the classical eight queens program of section 2.1 under spark&wait yields the parallel performance (on an ideal machine) given in Figure 9. We see that spark&wait performs much better on the classical pipeline algorithm than its fork-join counterpart: a speed-up of 99 versus 4.5. The performance of the divide&conquer algorithm under the spark&wait regime is presented in Figure 10.

We see that spark&wait performs better on the divide&conquer program than on the classical one: a speed-up of 423 versus 99, but the speed-up is less than that of the divide&conquer style version executed under fork-join policy (482). Note that the computation ends in a single sequential thread that runs from step 1709 until 2669. This sequential tail severely limits the overall performance since it accounts for 36% of the parallel execution time! Monitoring the task results showed that this is caused by the underlying lazy evaluation strategy which reduces sub-tasks to head normal, not full normal forms. In this particular case the sub-tasks return list structures with tails of unevaluated "append" expressions. Hence, the "main" task ends up evaluating those expressions sequentially.

A slight modification to the spark&wait semantics, to enforce reduction of sub-tasks to normal form, which we call spark-eager, resolves this problem. The speed-up

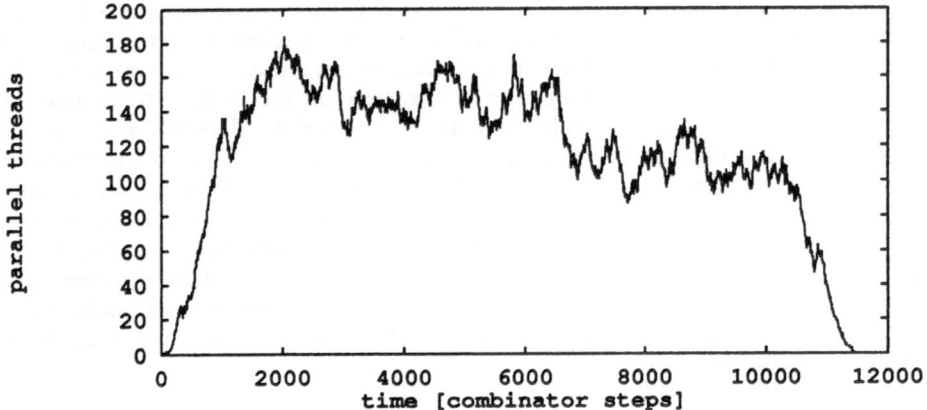

Figure 9: profile of spark&wait parallelism
speed-up = 98.8; number of tasks = 53056

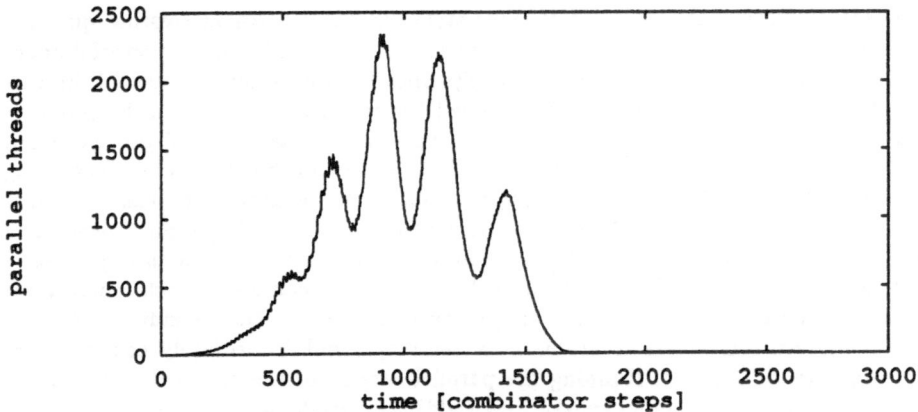

Figure 10: profile of spark&wait parallelism; divide&conquer algorithm
speed-up = 423; number of tasks = 46161

increases from 423 to 648, and the corresponding parallel profile is shown in Figure 11.

5   Discussion

The previous sections have shown that the transformed divide&conquer program performs significantly better on an ideal parallel machine than the original eight queens algorithm. When considering the difference between the two programs on real parallel machines we have to take into account the fixed number of processors, communication costs, and scheduling overheads. The short-sighted attitude in the previous analysis of generating as many parallel threads as possible to increase performance can have the anomalous effect of decreasing performance by swamping the finite machine with

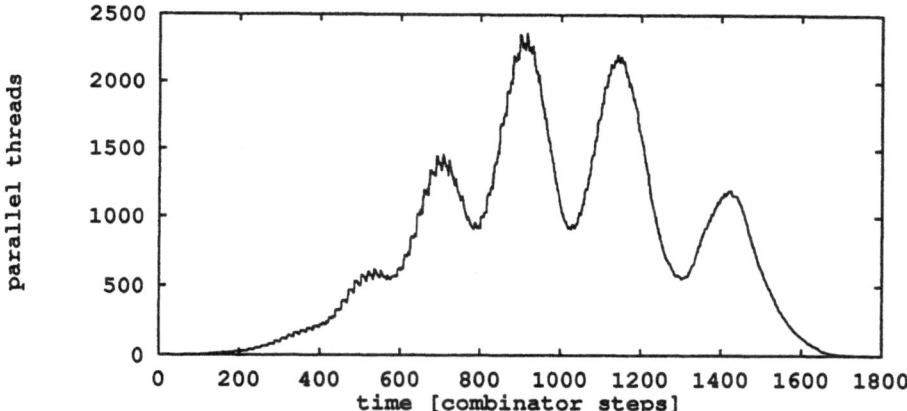

Figure 11: profile of spark-eager parallelism; divide&conquer algorithm
speed-up = 648; number of tasks = 46161

too many tasks. In general one has to limit the number of tasks and enforce some
minimal grain size on the tasks to overcome the scheduling and communication costs.

Both the classical algorithm and the divide&conquer program have far too many
small tasks for optimal execution on a real machine. At the moment each worker task
only computes a single "safe 1 q sub" check and we would like to adjust the programs to generate tasks of greater complexity. The obvious modification of the classical algorithm is to keep the inner loop ("q <- [1..8]") as one sequential task. This
roughly increases the grain size with a factor of 8. The transformed divide&conquer
algorithm offers a much more refined task control mechanism of pruning the task
tree at some user controlled depth; when the queens's recursion depth exceeds some
threshold the program switches to sequential execution:

```
main = par_queens 0 []

par_queens 8 sub = [sub]
par_queens n sub = loop n sub [1..8],   n < Threshold || in parallel
                   queens n sub,        otherwise     || sequential

loop n sub []        = []
loop n sub (q:lst) = sandwich append (extend n sub q) (loop n sub lst)
```

Another advantage of the divide&conquer program is that its tree shaped task
structure can be mapped efficiently onto a distributed memory machine, whereas
the pipeline of the classical algorithm typically causes communication hot spots at
the nodes that process the intermediate result lists. FRATS is designed for shared
memory systems where this advantage of local over central communication shows up
in the cache hit ratios.

6   Conclusion

The poor parallel performance of the classical eight queens puzzle solution is caused by the underlying pipeline process structure of the algorithm and the fork-join semantics of the FRATS parallel reduction strategy. The analysis that revealed the performance bottleneck has motivated the transformation of the classical algorithm into an efficient divide&conquer version. Running both versions under the less restrictive spark&wait sparking regime also showed the superiority of the divide&conquer program. The speed-ups of the two programs under various parallel sparking strategies are summarised in table 1.

8queens	annotation semantics		
version	fork-join	spark&wait	spark-eager
classical	4.49	98.8	36.5
divide&conquer	482	423	648

Table 1: Speed-ups on an ideal machine.

The table shows that the inside-out transformation of section 3 is very effective for the fork-join sparking strategy of FRATS. The commonly used spark&wait approach performs considerably better on the classical algorithm than fork-join because the less restrictive synchronisation mechanism allows concurrent processing in several stages of the recursive pipeline. Still, spark&wait benefits greatly from the transformation to a divide&conquer style program because the linear processing of partial results in the original pipeline approach is replaced by a more efficient tree structure. By reducing child tasks to normal form the spark-eager derivate overcomes an artifact of the lazy evaluation mechanism that results in the divide&conquer program executing a sequential tail under spark&wait. In case of the classical algorithm, however, spark-eager's stronger normalisation property has the opposite effect of performing worse than spark&wait because it enforces superfluous synchronisations between parent and child tasks.

The difference in speed-up of the divide&conquer program under fork-join (482) and spark-eager (648) is caused by some extra normalisation of FRATS before sparking the parallel tasks. This additional overhead is well worthwhile because it allows FRATS to remove synchronisation locks on graph nodes, so tasks can be equipped with private heaps. The advantage of having private heaps is that it allows local garbage collection per task and doesn't require expensive coherency protocols to keep caches consistent.

Besides the superior performance of the divide&conquer program on an ideal parallel machine, its tree-shaped task structure has several real-world advantages over the classical pipeline program as well. First, the divide&conquer algorithm provides a refined grain-size control mechanism of pruning the task tree at an arbitrary level by switching to sequential code. Second, the tree structure can be mapped efficiently onto most computer architectures, whereas the pipeline structure will often generate communication hot spots.

To quantify the abovementioned transformation advantages we plan to send the program codes to research groups that posses running parallel graph-reduction machines in order to get real-world measurements. We are particularly interested in the results of the grain-size controlled version of the divide&conquer program.

In this paper we have mainly looked at the famous eight-queens program, but the results can be generalised to functions with a comparable recursion pattern: the inside-out transformation of section 3 can be applied to derive divide&conquer versions of all applications that are defined as functions iterating over recursive results and another fixed set:

$$F \ x = [\ \ldots \ | \ i \ \texttt{<-} \ F \ (f \ x); \ j \ \texttt{<-} \ J; \ \ldots]$$

Examples of algorithms with this specific iteration pattern are: the instant insanity problem and map colouring. The *inside-out* transformation opens a new class of applications that can be run efficiently by divide&conquer reduction strategies like FRATS.

7 Acknowledgements

We like to thank Rutger Hofman and Henk Muller for the informal discussions in front of the blackboard that led to the divide&conquer 8queens program, and their valuable advice on the writing of this paper. Furthermore we like to thank Sjaak Koot for his comments on a draft version of this paper.

References

[Abelson87] H. Abelson and G.J. Sussman, *"Structure and Interpretation of Computer Programs"*, 6th printing, MIT Press, ISBN 0-262-01077-1, 1987.

[Augustsson89] L. Augustsson and T. Johnsson, *"Parallel Graph Reduction with the $< \nu, G>$-machine"*, Proc. Functional Programming Languages and Computer Architecture 1989, pp 202-213.

[Bird88] R.J. Bird and P. Wadler, *"Introduction to Functional Programming"*, Prentice Hall, ISBN 0-13-484189-1, 1988.

[Hammond90] K. Hammond and S.L. Peyton Jones, *"Some Early Experiments on the GRIP Parallel Reducer"*, Proc. of the second International Workshop on Implementation of Functional Languages on Parallel Architectures, Nijmegen, The Netherlands, 1990.

[Langendoen91] K.G. Langendoen and W.G. Vree, *"FRATS: A parallel reduction strategy for shared memory"*, Third International Symposium on Programming Language Implementation and Logic Programming, Passau, Germany August 1991.

[Partsch90] H.A. Partsch, *"Specification and Transformation of Programs"*, Springer-Verlag, ISBN 0-387-52356-1, 1990.

[PeytonJones87] S.L. Peyton Jones, *"The Implementation of Functional Languages"*, Prentice-Hall, ISBN 0-13-453325-9, 1987.

[Turner81] D.A. Turner, *"The semantic elegance of applicative languages"*, Proc. of the 1981 Conf. on Functional Programming Languages and Computer Architecture, pp 85-92, 1981.

[Turner85] D.A. Turner, "*Miranda: A non-strict functional language with polymor-phic types*", Functional Programming Languages and Computer Architecture, Springer-Verlag, LNCS 201, pp 1-16, 1985.

[Vree90] W.G. Vree, "*Implementation of Parallel Graph Reduction by Explicit Anno-tation and Program Transformation*", Mathematical Foundations of Computer Science 1990, LNCS 452, pp 135-151.

A Correctness proof

In this section we prove that the second step in the transformation of the eight queens program, which moves the recursive "queens" call inside the list comprehension, is correct. That is, we show that the following program:

```
main = queens 0 [[]]

queens 8 sub = sub
queens n sub = queens (n+1) [q:b | b<-sub; q<-[1..8]; safe 1 q b]
```

is equivalent with the next one:

```
Main = Queens 0 [[]]

Queens 8 sub = sub
Queens n sub = concat [Queens (n+1) [q:b|b<-sub;q<-[1..8];safe 1 q b]
```

The proof is based on manipulations of listcomprehesions according to the following rules:

```
(A1)  [x | x<-xs]              =  xs
(A2)  [f x | x<-xs]            =  map f xs
(A3)  [e | x<-xs; p x; ...]    =  [e | x <- filter p xs; ...]
(A4)  [e | x<-xs; y<-ys; ...]  =  concat [[e | y<-ys; ...] | x<-xs]
(R1)  [e | x <- [E | D]]       =  [e | D; x <- [E]]   if e does not use D

(L1)  concat (concat [E | D])  =  concat [concat E | D]
(L2)  [e | D]                  =  concat [[e] | D]
```

The axioms (A1) through (A4) can be found in [Bird88]. (R1), (L1), and (L2) can be proven by using the axioms in a straightforward induction on the structure of D.

The proof of queens n sub = Queens n sub uses induction on the (decreasing) value of n. The induction step amounts to unfolding the recursion twice, reorder-ing the resulting nested sets, and folding back into the other queens definition.

case 8:

```
queens 8 sub = sub = Queens 8 sub
```

case 7:

```
queens 7 sub
    = queens 8 [q:b | b <- sub; q <- [1..8]; safe 1 q b]
    = [q:b | b <- sub; q <- [1..8]; safe 1 q b]
(L2)
    = concat [[q:b] | b <- sub; q <- [1..8]; safe 1 q b]
    = concat [Queens 8 [q:b] | b <- sub; q <- [1..8]; safe 1 q b]
    = Queens 7 sub
```

case $0 \leq n < 7$:

```
queens n sub
    = queens (n+1) [q:b | b<-sub; q<-[1..8]; safe 1 q b]
(induction)
    = Queens (n+1) [q:b | b<-sub; q<-[1..8]; safe 1 q b]
    = concat [Queens (n+2) [Q:B] |
                    B<-[q:b | b <- sub; q <- [1..8]; safe 1 q b];
                    Q<-[1..8]; safe 1 Q B]
(A4)
    = concat (concat [[Queens (n+2) [Q:B]|Q<-[1..8];safe 1 Q B] |
                    B<-[q:b | b<-sub; q<-[1..8]; safe 1 q b]])
(R1, flatten inner listcomprehension)
    = concat (concat [[Queens (n+2) [Q:B]|Q<-[1..8];safe 1 Q B] |
                    b<-sub; q<-[1..8]; safe 1 q b; B<-[q:b]])
(A4)
    = concat (concat (concat
        [[[Queens (n+2) [Q:B]|Q<-[1..8];safe 1 Q B] | B<-[q:b]] |
                    b<-sub; q<-[1..8]; safe 1 q b]))
(L1)
    = concat (concat [concat
        [[Queens (n+2) [Q:B]|Q<-[1..8];safe 1 Q B] | B<-[q:b]] |
                    b<-sub; q<-[1..8]; safe 1 q b])
(A4)
    = concat (concat
        [ [Queens (n+2) [Q:B]|B<-[q:b];Q<-[1..8];safe 1 Q B] |
                    b<-sub; q<-[1..8]; safe 1 q b])
(L1)
    = concat [concat
            [Queens (n+2) [Q:B]|B<-[q:b];Q<-[1..8];safe 1 Q B] |
                    b<-sub; q<-[1..8]; safe 1 q b]
    = concat [Queens (n+1) [q:b] | b<-sub; q<-[1..8]; safe 1 q b]
    = Queens n sub
```

Intelligent Backtracking in And–Parallel Prolog

Andrew Verden and Hugh Glaser

University of Southampton,

Southampton,

England.

Abstract

In this paper we present an intelligent backtracking scheme for the independent and–parallel execution of Prolog. It is implemented for a distributed memory machine where an extended Warren Abstract Machine [1] is placed on each processor and can receive subgoals and spawn further subgoals to other processors.

The chosen scheme for the communication of bindings makes available additional run-time information which is incorporated into the execution. Our executor [2,3,4,5] is most notably derived from the execution schemes of Hermenegildo [6,7,8,9] and Lin [10] although both these other schemes are implemented for shared memory machines.

We present an incremental algorithm to support clause level intelligent backtracking. In our scheme intelligent backtracking will both select subgoal(s) attributable to the failure and prevent unnecessary re-execution of subgoals independent of the failure. We observe that a portion of the intelligent backtracking can be applied during forward execution and we introduce a notion of 'intelligent cutting'.

The effectiveness of our execution scheme and intelligent backtracking is demonstrated by an implementation based on an array of transputer processors.

1 Introduction

There are two main forms of parallelism to be exploited implicitly from Prolog: or–parallelism and and–parallelism. To execute efficiently 'general' Prolog programs it has been shown that both forms of parallelism are worthy of pursuit. Here we concentrate on a restricted form of and–parallelism, 'independent and–parallelism'.

Full and–parallel execution must solve the problem of multiple instantiation to variables in a clause when one or more subgoals have variables in common; the 'binding conflict problem'. In independent and–parallelism the 'binding conflict problem' is avoided by designating a variable generator subgoal ordering for each variable in a clause. Subgoals may then be executed independently when each variable in the call is either ground or the subgoal is the next designated generator for the variable. The subgoal ordering is usually encoded as a Data-Dependency Graph (*DDG*). The potential independent and–parallelism is detected at compile-time assuming a worst-case approximation to the actual execution, and is then encoded in a *DDG* [11,10,12,13].

The destination architecture is a distributed memory machine where a Prolog executor is placed on each processor; which is capable of receiving goals and spawning further subgoals to other processors. Our implementation is realised as an extension to the Warren Abstract Machine (*WAM*) [1] used extensively in sequential Prolog execution. When a subgoal is spawned to another processor, bindings are passed from parent processor to child processor by passing the total binding structure for the call; the communications alone justify this decision [3,5].

In other schemes further information is derived at run-time by traversing the incoming arguments for a call or performing ground and independence tests for specific variables. This overhead cannot normally be justified as the complexity of traversing these incoming structures is often worse than the complexity of the procedure they are intended to aid. In our scheme we are able to derive similar information at no additional overhead from the communication of bindings. This additional information is incorporated into the execution providing improvement over the compile-time prediction.

To incorporate information into the independent–parallel execution the *DDG* for a clause is constructed at run-time, in a lazy manner, as it is required. Much of the information derived for the forward execution can also be used to improve the selection of redo subgoals, 'intelligent backtracking'. We present an incremental algorithm to support clause level intelligent backtracking in parallel clauses. Individual failures are handled as distinct operations, removing the need for global time as in other schemes [10]. Our intelligent backtracking benefits execution in two ways: firstly, subgoals attributable to the cause of failure are selected for redo. Secondly, all other execution in the clause persists unless a head binding for a subgoal is re-instantiated by a redo subgoal.

During forward execution it is possible to 'prune' search space that would always be backtracked over by the intelligent backtracking, for any possible subsequent failure that may arise. We introduce a notion of 'intelligent cutting' and describe how *choice points* can be discarded where conventional *WAM* execution would retain them.

We first briefly describe the forward execution algorithm to show how additional information is laid down for the backward execution. We describe our intelligent backtracking scheme and illustrate it through an example execution. Finally, we present an analysis of our implementation based on an array of transputer processing elements. Performance results for a number of benchmark programs are given for execution on a multiprocessor machine. More comprehensive results for forward execution can be found in [4,5].

2 Parallel Clause Execution

The forward execution algorithm is described in greater detail in [3,5]. The execution of each Prolog parallel clause switches dynamically between two modes of operation. The execution mode is selected automatically according to the demand for tasks on that processor.

The *distribution mode* controls execution optimised towards the allocation of tasks (subgoals) to descendent processors until all assigned processors are allocated tasks.

The *serial mode* controls execution optimised towards execution on a single processor.

It is important that an executor be efficient in both modes. The *distribution mode* requires all the data–dependency information to spawn independent tasks. Once all the allocated processors are utilised, a switch to *serial mode* means that no data–dependency information is constructed and a parallel clause is executed in a similar way to a conventional sequential clause. It is still possible to spawn further tasks but this is no longer the primary mode of operation.

The forward execution of a parallel clause is derived at run-time from the static prediction held in the *DDG* and the run-time activation of the clause determined from binding communication. The dynamic generation of the *DDG* was first proposed by Conery [14] and has been shown to be efficient in the implementation of Lin [10]. In our scheme the activation mode of the initial call on a processor is known from the communication of the binding structure and is propagated further through descendent parallel clauses. The dynamic information is also incorporated into the parallel clause from which the task was spawned.

The *WAM* has been extended for independent and-parallel execution; the extra instructions provide table driven access to individual subgoals. Subgoals may then be executed locally or remotely depending on the run-time environment rather than simply their ordering within the clause. The *WAM* extensions include a number of additional data structures placed on the *local* stack during execution and an additional data area, the *dump*.

The new instructions center around the manipulation of a new data structure, the *parallel frame*, which is allocated each time a parallel clause is encountered. A *parallel frame* is used to hold run-time status information about each of the subgoals. The information for a single subgoal is stored in a *subgoal table* which is itself, a sub-component of the *parallel frame*. The *parallel frame* is placed on the *local* stack amid *choice points* and *environments*; our *parallel frame* is similar, in concept, to that of [6].

Information derived at compile-time for each subgoal in a parallel clause is held in the corresponding *static table*. The *static table* encodes both the *DDG* and information describing the static prediction for when variables become *ground*. The *static table* is part of the bytecode program and is not altered during execution. The selection algorithm uses both compile-time information from the *static table* and run-time information in the *parallel frame* to determine whether a subgoal can be executed independently, possibly sharing ground variables.

Redo's are coordinated from parent to child by passing messages; these are similar to those used in Conery's *AND/OR* process model [14].

2.1 New Control Registers

A number of new registers have been added to the *WAM*; these control the *parallel frames* and the *dump*.

PF   Pointer to the topmost parallel frame
sPF   Pointer to the spawn parallel frame
tPF   Pointer to the topmost spawn parallel frame
D   Pointer to the top of the dump

The *PF* register points to the parent *parallel frame* which is always the topmost active *parallel frame*. The *sPF* register points to the topmost *parallel frame* searched when allocating tasks to waiting processors. The *tPF* register points to the topmost *parallel frame* from which a task was allocated. A simple comparison between the *PF* register and the *tPF* register determines the execution mode. *Serial mode* when the *PF* register is greater than the *tPF* register. The *dump* is operated as a stack; the top of which is determined by the *D* register.

There are also a number of control flags which make forward execution more efficient, and support the 'tail recursion optimisation' in parallel clauses. In *serial mode*, *parallel frames* can be efficiently operated without the need to re-traverse previous *subgoal tables* to find the next available task in the *parallel frame*; this significantly reduces the overhead of executing *parallel code* sequentially.

2.2 The Parallel Frame

The *parallel frame* is a data structure used to allow independent execution of 'firable' subgoals. Within each *parallel frame* there are several active fields: The *subgoal index* field denotes the subgoal on the active branch. This represents the last subgoal executed by the parent when another parallel clause is encountered. There are three bitmap cells used to control the execution in a parallel clause:

The *free variables cell* contains the variables in the parallel clause which are available to any *dependent* subgoal. Note that all ground variables are free variables.

The *grounds cell* contains the variables in the parallel clause which are currently ground.

The *ungrounds cell* contains the variables in the parallel clause which are currently unground.

During *distribution mode* execution the *free variables* cell is masked with information in subgoal's *static table* entry, to determine whether or not the subgoal can be executed independently. In *serial mode* the *free variables cell* remains unused and simply the next subgoal in the clause can be selected providing it has not persisted from an intelligent backtrack. A slight overhead is thus encurred in executing a parallel clause in both *serial mode* and *distribution mode*.

2.3 Subgoal Execution

For each subgoal in the *parallel frame* the subgoal's *subgoal table* holds information concerning its current run-time status. There are several fields associated with each subgoal in a parallel clause:

The *subgoal status* holds the status of the subgoal corresponding to those mentioned in *figure* 1.

The *generator variables* are those which are passed to the subgoal and are not in the *grounds cell*. These are a safe approximation to the variables the subgoal may generate bindings for.

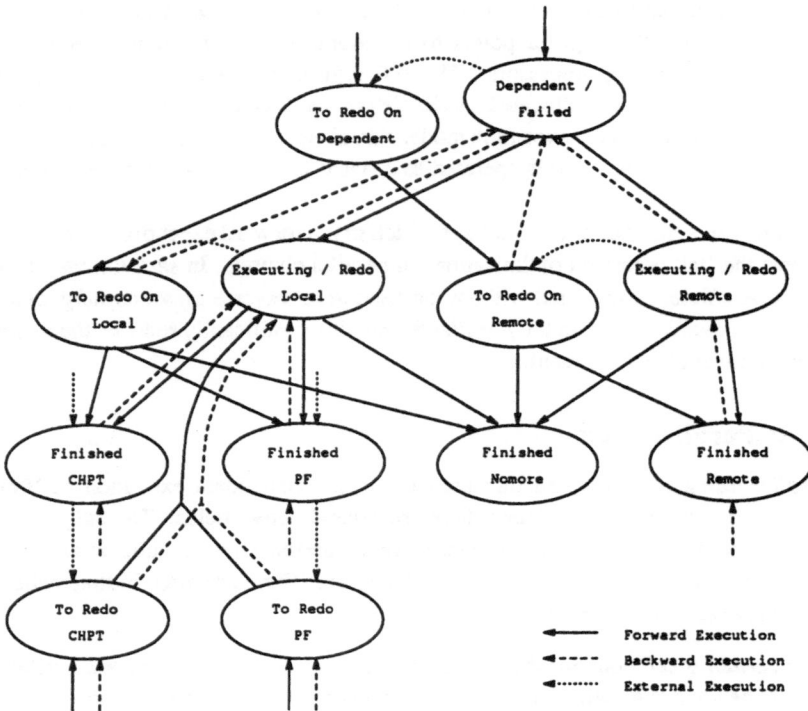

Figure 1: Subgoal Execution States

The *cause variables* are those which are passed to the subgoal and are not in the *ungrounds cell*. These are a safe prediction to the variables which could possibly cause the failure should the subgoal fail.

Other fields in the *subgoal table* hold further information so that completed subgoals can be redone.

A subgoal traverses the states in *figure* 1 starting from the *dependent* state. The subgoal may then be executed locally or remotely. From either of these states the subgoal may have its state changed when another subgoal in the clause backtracks and is forced to wait for the outcome of the subgoal.

When a subgoal completes (either succeeds or fails) what backtracking occurs is dependent on the subgoal's current state. If marked *to_redo_on* the dependent failure is processed along with any failure that may have occurred when the subgoal completed. The backtracking mechanism is described in detail in the next section.

The *finished* states are tagged with further information required to redo the subgoal. A subgoal may complete either with *more* or with *nomore* according to whether or not the subgoal contains further unexplored branches, (*choice points* or *parallel frames*). The *nomore* tag is used to improve the efficiency of redoing. A remote redo is not started unless there are further unexplored branches for the subgoal. A subgoal completed with *nomore* may discard the task when it completes.

The *to_redo* states are used to indicate that a task executed locally must be redone. The local processor is currently executing its own independent task and will encounter the *to_redo* subgoal when it re-enters the *parallel frame* in *distribution mode*.

3 Clause Level Intelligent Backtracking

The backward execution algorithm is invoked when the forward execution algorithm has resulted in the failure of a subgoal. In Prolog the next alternative is selected according to the depth–first left–right procedural interpretation. In many Prolog programs this execution strategy will redo subgoals which are out of context with that of the failed subgoal and variables not attributable to the cause of failure are re-instantiated. In our backward execution algorithm we aim to improve the selection of redo subgoal(s) in a parallel clause by taking into account the cause of failure. Where possible forward execution is allowed to continue in parallel with backward execution. Subgoals are terminated only if they are dependent on a variable which has both been attributed to the cause of failure and is being re-instantiated by the redo subgoal(s). Failure on an individual processor in the system can occur from three sources: locally on the parent processor, remotely from any of the child processors or when another failure is dependent on the completion of the subgoal.

In our scheme, processing of a failure is delayed until all subgoals to the left of the failed subgoal with variables in common have completed. Consider the clause:

$$p(X,Y) :- a(X,Y), b(X).$$

Subgoal $p(X,Y)$ is called with variable X ground so that $a(X,Y)$ and $b(X)$ are executed independently in parallel. If $b(X)$ fails before $a(X,Y)$ has completed then the processing of $b(X)$'s failure is delayed until $a(X,Y)$ completes. If $a(X,Y)$ were to fail then the the the cause of the failure would be both variables X and Y rather than just X. A more accurate selection of redo subgoals could then be made.

Thus, the backtrack subgoal is selected from all available information; the selection corresponds exactly to the selection that Prolog execution would reach after executing all the non-attributable subgoals. This is more accurate than other schemes.

The maintenance of a failure history is an essential part of any backward execution algorithm and it necessity is illustrated by the following clause:

$$p(X,Y) :- a(X,Y), b(X), c(Y), d(X,Y).$$

Execution has progressed successfully up to subgoal $d(X,Y)$. Subgoals $a(X,Y)$, $b(X)$ and $c(Y)$ are generators of all their parameter variables. The failure of $d(X,Y)$ has attributed cause variables X and Y.

The failure of $d(X,Y)$ leads to the redo of $c(Y)$ as this is the last designated generator of any of the cause variables. $c(Y)$ is then redone, it's execution fails, invoking the backward execution algorithm once more. With no failure history the cause of failure is attributed only to the Y variable and $a(X,Y)$ is selected to redo. This is incorrect. The original failure stemmed from $d(X,Y)$ attributing variables X and Y; clearly the next correct selection would redo $b(X)$ rather than $a(X,Y)$.

A failure history must be maintained so that when $c(Y)$ fails the next redo subgoal is selected from the cause of $d(X,Y)$, the original failure resulting in the selection of $c(Y)$. In our scheme the redo of $c(Y)$ is tagged with the original failure, $d(X,Y)$.

Our backward execution algorithm operates in two execution modes corresponding to forward execution. In *serial mode* a more efficient algorithm is implemented; the same level of 'intelligence' in backtracking is met by this algorithm but the possible scenarios resulting from failure are greatly reduced.

The backward execution scheme consists of three phases of operation: first, determine which subgoals must be satisfied by the processing of this failure, then determine the set of subgoals that must be redone and finally, terminate any other subgoals dependent on any of the variables re-instantiated by any subgoals in the redo set.

3.1 Backward Execution in a Parallel Frame

Backward execution is simplified in *serial mode* as a *serial mode* parallel clause has only one executing subgoal. There are no subgoals to terminate once the redo subgoal has been selected as no independent parallel execution occurs in the parallel clause. A failure can only lead to a single redo subgoal being selected.

3.1.1 Supporting Failure History

If a failure is an original failure, determined by the subgoal executing in *executing* status rather than *redo* status, the set of subgoals to be satisfied is simply the failed subgoal. If the subgoal is executing in *redo* status then the set of subgoals to be satisfied are those which have previously selected the now failed subgoal, for redo.

In our algorithm the failure history is maintained by using an index for each subgoal in the clause, numbered in a similar manner to the variable numbering scheme.

A field in the *subgoal table* for the redo subgoal is marked with the subgoal index(es) for all failed subgoals satisfied by the selection of this redo subgoal. The *subgoal table cause variables* for each satisfied subgoal is added to the *cause variables* for the redo subgoal. In this way solutions generated indirectly through the previous redo subgoal will also be taken into account.

3.1.2 Failure in a Parallel Clause Distribution Mode

The failed subgoal set is determined according to the execution state of the current subgoal, as described in the previous section. The backtrack algorithm starts by searching backward through the parallel clause from the most recently failed subgoal; when the search encounters a subgoal in the following states the corresponding actions are taken:

dependent status means that the searched subgoal has not yet started executing. If there are variables in common with cause variables for any failed subgoals then the failed subgoal's index is added to a field in the current subgoal's *subgoal table*; the current subgoal is then marked *to_redo_dependent*. The potential generators for the subgoal are determined from the *static table*.

executing or *to_redo_on* status means that a subgoal to the left has yet to complete. If this subgoal has variables in common with any of the failed subgoals and upon it's failure further cause variables are added to the current cause variables, then the current failure is dependent on the outcome of this execution. The subgoal's subgoal index is placed in the subgoal's *subgoal's table*. The state of the searched subgoal is changed to *to_redo_on*.

finished_PF, *finished_CHPT* or *finished_remote* status means there are further branches to be explored by redoing this subgoal. The subgoal is marked *to_redo* and the failure history is maintained.

finished_nomore status means that there are no further branches to be explored by redoing this subgoal; the *cause variables* for the searched subgoal are added to the *cause variables* of the failed subgoal(s).

Failed status means that the subgoal has failed and is waiting for another to complete before the failure can be processed any further. The status prevents re-execution of the subgoal until its failure is handled.

Subgoals dependent on any variables generated by the any of the subgoals in the redo set are altered according to their state as follows:

executing_remote, *redo_remote*, *to_redo_on* or *finished_remote* status means that a subgoal executed independently must be cancelled by sending a message.

finished_PF or *to_redo_PF* status means that a subgoal which completed locally and which may contain remote execution must be reset.

finished_CHPT or *to_redo_CHPT* status means that the list of *choice points* corresponding to this branch of execution is reset.

finished_nomore status means that the *trail* corresponding to the execution is reset.

In all above cases the subgoal is then marked *dependent*.

3.1.3 Failure in a Parallel Clause Serial Mode

The possibilities in backward execution in *serial mode* execution are greatly reduced; the execution has only to consider a subset of the states for *distribution mode*. In *serial mode* there can only be one failure history as parallel execution only occurs in clauses executing in *distribution mode*. The simplified *serial mode* backward execution algorithm performs an equivalent backward search but at reduced complexity. The complexity of the *distribution mode* algorithm is $O(n^2)$ whereas the complexity of the *serial mode* algorithm is $O(n)$. Where n is the number of tests to determine whether a subgoal generates any cause variables for a single failed subgoal.

3.2 Intelligent Cutting

During backward execution, a subgoal where the worst-case approximation to the variables the subgoal generates is none, is never selected for redoing. The only possibility is that the corresponding search space will be reset if the subgoal is dependent upon the variables generated by any subgoals in the redo set. If it were possible to determine during forward execution whether the subgoal execution contributed to any variable bindings, as a worst-case approximation, the search space could be 'cut' 'intelligently'.

In our execution scheme this is possible, at run-time we maintain a worst-case approximation for generated variables for each subgoal in a parallel clause. This is used during backward execution to select the last generator subgoal for the cause variables for any subgoal in the failed set. When the execution for the current subgoal is completes, a simple test is made comparing the *subgoal table generates* field with *null*; if the subgoal execution generates no variable bindings then the search space can be discarded. *Choice points* and *parallel frames* retained by the execution of the subgoal are 'cut' from the *local* stack. The subgoal is then marked *finished nomore*.

This saving in search space is of particular relevance to the 'generate and test' programming paradigm, where in our scheme all 'test' subgoals have their search space removed once they have completed successfully.

4 An Example Execution

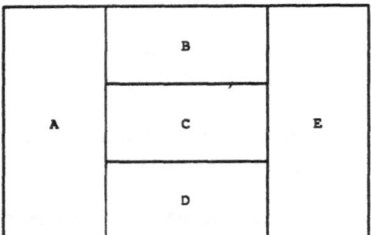

Figure 2: A Map Colouring of Five Regions

To illustrate both the forward and backward execution algorithms within a single parallel frame we consider a simple map colouring problem of five regions (see *figure* 2). In Prolog the map colouring problem is represented by the following code:

```
colour(A,B,C,D,E) :-   next(A,B), next(A,C), next(A,D),
                       next(B,C), next(C,D), next(B,E),
                       next(C,E), next(D,E).
next(red,blue).
next(red,green).
next(blue,red).
next(blue,green).
next(green,red).
next(green,blue).

?- colour(A,B,C,D,E).
```

The parallel execution steps for the neutral query are given in *figure* 3. The execution starts by executing subgoal *next(A,B)* alone on the parent processor, subgoals *next(C,D)*, *next(C,E)* or *next(D,E)* are not 'firable' as they are not the first generators of all their variables. The completion of *next(A,B)* free's variables A and B.

In *step 2* subgoals *next(A,C)*, *next(A,D)* and *next(B,E)* are 'firable'. *next(A,C)* is selected for execution on the parent and assuming sufficient other processors are waiting for tasks,

Step	Execution	Comments	Variable Bindings				
			A	B	C	D	E
1.	next(A,B)		red	blue			
2.	next(A,C)		red		blue		
	next(A,D)		red			blue	
	next(B,E)			blue			red
3.	next(B,C)	Fails		blue	blue		
	next(C,D)	Fails			blue	blue	
	next(C,E)				blue		red
	next(D,E)					blue	red
4.	next(A,C)		red		green		
5.	next(B,C)			blue	green		
	next(C,D)				green	blue	
	next(C,E)				green		red

Figure 3: Parallel Execution of *colour*

subgoals *next(A,D)* and *next(B,E)* are executed remotely. Then, the remaining subgoals *next(B,C)*, *next(C,D)*, *next(C,E)* and *next(D,E)* are executed in parallel. Subgoals *next(B,C)* and *next(C,D)* fail, invoking the backward execution algorithm.

There are two possible scenarios when the parallel clause is executed in *distribution mode*: the *next(B,C)* subgoal fails first or the *next(C,D)* subgoal fails first. In either case the correct redo subgoal (*next(A,C)*) must be selected. It is not possible to predict which subgoal will fail first and so both possibilities are considered here.

4.1 First Failure from the next(B,C) Subgoal

The *next(B,C)* subgoal fails attributing the cause to variables *B* and *C*. The backward execution algorithm selects the last generator for either of these variables, the *next(A,C)* subgoal. This subgoal is redone resulting in the re-instantiation of variable *C*. Subgoals *next(C,D)* and *next(C,E)* are terminated as there binding for variable *C* is no-longer valid.

Forward execution may now continue with the redoing of *next(A,C)* followed by the re-execution of *next(B,C)*, *next(C,D)* and *next(C,E)*. All of which succeed and the query is solved.

4.2 First Failure from the next(C,D) Subgoal

Failure of the *next(C,D)* subgoal interrupts the parent execution so that this failure may be processed. Variables *C* and *D* are attributable to the failure which in other backtracking schemes [10] would result in the immediate redo of *next(A,D)* as variable *C* is not generated by *next(B,C)*. In our scheme a slightly different approach is taken. The attributed variables (*C* and *D*) are in common with those passed to *next(B,C)*. The *subgoal table redo* field for the *next(B,C)* subgoal is marked with the subgoal index of subgoal *next(C,D)*. The *subgoal table status* field for the *next(B,C)* subgoal is changed to *To_Redo_On*. The failure of *next(C,D)* has now been handled and the parent can return to the execution of *next(B,C)*.

The *next(B,C)* subgoal may complete with success or failure; in this case it completes with failure but let us consider both.

4.2.1 next(B,C) Fails

When the subgoal *next(B,C)* fails, a redo subgoal must be found to satisfy both the failure of *next(B,C)* and *next(C,D)*. The failure of *next(C,D)* can possibly be corrected by the redoing of the *next(A,D)* subgoal, and this is noted in the *subgoal table redo* field for the *next(C,D)* subgoal. The *next(B,C)* subgoal is not satisfied by this redo and so the search continues. The next subgoal (*next(A,C)*) will generate a new binding for variable *C*. This redo will satisfy both subgoals *next(B,C)* and *next(C,D)* and this is noted in the *subgoal table* for both subgoals *next(B,C)* and *next(C,D)*. This overwrites the previously selected redo subgoal for *next(C,D)*. As before the *next(C,E)* subgoal is terminated and forward execution is restarted.

4.2.2 next(B,C) Succeeds

Straying slightly from this example, if the subgoal *next(B,C)* were to succeed then only the *next(C,D)* subgoal need be satisfied. The *next(A,D)* subgoal would be selected to be redone. This is the correct course of action for this failure.

5 Evaluation of Our Implementation

Our implementation places a Prolog bytecode emulator written in occam and capable of 8 KLIPS on each processor. Results were obtained on an array of transputer processing elements using the *ECCL* communications harness [15].

We consider several aspects of our implementation: the efficiency of execution in *serial mode*, *distribution mode* and any benefit from intelligent backtracking on a single processor. We also present results for the parallel execution of algorithms which also exhibit intelligent backtracking.

5.1 Serial Mode vs Distribution Mode Execution

To compare *serial mode* and *distribution mode* execution we consider programs which exhibit varying degrees of potential parallelism in their execution. The *nfib* program calculates the fibonacci number plus one at each recursive iteration, for *nfib(20)*. The program exhibits a large amount of parallelism preceded in each clause by simple arithmetic operations. The *quicksort* program exhibits similar divide and conquer parallelism but at each recursive iteration, the incoming argument list must first be split into two parts; a list of 200 random elements is sorted. The *reverse* benchmark reverses a list of 30 elements.

There is an overhead associated with executing parallel encoded clauses sequentially and this shows up in the performance results where benchmark programs with very 'fine grained' parallelism (*nfib*) execute less efficiently than those with courser grained and-parallelism (*quicksort*) (see *table* 1). The results are very encouraging and show that even the finest granularity benchmark programs execute at above 80% *WAM* speed in *serial mode* and above 70% in *distribution mode*.

Benchmark Program	Sequential Code	Parallel Code Serial Mode		Parallel Code Distribution Mode		Intelligent Backtracking
			actual		actual	attrib.
	(msec)	(msec)	speedup	(msec)	speedup	speedup
nfib	8761	10944	0.80	12160	0.72	
quicksort	7821	8576	0.91	9088	0.86	
reverse	63	63	1.00	63	1.00	
colour_A	4.48	4.41	1.01	4.93	0.91	1.25
colour_B	5.95	4.80	1.24	5.38	1.11	1.53
colour_C	9.47	9.28	1.02	10.94	0.87	1.26
colour_D	18.88	12.80	1.47	14.87	1.27	1.81

Table 1: The Efficiency of Single Processor Execution

The use of two modes of execution has contributed approximately a 10% improvement over execution which derives all the data-dependency information. This is significant as it is vital to maintain a high efficiency for the sequential execution of parallel clauses.

To show the effectiveness of our intelligent backtracking scheme we consider four variations of the map colouring algorithm presented earlier. We choose to colour the map in *figure* 2 but alter the subgoal ordering within the *colour* clause. A more naive arrangement (*colour_D*) requires more backtracking to reach solution than a near optimal arrangement (*colour_A*). The code for the four *colour* programs is given in the appendix.

A map colouring problem was chosen as each individual subgoal execution is as 'fine grained' as is possible in Prolog execution. Any benefit in the execution is attributable only to the intelligent backtracking. Our scheme benefits from both the 'intelligent' selection of redo subgoals, and by only terminating subgoals dependent on reinstantiated variables.

In *table* 1 shows performance results for the execution on a single processor. Programs with a large amount of potential parallelism (*nfib*) execute less efficiently than programs with no potential parallelism (*reverse*).

In the map colouring results, the last column calculates the speedup attributable to the intelligent backtracking, taking into account the loss of efficiency for parallel execution in the clause. Significant speedup is attained for nearly all of the benchmarks. *colour_C* is unusual in that the intelligent backtracking also results in a rather naive execution. It is anticipated that for more 'general' programs the intelligent backtracking will effectively pay for the parallel execution.

5.2 Parallel Intelligent Backtracking

To measure the effectiveness of the combination of and–parallel execution and intelligent backtracking we consider the most complex map colouring problem *colour_D*. We consider the parallel execution with varying weight to the *next* subgoal. Weight is measured in recursive iterations; a weight of 5 corresponds to the *next* subgoal calling a procedure which performs 5 recursive iterations. This will provide us with some indication as to how the and–parallelism and intelligent backtracking behave in combination and also provide an indication of the complexity a task must have to justify its remote execution.

Benchmark Program	Sequential Code (msec)	Parallel Code Execution			
		Number of Processors	(msec)	Speedup	Utilisation
colour_D weight(0)	18.88	1	12.80	1.47	100%
		2	57.01	0.33	56%
		3	51.26	0.37	40%
colour_D weight(5)	82.69	1	51.78	1.14	100%
		2	73.73	1.12	61%
		3	63.23	1.31	48%
colour_D weight(10)	143.42	1	88.90	1.61	100%
		2	100.74	1.42	66%
		3	86.72	1.65	51%

Table 2: Parallel Intelligent Backtracking

Table 2 gives results for the parallel execution of the *colour_D* benchmark. With no additional weighting to the *next* subgoal the performance degrades when executed on a parallel machine. So 'light' are the remote tasks, that when 3 processors are used the first to receive a task completes it before the parent processor has finished allocating a task to the second. Execution continues in this way until no further tasks are available, only then is the parent able to execute its own task.

As the weight of the tasks is increased so the performance on the parallel machine is improved. Execution on 2 processors never betters execution on 1 processor; this is probably due to the more efficient execution on 1 processor (in *serial mode*).

From these results it is not possible to make an accurate measurement of the weight required to justify remote execution of a task, but the weight is believed to be around 5 recursive iterations.

6   Conclusions

We have demonstrated that independent and–parallel execution can be augmented with intelligent backtracking to provide an effective parallel execution scheme on a distributed memory machine. Our scheme aims to be both scalable and efficient so that Prolog programs can be executed dynamically on arbitrary numbers of processors.

Our intelligent backtracking algorithm can give surprisingly good results on a single processor, and should be capable of paying for the dynamic construction of *DDG*'s in parallel clauses for more 'general' programs.

The parallel benchmarks show that providing an excess amount of parallelism exists in the program good utilisation can be made of the processors. By dynamically switching between *serial mode* and *distribution mode* the scheme also maintains 'near *WAM* performance' on each processor.

When the benchmark program constrains the amount of parallelism in the execution, it is encouraging to see that performance is maintained for increasing numbers of processors in the system.

In the future we intend to execute more 'general' Prolog programs and considering issues such as I/O and scheduling in greater detail.

Appendix

colour_A

```
colour(A,B,C,D,E) :-  next(A,B), next(A,C), next(A,D),
                      next(B,C), next(C,D), next(B,E),
                      next(C,E), next(D,E).
```

colour_B

```
colour(A,B,C,D,E) :-  next(A,B), next(B,E), next(A,C),
                      next(C,E), next(A,D), next(D,E),
                      next(B,C), next(C,D).
```

colour_C

```
colour(A,B,C,D,E) :-  next(A,B), next(D,E), next(B,C),
                      next(C,D), next(A,C), next(C,E),
                      next(A,D), next(B,E).
```

colour_D

```
colour(A,B,C,D,E) :-  next(C,D), next(A,B), next(D,E),
                      next(A,D), next(B,C), next(C,E),
                      next(B,E), next(A,C).
```

References

[1] D. H. D. Warren, "An abstract prolog instruction set," Tech. Rep. 309, Artificial Intelligence Center, SRI International, (1983).

[2] A. Verden, A. King, and W. Hall, "An implementation of prolog for the inmos t800 transputer," in *Proceedings of the 1st North American Transputer User Group*, (Salt Lake City, Utah, USA), (1989).

[3] A. R. Verden and H. Glaser, "Independent and-parallel prolog for distributed memory architectures," Tech. Rep. 90-17, Dept. of Electronics and Computer Science, University of Southampton, Southampton, England, (1990).

[4] A. R. Verden and H. Glaser, *An And-Parallel Prolog Executor, In Distributed Prolog, ed P. Kacsuk and M. J. Wise.* John Wiley & Sons, April (1991).

[5] A. R. Verden, *And–Parallel Implementation of Prolog On Distributed Memory Machines.* PhD thesis, University of Southampton, April (1991).

[6] M. Hermenegildo and R. Nasr, "Efficient management of backtracking in and-parallelism," in *Proceedings of the Third International Conference on Logic Programming*, (London), (1986).

[7] M. Hermenegildo, "An abstract machine for restricted and-parallel execution of logic," in *Proceedings of the Third on International Conference on Logic Programming*, (London), (1986).

[8] M. Hermenegildo and F. Rossi, "Non-strict independent and-parallelism," in *Proceedings of the 1990 International Conference on Logic Programming*, (1990).

[9] M. Hermenegildo and K. Green, "&-prolog and its performance: Exploiting independent and-parallelism," in *Proceedings of the 1990 International Conference on Logic Programming*, (1990).

[10] Y. J. Lin, *A Parallel Implementation of Logic Programs*. PhD thesis, University of Texas at Austin, (1988).

[11] D. DeGroot, "Restricted and-parallelism and side effects," in *Proceedings of the 1987 Symposium on Logic Programming*, vol. I, pp. 80–89, (1987).

[12] Z. Hwang and S. Hu, "A compiling approach for exploiting and-parallelism in parallel logic programming systems," in *Proceedings of PARLE*, vol. II, pp. 335–345, (1989).

[13] H. Xia, *Analyzing Data Dependencies, Detecting AND-Parallelism and Optimizing Backtracking in Prolog Programs*. PhD thesis, University of Berlin, (1989).

[14] J. Conery, *The AND-OR Process Model for Parallel Interpretation of Logic Programs*. PhD thesis, U. C. Urvine, (1983).

[15] M. Surridge, "The eulerian channel configuration language and message-passing system," tech. rep., S.E.R.C./D.T.I. Transputer Initiative, (1989). Report for E.M.R. Contract N2A-8R-1756 (Phase II).

Modules and Types

Parameterized Interfaces are Interfaces – AIAS

Sophia Drossopoulou   Ross Paterson*   Susan Eisenbach

Department of Computing
Imperial College
London SW7, UK

Abstract

We introduce AIAS, a proposal for expressing higher order parameterization and abstraction for modules. A module consists of an interface and an implementation. Both interfaces and implementations can be parameterized, and they are first class citizens, *i.e.* any order of parameterization is possible. The interface of the application of a parameterized implementation may depend on the interface of its arguments, *i.e.* we have a weaker form of dependent product types.

AIAS is conceptually very simple because, in contrast to other systems, it does not distinguish between an interface of a parameterized implementation and a parameterized interface. Consequently, fewer entities need to be declared using AIAS than would be necessary for the same problem using comparable systems. AIAS also permits a solution to the witness problem, allowing a mixture of the abstract and transparent witness models.

1   INTRODUCTION

Module systems aim to provide a framework for the expression of abstract data types, and to support decomposition and hierarchy in large programs. Modules offer means for information hiding (abstraction). More sophisticated systems offer means for module reuse (parameterization). The combination of these two issues, abstraction and parameterization, in module (type) systems has been tackled in various ways, *e.g.* generics [13], theories and views [3], polymorphism [8] and functors [7]. Most of these systems impose restrictions on the level of parameterization, but lately more interest has been shown in higher-order parameterization for types [1, 5, 12].

---

*This work was supported by Esprit Basic Research Action 3147: PHŒNIX.

AIAS[1] is a proposal for expressing parameterization and abstraction in a module system. The module system views programs as built out of several implementations combined according to their interfaces. Interfaces may be parameterized, and the application of such interfaces yields an interface. Implementations may be parameterized with implementation parameters. The interface of the application of such a parameterized implementation may depend on the interface of the arguments. Therefore, in AIAS, parameterized interfaces are a special kind of interface and they have implementations which satisfy them. A preorder among interfaces, the sub-interface relationship, allows one implementation to have several interfaces. Since our system imposes only loose conditions on this relation, it may give the programmer the flexibility to decide whether a particular type will be exported opaquely or transparently, allowing for a mixture of the abstract and transparent witness model. Our proposal makes only restricted use of dependent product types, yielding what we believe to be a simpler system.

The most important feature of AIAS is that, in contrast to other systems, it does not distinguish between an interface of a parameterized implementation and a parameterized interface. This is a novel approach, since in most other systems for module parameterization the distinction between parameterized type (or interface) and type of parameterized value (interface of parameterized implementation) is carefully maintained. This distinction stems from the equation of types to sets. However, this distinction is difficult to explain to a programmer, and it is counterintuitive, when comparing with value parameterization. Dropping the distinction leads to a conceptually simpler system, especially when we consider higher order parameterization. Also, fewer entities need to be declared using AIAS than would be necessary for the same problem with comparable systems. In AIAS interface parameterization is explicit. This provides a solution to the witness problem with a mixture of the abstract and transparent witness model. The system makes only use of a very weak form of dependent types (no value parameters to types) which is easy to understand.

AIAS is independent of the programming paradigm, and it can be incorporated into any basic language or system which provides strong typing and the basic concepts of interface and implementation and a preorder among interfaces. This is interesting, since most of the powerful module parameterization possibilities are explained in terms of some underlying language or calculus. In fact, AIAS is even independent of the programming paradigm: in this paper we use as a language to illustrate AIAS the functional language ML. A case study [10] in FALCON [4] (a functional-logic language based on Haskell [6]) makes use of the AIAS abstract data type parameterization facilities, leads to a clear and short program.

---

[1] AIAS was a Greek warrior of the Trojan war, he was valiant and simple. The name can surely can be made into as unconvincing an acronym as any other.

The rest of the paper is organized as follows. In section 2 we describe AIAS at the programming language level, that is we illustrate the concepts using a series of examples: ordering, set and graph abstract data types. The examples are expressed in an enhanced ML syntax. In section 3 we compare AIAS with other parameterization and abstraction systems, both from the practical and the conceptual point of view. We also discuss the views from [11] which advocate maintaining the distinction between parameterized specification and specifications of parameterized programs, in their words:

parameterized (program specification) $\neq$ (parameterized program) specification

We transform the arguments to the case of interfaces. We explain why, in our view, this distinction need not be made, at least when dealing with interfaces rather than specifications. In section 4 we then give the type inference system for AIAS. Finally, we give our conclusions and outline further areas of research.

2 AIAS: A MODULE PARAMETERIZATION SYSTEM

We describe AIAS using three examples: ordering, parameterized set and graph abstract data types. The example is expressed in an enhanced ML syntax. We chose ML because it is widely known, especially among the community interested in modules and types, and because it has a succinct syntax. Nevertheless, our proposal can be incorporated into any language with strong typing, including languages from other paradigms. Rather than the Standard ML concepts of signatures, structures and functors, we shall speak of interfaces and implementations, to emphasise the differences.

We follow the naming convention that interfaces start with an upper case letter (*e.g.* *Integers*), implementations start with a lower case letter (*e.g. integers*), parameterized interfaces carry the suffix "*-Of*", and parameterized implementations carry the prefix "*make-*".

2.1 Interfaces and Implementations: Order

In this section we describe a very basic system with interfaces, implementations, a satisfaction relation among implementations and interfaces and a preorder among interfaces. Such concepts can be found in several languages (like Fun [2], Quest [1], Standard ML [9] *etc*), but, as can be seen seen in this section, it is easy to extend a language with strong typing to incorporate these concepts.

Interfaces characterize a group of implementations, namely all implementations which provide definitions for the entities "required" by this interface. For example, the following interface describes a type with two comparison operations, intended to be a total ordering and equality:

```
interface Order =
  Begin
    type t
    val lt : t × t → bool
    val eq : t × t → bool
  End
```

Here the type t is exported in an opaque manner, which means that only the identifier of the type is exported, and no details about the representation of the values of this type are given. It is also possible to export types transparently, as in the following interfaces:

```
interface Integers =
  Begin
    datatype t = 0 | succ of t
    val lt : t × t → bool
    val eq : t × t → bool
  End
interface Characters =
  Begin
    datatype t = 'a' | 'b' | ...
    val lt : t × t → bool
    val eq : t × t → bool
  End
```

There exists a partial ordering between interfaces, namely the sub-interface relation. An interface $Interf_1$ is said to be a sub-interface of another interface $Interf_2$, written $Interf_1 \leq Interf_2$, if it provides more information (and therefore has fewer implementations, as we shall see later).

In our example, $Integers$ is a sub-interface of $Order$, that is: $Integers \leq Order$. Similarly we also have $Characters \leq Order$. Further, if we define

```
interface Equality =
  Begin
    type t
    val eq : t × t → bool
  End
interface Trivial =
  Begin
```

    type *t*
  End

then we also have *Order* ≤ *Equality* ≤ *Trivial*.

Every implementation is introduced together with its initial interface, that is the most specific interface it satisfies. In that sense, every implementation has "in-built" its initial interface, and it inherits information (the type and value declarations) from it. An implementation satisfies an interface if it provides a complete type declaration for every opaque type from the interface, and a value for every entity introduced in the interface. The implementation *integers* has the initial interface *Integers*:

  implementation *integers* : *Integers* =
    begin
      fun *lt*(*n*, 0) = *false*
    | *lt*(0, *succ*(*n*)) = *true*
    | *lt*(*succ*(*n*), *succ*(*m*)) = *lt*(*n*, *m*)
      fun *eq*(0, 0) = *true*
      ⋮
    end

whereas the implementation *characters* satisfies the interface *Characters*:

  implementation *characters* : *Characters* =
    begin
      fun *lt*('a', 'a') = *false*
    | *lt*('a', 'b') = *true*
      ⋮
      fun *eq*('a', 'a') = *true*
      ⋮
    end

If *Interf₁* ≤ *Interf₂*, then any implementation *impl* which satisfies *Interf₁* (*impl* : *Interf₁*), satisfies *Interf₂* as well (*impl* : *Interf₂*). Thus, for example, since *integers* : *Integers*, we also have *integers* : *Order*, *integers* : *Equality* and *integers* : *Trivial*.

2.2 Parameterized Interfaces and Implementations: Sets

Parameterized interfaces can be applied to interfaces to build new interfaces. They have one or more interface parameters, each characterized by an interface of which the actual interface argument must be a sub-interface. For example, the following interface operator maps interfaces describing ordered types[2] to interfaces describing sets whose elements are of the original types, with operations to create an empty set, add an element to a set, and test whether a value belongs to a set:

>**interface** *Set-Of* =
>>**Lambda** *Element* $\leq$ *Order*
>>>**Begin**
>>>>**type** *set*
>>>>**val** *empty* : *set*
>>>>**val** *add* : *Element.t* $\times$ *set* $\rightarrow$ *set*
>>>>**val** *member* : *Element.t* $\times$ *set* $\rightarrow$ *bool*
>>>**End**

Parameterized interfaces may be applied to interfaces. Every interface argument must be a sub-interface of the characteristic interface of the corresponding formal interface parameter. The application of an interface operator to interface arguments is equivalent to the body of the interface operator with all interface parameters replaced by the corresponding interface arguments. For example, by applying *Set-Of* to *Integers* we obtain a new interface:

>**interface** *IntSet* = *Set-Of*(*Integers*)

This is equivalent to the interface *AnotherIntSet* defined as:

>**interface** *AnotherIntSet* =
>>**Begin**
>>>**type** *set*
>>>**val** *empty* : *set*
>>>**val** *add* : *Integers.t* $\times$ *set* $\rightarrow$ *set*
>>>**val** *member* : *Integers.t* $\times$ *set* $\rightarrow$ *bool*
>>**End**

Also, it is easy to see that *IntSet* $\leq$ *Set-Of*(*Order*).

In contrast to other systems with higher order type/module parameterization, parameterized interfaces are themselves interfaces, and therefore there can be implementations satisfying these parameterized interfaces. These are the parameterized implementations. Every parameterized implementation has as many (implementation) parameters as the (interface) parameters of its interface, and each implementation parameter must satisfy the characteristic interface of the corresponding interface parameter.

---

[2]The careful reader might expect that *Set-Of* requires an argument which is a subinterface of *Trivial*. The example of *Set-Of* was deliberately made more restrictive than necessary with view to the next examples and for the sake of brevity.

The simplest implementation of the interface *Set-Of* is *make-List-Set*, which uses lists of elements. The implementation parameter *element*, satisfies the interface *Element* and it corresponds to the interface parameter *Element* of the parameterized interface *Set-Of*:

> **implementation** *make-List-Set* : *Set-Of* =
>   **lambda** *element* : *Order*
>   **begin**
>   **datatype** *set* = *empty* | *add* **of** (*element.t* × *set*)
>   **fun** *member*(*x*, *empty*) = *false*
> | *member*(*x*, *add*(*y*, *s*)) = *element.eq*(*x*, *y*) **or** *member*(*x*, *s*)
>   **end**

A more sophisticated implementation of *Set-Of* might represent sets as ordered binary trees:

> **implementation** *make-Tree-Set* : *Set-Of* =
>   **lambda** *element* : *Order*
>   **begin**
>   **datatype** *set* = *empty* | *node* **of** (*element.t* × *set* × *set*)
>   **fun** *add*(*x*, *empty*) = *node*(*x*, *empty*, *empty*)
> | *add*(*x*, *node*(*y*, *l*, *r*)) =
>   **if** *element.eq*(*x*, *y*) **then** *node*(*y*, *l*, *r*)
>   **else if** *element.lt*(*x*, *y*)
>   **then** *node*(*y*, *add*(*x*, *l*), *r*)
>   **else** *node*(*y*, *l*, *add*(*x*, *r*))
>   **fun** *member*(*x*, *empty*) = *false*
> | *member*(*x*, *node*(*y*, *l*, *r*)) =
>   *element.eq*(*x*, *y*) **or**
>   *member*(*x*, **if** *element.lt*(*x*, *y*) **then** *l* **else** *r*)
>   **end**

A parameterized implementation can be applied to an implementation satisfying the given argument interface (here *Order*), to yield another implementation. The interface of the resulting implementation depends on the interfaces of the actual implementation parameters. For example, we have

> *make-List-Set*(*integers*) : *Set-Of*(*Integers*)
>
> *make-Tree-Set*(*characters*) : *Set-Of*(*Characters*)

In analogy to parameterized interfaces, the application is equivalent to the body of the parameterized implementation with each occurrence of the formal parameter replaced by the actual implementation parameter.

Note that besides *make-List-Set(characters)* and *make-Tree-Set(characters)* there are several more ways to construct an implementation of *Set-Of(Characters)*. For example, one could write an implementation *array-Char-Set*, which implements sets of characters as arrays of Booleans indexed by characters.

2.3   Higher-order Parameterization: Graphs

Our next example is the abstract data type of graphs with directed edges and nodes labelled with elements of some base type:

> **interface** *Graph-Of* =
>   **Lambda** *Label* ≤ *Trivial*
>   **Begin**
>   **type** *graph*
>   **type** *node*
>   **val** *empty* : *graph*
>   **val** *add-node* : *graph* × *Label.t* → *graph* × *node*
>   **val** *add-edge* : *graph* × *node* × *node* → *graph*
>   ⋮
>   **val** *search* : *graph* × *node* × (*Label.t* → *bool*) → *bool*
>   **End**

The intended behaviour of *search*(*g*, *n*, *cond*) is to determine whether any node reachable from the node *n* in graph *g* has a label which satisfies the condition *cond*. Typical implementations of this operation will maintain a set of nodes already visited in the search for a matching node, to avoid being trapped by loops in the graph. Any implementation *make-set* satisfying the interface *Set-Of* could be used for this purpose. The difficulty is that the implementation to which *make-set* must be applied, in particular the representation of the type *node*, is not visible outside the implementation of the graph. Thus the parameterized implementation must be passed as a parameter. We arrive at the following interface for implementations of graphs:

> **interface** *Make-Graph-Of* =
>   **Lambda** *Label* ≤ *Trivial*, *Set* ≤ *Set-Of*
>   *Graph-Of*(*Label*)

One implementation satisfying this interface represents nodes as integers:

```
implementation make-Graph : Make-Graph-Of =
    lambda label : Trivial, make-set : Set-Of
      begin
        type node = integers.t
        type edge = node × node
        type graph = int × label.t list × edge list

        val empty = (0, [], [])
        fun add-node((size, labels, edges), l) =
            ((succ(size), l::labels, edges), size)
        fun add-edge((size, labels, edges), x, y) =
            (size, labels, (x, y)::edges)
        ⋮

        implementation node-set = make-set(integers)
        fun search((size, labels, edges), start, cond) =
            ... node-set.empty ... node-set.add ...
      end
```

Now we can define implementations of the parameterized interface *Graph-Of* by supplying implementations of its parameter *Set-Of*:

```
implementation make-Slow-Graph : Graph-Of =
        lambda label : Trivial
            make-Graph(label, make-List-Set)

implementation make-Fast-Graph : Graph-Of =
        lambda label : Trivial
            make-Graph(label, make-Tree-Set)
```

These implementations may also be applied to parameters, yielding concrete implementations of particular kinds of graph:

```
implementation C-Slow-Graph : Graph-Of(Characters) =
        make-Slow-Graph(characters)

implementation I-Fast-Graph : Graph-Of(Integers) =
        make-Fast-Graph(integers)
```

2.4 Remarks

All of the above is independent of what language is inside the **Begin ... End** and **begin ... end** brackets. All that is required of the language is the sub-interface and satisfaction relations. This allows a great deal of flexibility in the design of these relations. For example, they can deal with algebraic data types, or permit both transparent and opaque export of types, as in the examples above.

Higher-order parameterization can also subsume the function of the sharing constraints of Standard ML—parameters with shared components can be restructured to accept the shared component as a parameter.

3   COMPARISON WITH OTHER APPROACHES

Here we compare AIAS with other schemes for higher-order modules.

The universe according to AIAS is simple and symmetrical (see figure 1); there are two classes of entities: interfaces and implementations. Implementations satisfy interfaces. Both interfaces and implementations can be parameterized. Parameterized interfaces take interfaces as arguments and produce new interfaces. Parameterized interfaces are satisfied by parameterized implementations, which take implementations as parameters and produce new implementations. These concepts may be imposed on top of any language for programming, specification or logic satisfying certain loose conditions. This flexibility allows a novel solution to the witness problem, as the underlying language may define the sub-interface relation as a mixture of the abstract and transparent witness models.

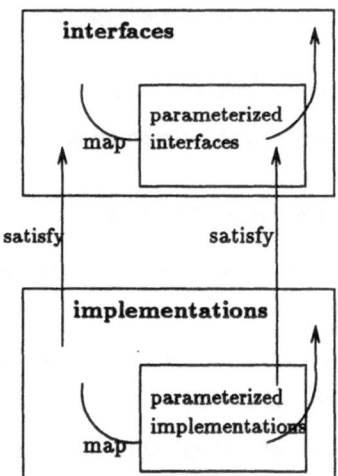

Figure 1: AIAS Classes of Entities

3.1 The Distinction between Parameterized Type and Type of Parameterized Values

Investigations of modules from the type-theoretic point of view have focussed on the analogy of interfaces and implementations with types and values, *i.e.* implementations satisfying an interface correspond to values belonging to a type. Also, most programmers' intuitive view of a type is that it represents a set of values. A parameterized type then stands for a mapping from sets to sets, whereas the type of parameterized values stands for a set of mappings. Therefore, it seems imperative to distinguish between parameterized types and the types of parameterized values. Especially, parameterized types are not types, and therefore they have no values.

This is the approach taken, for example, with polymorphic types, where the unary type constructor *list* is distinguished from the polymorphic type $\forall \alpha. \alpha \; list$. In the standard presentation (*e.g.* [8]), the former is not a type but a mapping from types to types, and thus has no values, while the latter does. This contrasts with the world of values, where a parameterized value is itself a value. However, although programmers are mostly not aware of this distinction, they are able to use the language correctly and elegantly. Therefore, we do not advocate dropping this distinction for programming in the small.

On the other hand, in our experience, this distinction, if applied to module parameterization, leads to a counterintuitive system. Indeed, interface operators always appear in the expression of interfaces of implementation operators. Even worse, this distinction leads to the necessity of allowing types as parameters to values, which "breaks" the original, simple classification into two classes of objects (values and types, or interfaces and implementations). We therefore unified interfaces and interface operators and thus arrived at a system which is conceptually much simpler.

3.2 Standard ML

In Standard ML module parameterization is confined to first order parameterization. Functors are mappings from structures (implementations) to structures (implementations), but, as functors have no signature (interface), they cannot be passed as parameters, nor can they be returned as results. Comparing with our example from section 2, Standard ML would not offer any way of expressing the parameterized interface *Set-Of* but one would be able to express the parameterized implementations *make-List-Set* and *make-Tree-Set*. It would be impossible to express parameterized implementations with parameterized implementation parameters like *make-Graph*.

3.3 Parameterized (Program Specification) =?= (Parameterized Program) Specification

In [11] Sanella, Sokolowski and Tarlecki recognize that there is a "natural connection between the semantic domain of parameterized specifications and the specifications of parametric algebras". Nevertheless, they argue for the maintenance of the distinction between them. This is expressed as: "parameterized (program specification) $\neq$ (parameterized program) specification".

Interfaces can be viewed as restricted forms of specifications (namely interfaces contain only signatures, and no axioms). Therefore, the arguments of [11] against the unification of parameterized specifications with specifications of parameterized programs can be "translated" to corresponding arguments against the unification of parameterized interfaces with interfaces of parameterized implementations:

- Parameterized program interfaces and interfaces of parameterized programs are not isomorphic. An interface corresponds to a set (namely the set of all implementations which satisfy this interface); an interface of parameterized implementations $INT1 \rightarrow INT2$ corresponds to the set of all mappings from an implementation in the set $INT1$ to an implementation in the set $INT2$; any monotonic mapping from sets representing interfaces to sets representing interfaces corresponds to a parameterized interface.

  These definitions we consider to be too broad. We clearly need to consider only the mappings that can be described in the language itself.[3] And considering only these mappings, as in AIAS by definition, the two classes are isomorphic[11].

- Considering parameterized program interfaces as interfaces of parameterized programs would unnecessarily restrict the possibilities to construct programs. An interface which is constructed by the application of a parameterized interface to another interface need not be implemented by the application of corresponding implementations. In other words, if we unified parameterized interfaces with interfaces of parameterized implementations, and if we now consider a parameterized interface P applied to another interface A, then the application $P(A)$ is a new interface which could only be satisfied by the application $p(a)$ where p is a program which satisfies P and a is a program which satisfies A.

---

[3]There exist mappings from implementations in a set to implementations in another set for which no corresponding parameterized implementation can be written in the programming language, *e.g.* the function $f : Equality \rightarrow Set\text{-}Of(Equality)$ with $x : X$ then $f(x):Set\text{-}Of(Equality)$ and for all $f(x)=make\text{-}Tree\text{-}Set(x)$ if $x=integers$ and $f(x)=make\text{-}List\text{-}Set(x)$ otherwise. Therefore, the mapping f is not a possible program in the language, and, we believe, it need not be considered as a possible parameterized implementation of any interface. Similar "impossible" parameterized interfaces can be constructed with corresponding arguments.

But this is not so in AIAS. We too share the belief that interfaces should only be prescriptions for the behaviour of their implementations, but they need not restrict the way to construct such implementations. This freedom is preserved in AIAS; *e.g.* in section 2.2 the application *make-Tree-Set(characters)* is an implementation of *Set-Of(Characters)*, but other implementations are also possible, *e.g.* the "tailor-made" implementation *array-Char-Set*, whose construction does not reflect the way its initial interface, *Set-Of(Characters)*, was constructed.

4 AN INFERENCE SYSTEM

In this section we give a more formal description of our system. For this purpose we shall use a more concise notation, though the connexion with the syntax of section 2 should be clear.

Interfaces are represented by A, B, C, *etc*, with interface variables written X, Y, Z, *etc.* Interface expressions are defined as follows:

Interface $\leftarrow$ *basic interface* $\mid X \mid \Lambda X \leq A.B \mid A(B)$

In an interface expression $\Lambda X \leq A.B$, the sub-expression is required to be closed. Occurrences of X in B are bound as usual.

The meta-notation $[B/X]A$ denotes the interface expression obtained by replacing each free occurrence of X in A by B, with the usual renaming of bound variables to avoid capture.

Implementations are represented by a, b, c, *etc*, with variables x, y, z, *etc.* Implementation expressions are defined as follows:

Implementation $\leftarrow$ *basic implementation* $\mid x \mid \lambda x : A.b \mid a(b)$

where the interface expression A is required to be closed.

The assertions of our system are of the form $\Gamma \vdash \gamma$, where γ has one of the following forms:

$A \leq B$ A is a sub-interface of B

$a : A$ a is an implementation of A

and Γ is a sequence of assertions of the forms $X \leq A$, for closed A, or $x : X$.

The relation $\leq$ is not reflexive on all interfaces; the assertion $A \leq A$ should be interpreted as meaning that A is a well-formed interface. We assume that for basic interfaces, whenever $A \leq B$, then also $A \leq A$ and $B \leq B$. It is easy to verify that the rules preserve this property.

The inference rules are listed in figure 2.

$$\frac{\Gamma \vdash A \leq B \quad \Gamma \vdash B \leq C}{\Gamma \vdash A \leq C}$$

$$\frac{\Gamma \vdash a : A \quad \Gamma \vdash A \leq B}{\Gamma \vdash a : B}$$

$$\frac{\Gamma \vdash A \leq A}{\Gamma, X \leq A \vdash X \leq X}$$

$$\Gamma, x : X \vdash x : X$$

$$\frac{\Gamma \vdash A \leq A}{\Gamma, X \leq A \vdash X \leq A}$$

$$\frac{\Gamma \vdash A' \leq A \quad \Gamma, X \leq A' \vdash B \leq B'}{\Gamma \vdash (\Lambda X \leq A.B) \leq (\Lambda X \leq A'.B')}$$

$$\frac{\Gamma \vdash A' \leq A \quad \Gamma, X \leq A', x : X \vdash b : B}{\Gamma \vdash (\lambda x : A.b) : (\Lambda X \leq A'.B)}$$

$$\frac{\Gamma \vdash A \leq A' \quad \Gamma \vdash B \leq B' \quad \Gamma \vdash B' \leq B'' \quad \Gamma \vdash A' \leq (\Lambda X \leq B''.C')}{\Gamma \vdash A(B) \leq A'(B')}$$

$$\frac{\Gamma \vdash a : A \quad \Gamma \vdash b : B \quad \Gamma \vdash B \leq B' \quad \Gamma \vdash A \leq (\Lambda X \leq B'.C)}{\Gamma \vdash a(b) : A(B)}$$

$$\frac{\Gamma \vdash A' \leq A \quad \Gamma \vdash (\Lambda X \leq A.B) \leq (\Lambda X \leq A.B)}{\Gamma \vdash (\Lambda X \leq A.B)(A') = [A'/X]B}$$

Figure 2: Inference system for parameterized interfaces and implementations

5 CONCLUSIONS

We have introduced AIAS, a module parameterization system which in our opinion combines expressive power with simplicity: The expression of higher order parameterization of interfaces and implementations is possible. It is conceptually very simple, because it requires only two classes of entities (interfaces and implementations) as opposed to four in other approaches. No dependencies between entities of different classes are possible (ie no type parameters to values, no value parameters to types).

Further work is planned in the areas of case studies, efficient checking algorithms, comparison of the power of AIAS with the other approaches, more abstract (*e.g.* categorical) descriptions of the system, and investigation of various possibilities for the sub-interface relation.

REFERENCES

[1] Luca Cardelli. Typeful programming. Technical Report 45, Digital, May 1989.

[2] Luca Cardelli and Peter Wegner. On understanding types, data abstraction and polymorphism. *ACM Computing Surveys*, 86, 1986.

[3] Joseph A. Goguen and Timothy Winkler. Introducing OBJ3. Technical Report SRI-CSL-88-9, SRI International, August 1988.

[4] Yike Guo and Helen Pull. FALCON: Functional and logic language with constraints – language definition. Technical Report IC/FPG/Phoenix/15/2, Department of Computing, Imperial College, February 1991.

[5] Robert Harper, John C. Mitchell, and Eugenio Moggi. Higher-order modules and the phase distinction. In *17th Annual ACM Symposium on Principles of Programming Languages*, pages 341–354, 1990.

[6] Paul Hudak, Philip Wadler, et al. Report on the programming language Haskell, a non-strict purely functional language (Version 1.0). Technical Report YALEU/DCS/RR777, Yale University, Department of Computer Science, April 1990.

[7] David MacQueen. Modules for Standard ML. In *ACM Symposium on Lisp and Functional Programming, Austin*, 1984.

[8] Robin Milner. A theory of type polymorphism in programming. *Journal of Computer and System Sciences*, 17(3):348–375, 1978.

[9] Robin Milner. Standard ML. Technical report, University of Edinburgh, 1987.

[10] Helen Pull, Sophia Drossopoulou, Yike Guo, and Ross Paterson. EXIS case study in FALCON. Technical Report IC/FPG/Phoenix/3/2, Department of Computing, Imperial College, February 1991.

[11] Don T. Sanella, Stefan Sokołowski, and Andrzej Tarlecki. Towards formal development of programs from algebraic specifications: Parameterisation revisited. Technical Report 6/90, FB Informatik, Universität Bremen, 1990.

[12] Donald Sanella and Andrzej Tarlecki. A kernel specification formalism with higher-order parameterisation. In *7th Workshop on Specification of Abstract Data Types*, Lecture Notes in Computer Science. Springer, 1991. to appear.

[13] US Department of Defense. *Reference Manual for the Ada Programming Language*, 1983. ANSI/MIL-STD-1815 A.

Type Classes are Signatures of Abstract Types

Konstantin Läufer[*]

New York University
251 Mercer Street
New York, NY 10012, USA
laufer@cs.nyu.edu

Martin Odersky

IBM T.J. Watson Research Center
P.O. Box 704
Yorktown Heights, NY 10598, USA
odersky@watson.ibm.com

Abstract

We present an extension of Haskell's type class concept in which a type class is identified with the signature of an abstract type. As shown by Mitchell and Plotkin, abstract types can be expressed using existential quantification. Unlike in Mitchell and Plotkin's work, an abstract type does not come with one — and only one — implementation. Rather, any concrete type can be declared to be an implementation by a clause that corresponds to an instance declaration in Haskell. We introduce F-bounded existential quantification, where an abstract type has the form:

$$\exists \alpha . C(\alpha) . \tau(\alpha).$$

Here, $C(\alpha)$ is a set of constraints that restricts the range of the bound variable α, and $\tau(\alpha)$ is a type constructed from α. The expression reads "some type $\tau(\alpha)$, where α is some arbitrary fixed type satisfying constraints $C(\alpha)$". The constraint set C corresponds to a type class. Just like a type class, it contains declarations for overloaded identifiers as well as conformity clauses that declare one abstract type to be more specific than another.

The generalization of type classes to abstract types has the advantage of greater expressiveness: We can model polymorphic abstract types and heterogeneous data structures, concepts which cannot be expressed in Haskell. An example of a polymorphic abstract type is $\forall \alpha . Bag \ \alpha$, the abstract type of all bags with elements of type α. In Haskell, we would either have to fix the element type, or we would have to fix the implementation of Bag.

Our extension shares the desirable properties of the type class approach in that it is fully static and in that type reconstruction is feasible.

---

[*]Supported by the Defense Advanced Research Projects Agency/Information Systems Technology Office under the Office of Naval Research contract N00014-90-J-1110

1   Introduction

Recently, many researchers have looked at the problem of systematic overloading resolution [8, 19, 1, 5]. All these approaches use predicates (called *type classes* in [19]) which assert that certain overloaded operations with given signatures are defined. Functions can be made dependent on these assertions using a form of bounded universal type quantification, in which the bound variable is restricted to range over the instances of a type class. In [19] it was noted that type classes and abstract data types [14, 3] are similar in that they both define a signature without its implementation. Because of this correspondence, Wadler and Blott called for a closer exploration of the relationship between type classes and abstract data types.

Here we describe the results of our exploration of this relationship. We show that type classes can indeed be generalized to a form of abstract data types, by identifying them with type signatures. Furthermore, the generalization is not simply a recast of the type class concept into another formalism; it allows us to model several new concepts. Among these are polymorphic abstract types and heterogeneous data structures.

Polymorphic abstract types are useful for modeling signatures which depend on other types. The abstract type $\forall \alpha. Bag\ \alpha$, for instance, cannot be represented as a type class, but it can be represented in our type system.

Heterogeneous data structures are useful in extensible software systems. An example is a window handler which provides central bookkeeping for windows of various types. In an extensible system, window types can be defined in clients as well as in the handler itself. Therefore, the type of any global data structure (say, one containing all active windows) cannot be a simple, finite sum type. What is needed is a heterogeneous structure whose elements are instances of an abstract type "Window".

Programming languages usually support heterogeneous data by adopting an object-oriented subtyping rule (it is no coincidence that the interest in object-oriented programming has spread in parallel with the use of windowing operating systems). Subtyping is not without problems, however. First, pervasive subtyping prevents the definition of polymorphic homogeneous data structures, which are useful in many circumstances. The function *maximum*, for instance, which finds the maximum of element a list, makes sense only on homogeneous lists whose elements are all of the same, ordered type. Another, more serious, problem stems from the subtype rule for method functions. Because the first argument to a method is implicit, and the others are subjected to the contravariance rule, method arguments are treated asymmetrically. This leads to counter-intuitive subtyping rules for methods with additional arguments of type "like current".

Several newer approaches try to overcome the problems caused by the contravariance rule in object-oriented programming. Descriptive classes [17] and F-bounded polymorphism [1] are in concept very similar to Haskell's type classes. Other methods, which generalize the subtyping concept, introduce "like current" parameters, which are checked type correct at runtime [4], or replace the subtyping rule by something rather more complex [16]. None of these latter approaches is both fully static and safe. A system that describes heterogeneous data types directly is [18]. Thatte uses partial types instead of existential quantification, which leads to less precise typings and requires runtime type checking in general. By contrast, our system follows the type class approach in that it is fully static; no type-related errors can occur at runtime. Another desirable property that our system shares with type classes is the existence of a type reconstruction algorithm.

The rest of this paper is organized as follows: Section 2 gives an informal overview of of abstract types. Section 3 discusses heterogeneous data structures, Section 4 sketches a runtime model, and Section 5 concludes. The formal typing rules are given in the Appendix.

2 Abstract Types

Following [14, 3], we identify abstract types with existential types. We use a bounded form of existential quantification. An abstract type is of the form

$$\exists \alpha. C(\alpha). \tau(\alpha).$$

Here, $C(\alpha)$ is a set of constraints which restricts the range of the bound variable α. $\tau(\alpha)$ is a type constructed from α. In the simplest case, $\tau = \alpha$. As an example, in our framework the abstract type of values admitting an order relation is

$$\exists \alpha . [(<), (\leq) : \alpha \to \alpha \to Bool] . \alpha,$$

which reads "some (concrete) type α, on which $(<)$ and $(\leq)$ are defined".

On the other hand, the unbound abstract type

$$\exists \alpha . . (\alpha \to \alpha \to Bool) \times \alpha$$

describes all pairs whose components are a function of type $\alpha \to \alpha \to Bool$ and a value of some (unconstrained) type α. Thus each value of this abstract type might have a different first (and second) component.

An example of an existential type with a more complex type component is:

$$\exists \alpha . [(<), (\leq) : \alpha \to \alpha \to Bool] . List\ (\alpha \times \alpha),$$

the type of all lists whose elements are homogeneous pairs whose components have both the same ordered type.

By contrast,

$$List\ ((\exists \alpha . [(<), (\leq) : \alpha \to \alpha \to Bool] . \alpha) \times$$
$$(\exists \alpha . [(<), (\leq) : \alpha \to \alpha \to Bool] . \alpha))$$

gives us a list of heterogeneous pairs, whose components are are arbitrary — possibly different — ordered types.

2.1 Abstract Type Declarations

In the concrete syntax of our example language, we use keywords **some ... where** instead of existential quantifiers. An abstract type is expressed as follows:

$$\tau = \textbf{some}\ a\ \textbf{where}\ C\ \textbf{in}\ \tau'$$

The bound variable a is a *placeholder*; it stands for all implementations of the abstract type. We adopt the convention that the signature part following **where** can be omitted if it is empty and that the type part following **in** can be omitted if it is just the placeholder.

The signature part corresponds to a type class. It consists of an arbitrary number of conformity clauses and definitions of overloaded identifiers. A conformity clause is of the form $\alpha :: \tau$, where α is the placeholder and τ is another abstract type. It reads: "Every implementation of the type being defined is also an implementation of τ". A definition of an overloaded identifier is of the form $x : \sigma$. It states that an identifier x of type $[\tau =: \alpha]\sigma$ is declared for all implementations τ of the defined type. Here, $[\tau =: \alpha]$ denotes substitution of τ for α.

Example 2.1 Some simple abstract type declarations are:

```
Eq    = some a where
           (=): a -> a -> Bool

Ord   = some a where
           a :: Eq
           (<), (<=) : a -> a -> Bool

Point = some p where
           p    :: Ord
           x, y : p -> Coord
           move : p -> (Coord * Coord) -> p
```

So far, we have used abstract types in ways which could just as well have been expressed with type classes. Abstract types are more general than type classes, however, since they are identified with types. Being types, they can be used in a more flexible way than predicates on types can. Two examples are the possibility to define values of an abstract type, and the possibility to construct abstract types which are parameterized by other types. Values of abstract types are important in connection with heterogeneous data structures (see Section 3). An example of a parameterized abstract type is the following:

Example 2.2 Bag is a type constructor which, given an element type a, yields the abstract type of bags of a.

```
a :: Eq => Bag a = some b where
    b :: Eq
    emptybag     : b
    singleton    : a -> b
    union,
    intersection,
    difference   : b -> b -> b
    elements     : b -> List a
```

2.2   The Implementation Relation

We have seen that an abstract type defines the interface of some data structure; it does not specify the data structure's implementation. To specify that a given type τ

is an implementation of an abstract type σ, we use a variant of a conformity clause, in which the implementations of all functions in σ's signature are given. Syntax:

$$impl \quad ::= \quad [cond \Rightarrow] \, \tau :: \sigma \text{ where } x_1 = e_1, \ldots, x_n = e_n$$
$$cond \quad ::= \quad [cond,] \, \alpha :: \sigma$$

Notes:

1. Every concrete or abstract type may occur in arbitrarily many implementation clauses. Hence, an abstract type can be implemented by several concrete types, and a concrete type can be the implementation of several abstract types.

2. Implementations can be conditional.

3. Each implementing expression e_i must be of type $[\tau =: \alpha]\tau_i$, where the declaration $x_i : \tau_i$ forms part of the signature of σ and α is σ's placeholder variable.

Example 2.3 Lists conditionally implement the Eq abstract type:

```
a :: Eq => List a :: Eq where
    (=) = listeq

listeq : List a -> List a -> Bool
listeq = ...
```

In the same style we can state that List conditionally implements the Ord abstract type. Lists of elements with equality also implement bags; a simple, albeit inefficient implementation would be:

```
a :: Ord => List a :: Bag a where
    (=) xs ys            = sort xs = sort ys
    emptybag             = []
    singleton x          = [x]
    union                = (++)
    intersection         = isect
    difference           = (--)
    elements             = id

isect [] ys     = []
isect (x:xs) ys = (if x 'in' ys then [x] else [])
                    ++ isect xs (ys -- [x])
```

Note that List implements the abstract type Eq in two different ways: Once directly, meaning lexical ordering, and another time indirectly, via Bag. Having two different implementations of equality raises the question which implementation is meant by (=) We disambiguate by the rule that left-hand side occurrences of (=) refer to the newly defined type (i.e. Bag), whereas right-hand side occurrences refer to the implementing type (i.e. List). As a consequence, the definitions of a signature are not known in the expressions that implement the signature. In our example, intersection had to be defined in terms of an auxiliary, recursive function isect. This is admittedly rather crude, but the only route open to us if we want to avoid atrocities like CLU's **rep** and **cvt**.

2.3 F-Bounded Polymorphism

Like existential types, universal types are bounded, having the form:

$$\forall \alpha. C(\alpha).\tau(\alpha)$$

C is a set of conformity constraints. A conformity constraint $\alpha :: \tau$ restricts the bound variable α to range only over implementations of abstract type τ. Again, this is similar to the predicated types in [19]. It is strictly more expressive than universal polymorphism with type class bounds since bounds are types and therefore can be parameterized.

Example 2.4 A function to compute the symmetric difference between two bags:

symdiff : $\forall \alpha.\forall \beta \,.\, (\beta :: Bag\ \alpha)\,.\, \beta \times \beta \to \beta$

```
symdiff b1 b2 = union (difference (b1, b2), difference (b2, b1))
```

In other type systems such as the ones of Haskell, ML [12], or XML+ [13], we either have to fix the element type α, or we have to fix the implementation of Bag, whereas our system allows to abstract on both element type and implementation.

2.4 Abstract Types are Large

Not all types have equal status in the Hindley/Milner system. Universally quantified types are second class citizens, since they cannot be substituted for a type variable. The reason for this restriction is that type reconstruction is conjectured to be undecidable if quantifiers range over polymorphic as well as monomorphic types [7]. In [10], the types over which quantifiers range are called small types, and all other types are called large types. Universally quantified types would be considered large by that definition. As far as existential types go, we have a choice. To see the distinction, consider the type expression (from [3])

$$\exists \alpha. \alpha \times \alpha.$$

If abstract types are large, this expression denotes the type of pairs where both elements have the same, unknown type. On the other hand, if abstract types are small, we can substitute $\exists \alpha. \alpha$ for α and write:

$$\exists \alpha. \alpha \times \alpha \;=\; (\exists \alpha. \alpha) \times (\exists \alpha. \alpha)$$

Hence, we see that the abstract type $\exists \alpha. \alpha \times \alpha$ stands now for pairs whose elements have arbitrary, possibly different types.

In this work, we have chosen abstract types to be large. That is, quantifiers do not range over abstract types, and abstract types cannot be substituted for type variables. This makes automatic type reconstruction possible (an inference algorithm is given in [9]). For the general case, with quantifiers ranging over abstract as well as concrete types, the problem of type inference is still open.

One consequence of abstract types being large is that the form of types taking part in the proof of a typing is restricted. The typing rules in Appendix A force all existential quantifiers to occur only at the outermost level, as element types of an algebraic type, or as function results. While we regard the syntax of types required by the typing rules as their "normal form," we use abstract types more liberally in our programming examples. The examples can be "de-sugared" to normal form using laws (P1) – (P3):

(P1) $(\exists \alpha. C.\tau) \to \tau' = \forall \alpha. C.(\tau \to \tau')$

(P2) $(\exists \alpha. C.\eta_1) \times \eta_2 = \exists \alpha. C.\eta_1 \times \eta_2$ if α is not free in η_2
$\eta_1 \times (\exists \alpha. C.\eta_2) = \exists \alpha. C.\eta_1 \times \eta_2$ if α is not free in η_1

(P3) $\exists \alpha.(\alpha :: \exists \beta. C.\beta).\alpha = \exists \alpha. C.\alpha$

3 Heterogeneous Data Types

Abstract types with more than one implementation give us heterogeneous data structures for free. If we declare a data structure with a field of an abstract type, every occurrence of this field can be represented by a different implementation of the abstract type. That is, the structure is (boundedly) heterogeneous.

Example 3.1 A heterogeneous list of windows.
Assume the following hierarchy of window types to be given:

```
Window      = some w where
                  handle  : w -> Event -> w
                  display : w -> DisplayList
                  ...

TextWindow  = some w where w :: Window
                  ...

GraphWindow = some w where w :: Window
                  ...
```

We can then declare a type `WindowList` in terms of the abstract type `Window`. Note that unlike `List`, `WindowList` is a type, not a type constructor, since there are no variables on the left hand side of the declaration.

```
WindowList  = WNil | WCons (Window * WindowList)
```

Then, in the expression

```
case wl of WCons (win, ws) => ...
```

the pattern `win` is typed `Window`. This means that `win` can be passed to every function which expects an arbitrary implementation of `Window` as argument.

The constructor aspect of the above type declaration is in some sense the reverse of the pattern matching aspect. With properties P1, P2, and P3, we have:

```
WCons   :   Window × WindowList → WindowList
        = (P3)
```

$$(\exists w \,.\, w :: Window \,.\, w) \times WindowList \rightarrow WindowList$$
$$= \text{(P2)}$$
$$(\exists w \,.\, w :: Window \,.\, w \times WindowList) \rightarrow WindowList$$
$$= \text{(P1)}$$
$$\forall w \,.\, w :: Window \,.\, (w \times WindowList \rightarrow WindowList).$$

Hence, we see that, first, the quantifier changes between constructors and pattern matching, and, second, that WCons indeed may be passed an arbitrary implementation of Window. This means that (implementations of) TextWindows or GraphWindows, for example, can also be included in window lists, or, put in other words, that WindowList is a heterogeneous data structure. This solves the extensibility problem described in the introduction. For example, a broadcast function, which passes an event to all windows in a WindowList could be expressed as follows:

```
broadcast : WindowList -> Event -> WindowList

broadcast WNil e            = WNil
broadcast (WCons (w, ws)) e = WCons (handle w e, broadcast ws e)
```

4 Runtime Model

Since the implementation of the operations defined in an abstract type is not known statically, we have to maintain this information at runtime, in the form of "method dictionaries". Our runtime model is an extension of the one introduced by Wadler and Blott [19]. They present a scheme for the translation of expressions with type classes into equivalent ML expressions.

Every implementation of an abstract type defines a dictionary, i.e. a tuple which contains the definition of all operations in the type's signature. Dictionaries are passed to polymorphic functions as additional arguments. A dictionary is passed for every conformity constraint in the function's type. A function such as

```
redefine  : ∀w . (w :: Window) . w → w
```

would be translated to a function with two arguments, a dictionary and a window. The additional dictionary arguments are passed at the point in the program text where the polymorphic type is instantiated. An expression such as redefine tw, where tw is a TextWindow, would be translated to (we mark translated versions of original identifiers with an apostrophe):

```
redefine' textWinDict tw.
```

This method is identical to the one described in [19], with conformity constraints replacing instance constraints in Haskell. For abstract types, an extension to the scheme is needed.

We map values of an existential type into dictionary/value tuples, similarly to the memory layout for object-oriented languages. A WindowList would thus be translated into a data structure which is decorated with one dictionary table per element:

```
WindowList' = WNil'
            | WCons' (WindowDict, (WindowData, WindowList'))
```

Since existential polymorphism in the type becomes universal polymorphism in its constructors, all constructors already have the needed dictionaries as arguments. The original WCons, for example, is of type

$$\text{WCons} \quad : \quad \forall \alpha . (\alpha :: Window) . \alpha \times WindowList \rightarrow WindowList,$$

and would hence be translated to a function whose signature matches the second alternative in type WindowList:

$$\text{WCons}' \quad : \quad WindowDict \times (WindowData \times WindowList') \rightarrow WindowList'$$

If a value of an existential types is passed to a function, all needed dictionary components are extracted and passed as additional arguments. Hence, the expression

```
redefine w
  where WCons (w, ws) = wlist,
```

would be translated to

```
redefine' wdict w
  where WCons' (wdict, (w, ws)) = wlist.
```

5 Conclusion

We have introduced a form of abstract data type that extends the type class concept of Haskell and allows us to model heterogeneous data structures, useful for extensible software systems. The type system is fully static, that is, no type-related errors can occur at runtime. Types are reconstructible using a variant of the ML type inference algorithm.

Since abstract types are large, our type discipline is polymorphic over concrete types only. An interesting extension, which we are currently investigating, would be a theory that is is polymorphic over abstract types as well. We could then abstract over properties of types; a concept such as *List T*, the list of objects which are instances of the given abstract type *T*, could be defined. This expression could then be instantiated to yield *List Window*, or *List Order*, for example. We see two ways to achieve that extension: We could either introduce explicit typing for abstract types in the style of the ML Module system [10], or we could generalize our system by considering existential types to belong to the universe of small types. The problem of type inference in such an extension remains to be solved, however.

Acknowledgements

We would like to thank Ben Goldberg, Fritz Henglein, Kim Marriott, and Satish Thatte for helpful comments and discussions.

A Typing Rules

This section presents the formal typing rules for abstract data types. For the kernel language, these rules are similar to the ones of the Hindley/Milner system [11, 6]. In their overloading and implementation aspects, they are derived from the rules in [19]. New rules for existential quantification and the formal treatment of algebraic data types have been added.

A.1 Language

The example language is designed such that common functional languages can be mapped into it. It consists of expressions of the following forms:

Expressions e ::= x (identifier)
          | $e\ e'$ (function application)
          | $\lambda x.e$ (function abstraction)
          | **let** $x = e$ **in** e' (local declaration).
          | **data** σ **in** e (data declaration)
          | **over** $x :: \sigma$ **in** e (overloaded identifier)
          | **inst** $x :: \sigma = e$ **in** e' (instance declaration)

Predefined:

fix : $\forall\alpha.(\alpha \to \alpha) \to \alpha$
if   : $\forall\alpha.Bool \to \alpha \to \alpha \to \alpha$
$(\cdot\,,\cdot)$: $\forall\alpha.\forall\beta.\alpha \to \beta \to \alpha \times \beta$
fst : $\forall\alpha.\forall\beta.\alpha \times \beta \to \alpha$
snd : $\forall\alpha.\forall\beta.\alpha \times \beta \to \beta$

The first four productions describe a conventional λ-calculus language, similar to *Exp* [11] Instead of having a set of primitive types, we augment *Exp* by **data** clauses defining algebraic types (types are discussed in the next subsection). We also add declarations for overloaded identifiers and their instances in the style of [19].

Example A.1 The overloaded identifiers of the abstract types *Eq* and *Bag* are declared by:

> **over** $eq :: \forall\alpha$. $EqSig\ \alpha$ **in**
> **over** $bag :: \forall\alpha$. $(eq :_i EqSig\ \alpha)$. $\forall\beta$. $BagSig\ \alpha\ \beta$ **in** ...

The lower-case identifiers *eq* and *bag* name the defined operations. That is, *eq* is just the equality function, and *bag* is a tuple of all functions defined in the abstract type **Bag** (see Example 2.2). *EqSig* and *BagSig* are used as shorthands for the signatures of the abstract type. That is,

$EqSig\ \alpha$ $=$ $\alpha \to \alpha \to Bool$
$BagSig\ \alpha\ \beta$ $=$ $\beta\times$ (emptybag)
                    $(\alpha \to \beta)\times$ (singleton)
                    $(\beta \to \beta \to \beta)\times$ (union)
                    $\cdots$

The conformity declaration that *List* α implements *Bag* α is translated as follows:

> **inst** bag :: $\forall\alpha$. $(eq :_i EqSig\ \alpha)$. $BagSig\ \alpha\ (List\ \alpha)$
> $=$ $(Nil,$
> $\lambda x.Cons\ x\ Nil,$
> $\lambda xs.\lambda ys.append\ xs\ ys,$
> $\ldots)$

More detailed examples are found in [19].

Remark on naming: All variable identifiers defined in a **let** or **over** clause, and all type and constructor identifiers defined in a **data** clause are assumed to be different from each other.

A.2 Types

We augment Hindley/Milner types with algebraic data types and bounded universal and existential quantification:

Type Identifiers	T		
Constructors	K		
Types	τ ::=	α	(variable)
	|	$\tau \rightarrow \eta$	(function)
	|	$\tau_1 \times \tau_2$	(product)
	|	$\mu T.K_1\, \eta_1 + \ldots + K_n\, \eta_n$	(algebraic type)
Abstract Types	η ::=	$\exists \alpha.\chi.\eta \mid \tau$	
Type Schemes	σ ::=	$\forall \alpha.\chi.\sigma \mid \eta$	
Constraints	χ ::=	$\chi_1.\chi_2$	(conjunction)
	|	$x :_i \tau$	(is-instance)

An algebraic data type is given by a type expression of the form $\mu T.K_1\, \eta_1 + \ldots + K_n\, \eta_n$. Here, T is the type's name and $K_1, \ldots, K_n$ are its constructors. For every such algebraic type, we assume injection functions K_i, projection functions $\downarrow K_i$, and test functions $?K_i$ to be given. The types of these function are determined by rules INJ, PROJ, and TEST in Section A.4.

Example A.2 Type *List* α can be written as follows:

$$\forall \alpha \,.\, \mu\ List\ .\ Nil + Cons\ (\alpha \times List)$$

The deduction rules in Section A.4 ensure that only algebraic types declared in a **data** clause take part in a typing.

An abstract type is defined by a type expression of the form $\exists \alpha.\chi.\eta$. Here, η is a (possibly abstract) type, and χ is a constraint which restricts the range of the quantifier. Constraints are finite sets of instance assertions $x :_i \tau$. If the constraint set is empty it can be omitted, dropping one of the two delimiting period signs. Note that this is different from the concrete example language, where constraints were written in the reverse way.

Example A.3 Type *Bag* α can be translated as follows:

$$\forall \alpha \,.\, \exists \beta \,.\, (bag :_i BagSig\ \alpha\ \beta) \,.\, \beta$$

A.3 Assumptions

Assumptions are sets of type predicates.

Assumptions	A	$::=$	$A_1.A_2$	(conjunction)
		$\mid$	$\pi(\sigma)$	(predicate in σ)
Predicates in σ	$\pi(\sigma)$	$::=$	$x :_o \sigma$	(overloaded identifier)
		$\mid$	$x :_i \sigma$	(instance)
		$\mid$	$x : \sigma$	(has-type)
		$\mid$	$! \sigma$	(is-type)

A.4 Typing Rules

Logical rules

TAUT
$$\frac{}{A \vdash \pi(\sigma)} \quad (\pi(\sigma) \in A)$$

AND
$$\frac{A \vdash \pi_1(\sigma_1) \qquad A \vdash \pi_2(\sigma_2)}{A \vdash \pi_1(\sigma_1).\pi_2(\sigma_2)}$$

∀-ELIM
$$\frac{A \vdash \pi(\forall\alpha.\chi.\sigma) \qquad A \vdash [\tau =: \alpha]\chi}{A \vdash \pi([\tau =: \alpha]\sigma)}$$

∀-INTRO
$$\frac{A . \chi \vdash \pi(\sigma)}{A \vdash \pi(\forall\alpha.\chi.\sigma)} \quad (\alpha \notin FV(A))$$

Rules ∀-ELIM and ∀-INTRO are generalized to cover all forms of type predicates in Section A.3, instead of just predicates of the form $e : \tau$. Note that type variables can be instantiated only with concrete types.

∃-ELIM
$$\frac{A \vdash \pi(\exists\alpha.\chi.\eta)}{A \vdash \pi(\eta)} \quad (\alpha \notin FV(\eta))$$

SKOLEM
$$\frac{A \vdash \pi(\exists\alpha.\chi.\eta) \qquad A . \pi([\beta =: \alpha]\eta) . [\beta =: \alpha]\chi \vdash \pi'(\eta')}{A \vdash \pi'(\exists\alpha.\chi.[\alpha =: \beta]\eta')} \quad \begin{array}{l}(\beta \notin FV(A, \chi, \eta), \\ \alpha \notin FV(\eta'))\end{array}$$

With rule ∃-ELIM, "superfluous" existential quantifiers, which do not bind anything, may be dropped. Rule SKOLEM eliminates an existential quantifier in a subproof, replacing it with a "Skolem" variable (written β in the rule above). There is no rule for introducing an existential quantifier. Loosely speaking, the only way for an existential quantifier to enter a proof of ($\vdash e : \tau$) is via an explicitly given abstract type in e. Type reconstruction is thus greatly simplified.

Rules for the base language

The rules for the base language (excluding **data** clauses and overloading) are fairly conventional:

$$\text{APP} \quad \frac{A \vdash e : \tau \to \eta \qquad A \vdash e' : \tau}{A \vdash (e\ e') : \eta}$$

$$\text{ABS} \quad \frac{A \cdot (x : \tau) \vdash e : \eta}{A \vdash (\lambda x.e) : \tau \to \eta}$$

$$\text{LET} \quad \frac{A \vdash e : \sigma \qquad A \cdot (x : \sigma) \vdash e' : \tau}{A \vdash (\text{let } x = e \text{ in } e') : \tau}$$

Rules for algebraic type declarations and pattern matching

$$\text{DATA} \quad \frac{A \cdot (!\,\sigma) \vdash e : \tau}{A \vdash (\text{data } \sigma \text{ in } e) : \tau}$$

$$\text{INJ} \quad \frac{A \vdash !\,\mu T.K_1\,\eta_1 + \ldots + K_n\,\eta_n}{A \vdash K_i : shallow(\eta_i \to \mu T.K_1\,\eta_1 + \ldots + K_n\,\eta_n)} \quad (1 \le i \le n)$$

$$\text{PROJ} \quad \frac{A \vdash !\,\mu T.K_1\,\eta_1 + \ldots + K_n\,\eta_n}{A \vdash \downarrow K_i : \mu T.K_1\,\eta_1 + \ldots + K_n\,\eta_n \to \eta_i} \quad (1 \le i \le n)$$

$$\text{TEST} \quad \frac{A \vdash !\,\mu T.K_1\,\eta_1 + \ldots + K_n\,\eta_n}{A \vdash ?K_i : \mu T.K_1\,\eta_1 + \ldots + K_n\,\eta_n \to Bool} \quad (1 \le i \le n)$$

Rules INJ, PROJ, and TEST give types to injections, projections and test functions which are associated with an algebraic data type. Function *shallow* in INJ converts a function signature of the form $\eta \to \eta'$ (which is syntactically illegal if η is quantified) to an equivalent shallow function signature [2]. Existential quantifiers in argument position are converted to universal quantifiers over the whole function.

$$\begin{aligned} shallow\ ((\exists\alpha.\chi.\eta) \to \eta') &= \forall\alpha.\chi.shallow\ (\eta \to \eta') \\ shallow\ (\tau \to \eta) &= \tau \to \eta \end{aligned}$$

Rules for overloading

$$\text{OVER} \quad \frac{A \cdot (x :_o \sigma) \vdash e : \tau}{A \vdash (\text{over } x :: \sigma \text{ in } e) : \tau}$$

$$\text{INST} \quad \frac{\begin{array}{c} A \vdash x :_o \sigma \\ A \vdash e : \sigma \\ A \cdot (x :_i \sigma) \vdash e' : \tau \end{array}}{A \vdash (\text{inst } x :: \sigma = e \text{ in } e') : \tau} \quad \begin{array}{l} \text{(for all } (x :_i \sigma') \in A: \\ \sigma, \sigma' \text{ not unifiable)} \end{array}$$

$$\text{ITYPE} \quad \frac{A \vdash x :_i \sigma}{A \vdash x : \sigma}$$

The last three rules are essentially equivalent to rules for overloading resolution in [19]. Wadler and Blott's definition of "valid assumption set" corresponds to our "not unifiable" condition in rule INST.

Wadler and Blott conjectured that principal types exist in their system, provided all **over** and **inst** declarations are global. This was subsequently shown correct in [15]. We conjecture that the extended system with existential type shares the principal type properties of type classes.

References

[1] P. Canning, W. Cook, W. Hill, W. Olthoff, and J. Mitchell. F-bounded polymorphism for object-oriented programming. In *Proc. Functional Programming and Computer Architecture*, pages 273–280, 1989.

[2] L. Cardelli. Basic polymorphic typechecking. *Science of Computer Programming*, 9(8):147–172, 1987.

[3] L. Cardelli and P. Wegner. On understanding types, data abstraction and polymorphism. *ACM Computing Surveys*, 17(4):471–522, Dec. 1985.

[4] W. Cook. A proposal for making Eiffel type-safe. *Computer Journal*, 32(4):305–311, 1989.

[5] G. Cormack and A. Wright. Type-dependent parameter inference. In *Proc. SIGPLAN'90 Conf. on Programming Language Design and Implementation*, pages 127–136, White Plains, NY, June 1990.

[6] L. Damas and R. Milner. Principal type schemes for functional programs. In *Proc. 9th Annual ACM Symp. on Principles of Programming Languages*, pages 207–212, Jan. 1982.

[7] F. Henglein and H. Mairson. The complexity of type inference for higher-order typed lambda calculi. In *Proc. 18th ACM Symp. on Principles of Programming Languages (POPL)*, Orlando, Florida, Jan. 1991.

[8] S. Kaes. Parametric overloading in polymorphic programming languages. In H. Ganzinger, editor, *Proc. 2nd European Symosium on Programming, Lecture Notes in Computer Science, Vol. 300*, pages 131–144, Nancy, France, March 1988. Springer-Verlag.

[9] K. Läufer and M. Odersky. Type inference for an object-oriented extension of ML. NYU-CIMS Report, New York University, Department of Computer Science, in preparation.

[10] D. MacQueen. Using dependent types to express modular structure. In *Proc. 13th ACM Symp. on Principles of Programming Languages*, pages 277–286. ACM, Jan. 1986.

[11] R. Milner. A theory of type polymorphism in programming. *J. Computer and System Sciences*, 17:348–375, 1978.

[12] R. Milner, M. Tofte., and R. Harper. *The Definition of Standard ML.* MIT Press, 1990.

[13] J. Mitchell, S. Meldal, and N. Madhav. An extension of Standard ML modules with subtyping and inheritance. In *Proc. ACM Symp. on Principles of Programming Languages*, Jan. 1991.

[14] J. Mitchell and G. Plotkin. Abstract Types have Existential Type. In *Proc. 12th ACM Symp. on Principles of Programming Languages*, pages 37–51. ACM, Jan. 1985.

[15] T. Niphow and G. Snelting. Type classes and overloading resolution via order-sorted unification. Technical Report PI-R8/90, Technische Hochschule Darmstadt, Praktische Informatik, July 1990.

[16] J. Palsberg and M. Schwartzbach. Type substitution for object-oriented programming. In N. Meyrowitz, editor, *Proc. Conf. Object-Oriented Programming: Systems, Languages, and Applications and European Conf. on Object-Oriented Programming*, pages 151–160, Ottawa, Canada, Oct. 1990. ACM Press.

[17] D. Sandberg. An alternative to subclassing. In *Proc. Object-Oriented Programming: Languages, Systems and Applications*, pages 424–428, 1986.

[18] S. Thatte. Type inference with partial types. In *Proc. Int'l Conf. on Algorithms, Languages and Programming*, pages 615–629, 1988.

[19] P. Wadler and S. Blott. How to make ad-hoc polymorphism less ad hoc. In *Proc. 16th Annual ACM Symp. on Principles of Programming Languages*, pages 60–76. ACM, Jan. 1989.

Syntactic and Semantic Inheritance in Logic Programming

Luís Monteiro
António Porto

Departamento de Informática
Universidade Nova de Lisboa
2825 Monte da Caparica
Portugal

{ lm, ap }@fct.unl.pt

Abstract

This paper aims at a deeper understanding of how inheritance can fit into a logic programming framework, by considering inheritance systems in terms of partially ordered sets of logic program units. We develop for such systems operational, declarative and fixed point semantics which are proven equivalent.

We begin by discussing, in logic programming terms, the basic types of inheritance that can be achieved. We identify two kinds, semantic and syntactic inheritance, which can occur in two modes, extension and overriding. We then present a (abstract) language for programming systems with combinations of these various types of inheritance. These combinations are obtained through a signature that assigns to each unit the sets of predicates for semantic and syntactic inheritance, extension and overriding becoming implicit. We define and characterize the operational, declarative, and fixed-point semantics, and we prove their equivalence. The equivalence between declarative and operational semantics is based on a two-step reduction of inheritance systems to non-inheritance systems, i.e. systems of standard logic programs, by eliminating first syntactic inheritance and then semantic inheritance. Through equivalence results along the way and using the well-known equivalence of semantics for standard logic programs we achieve the main result. Then we extend the language with inheritance control at the level of individual goal calls, using two new connectives *super* and *self*, and define the corresponding extension of the semantic definitions, showing that the equivalence is still preserved.

The semantics presented provide simple direct insights into inheritance phenomena. The reduction technique used in the main equivalence proof actually suggests that inheritance really adds no extra conceptual power to standard logic programs, although remaining a highly convenient structuring technique with implications for software engineering.

Introduction

Languages for object-oriented programming, knowledge representation, and conceptual modelling for databases, to name a few representative areas, all share a common feature usually referred to as *inheritance*. Programs in these languages have structure, and inheritance means that at some locations in the structure (objects, frames, entities, ...) some properties (operational, declarative or both) are implicitly obtained from other locations in the structure.

In logic programming, although there have been proposals for generic structuring [O'K 85] [Mil 89] [Mon Por 89] and also for more specific inheritance schemes [Zan 84] [Gal 86] [Kau Gru 86] [A-K 86] [McC 88] [Mel 89], there has been no satisfactory account of inheritance giving us a simple declarative semantics and equivalent operational semantics that capture the phenomena found in typical inheritance languages. Preliminary work in that direction was presented in [Mon Por 90]. Here we present more coherent and substantial results.

The organization of the paper is as follows. We first study how various inheritance concepts can be expressed in logic programming terms, producing a classification of the corresponding inheritance types, in which stand out the notions of semantic and syntactic inheritance. Then we present a language allowing for combinations of those types of inheritance, and define and characterize its operational, declarative, and fixed-point semantics. Then we prove the equivalence between the semantics. We start with that between fixed point and declarative semantics, and then establish the main result of the equivalence between declarative and operational semantics, defining two semantic-preserving program transformations that reduce inheritance programs to standard logic programs, by first eliminating syntactic inheritance and then semantic inheritance. We conclude with some final remarks.

Kinds and modes of inheritance

The typical structure of inheritance systems is given by a partial order relation on a set of units. The intransitive relation giving rise to the partial order is usually referred to as *isa*.

We consider units in the structure as being logic programs, i.e. sets of clauses. We assign an atomic name to each unit in the structure, and consider *isa* to be a relation over these names. The clauses in a unit define predicates (those appearing in the heads of the clauses), and these predicates denote relations in the intended interpretation of the unit.

Now the question of inheritance can be posed as follows. In general, the predicates we want to associate with a given unit u do not correspond to those in the least model of u taken as a single logic program. The *isa* structure will generally induce a composition of information in u with "inherited" information from "super" units in order to get at the predicates we want u to stand for. What types of such compositions can there be?

We consider two basic kinds of inheritance. One we call *semantic*, *relational* or *predicate* inheritance, and the other we call *syntactic, definitional* or *clause* inheritance.

Consider two units u and v such that u *isa* v. With predicate inheritance we can imagine u inheriting *relations* corresponding to certain predicates from v, i.e. compositionality is done at the semantic level by using relations from the model of v in order to construct the model of u. On the other hand, if we have clause inheritance u inherits *clauses* from v, i.e. one must compose syntactic definitions from u and v in order to construct the model of u. It should be obvious that syntactic inheritance cannot be reduced to semantic inheritance when considering the usual Herbrand model semantics.

Orthogonally to the semantic and syntactic kinds we can also distinguish two inheritance modes: *extension* and *overriding*. In extension mode one is adding all tuples/clauses from v to those in u, whereas in overriding mode relations/definitions in u are regarded as complete for the corresponding predicates and only those for other predicates are inherited from v.

The kinds and modes being independent, we then have four basic types of inheritance:

	Extension	Overriding
Predicate	PE	PO
Clause	CE	CO

We can show with a small example that in general all four types of inheritance can give different results. Consider the two units

$u:$
$q(1)$

isa

$v:$
$p(X) \leftarrow q(X)$
$q(2)$

The values for the arguments of the predicates in u, in the four possible inheritance cases, are as follows:

	p	q
PE	2	1, 2
CE	1, 2	1, 2
PO	2	1
CO	1	1

An inheritance language

Assigning an inheritance type to each unit u or to each pair of units u and v such that u *isa* v is usually not expressive enough. Rather than having inheritance defined at the *unit* level, we may wish to have it defined at the *predicate* level, thus allowing for combinations of the four inheritance types in the same unit. To this end we will now present an abstract language, in which inheritance is defined by partitioning the predicate space in each unit according to the intended inheritance types.

Syntax

The basic structure in our language is an ordered set of unit names $\mathbf{U} = (U, <)$, where U is a finite set of unit names and $<$ is an intransitive acyclic binary relation on U (the *isa* relation).

The language defines a signature over $\mathbf{U}$, $\Sigma = (F, P, (R_u, D_u)_{u \in U})$. F is the finite set of function symbols and P the finite set of predicate symbols. We now define the well-formed expressions over Σ.

A *term* is either a variable or $f(t_1, \ldots, t_n)$ where $f \in F$, $n \geq 0$ is the arity of f and $t_1, \ldots, t_n$ are terms.

An *atomic formula* is $p(t_1, \ldots, t_n)$ where $p \in P$, $n \geq 0$ is the arity of p and $t_1, \ldots, t_n$ are terms. Given an atomic formula $g \equiv p(t_1, \ldots, t_n)$ we use the notation $\hat{g}$ to denote p.

A *goal* is $g_1, \ldots, g_n$ where $n \geq 0$ and $g_1, \ldots, g_n$ are atomic formulæ. When $n = 0$ we have the empty goal, which we denote by $\triangle$.

A *clause* is $h \leftarrow G$ where h is an atomic formula and G is a goal.

A *unit* is $u : C$ where $u \in U$ and C is a finite set of clauses.

An *inheritance system* is a set of units, one for each $u \in U$.

Given an inheritance system $\mathcal{U}$, we use the notation C_u to refer to the set of clauses C in the unit $(u : C) \in \mathcal{U}$.

In the signature $\Sigma = (F, P, (R_u, D_u)_{u \in U})$, R_u and D_u are subsets of P meant to denote the predicate symbols for which inheritance is to be had in u, respectively of the relational and definitional kind. Naturally we must have $R_u \cap D_u = \emptyset$. In u, predicates from $R_u \cup D_u$ are inherited in extension mode; overriding is implicit for all other predicates in P defined in u.

Recasting our initial example in this language, we can see that different possibilities can be achieved through different signatures:

$$
\begin{array}{ccc}
\boxed{\begin{array}{l} u: \\ \\ q(1) \end{array}} & < & \boxed{\begin{array}{l} v: \\ p(X) \leftarrow q(X) \\ q(2) \end{array}}
\end{array}
$$

R_u	D_u	p	q
$\{p\}$	$\{q\}$	2	$1, 2$
$\{q\}$	$\{p\}$	$1, 2$	$1, 2$
$\{p\}$	$\emptyset$	2	1
$\emptyset$	$\{p\}$	1	2

Operational semantics

The intuitive understanding of how inheritance works can be given a precise characterization by defining the operational semantics. We shall do it by presenting structural rules for the top-down derivation relation. This relation will naturally involve a goal G and a computed answer substitution θ, but in our case has to be doubly indexed by an inheritance system $\mathcal{U}$ and a unit $u \in \mathcal{U}$ for which the goal is intended. We represent this relation by

$$\vdash_{\mathcal{U},u} G\,[\theta]$$

but will omit one or both indices when unnecessary in the context. We use ϵ to denote the empty substitution.

The rules are split in two groups: the *local* derivation rules, corresponding to the standard logic programming inference rules, and the *inheritance* derivation rules dealing with inheritance.

Local derivation rules

Empty goal

$$\frac{}{\vdash \triangle\,[\epsilon]} \qquad\qquad (E)$$

Conjunction

$$\frac{\vdash g\,[\theta] \qquad \vdash G\theta\,[\sigma]}{\vdash g,G\,[\theta\sigma]} \qquad\qquad (C)$$

Atomic formula — local reduction

$$\frac{\vdash_u G\theta\,[\sigma]}{\vdash_u g\,[\theta\sigma_{(g)}]} \quad \left\{ \begin{array}{l} (h \leftarrow G)' \in C_u \\ \theta = mgu(g,h) \end{array} \right\} \qquad\qquad (R)$$

We are using $(h \leftarrow G)'$ to represent a variant of the clause $h \leftarrow G$ and $\theta\sigma_{(g)}$ to denote the restriction of the substitution $\theta\sigma$ to the variables of g.

Inheritance derivation rules

Atomic formula — predicate inheritance

$$\frac{\vdash_v g\,[\theta]}{\vdash_u g\,[\theta]} \quad \left\{ \begin{array}{l} \hat{g} \in R_u \\ u < v \end{array} \right\} \qquad\qquad (PI)$$

Atomic formula — clause inheritance

$$\frac{\vdash_u G\theta\,[\sigma]}{\vdash_u g\,[\theta\sigma]} \quad \left\{ \begin{array}{l} \hat{g} \in D_u \\ (h \leftarrow G)' \in C{\downarrow}_u \\ \theta = mgu(g,h) \end{array} \right\} \qquad\qquad (CI)$$

Here $C{\downarrow}_u$ denotes the set of clauses inherited by u, i.e. acessible in u via definitional inheritance. In order to formally define it, we introduce the notion of *restriction* $C{\lceil}_Q$ of a set of clauses C to the predicates in the set Q:

$$C{\lceil}_Q = \{\,(h \leftarrow G) \in C \ : \ \hat{h} \in Q\,\}$$

Then the set of clauses inherited by $u \in U$ is

$$C{\downarrow}_u = \bigcup_{u<v} (C_v \cup C{\downarrow}_v){\lceil}_{D_u}$$

A *computed answer substitution* for G at u is a substitution θ such that $\vdash_{\mathcal{U},u} G[\theta]$. The *operational semantics* of inheritance systems is a function that assigns to each triple $\mathcal{U}, u, G$ the set $O_{\mathcal{U},u}(G) = \{ \theta : \vdash_{\mathcal{U},u} G[\theta] \}$ of computed answer substitutions for G at u.

Declarative semantics

The declarative semantics of a logic programming language is based on the model theory of the underlying logic, and explains the meaning of programs in terms of the set of its logical consequences. The basic notions on which the declarative semantics rests are, accordingly, those of interpretation and model. The appropriate notion of interpretation for our inheritance language is a straightforward generalization of the corresponding notion for Horn clause logic, the only difference being that it assigns a subset of the Herbrand base to every unit.

Let B be the Herbrand base defined by the sets F and P of function and predicate symbols, respectively. An *interpretation* of an inheritance language is a family

$$I = (I_u)_{u \in U}$$

of subsets I_u of B. The set $\mathcal{I}$ of all interpretations is a complete lattice for the order defined componentwise: $I \leq J$ if and only if $I_u \leq J_u$ for every $u \in U$.

Let I be an interpretation, u a unit name and f a formula, which may be a goal or a clause. The *satisfaction* of f by I_u is defined in the usual way:

- I_u satisfies f if I_u satisfies every ground instance f_0 of f.

- For a ground goal, I_u satisfies G if $G \subseteq I_u$.

- For a ground clause, I_u satisfies $h \leftarrow G$ if $h \in I_u$ or $G \not\subseteq I_u$.

A model is an interpretation satisfying some additional conditions. In the first place, each I_u must satisfy all the clauses in the unit u, namely the clauses in the set C_u. But since u may inherit clauses through every unit v such that $u < v$, I_u must also satisfy those clauses, which form the set $C{\downarrow}_u$. Finally, relational inheritance implies that, whenever $u < v$, I_u must satisfy all atomic formulæ for predicate symbols in R_u satisfied by I_v.

Before we characterize models formally, we need two auxiliary definitions. Let the set of clauses *available* in $u \in U$ be $\overline{C}_u = C_u \cup C{\downarrow}_u$. Given a set of ground atomic formulæ $J \subseteq B$ and a set of predicate symbols $Q \subseteq P$, let the *restriction* of J to Q be defined by

$$J{\lceil}_Q = \{ g \in J : \hat{g} \in Q \}.$$

A *model* of an inheritance system is an interpretation I satisfying the following two conditions:

- $I_v{\lceil}_{R_u} \subseteq I_u$ whenever $u < v$.

- I_u satisfies all the clauses in $\overline{C}_u$ for every $u \in U$.

If $\mathcal{U}$ is an inheritance system, $u \in U$ and G is a goal, G is said to be a *consequence* of $\mathcal{U}$ at u, written $\mathcal{U} \models_u G$, if I_u satisfies G for every model I of $\mathcal{U}$. Notice that the notions of model and consequence presented here are less general than is the case for classical logic. However, for the results in this paper this difference is irrelevant provided that the set of function symbols F is infinite.

A *correct answer substitution* for G at u is a substitution θ such that $\mathcal{U} \models_u G\theta$. The *declarative semantics* of inheritance systems is a function that assigns to each triple $\mathcal{U}, u, G$ the set $D_{\mathcal{U},u}(G) = \{\theta : \mathcal{U} \models_u G\theta\}$ of correct answer substitutions for G at u.

It is easy to see that the greatest lower bound of any non-empty set of models of $\mathcal{U}$ is also a model. Since the interpretation I with each I_u equal to B is easily seen to be a model, it follows that $\mathcal{U}$ has a least model.

Proposition 1 *Every inheritance system $\mathcal{U}$ has a least model $M_{\mathcal{U}}$.*

The importance of $M_{\mathcal{U}}$ is that it allows to simplify the definition of the declarative semantics: instead of requiring that $G\theta$ be satisfied by I_u for every model I of $\mathcal{U}$, it is enough that it be satisfied by $M_{\mathcal{U},u}$. Indeed, this is a simple consequence of the fact that if I and J are interpretations such that $I \leq J$ and I_u satisfies G then J_u also satisfies G.

Proposition 2 *One has $D_{\mathcal{U},u}(G) = \{\theta : M_{\mathcal{U},u} \text{ satisfies } G\theta\}$.*

Fixed-point semantics

Analogously to standard logic programs, we can introduce an immediate consequence operator associated with an inheritance system $\mathcal{U}$, which is a mapping $T_{\mathcal{U}} : \mathcal{I} \to \mathcal{I}$ from interpretations to interpretations. $T_{\mathcal{U}}(I)$ is defined as being the interpretation $J = (J_u)_{u \in U}$ such that

$$J_u = \{ h : \exists(h \leftarrow G) \in ground(\overline{C}_u) . G \subseteq I_u \} \cup \bigcup_{u < v} I_v \lceil_{R_u}$$

Let $T_{\mathcal{U},u}$ be the "projection" of $T_{\mathcal{U}}$ on the "coordinate" u, that is $T_{\mathcal{U},u}(I) = J_u$ if $T_{\mathcal{U}}(I) = J$. $T_{\mathcal{U},u}$ is defined by the union of two continuous functions and therefore is itself continuous, hence $T_{\mathcal{U}}$ is continuous. Indeed, the first function is analogous to the immediate consequence operator for Horn clause logic, and is continuous for the same reason. The continuity of the second function results from the fact that restriction and union are continuous. Thus we can state

Proposition 3 *$T_{\mathcal{U}}$ is continuous.*

It is easy to verify that an interpretation I is a model if and only if $T_{\mathcal{U}}(I) \leq I$, so that we have the following expected result.

Proposition 4 *The least model $M_{\mathcal{U}}$ of $\mathcal{U}$ is the least fixed point of $T_{\mathcal{U}}$.*

Denoting by $lfp(T_{\mathcal{U}})$ the least fixed point of $T_{\mathcal{U}}$, we have the following equivalent characterization of the semantics of inheritance systems.

Proposition 5 *One has $D_{\mathcal{U},u}(G) = \{\theta : lfp(T_{\mathcal{U}})_u \text{ satisfies } G\theta\}$.*

Eliminating syntactic inheritance

This and the next subsections show that the types of inheritance that have been studied in this paper are at most a programming convenience and do not add to the power of Horn clause logic. They can both be eliminated, transforming a given inheritance system to an equivalent ordinary Horn clause logic program. This result will then be used to establish the equivalence between the operational and the declarative semantics of inheritance systems. We start in this subsection by eliminating syntactic inheritance.

Given a signature $\Sigma = (F, P, (R_u, D_u)_{u \in U})$ and an inheritance system $\mathcal{U}$, consider the new signature $\overline{\Sigma} = (F, P, (R_u, \emptyset)_{u \in U})$ in which the set D_u of predicate symbols associated with syntactic inheritance have been eliminated. Let $\overline{\mathcal{U}}$ be the inheritance system for $\overline{\Sigma}$ obtained from $\mathcal{U}$ by replacing every unit $u : C_u$ by $u : \overline{C}_u$, where $\overline{C}_u$ is the set of all clauses available in u in the system $\mathcal{U}$.

Note that in the new system $\overline{\mathcal{U}}$ there is no need for syntactic inheritance since the clauses inherited by u in $\mathcal{U}$ are now part of the clauses in the unit. Thus it is not surprising to find that the two systems are equivalent, in the sense made precise by the following proposition.

Proposition 6 $\mathcal{U}$ and $\overline{\mathcal{U}}$ have exactly the same interpretations and models. Furthermore, $\vdash_{\mathcal{U},u} G[\theta]$ if and only if $\vdash_{\overline{\mathcal{U}},u} G[\theta]$ for all $\mathcal{U}, u, G$. As a consequence, $O_{\mathcal{U},u}(G) = O_{\overline{\mathcal{U}},u}(G)$ and $D_{\mathcal{U},u}(G) = D_{\overline{\mathcal{U}},u}(G)$, that is $\mathcal{U}$ and $\overline{\mathcal{U}}$ are equivalent from the point of view of both the operational and the declarative semantics.

Eliminating semantic inheritance

We now show how semantic inheritance can also be eliminated in a way that preserves the operational and the declarative semantics of the original inheritance system. We assume given a signature $\Sigma = (F, P, (R_u, \emptyset)_{u \in U})$, already disallowing syntactic inheritance, and define a new signature $\Sigma^* = (F, P^*, (\emptyset, \emptyset)_{u \in U})$, based on a new set P^* of predicate symbols, from which semantic inheritance has also been eliminated. Next, for any inheritance system $\mathcal{U}$ over Σ we show how to build an equivalent inheritance system $\mathcal{U}^*$ over Σ^*.

Each new predicate symbol is obtained by concatenating sequences of unit names and old predicate symbols:

$$P^* = P \cup \{v_1 \cdots v_n p : v_1, \ldots, v_n \in U, v_1 < \cdots < v_n \ (n > 0), p \in P\}.$$

The idea is that if $p \in R_v$ and $v < w$ then the predicate symbol wp may be used in v to simulate the predicate p in w. If also $p \in R_u$ and $u < v$, vwp may be used in u to simulate p in w, and so on. In defining $\mathcal{U}^*$ we must make sure that each u contains clauses for the new predicate symbols like vwp, defining the predicate that u inherits from w through v in $\mathcal{U}$. We need an auxiliary function $\Pi_v : P^* \to P^*$ prefixing every new predicate symbol p with $v \in U$, that is $\Pi_v(p) = vp$. This function can be extended in the obvious way to atomic formulæ, goals, clauses and sets of clauses.

$\mathcal{U}^*$ is the set of all units $u : C_u^*$ where C_u^* is defined from C_u as follows:

$$C_u^* = C_u \cup C_u^R \cup \bigcup_{u < v} \Pi_v(C_v^*).$$

The set C_u is just the set of clauses of the original unit in $\mathcal{U}$. The set C_u^R is defined by

$$C_u^R = \{ \quad p(X_1, \ldots, X_n) \leftarrow vp(X_1, \ldots, X_n) :$$
$$p/n \in R_u, \, u < v, \, X_1, \ldots, X_n \text{ distinct variables} \quad \}.$$

These clauses extend the original predicates with the predicates that simulate relational inheritance. The last set is an encoding of the definitions of the predicates that may be relationally inherited so that they may be used directly in u.

It is not difficult to verify that $\mathcal{U}$ and $\overline{\mathcal{U}}$ are equivalent from the point of view of the operational semantics, as stated in the next result.

Proposition 7 *For every $u \in U$ and every goal G over P (and therefore over P^*), $\vdash_{\mathcal{U},u} G[\theta]$ if and only if $\vdash_{\mathcal{U}^-,u} G[\theta]$, hence $O_{\mathcal{U},u}(G) = O_{\mathcal{U}^-,u}(G)$.*

The equivalence from the point of view of the declarative semantics is also easy to establish.

Proposition 8 *The mapping $I \mapsto I^*$ is an order-preserving bijection between models $I = (I_u)_{u \in U}$ of $\mathcal{U}$ and models $I^* = (I_u^*)_{u \in U}$ of $\mathcal{U}^*$, where each I_u^* is given by*

$$I_u^* = I_u \cup \bigcup_{u < v} \Pi_v(I_v^*).$$

Conversely, I is uniquely determined from I^* by the formula $I_u = I_u^* \lceil P$ for every $u \in U$. Thus for every $u \in U$ and every goal G over P, I_u satisfies G if and only if I_u^* satisfies G, so that $D_{\mathcal{U},u}(G) = D_{\mathcal{U}^-,u}(G)$.

We are now in a position to state and prove the equivalence between the operational and the declarative semantics of inheritance systems. As a matter of notation, given a set Θ of substitutions let $\Theta^\dagger$ denote the set of substitutions of the form $\theta\sigma$ where $\theta \in \Theta$ and σ is an arbitrary substitution.

Theorem 9 *Let $\mathcal{U}$ be an inheritance system over a signature Σ. For every goal G, unit name u and substitution σ, $\mathcal{U} \models_u G\sigma$ if and only if $\vdash_{\mathcal{U},u} G[\theta]$ for some θ more general then σ. In other words, $D_{\mathcal{U},u}(G) = O_{\mathcal{U},u}(G)^\dagger$.*

Proof: We have $\mathcal{U} \models_u G\sigma$ if and only if $M_{\mathcal{U},u}$ satisfies $G\sigma$, if and only if $M_{\mathcal{U},u}^*$ satisfies $G\sigma$. Since the units in the inheritance system $\overline{\mathcal{U}}^*$ are ordinary Horn clause programs, by a result due to Clark (see [Cla 79, Llo 87]) it follows that there exists a substitution θ more general than σ such that $\vdash_{\overline{\mathcal{U}}^*,u} G[\theta]$. By the equivalence results on the elimination of syntactic and semantic inheritance, this is firstly equivalent to $\vdash_{\overline{\mathcal{U}},u} G[\theta]$, and then to $\vdash_{\mathcal{U},u} G[\theta]$, as desired. □

Conclusions and further work

We have shown that the common inheritance notions of other languages can be naturally incorporated into a logic programming language that provides for inheritance control at the predicate level. Furthermore, we have shown that the inheritance phenomena can in this way be enlightened by direct semantic characterizations of the operational, declarative and fixed point styles, which as should befit a logic programming framework we have proven equivalent. This very proof, being carried out through simple reductions of inheritance systems to regular logic programs without inheritance, suggests that inheritance is in fact a convenience carrying no major conceptual role.

In terms of further work we intend to study an alternative language where inheritance is expressed by annotating not the "caller" but the "code". This will correspond to the use of the feature of 'self' annotations in some inheritance languages (for example [McC 88]) and of a dual concept. The declarative semantics for this language will have to be develop differently from that presented here, and will be based on associating subsets of the Herbrand base to *pairs* of unit names in the hierarchical ordering.

Acknowledgements

We thank the support of Esprit BRA 3020 "Integration", Instituto Nacional de Investigação Científica, and Junta Nacional de Investigação Científica e Tecnológica.

References

[A-K 86]   H. Aït-Kaci, R. Nasr. LOGIN: A logic programming language with built-in inheritance. *J. Logic Programming*, vol.3, no.3, 1986.

[Cla 79]   K.L. Clark. *Predicate Logic as a Computational Formalism*. Research Report Doc. 79/59, Department of Computing, Imperial College, 1979.

[Gal 86]   H. Gallaire. Merging objects and logic programming: relational semantics. *Proc. AAAI-86*, Philadelphia, PA, 1986.

[Kau Gru 86] H. Kauffman, A. Grumbach. MULTILOG: MULTIple worlds in LOGic Programming. *Proc. ECAI-86*, North-Holland, 1986.

[Llo 87]   J.W. Lloyd. *Foundations of Logic Programming*. Second edition, Springer-Verlag, Berlin, 1987.

[McC 88]   F. McCabe. *Logic and objects*. Imperial College, London, 1988.

[Mel 89]   P. Mello. Inheritance as a Combination of Horn Clause Theories. *Inheritance Hierarchies in Knowledge Representation*, J. Wiley and Sons, 1989.

[Mil 89]   D. Miller. A Logical Analysis of Modules in Logic Programming. *Journal of Logic Programming*, Vol. 6, pp. 79-108, 1989.

[Mon Por 89] L. Monteiro, A. Porto. Contextual Logic Programming. *Logic Programming, Proc. 6th International Conference*, eds. G. Levi and M. Martelli, MIT Press, Cambridge, MA, 1989.

[Mon Por 90] L. Monteiro, A. Porto. A Tranformational View of Inheritance in Logic Programming. *Logic Programming, Proc. 7th International Conference*, eds. P. Szeredi and D. H. D. Warren, MIT Press, Cambridge, MA, 1990.

[O'K 85] R. O'Keefe. Towards an Algebra for Constructing Logic Programs. *Proc. 1985 Symposium on Logic Programming*, IEEE Computer Society Press, 1985.

[Zan 84] C. Zaniolo. Object oriented programming in Prolog. *Proc. International Symposium on Logic Programming*, IEEE Press, 1984.

Implementation

A survey of the implementations of narrowing*

P.H. Cheong   L. Fribourg

LIENS, URA 1327 du CNRS
45, rue d'Ulm, 75005 Paris, FRANCE
e-mail: {cheong,fribourg}@dmi.ens.fr

1   Introduction

Recently, there has been a lot of interest in the integration of functional programming and logic programming. A natural framework would be to consider a program as a conditional term rewriting system, with conditional narrowing as the goal-solving mechanism. If EQLOG [14] is one of the earliest proposals in that direction, many others have since then followed the trend, including SLOG [10], K-LEAF [12], ALF [15], BABEL [18] and many others.

The relative popularity of narrowing can be attributed to its ambivalence, for it extends not only the basic computational mechanism of functional languages but also that of logic languages. Some critics may perhaps ask: is narrowing too powerful to be feasible in practice? To implement narrowing efficiently is certainly quite a difficult task, but a worth-while one, not only for the field of functional logic programming, but also for other closely related areas like algebraic programming, constraint logic programming, theorem proving, etc. Moreover, recent breakthroughs have shown that, with suitable restrictions and refinements, narrowing can be implemented as efficiently as—and, for some problems, even more efficiently than—SLD-resolution.

It is our intention here to provide a state-of-the-art in the field. By this, we hope to understand how narrowing can be made efficient and, having this in mind, it seems rather natural to give priority to ideas than to technical details, which are otherwise contained in the specific references. We shall also limit ourselves to the domain of functional logic programming.

---

*This work has been partially supported by ESPRIT project BRA 3020.

2 Strategy refinements

A very important ingredient in an efficient narrowing implementation is a suitable strategy refinement, for narrowing in general has a high degree of don't-know nondeterminism. Except for a few implementations, like [6] and [22], all practical implementations impose some kind of strategy refinement.

Actually, the inherent inefficiency of narrowing stems from two principal sources of don't-know nondeterminism, namely, (1) the choice of the redex, and (2) the choice of the rewrite rule. Strategy refinements consist then in reducing some don't-know choices to don't-care choices.

Before we proceed to examine some of the existing proposals, some comments are in order:

- Not all arbitrary refinements are admissible, since completeness is not necessarily preserved. Completeness is an important requirement and hence we are mainly interested in strategies that possess some rigorous completeness result.

- Although many types of refinements are proposed, it is hard and certainly unfair to compare their merits in absolute terms, since all depends on the types of problems we want to express and solve. Moreover, some refinements are not intended to be used alone, but in conjunction with others.

- It seems better to use a *good* narrowing strategy which has an easy implementation than a *better* strategy which requires a highly complex implementation. On the one hand, this is in keeping with the RISC philosophy. On the other hand, our experience is that efficient narrowing implementations are those that can be implemented, with little or no extension, on classical abstract machines for functional or logic languages. For these reasons, we shall mainly favor strategies that have straightforward implementation.[1]

2.1 Basic narrowing

Basic narrowing goes back to Hullot [17]. The idea is to limit narrowing to subterms that are not introduced by instantiation, therefore preferring inner redexes to outer redexes (i.e. a kind of "inner-before-outer" strategy). Basic narrowing is seldom used alone, and further restrictions are usually imposed.

---

[1]More complex strategies are interesting in themselves, and they should find more a favorable audience in other areas, such as theorem proving.

For instance, leftmost-innermost basic narrowing, which is used in ALF, may be viewed as a further refinement of basic narrowing.

The completeness of basic narrowing has been studied by various authors, namely, [17] in the unconditional context, [16] and [13] in the conditional context; unconditional basic narrowing has also been studied in conjunction with rewriting [23], but wrt the initial semantics. These results are summarized as follows:

- Basic narrowing is complete for canonical term rewriting systems (or TRS for short).

- Basic narrowing is complete for level-canonical conditional term rewriting systems (or CTRS for short). Moreover, extra-variables are allowed in the conditions.

Some counter-results have recently been given by [20]:

- Basic narrowing is not complete wrt normalizable solutions for weakly-canonical TRS.

- Basic narrowing is not complete for canonical CTRS without extra-variables. This refutes a previous claim in [16].

Basic narrowing is interesting because simple implementation exists in practice. One method consists in separating a goal into a skeleton part and an environment part, so that narrowing is only performed on the skeleton part [15].

2.2 Normalized narrowing

Normalized narrowing can be traced back to [9]. The idea is to perform a normalization step after each narrowing step, therefore enforcing the priority of determinate computations over nondeterminate ones.

It has often been remarked that normalized narrowing can turn an infinite narrowing tree into a finite one [7, 10]. However, completeness of normalized narrowing is hard to obtain, especially when it is used in conjunction with the basic strategy. In general, it may be necessary to move the terms from the environment part to the skeleton part. However, under the initial semantics,[2] it has been shown that these terms can be safely moved back to the environment part [23]. It remains to check whether this result extends to the conditional case.

---

[2]I.e., one is mainly interested in ground solutions.

But the conditional case also presents an additional difficulty, since reducibility is then undecidable. This means that, unless strong restrictions are imposed, there is no way to ensure the termination of the normalization step. Nontermination would delay the next narrowing step indefinitely, hence leading to incompleteness. A reasonable compromise in this case would consist in normalizing only via the *unconditional* rules.

2.3 Selection narrowing

Selection narrowing has been introduced in two different contexts, namely, in the flattening context [2] and also in the ordinary term context [24, 8]. We examine these two variants in order.

Literal-selection narrowing

In this variant, programs and goals are considered as syntactic sugar for their flat form, and selection narrowing (we shall call this literal-selection narrowing) is simply taken to be SLD-resolution on the flat form. The flat form can be obtained by a process commonly known as flattening [26], which consists in replacing functional nestings by logical conjunction. For instance, flattening the program

$$
\begin{aligned}
0 + y &= y \\
s(x) + y &= s(x + y)
\end{aligned}
$$

yields

$$
\begin{aligned}
x &= x \\
0 + y &= y \\
s(x) + y &= s(z) \leftarrow x + y = z
\end{aligned}
$$

Note that the reflexive axiom $x = x$ has been added. Although the above program is constructor-based, flattening can actually be applied to any program [2].

Literal-selection narrowing is interesting due to the following reasons.

- There already exists efficient implementations of SLD-resolution and more efficient ones are likely to be developed in the future.

- Terms are shared and not duplicated, in the sense that when a term is narrowed, all its copies are also simultaneously narrowed to the same term. Although it is possible to introduce term sharing without recourse to flattening, the formal treatment involved would otherwise be quite tedious and clumsy.

- Literal-selection narrowing can be considered a refinement over basic narrowing [2]. In fact, in terms of search space, the former is more efficient than the latter, although they are strictly equivalent in terms of completeness (i.e. the former is complete under the same conditions as the latter).

However, there are also some inconveniences:

- The original functional dependency among the data is now present in a nontrivial partial ordering on literals, hence making it harder to exploit.

- A new variable is introduced for each nested expression. This means the requirement of more runtime space and garbage-collection.

In SLD-resolution, any literal-selection strategy can be arbitrary chosen. Of special interests are the innermost strategy[3] and the outermost strategy, which mimic the strict and lazy evaluation strategies known from functional programming languages. The innermost strategy can be simply implemented as the leftmost computation rule of Prolog. The outermost strategy however requires a dynamic computation rule that is based on the (functional) partial ordering on literals [12].

Redex-selection narrowing

In this variant, the idea is to select, at each step, only a redex for narrowing, while discarding other choices of redex (we shall call this redex-selection narrowing). Redex-selection narrowing is different from literal-selection narrowing, as the following points show:

- Terms are not shared in redex-selection narrowing. As such, it is sometimes less efficient than basic narrowing. This is especially the case when an outermost redex-selection strategy is used and when there are rules that duplicate variables on the right-hand sides.

- Redex-selection narrowing is less complete than literal-selection narrowing.

The following example, due to You [28], shows the incompleteness of innermost and outermost redex-selection narrowing for canonical TRS. Consider

$$P = \{f(y, a) = true, f(c, b) = true, g(b) = c\}$$

---

[3]Strictly speaking, two innermost strategies are possible: one that use the reflexive axiom and one that does not. The latter is more efficient and its completeness can be established with the help of some stronger conditions [10].

The program P is canonical, but innermost narrowing of $f(g(x), x)$ to *true* yields the binding $\{x/b\}$, whereas outermost narrowing yields $\{x/a\}$. The innermost and the outermost strategies yield uncompared results and hence neither is complete.

Completeness of redex-selection narrowing has been studied by [24] and [8]. The latter has shown how a simple transformation of the given rewriting system can restore completeness in some cases. The problem with the previous example can be attributed to the fact that the first and the second f-rule do not demand the evaluation of the first argument at the same time. However, simply transforming the problem P into

$$P' = \{f(y, a) = true, f(y, b) = h(y), g(b) = c, h(c) = true\}$$

allows to restore completeness: we can verify that outermost narrowing of $f(g(x), x)$ to *true* yields the bindings $\{x/a\}$ and $\{x/b\}$.

Hence, [8] suggested the transformation of programs into some homogeneous form, in order to guarantee the completeness of redex-selection narrowing. It is of interest to note that the transformation into homogeneous form is actually implicit in the flattening approach. Also, lazy narrowing [25] and outer narrowing [28] can be understood as outermost redex-selection narrowing, modulo the transformation into homogeneous form.

2.4 Other refinements

Another simple refinement is the idea of determinate computations [19], which consists in detecting if a narrowing step is indeed a rewriting step and, if so, prunes all don't know choices introduced during that step. The idea of determinate computations is closely related to that of normalized narrowing. The essential difference is that the former prunes the search space *after* each narrowing step, whereas the latter prunes the search space *before* each narrowing step. Also, the former simulates rewriting at a particular redex, whereas the latter rewrites at all possible redexes.

In practice, this refinement is easy to implement on top of selection narrowing, and its correctness is immediate for any nonambiguous and left-linear CTRS.

3 Semantic Restrictions

The difficulty of ensuring completeness of narrowing is a result of the difficulty of handling classical equality. This has motivated many authors to consider semantic restrictions to classical equality, for which complete and efficient implementations may be obtained more easily. For instance, [23] used the initial semantics approach and [29] used a weaker notion of equality.

But it is natural in the context of functional logic programming to consider the restriction to theories with constructors. The advantages to this approach are:

- The declarative semantics can be defined in terms of Herbrand models, similarly to ordinary logic programs.

- Completeness can be achieved with less conditions, even in absence of the termination property. For instance, lazy narrowing is complete for a left-linear and nonambiguous CTRS [12, 18] that use the constructor-equality in the conditions.

- The implementation of narrowing can be simplified and made more efficient, thanks to the syntactic distinction between reducibles and canonicals.

Note that, functional logic languages like ALF, BABEL, K-LEAF and SLOG all impose the constructor-discipline, in contrast to EQLOG which can be better qualified as an equational logic language.

4   WAM-based implementations of narrowing

The Warren Abstract Machine (WAM) [27] is definitely the state-of-the-art for implementing Prolog compilers, and its remarkable design, especially regarding the handling of unification and nondeterminism, has influenced and inspired in many ways the design of narrowing implementations.

One obvious possibility is to implement narrowing directly on a WAM. The necessary extension concerns the support of nested expressions, which can be obtained for free if the flattening approach is used. It is known that, after flattening, the innermost strategy of narrowing can be simulated by the leftmost computation rule known from Prolog. Hence, WAM can be used to implement innermost narrowing without any extension.

The lazy strategy, however, requires an outermost computation rule, which is used for instance in K-LEAF [12]. The dynamic nature of the outermost rule has motivated an extension of WAM, called K-WAM [1], that is specially tailored for it. But it is also possible to compile the program in such a way that the leftmost rule directly simulates the outermost rule [4]. Hence, WAM can also be used to implement lazy narrowing without any extension.

A disadvantage with the flattening approach is that rewriting cannot be easily simulated by SLD-resolution. This is mainly due to the possible deletion of terms by rewrite rules. For example, the expression $0 \times (y+z) = 0$ is reduced to $0 = 0$ using the rule $0 \times x = 0$, while its flat form $y + z = w \& 0 \times w = 0$ is transformed to $y + z = w$ by SLD-resolution with $0 \times x = 0$. This has motivated a weaker notion of rewriting, called simplification [11], which seems to be more suited to the flat form. [5] contains the account of an efficient integration of simplification into Prolog.

In contrast, the A-WAM machine [15] does not handle nested expressions by flattening. Instead, narrowing redexes are kept on a new stack called the occurrence stack. (An auxiliary stack is later added for further optimizations.) A-WAM implements the leftmost-innermost basic narrowing strategy. Moreover, conditional normalization is performed (on the leftmost atom) after each narrowing step.

5 Implementations of narrowing based on functional machines

The basic computational mechanism of functional languages is rewriting, for which powerful implementation techniques (graph reduction machines, stack reduction machines, etc) have also been largely explored and developed. It is hence an attractive idea to implement narrowing on functional abstract machines. The necessary extensions are:

1. replacing pattern matching by unification, and

2. handling nondeterminism.

Note that (1) implies the use of logical variables and (2) the use of choice points and a trail. The good performance of the WAM strongly suggests that these extensions can be efficiently integrated into a functional abstract machine.

Several machines have now appeared and they all implement lazy narrowing. These are the JUMP machine [3], the LBAM machine [21] and the machine in [19], the last two being designed for the BABEL language. The LBAM is a graph-based machine, whereas the other two are stack-based. However, JUMP seems to have the simpliest design, requiring only a small instruction set. Both JUMP and the machine in [19] support the dynamic detection of determinate computations, and hence support pure functional reductions efficiently.

It is worthy to note that, in these machines, clauses are first transformed to homogeneous form, and lazy narrowing is then implemented as the leftmost-outermost (redex-selection) strategy. The transformation to homogeneous form generally requires the introduction of new functions, but that is avoided in the JUMP machine by using machine instructions that dynamically allocates choice points.

The techniques used in these machines to handle unification and backtracking are otherwise quite similar to the WAM. Their performance can be further improved if optimizations like clause indexing or classification of variables are fully implemented. Clause indexing is an essential tool to ease the burden of handling backtracking, and classification of variables is particularly important for reducing the number of memory accesses.

6 Final remarks

Although narrowing is inefficient in general, efficient implementations may be obtained when we restrict to the domain of functional logic programming. This is mainly due to the fact that suitable strategy refinements, semantic restrictions, as well as powerful implementation techniques are available in that particular context.

Preliminary experiments have been conducted by various authors to demonstrate the feasibility of narrowing [1, 15], and the available benchmarks indicate that narrowing compares very favorably with SLD-resolution.

Acknowledgements

We would like to thank Hendrick Lock for his helpful comments on an earlier draft of this paper.

References

[1] P.G. Bosco, C. Cecchi, and C. Moiso. An extension of WAM for K-LEAF. In *Proceedings of the 6th International Conference on Logic Programming, Lisboa*, pages 318–333, 1989.

[2] P.G. Bosco, E. Giovannetti, and G. Moiso. Refined strategies for semantic unification. In *TAPSOFT'87, LNCS 150*, pages 276–290, 1987.

[3] M.M.T. Chakravarty and H.C.R. Lock. The implementation of lazy narrowing. *To appear in Proceedings of PLILP'91, LNCS*, 1991.

[4] P.H. Cheong. Compiling lazy narrowing into prolog. Technical Report 25, LIENS, 1990. To appear in *Journal of New Generation Computing*.

[5] P.H. Cheong and L. Fribourg. Efficient integration of simplification into prolog. Technical Report 26, LIENS, 1990. To appear in *proceedings of PLILP'91*, LNCS.

[6] N. Dershowitz and A. Josephson. An implementation of narrowing, the RITE way. In *Proceedings of the IEEE Symposium on Logic Programming, Salt Lake City*, pages 187–197, 1986.

[7] N. Dershowitz and D.A. Plaisted. Logic programming cum applicative programming. In *Proceedings of the IEEE Symposium on Logic Programming, Boston*, pages 54–66, 1985.

[8] R. Echahed. On completeness of narrowing strategies. In *Proceedings of CAAP 88, LNCS 299*, pages 89–101, 1988.

[9] M. Fay. First-order unification in an equational theory. In *Proceedings of the 4th workshop on Automated Deduction*, 1979.

[10] L. Fribourg. SLOG: A logic programming language interpreter based on clausal superposition and rewriting. In *Proceedings of the IEEE Symposium on Logic Programming, Boston*, pages 172–184, 1985.

[11] L. Fribourg. Prolog with simplification. In K. Fuchi and M. Nivat, editors, *Programming of future generation computers*, pages 161–183. Elsevier Science Publishers B.V. (North Holland), 1988.

[12] E. Giovannetti, G. Levi, C. Moiso, and C. Palamidessi. Kernel LEAF: a logic plus functional language. *Journal of Computer and System Sciences*, 42, pages 139–185, 1991.

[13] E. Giovannetti and C. Moiso. A completeness result for E-unification algorithms based on conditional narrowing. In *Foundations of Logic and Functional Programming, LNCS 306*, pages 318–334, 1987.

[14] J. Goguen and J. Meseguer. EQLOG: equality, types and generic modules for logic programming. In D. DeGroot and G. Lindstrom, editors, *Functional and Logic Programming*, pages 295–363. Prentice-Hall, 1986.

[15] M. Hanus. Compiling logic programs with equality. In *PLILP'90, LNCS 456*, pages 387–401, 1990.

[16] S. Hölldobler. From paramodulation to narrowing. In *Proceedings of the 5th International Conference on Logic Programming, Seattle*, pages 327–342, 1988.

[17] J.M. Hullot. Canonical forms and unification. In *Proceedings of the 5th Conference on Automated Deduction, LNCS 87*, pages 318–334, 1980.

[18] H. Kuchen, R. Loogen, J.J. Moreno, and M. Rodríguez. Graph-based implementation of a functional logic language. In *Proceedings of ESOP'90, LNCS 432*, pages 271–290, 1990.

[19] R. Loogen. From reduction machines to narrowing machines. In *Proceedings of TAPSOFT'91, LNCS 494*, pages 438–457, 1991.

[20] Aart. Middletorp. Private communication, 1991.

[21] J.J. Moreno, H. Kuchen, R. Loogen, and M. Rodríguez. Lazy narrowing in a graph machine. In *Algebraic and Logic Programming, LNCS 463*, pages 298–317, 1990.

[22] A. Mück. The compilation of narrowing. In *Proceedings of PLILP'90, LNCS 456*, pages 16–29, 1990.

[23] W. Nutt, P. Réty, and G. Smolka. Basic narrowing revisited. *Journal of Symbolic Computation*, 7, pages 295–317, 1989.

[24] P. Padawitz1. Strategy controlled reduction and narrowing. In *Proceedings of RTA'87, Bordeaux, LNCS 256*, pages 242–255, 1987.

[25] U.S. Reddy. Narrowing as the operational semantics of functional languages. In *Proceedings of the IEEE Symposium on Logic Programming, Boston*, pages 138–151, 1985.

[26] M.H. van Emdem and K. Yukawa. Logic programming with equations. *Journal of Logic Programming*, 4, pages 265–288, 1987.

[27] D.H.D. Warren. An abstract Prolog instruction set. Technical Report 309, SRI International, 1983.

[28] Y.H. You. Enumerating outer narrowing derivations for constructor-based term rewriting systems. *Journal of Symbolic Computation*, 7, pages 319–343, 1989.

[29] Y.H. You. Unification modulo an equality theory for equational logic programming. *Journal of Computer and System Sciences*, 42, pages 54–75, 1991.

A Systematic Method for Designing Abstract Narrowing Machines

Hendrik C.R. Lock

Forschungstelle der GMD an der Universität Karlsruhe
Vincenz-Prießnitz-Str. 1, 75 Karlsruhe 1, FRG

Abstract

In this paper we present a first step towards a general implementation technique for narrowing using abstract machines as a means to structure the mapping of functional logic languages to (sequential) target machines. A framework is given for describing, designing and classifying abstract machines. Its core is a design space over basic concepts which have been extracted from existing machines. The design of an abstract machine is obtained by combining these basic concepts. As a result, we are able to demonstrate the design of a machine which supports narrowing, reduction, lazy and innermost strategies, and higher order functional features.

1 Introduction

Narrowing has become established as the operational model of functional logic programming languages. Despite various language implementations no general technique for implementing narrowing exists which is language independent and which covers different evaluation strategies. This paper contributes to such a general technique.

A functional logic program consists of a set of rewrite rules and a main expression. Narrowing transforms the main expression to a normal form. Thereby, each narrowing step selects some subexpression and a rewrite rule. If a syntactic unifier (a substitution) exists which makes the subexpression and the head of the selected rule equal, this subexpression is replaced by the body of the rule. Then, the unifier is applied to the result expression.

It is established that narrowing subsumes SLD-resolution and reduction. This suggests that a narrowing machine can be modeled by means of those machine concepts which appear in the implementation of these two operational models. Following this idea, we have developed a novel framework which comprises a design space over basic concepts whose combination provides a systematic method to design machines. Furthermore, the framework is a means to describe machines in a uniform way and to classify existing machines.

To achieve independence from functional logic source languages we provide a simple language $\mathcal{L}_0$. It captures their essential operational features and makes them explicit. $\mathcal{L}_0$ serves as an intermediate level in the translation of languages to machines.

The contributions of this paper are $\mathcal{L}_0$, the design space, the systematic development of a narrowing machine in this framework, and a classification of a selection of existing machines. Furthermore, a relation to the conventional stack-based architecture is established which has great importance for an efficient implementation on stock hardware.

We have greatly benefited from a wealth of work on abstract machines. In particular, our work incorporates Meijer's classification of functional machines [Mei88]. The language $\mathcal{L}_0$ is an enriched form of Paterson's non-deterministic λ-calculus [Pat90] with the difference that $\mathcal{L}_0$ directly supports translation techniques. Recently, Meijer has developed a formal framework based on denotational semantics in which it is possible to derive correct denotational descriptions of abstract machines [Mei92]. A formal derivation of the backtracking part of the WAM [War83] is given there. Where Meijer's interest is the correctness, our approach is oriented towards a detailed operational description and realization of the machine concepts. To achieve compact and precise machine specifications, we used the ideas and notation of Osborne's *Update Schemes* [Osb91].

The second section briefly introduces the intermediate language $\mathcal{L}_0$; section three discusses basic machine concepts and the design of abstract machines, and section four gives a classification of a selection of abstract machines.

2 The Intermediate Language $\mathcal{L}_0$

$\mathcal{L}_0$ is a simple language capturing the essential features of functional logic languages and serving as an intermediate stage in the implementation to which these source languages can be translated. $\mathcal{L}_0$ extends the usual notation of the λ-calculus by a choice operator $\llbracket$ to make the choice between rewrite rules explicit, a guard $\rightarrow$ which behaves as a conditional, a conjunction $\wedge$ with the usual meaning, $\exists x$ in order to denote logical variables, and an equality operator $\doteq$ which makes unification steps explicit.

Let Σ_f, Σ_c and V be disjoint alphabets of function symbols, constructors and variables, further, *arity* s maps an identifier $s \in \Sigma_f \cup \Sigma_c$ to its arity. In the following sections, $f, g, \ldots$ denote function symbols, $c, d, \ldots$ constructors, and $x, y, \ldots$ variables. $\mathcal{L}_0$ is defined by:

$$
\begin{aligned}
program \quad &::= \quad (f = exp)^* \ exp \\
exp \quad &::= \quad \lambda x.exp \mid \exists x.exp \mid exp \ \llbracket \ exp \mid exp \ exp \mid c \mid f \mid x \mid \\
&\qquad gexp \rightarrow exp \mid \text{FAIL} \mid \text{TRUE} \mid \text{strict } exp \mid \text{shared } exp \\
gexp \quad &::= \quad exp \doteq pat \mid gexp \wedge gexp \\
pat \quad &::= \quad c \ x_1 \ .. \ x_n \qquad \text{if } arity \ c = n
\end{aligned}
$$

$\mathcal{L}_0$'s operational semantics is based on narrowing. Its formal specification is beyond the scope of this paper, but can be found in [Loc91]. It comprises the following ideas: expression are evaluated in normal order (call-by-need). Arguments annotated by strict are evaluated before the application; this corresponds to call-by-value. Applicative order reduction (call-by-value) is obtained when all arguments are annotated by strict. As usual, the application of a lambda abstraction is reduced to an instance of the body of the abstraction in which all occurrences of the formal parameter are substituted by the argument. When the argument is annotated by shared, then the occurrences of the formal parameter are replaced by the reference to the argument; hence, it becomes shared. When this argument once becomes evaluated, the reference will point to its result. By this means lazy evaluation can be established which is explained as normal order reduction with sharing.

Furthermore, a guarded expression $c \rightarrow e$ expresses how the selection of e depends on the success of a condition c. Usually, c encodes an unification operation which is composed of equations using $\doteq$ and $\wedge$. *TRUE* and *FAIL* are used to indicate success and failure of these conditions. A failure propagates through conjunctions and guards to the next (innermost) choice operator with the effect that this choice expression is reduced to its second alternative.

Different language approaches can be translated to $\mathcal{L}_0$, examples are functional programs, general term rewriting systems and Horn logic programs. This topic is beyond the intention of this paper and discussed in [Loc91]. We briefly illustrate how to translate text source to $\mathcal{L}_0$:

```
concat nil R          = R
concat (cons X L) R = cons X (concat L R)
```

$$concat = \lambda p_1.\lambda p_1. \quad (p_1 \doteq nil \wedge p_2 \doteq r) \rightarrow r$$
$$\llbracket \ ((\ p_1 \doteq (cons \ z_1 \ z_2) \wedge z_1 \doteq x \wedge z_2 \doteq l \wedge p_2 \doteq r) \rightarrow cons \ x \ (concat \ l \ r))$$

3 The Design Space

The idea of the design space is relating operational features of functional logic languages to basic machine concepts, and further, constructing abstract machines from their combination. A machine concept is an abstract data type that provides a number of instructions for the operations on the data structure. The translation of $\mathcal{L}_0$ to these instructions establishes the relation between operational features (which are made explicit in $\mathcal{L}_0$) and machine concepts.

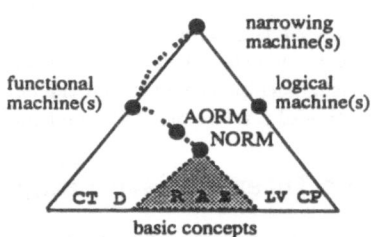

The design space is illustrated as a lattice with the shape of a triangle that represents all possible combinations of machine concepts. The above triangle serves as a guideline for the design and classification of machines in the remainder of this paper.

Our starting point in the triangle will be a machine supporting a functional subset of $\mathcal{L}_0$ with normal order reduction. This machine (NORM) is constituted by combining the basic concepts *compiled graph reduction, registers ($\mathcal{R}$), argument stack ($\mathcal{A}$), and environments ($\mathcal{E}$)*. From there we walk through the triangle towards the top by subsequently adding new concepts to the previous machines, thus supporting larger subsets of $\mathcal{L}_0$. The next machine (AORM) is obtained by adding a *dump stack ($\mathcal{D}$)* that additionally supports applicative order reduction. The development of functional machines is completed by means of the basic concept *closure technique ($\mathcal{CT}$)*; the resulting machine supports all functional features, including higher order functions and lazy evaluation. From this point we start to add logical concepts, such as the logical variable ($\mathcal{LV}$), which can be already realized by $\mathcal{CT}$, and a choice point technique ($\mathcal{CP}$) which supports backtracking. Then, we will have found a narrowing machine at the top of the design space which integrates all introduced basic concepts and which supports $\mathcal{L}_0$ entirely. Taking different paths would lead to other machines, some of them being existing machines. We will address this topic in section 4.

The subsequent parts introduce a set of basic machine concepts and the design of the narrowing machine.

3.1 Pure graph reduction

"Graph reduction machine" (GRM) is a technical term for those abstract machines which operate on some graph representation of functional programs. Thereby, applicative expressions which consist of λ-abstractions, constants, variables and applications are represented by directed cyclic graphs. During reduction, expression trees are transformed to graphs. The purpose of graphs is to share the results of evaluation and hence to achieve lazy evaluation. Cycles are used to model recursion. The graph reduction machine continuously transforms a graph until a normal form is reached. A graph is said to be in normal form if no more transformation steps can be applied. The major transformation step is the reduction of an application, e.g. $\lambda x.e\ a$. This involves substituting the argument a for all occurrences of the formal parameter x in e. A comprehensive presentation of the design and implementation of graph reduction machines can be found in the text books [Pey87] and [FH88].

In our framework, this means to represent an $\mathcal{L}_0$-expression as a graph and to realize an interpreter that transforms the graph to its normal form. The interpreter would be a direct realization of the operational semantics of $\mathcal{L}_0$. This interpretive approach might be interesting for a parallel implementation, but is hopeless inefficient on sequential stock hardware.

3.2 Compiled graph reduction

The pure graph reduction machine is inefficient since it repeatedly traverses and interprets graph nodes. It is commonly accepted that compilation to linear code and its execution is superior to interpretation. To achieve efficiency we introduce the basic concepts *compiled graph reduction, registers, argument stack, environments,* and *dump stack.* A full discussion of the derivation of these basic concepts, starting from the pure interpretative machine, is given in [Loc91]. The relation between the pure GRM and the concepts is as follows:

In **compiled graph reduction**, the functional program is represented by code of the abstract machine. Graphs are created only when it is necessary to represent data terms or suspensions. The program is stored in a static code area at which a program counter $\mathcal{PC}$ points. The machine executes that code and maintains a code pointer $\mathcal{PC}$.

Registers $\mathcal{R}$ are used in order to store intermediate results. The idea is that each register denotes a unique value and that an unbound number of registers exists. Each register is assigned at most once a value, and this assignment is called its definition.

The **argument stack** $\mathcal{A}$ replaces the spine of application nodes which carries the arguments.

Environments $\mathcal{E}$ are the means to postpone the direct substitution of an argument for a formal parameters until it is definitely demanded by the evaluation. With that, it becomes unnecessary to construct instances of graphs which is an expensive operation.

The **dump stack** $\mathcal{D}$ provides a means to recursively start the machine on argument graphs and to return to the main evaluation afterwards.

Using these concepts eliminates the majority of interpretative steps and decreases the amount of generated graphs. The advantage of using registers is that the allocation phase of a compiler which associates a concrete memory location with a variable can be kept flexible. Hence, a real machine register, a location in the main store or on a stack can be assigned to a register. Furthermore, different registers can be mapped to the same location provided that their lifetimes do not overlap. Therefore, the allocation should not be specified as part of the abstract machine's operational semantics, as many author's did in the past, but it should be part of some final code generation phase.

3.2.1 The model of the compiled graph reduction machine

These basic concepts can be realized by distinct machine components, which we do, but it is also possible to merge the stacks thus obtaining different abstract machines.

The compiled graph reduction machine incorporates the following components: an argument stack, a dump stack, a heap, several registers pointing into them, and a store. The argument stack contains references to graph nodes in the heap, the dump stack saves registers, the store contains the registers, and the heap stores environments and graph nodes.

Notation   All stacks will be represented by lists, where [] denotes the empty stack and $v : s$ denotes a stack s with item v on its top. As usual, the following notational equivalences hold: $v : s \equiv [v|s]$, $a_1 : .. : a_n : [] \equiv [a_1, .., a_n]$ and $a : [] \equiv [a]$. The contence v of a register l is denoted by $l[v]$, and this should not be confused with a list. The register identifies an arbitrary, but unique location in the store. An environment is a structure of consecutive fields on the heap, and l being its reference, $l[v_0..v_n]$ denotes this structure and $l + i[v_i]$ denotes the contents of its i-th location. Sometimes l and $l + i$ are called *locators.* Again, this notation should not be confused with lists.

A machine specification, such as in 3.2-1, defines the operational semantics of instructions in term of state transition rules $l ==> r$ whose left hand side specifies a valid configuration (state) of the machine and the right hand side specifies the changes after the transition step.[1]

Below, we first present the translation of $\mathcal{L}_0$-expressions to abstract machine code and then we specify the operational semantics of the machine executing that code.

The translation The translation is defined in terms of compilation schemes $\mathcal{F}$, $\mathcal{C}$ and $\mathcal{B}$ which map $\mathcal{L}_0$-expressions to abstract machine code.

$$
\begin{array}{rcl}
\mathcal{F}[\![\,\cdot\,]\!] & :: & program \longrightarrow Code \\
\mathcal{C}[\![\,\cdot\,]\!] & :: & exp \;\; identifier \;\; \phi \;\; \tau \longrightarrow Code \\
\mathcal{B}[\![\,\cdot\,]\!] & :: & exp \;\; \phi \;\; \tau \longrightarrow Code
\end{array}
$$

The task of list ϕ is to map a variable to a location in an environment, and list τ assigns a variable to a register. Since a value may reside at the same time in an environment and in a register, its variable may appear in both ϕ and τ. If the pair (x, l) appears in ϕ (respectively τ) we write x in ϕ, and then it holds that $\phi(x) = l$ (resp. $\tau(x) = l$).

We start with translating a functional subset of $\mathcal{L}_0$ which does not allow partial applications. This translation will be extended in the following subsections in order to accept larger parts of $\mathcal{L}_0$; a solution to partial applications will be given in part 3.3. After the translation schemes we will give the precise meaning of the instructions. We define:

$$
\begin{array}{rcll}
\mathcal{F}[\![f = e]\!] & = & f[\; \mathcal{C}[\![e]\!]\; l\; [\,]\; [\,];\; ENTER\; l;\;] & \\
\mathcal{B}[\![c]\!]\; \phi\; \tau & = & TERM\; c;\; RET & \\
\mathcal{B}[\![f]\!]\; \phi\; \tau & = & ENTER\_F\; f & \\
\mathcal{B}[\![x]\!]\; \phi\; \tau & = & ENTER\; \tau(x); & \text{if } x \text{ in } \tau \\
\mathcal{B}[\![x]\!]\; \phi\; \tau & = & GET\_E\; \phi(x)\; l\; ; ENTER\; l & \text{if } x \text{ in } \phi \\
\mathcal{B}[\![\lambda x.e]\!]\; \phi\; \tau & = & POP\; l;\; \mathcal{B}[\![e]\!]\; \phi\; (x, l) : \tau & \\
\mathcal{B}[\![a\; b]\!]\; \phi\; \tau & = & \mathcal{C}[\![b]\!]\; l\; \phi\; \tau;\; PUSH\; l;\; \mathcal{B}[\![A]\!]\; \phi\; \tau & \\
\mathcal{C}[\![x]\!]\; l\; \phi\; \tau & = & l := \tau(x); & \text{if } x \text{ in } \tau \\
\mathcal{C}[\![x]\!]\; l\; \phi\; \tau & = & GET\_E\; \phi(x)\; l & \text{if } x \text{ in } \phi \\
\mathcal{C}[\![exp]\!]\; l\; \phi\; \tau & = & CopyCode;\; SUSP\; l\; \gamma\; \{\mathcal{B}[\![exp]\!]\; \phi'\; [\,]\} &
\end{array}
$$

Please note that the function symbol f has been overloaded with the label of f's code area.

CopyCode is a sequence of assignments which moves all (currently) free variables also appearing free in exp to registers. Let $\mathcal{FV}(exp) = \{y_1, .., y_n\}$ be the set of free variables in exp, and let $temp_i$ denote new registers: With that, we define:

$\phi' = [(y_1, 1), .., (y_n, n)]$
$\gamma = [l_1, .., l_n]$ where for $i \in \{1..n\} : (l_i = temp_i$ if y_i in $\phi)$ or $(l_i = \tau(y_i)$ if y_i in $\tau)$
CopyCode contains $GET\_E\; \phi(y_i)\; temp_i$ for each y_i if not y_i in τ

A normal order machine Let e be a first order closed expression, and *init* a code label defined by: $init[\mathcal{B}[\![e]\!]\; l\; [\,]\; [\,]\,]$. The machine is started with the $\mathcal{PC}$ set to *init* and with empty argument stack $\mathcal{A} := [\,]$, environment $\mathcal{E} := [\,]$, empty register store $\mathcal{R}$ and heap $\mathcal{HP}$.

---

[1]In the remainder of this paper, machine components can be omitted when they do not contribute to a specification.

Machine Specification 3.2-1: *Compiled graph reduction with* $\mathcal{A}, \mathcal{E}$

$\mathcal{PC}$	$\mathcal{E}$	$\mathcal{A}$	$\mathcal{R}$		$\mathcal{PC}$	$\mathcal{E}$	$\mathcal{A}$	$\mathcal{R}$
$x := y; c$			$y[v]$	$==>$	c			$x[v]$
$POP\ x; c$		$v : as$		$==>$	c		as	$x[v]$
$GET\_E\ j\ l; c$	e			$==>$	c	e		$e + j[v]\ l[v]$
$PUSH\ l; c$		as	$l[v]$	$==>$	c		$v : as$	
$TERM\ \ d; c$		as		$==>$	c		$v : []$	$v[\diamond d\ as]$
$ENTER\ \ x$		as	$x[l]\ \ l[\bullet\ c\ e]$	$==>$	c	e	as	
$ENTER\ \ x$		$[]$	$x[l]\ \ l[\diamond\ d\ e]$	$==>$	RET		$x : []$	
$ENTER\_F\ f$				$==>$	f			
$SUSP\ l\ [y_1, .., y_n]\ d; c$			$y_1[v_1]..y_n[v_n]$	$==>$	c			$l[o]\ o[\bullet\ d\ e]$
								$e[v_1..v_n]$

The two tags $\bullet$ and $\diamond$ distinguish the node types closure and data term (using fancy symbols instead of numbers). The machine halts when it encounters a RET instruction. The result term is returned on the $\mathcal{A}$-stack

3.2.2 A CGRM with applicative order evaluation

We now extend the machine specification 3.2-1 by the concept *dump stack* such that arguments can be called by value. To evaluate an argument before the main application requires that the current machine state is stored on the dump stack. Since the store may be changed by subcomputations it also becomes necessary to save registers on the dump stack and to restore them after the call.

by the prefix **strict**. Let $[l_1, ..l_n]$ be the list of registers which will be still used after the evaluation of the argument. It suffices to save only those registers. In $\mathcal{L}_0$ each argument expression which is passed by value is annotated

$$\mathcal{B}[\![a\ (\text{strict}\ b)]\!]\ \phi\ \tau\ =\ SPILL\ [l_1, ..l_n]; \mathcal{A}[\![b]\!]\ l\ \phi\ \tau;\ UNSPILL\ [l_1, ..l_n];\ \mathcal{B}[\![A]\!]\ \phi\ \tau$$

Scheme $\mathcal{A}$ is identical to scheme $\mathcal{B}$ except that it uses a $CALL$ (resp. $CALL\_F$) instead of an $ENTER$ (resp. $ENTER\_F$) instruction.

Machine Specification 3.2-2: *Compiled graph reduction with* $\mathcal{A}, \mathcal{E}, \mathcal{D}$ *(additional rules)*

$\mathcal{PC}$	$\mathcal{E}$	$\mathcal{A}$	$\mathcal{D}$	$\mathcal{R}$
$SPILL\ [l_1, ..l_n]; c$			d	$l_1[v_1] \ldots l_n[v_n]$
$==>\ \ c$			$[v_1, .., v_n	d]$	
$UNSPILL\ [l_1, ..l_n]; c$	e	as	$[v_1, .., v_n	d]$	
$==>\ \ c$	e	as	d	$l_1[v_1] \ldots l_n[v_n]$
$CALL\ x; c$	e	as	d	$x[l]\ \ l[\bullet\ code\ env]$
$==>\ \ code$	env	$[]$	$[c, e, as	d]$	
$CALL\_F\ f; c$	e	as	d	
$==>\ \ f$	e	as	$[c, e, as	d]$	
RET		$v : []$	$[c, e, as	d]$	
$==>\ \ c$	e	$v : as$	d	

The machine halts when it encounters a RET instruction and an empty dump stack.

3.3 The closure technique

In the previous part we presented the design of a machine that implements a simple fragment of functional programs. To obtain a machine that executes all functional features of $\mathcal{L}_0$ requires additional support for: data terms, pattern matching, partial applications, and sharing. Below, we look at a basic concept called *closure technique* that provides a means for realizing these features. Moreover, as we will se, the closure technique already includes the treatment of logical variables and unification which is a first step towards a logical machine. In terms of our triangle on page 3, we are moving to the left edge.

The closure technique developed here incorporates the following idea: a pair of code and environment constitutes a closure. The environment stores the values of all variables being accessed by the closure's code. Then, all types of graph nodes will be encoded by closures, for instance suspensions, data terms, and partial applications. The great advantage of this technique is that all objects (graph nodes) have a uniform representation, and accordingly an object is evaluated by executing its code. Furthermore, this uniform representation supports the integration of functional and logical concepts, in particular because unbound logical variables can be represented by closures. Five closure types are used:

suspension: The essence of call-by-need is to postpone the evaluation of arguments until their value is absolutely needed. This is achieved by representing the argument by a closure of type *suspension* which is formed by the code obtained from compiling the argument along with an environment for the free variables in that code. When the value is demanded the code is executed in the context of that environment.

data term: An application of a data constructor to arguments is called data term. A closure is constituted when its constructor is represented by code and its argument list is stored in an environment. The code, when executed, is required to pass the constructor and the arguments to the calling context.

logical variable: An unbound logical variable is represented by a closure whose code indicates to any caller that the variable is unbound. The environment consists of a single, undefined field which later stores the binding reference.

indirection node: In lazy evaluation, a suspension is updated by the result of its evaluation. This is achieved by converting the suspension into an indirection node which points to the result object (which itself is a closure). In the same way, binding a logical variable is achieved by converting it into an indirection node which points to the binding value.

partial application: A partial application is obtained when a function (or a λ-abstraction) is applied to less arguments than it has formal parameters. For instance in the compiled GRM (part 3.2-1) this situation arises when a *POP*-instruction encounters an empty argument stack. We had excluded this problem previously.

Since its code represents a λ-abstraction over pending parameters it needs to test whether any further application is again undersupplied, or not. This is performed by an *uncurry* operation which reduces a single application, extends the current environment by the consumed argument and invokes uncurry again. If the uncurry operation finds no argument it creates and returns a new partial application. As soon as all arguments are available the function's body is invoked. Here, the role of the environments is to collect arguments.

In the following we define instructions for creating and evaluating closures. Additional components are required: a node pointer $\mathcal{N}$ to the closure being in evaluation, and a value register $\mathcal{V}$ and a tag register CT for returning the value of the closure. The heap area $\mathcal{HP}$ stores closures, and we omit the details of how new closures are allocated.

First of all, we redefine the instruction $ENTER$ ($CALL$ can be redefined analogously).

Machine Specification 3.3-1: *Closure evaluation*

$\mathcal{PC}$	$\mathcal{N}$	$\mathcal{E}$	$\mathcal{A}$	$\mathcal{R}$	$\mathcal{G}$		$\mathcal{PC}$	$\mathcal{N}$	$\mathcal{E}$	$\mathcal{A}$	$\mathcal{R}$	$\mathcal{G}$
$ENTER\ x$		as	$x[l]$	$l[d\ e]$	$==>$	d	l	e	as		

Data terms The scheme B is changed. Let for some data constructor c be $n = arity(c)$.

$$B[\![c]\!]\ \phi\ \tau\ =\ TERM\ n\ Termcode[\![c]\!]$$
$$Termcode[\![c]\!]\ =\ ltc\ where\ ltc[TCc]\ and\ TCc\ is\ defined\ below$$

Machine Specification 3.3-2: *data terms*

$\mathcal{PC}$	$\mathcal{N}$	$\mathcal{V}$	CT	$\mathcal{E}$	$\mathcal{A}$	$\mathcal{D}$	$\mathcal{R}$	$\mathcal{HP}$
$TERM\ n\ c$				e	$[a_1,..,a_n]$			
$==>\ \ c$	n				as			$n[p\ e]\ e[a_1..a_n]$
TCc	n					$[c,e,as|d]$		$n[ltc\ e]$
$==>\ \ p$	n	c	$\diamond$	e	as	d		
$GET\_A\ i\ l;c$	n							$n[c\ e]\ e + i[a]$
$==>\ \ c$	n						$l[a]$	

To each constructor c a code sequence TCc is associated which returns a binary value c and a tag value to the calling context. The tag $\diamond$ indicates a term (in contrast to, for instance, a logical variable). Please note that the constructor symbol c is overloaded with its binary coding. The value c and the tag value can be subsequently used for pattern matching and unification.

The instruction $GET\_A\ i\ l$ takes the i-th argument of the term and assigns it to register l. This is cheaper than first pushing the term arguments back to the $\mathcal{A}$-stack from where they could be transferred to registers. Furthermore, $GET\_A\ i\ l$ accesses the arguments via the node register $\mathcal{N}$, not via $\mathcal{E}$ which contains the current environment. This provides a base to define the operational semantics of pattern matching.

Pattern matching We remember that pattern matching is expressed in terms of the operators $\doteq$, $\wedge$ and $\rightarrowtail$. It will be assumed that the left argument y in an equation $y \doteq pat$ is an identifier and that the translation guarantees that y is located in a register. Let $\oplus$ denote either the guard operator $\rightarrowtail$ or the conjunction operator $\wedge$. We now extend B:

$$B[\![y \doteq c\ x_1\ ..\ x_n \oplus e]\!]\ \phi\ \tau\ =\ ENTER\ \tau(y);\ MATCH\ c\ n;\ B[\![e]\!]\ \phi\ (x_1,l_1):..:(x_n,l_n):\tau$$
$$B[\![y \doteq x \oplus e]\!]\ \phi\ \tau\ =\ l := \tau(y);\ B[\![e]\!]\ \phi\ (x,l):\tau$$

where $l, l_1, .., l_n$ are new registers.

Let $c_1 \neq c_2$ be two different constructors and $n = arity(c_1)$.

Machine Specification 3.3-3: *pattern matching*

$\mathcal{PC}$	$\mathcal{N}$	$\mathcal{V}$	$\mathcal{CT}$		$\mathcal{PC}$	$\mathcal{N}$	$\mathcal{V}$	$\mathcal{CT}$
$MATCH\ c_1\ n; co$	c_1	$\diamond$	==>	co	c_1	$\diamond$	
$MATCH\ c_1\ n; c$	c_2	$\diamond$	==>	$RETRY$	c_2	$\diamond$	
$MATCH\ c_1\ n; c$		$\odot$	==>	$RETRY$			

The $RETRY$ operation reflects that the match failed and will be defined in part 3.4. A match fails if the constructors are unequal or if the tag value $\odot$ indicates that $\mathcal{N}$ references a closure which is not a term, for instance a partial application. The comparison of tag values realizes a run-time type check. In a strongly typed language, however, the type system provides this distinction at compile-time. By that means, the tag values of data terms, binary values and partial applications can collapse. Then, the only types to be distinguished at run-time are terms and logical variables. The case of an unbound logical variable will be discussed later.

Partial application The scheme $\mathcal{B}$ is changed for λ-abstraction. Let m be the size of ϕ.

$$\mathcal{B}[\![\lambda x.a]\!]\ \phi\ \tau\ =\ POP\ l;\ PUT\ l;\ \mathcal{B}[\![a]\!]\ (x, m+1): \phi\ (x, l): \tau$$

Since $a' = \lambda x.a$ may suspend on an empty $\mathcal{A}$-stack all arguments consumed previously need to be stored in an environment which is passed along with the code for a'. This is achieved by copying the recently popped argument into a new environment which extends the old one (specified by ϕ). With that, a' can be represented by a closure of the type partial application consisting of the current environment and code label UC where $UC[\mathcal{B}[\![\lambda x.a]\!]] = UC[POP\ x; c]$. The POP performs an uncurry operation. Note, that POP pops an argument if there is one. Otherwise, a partial application is created and returned, which is indicated through the tag value $\triangleleft$.

Machine Specification 3.3-4: *partial application*

$\mathcal{PC}$	$\mathcal{N}$	$\mathcal{CT}$	$\mathcal{E}$	$\mathcal{A}$	$\mathcal{R}$	$\mathcal{HP}$		$\mathcal{PC}$	$\mathcal{N}$	$\mathcal{CT}$	$\mathcal{E}$	$\mathcal{A}$	$\mathcal{R}$	$\mathcal{HP}$
UC			e	$[\ ]$			==>	RET	n	$\triangleleft$			$[n]$	$n[UC\ e]$
$PUT\ x; c$			e	$x[v]$	$e[a_1..a_m]$		==>	c			e'			$e'[a_1..a_m\ v]$

Sharing In the CGRM subgraphs may become shared by reducing an application; the result of evaluating a subgraph, however, is not yet shared. For instance, when reducing the expression $(\lambda x.(\lambda y\ z.e)\ x\ x)\ a$ both y and z share a. Since the evaluation of y and z can be demanded independently a may be evaluated twice. Sharing is achieved when the closure representing a is updated by the result of a's first evaluation. Then, any further demand to a directly returns this result.

We change scheme $\mathcal{C}$ such that an instruction is inserted which performs the update of a closure. As shown before the scheme works perfectly well without that update. This means that the update instruction needs only be inserted for those subexpressions which are statically known to be shared. The sharing information can be obtained by static program analysis and incorporated by source code annotations. It is sound to annotate conservatively since the update of an unshared closure does no harm, although it leads to unnecessary overhead.

$$\mathcal{C}[\![\mathbf{shared}\ exp]\!]\ l\ \phi\ \tau\ =\ CopyCode;\ SUSP\ l\ \gamma\ \{WIRE\ ;\mathcal{B}[\![exp]\!]\ \phi'\ [\ ]\}$$

where *CopyCode* moves part of the current environment to registers, γ specifies the contents of the new environment and ϕ' maps the free variables of *exp* to locations in that environment.

The updates are performed by means of a tripwire which is a linked list of pairs residing on the argument stack. Each pair contains a reference to the closure to be updated and a link to the next pair. The top of the tripwire is referenced by the new component $\mathcal{W}$.

Machine Specification 3.3-5: *sharing and updates*

$\mathcal{PC}$		$\mathcal{N}$	$\mathcal{W}$	$\mathcal{V}$	$\mathcal{CT}$	$\mathcal{E}$	$\mathcal{A}$	$\mathcal{D}$	$\mathcal{R}$	$\mathcal{HP}$
WIRE; c		n	w			e	as			
==>	c	n	w'			e	$w' : as$			$w'[n\ w]$
POP x; c		n	w'			e	$w' : as$			$w'[r\ w]$
==>	*POP* x; c	n	w			e	as			$r[rc\ n]$
RET		n	w'	$\diamond$			$[w', n]$			$w'[r\ w]$
==>	c	n	w	$\diamond$			$n : as$			$r[rc\ n]$

The closure referenced by the top of the wire is converted into an indirection node which points to the active closure. Note that rc is the label defined by $rc[RC]$. If $\mathcal{W}$ points to an entry below the top of the $\mathcal{A}$-stack the normal *POP*-instruction is executed.

The application of a function being fully supplied either returns a partial application or a data term. A pending tripwire during a return indicates that this application needs to be by updated the returned data term. The other case, a partial application, is properly handled by *POP*.

Logical variables The expression $\exists x.e$ denotes that x is a logical variable in e.

$$\mathcal{B}[\![\exists x.e]\!]\ \phi\ \tau\ =\ LVAR\ l;\ \mathcal{B}[\![e]\!]\ \phi\ (x, l) : \tau$$

Machine Specification 3.3-6: *logical variables*

$\mathcal{PC}$		$\mathcal{N}$	$\mathcal{V}$	$\mathcal{CT}$	$\mathcal{E}$	$\mathcal{A}$	$\mathcal{D}$	$\mathcal{R}$	$\mathcal{HP}$
LVAR l; co									
==>	co							$l[var]$	$var[lc\ -]$
LC		n					$[c, e, as\vert d]$		$n[lc\ e]$
==>	c	n		$\diamond$	e	as	d		

The tag $\circ$ indicates that $\mathcal{N}$ references an unbound logical variables.

Linear unification Linear unification is a restricted form of the usual (syntactic) unification. Whenever a variable appears less than once in the patterns of a conjunction of match operators the unification problem is linear. For instance, $x \doteq y \wedge z \doteq y$ is non-linear, and as a consequence two statically unknown values need to be unified by means of a general unification procedure. Its definition can be found in [AK90, LM91], among others. In the linear case, the rules for pattern matching and binding of logical variables suffice.

Let lc and rc be the labels defined by $lc[LC]$ and $rc[RC]$, and further, let tcc be the code label belonging to constructor c_1, i.e. $tcc = Termcode[\![c_1]\!]$. With machine specification 3.3-7 the code obtained from translating $\doteq$ now executes unification instead of pattern matching.

Machine Specification 3.3-7: *binding logical variables and indirection nodes*

$\mathcal{PC}$		$\mathcal{N}$	$\mathcal{V}$	$\mathcal{CT}$	$\mathcal{E}$	$\mathcal{A}$	$\mathcal{D}$	$\mathcal{R}$	$\mathcal{HP}$
$MATCH\,c_1\,n; co$		n		$\circ$					$n[lc\,-]$
$==>$	co	t							$n[rc\,t]\,t[tcc\,e]\,e[r_1..r_n]\,r_1[lc\,-]\,..\,r_n[lc\,-]$
RC		n					d		$n[rc\,v]\,v[c\,e]$
$==>$	c	v			e		d		

In this case, a term is created on the fly whose arguments are unbound logical variables. The unbound variable referenced by $\mathcal{N}$ is converted into an indirection node which points to the new term. An indirection node represents a bound logical variable. Its code switches to the referenced closure.

3.4   Choice points and the trail stack

Backtracking is a control structure which provides a means to perform a sequential ordered search through a space of alternatives. Languages such as Snobol, Icon and Prolog, just to mention a few, rely on backtracking.

This part presents a choice point technique which realizes backtracking. A prototype for that is the WAM [War83, AK90] which provides a very efficient implementation of the choice point technique. It may surprise the reader that we specify a choice point technique in a framework of functional graph reduction machines. In fact, the WAM and graph reduction machines possess a common core, as will be discussed in part 4.1, and early interpretative implementations of Prolog such as [Emd82] or CProlog operate on graph representations of programs.

We start with an extension of scheme $\mathcal{B}$ in order to translate expressions which contain the choice operator $\|$.

$$\mathcal{B}[\![a \parallel b]\!]\,\phi\,\tau \;=\; SPILL\,[l_1,..,l_k];\; MAKECPT\,alternative;\; \mathcal{B}[\![a]\!]\,\phi\,\tau$$
$$where \qquad alternative[SETCPT\,failure;\; UNSPILL\,[l_1,..,l_k];\; \mathcal{B}[\![b]\!]\,\phi\,\tau]$$
$$failure[UNDO;\; RETRY\;]$$

All active registers $[l_1,..,l_k]$ which will be used in the alternative b need to be spilt before the first choice is executed.

The choice point technique comprises a stack which stores choice points and a trail stack which records those side effects which need to be reversed during backtracking. The update operation and the binding of a logical variable cause such side effects. The pointers to the top of both stacks are denoted by $\mathcal{CP}$ and $\mathcal{T}$. A choice point is a data structure which stores a state of the machine and a code label at which the machine continues after it has restored to the old state.

Machine Specification 3.4-1: *choice points and backtracking*

$\mathcal{PC}$		$\mathcal{N}$	$\mathcal{W}$	$\mathcal{V}$	$\mathcal{CT}$	$\mathcal{E}$	$\mathcal{A}$	$\mathcal{D}$	$\mathcal{CP}$		$\mathcal{T}$
$MAKECPT\,l;\,c$		n	w			e	as	d	cp		t
$==>$	c	n	w			e	as	d	$[l,t,n,w,e,as|d]$		t
$SETCPT\,l;\,c$									$[-|cpt]$		
$==>$	c								$[l|cpt]$		
$RETRY$									$[l,t,n,w,e,as|cpt]$		
$==>$	l	n	w			e	as	d	cpt		t

The whole machine state is conceptually copied into a choice point since the calling context will deallocate the stacks after the first alternative returns. Obviously, copying is hopelessly inefficient. It is known that copying can be avoided if the stacks are not discarded by return operations (see also part 4.2). Then, the older stack segments can be shared and, hence, it suffices that a choice point stores references to stacks.

The update of a suspension is recorded on the trail stack by its reference, code and environment. To record the binding of a variable it suffices to store its reference. This requires straightforward extensions of the *POP* and *MATCH*-instructions which will be omitted here. The *UNDO*-operation takes this information from the trail stack in order to restore the old value of a closure.

Machine Specification 3.4-2: *trail stack and reversing side effects*

$\mathcal{PC}$	$\mathcal{N}$	$\mathcal{W}$	$\mathcal{V}$	$\mathcal{CT}$	$\mathcal{E}$	$\mathcal{A}$	$\mathcal{D}$	$\mathcal{CP}$	$\mathcal{T}$	$\mathcal{HP}$
$UNDO; c$								$[l,t\lvert cpt]$	st	
$?\ st = t\ ==>\ c$								$[l,t\lvert cpt]$	st	
$UNDO; c$								$[l,t\lvert cpt]$	$[\sigma^3\,c\,e\,n\lvert st]$	
$?\ st \geq t\ ==>\ UNDO; c$								$[l,t\lvert cpt]$	st	$n[c\ e]$
$UNDO; c$								$[l,t\lvert cpt]$	$[\sigma^1\,n\lvert st]$	
$?\ st \geq t\ ==>\ UNDO; c$								$[l,t\lvert cpt]$	st	$n[lc\ -]$

A guard like $?st \geq t$ imposes an additional condition on the applicability of a transition rule. The tags σ^1 and σ^3 indicate that a single reference or a triple of references is stored.

We are now in the state to demonstrate how a function application is reduced, in particular how to select a rule from a function definition whose head unifies the application. The definition of *concat* from part 2 is translated as follows:

$concat\ [SUSP\ l_1\ []\ thunk_1;\ ENTER\ l_1]$
$thunk_1\ [POP\ l_2;\ PUT\ l_2;\ POP\ l_3;\ PUT\ l_3;$
        $MAKECPT\ alt_1;\ ENTER\ l_2;\ MATCH\ Termcode[\![nil]\!]\ 0;\ l_4 := l_3;$
        $\mathcal{B}[\![r]\!]\ [(p_1,1),(p_2,2)]\ [(p_1,l_2),(p_2,l_3),(r,l_4)]\ ]$
    $alt_1\ [SETCPT\ alt_2;\ GETE\ 1\ l_5;\ ENTER\ l_5;\ MATCH\ Termcode[\![cons]\!]\ 2;$
        $GET\_A\ 1\ l_6;\ GET\_A\ 2\ l_7;\ GET\_E\ 2\ l_8;\ l_9 := l_8;$
        $\mathcal{B}[\![cons\ x\ concat\ l\ r]\!]\ [(p_1,1),(p_2,2)]\ [(p_1,l_5),(p_2,l_8),(x,l_6),(l,l_7),(r,l_9)]\ ]$
    $alt_2\ [UNDO;\ RETRY\ ]$

In this case the spill and unspill-operations can be omitted. It is important to notice that the choice between the two function rules is implemented by a choice point. Consequently, the call **concat cons 1 2** fails in its first alternative which matches *nil*. Then, the machine backtracks to the second alternative which succeeds. Note that the application **concat 1** would lead to a total failure; however, this could be already refuted by a type-checker.

The code in alt_2 gives an example where a source variable, e.g. p_1, is located both in the environment and in a register. This information can be used to produce good code which accesses the register as long as possible and which avoids spilling.

Furthermore, function *concat* can be called with a logical variable, e.g. in $\exists x.concat\ x\ e$.

$$[LVAR\ l_1;\ PUSH\ l_1;\ C[\![e]\!]\ l_2\ \phi\ \tau;\ PUSH\ l_2;\ ENTER\_F\ concat]$$

Then, the match operation creates a closure term *nil* and binds it to the logical variable identified by l_1. After backtracking by a retry-operation, the term *cons* $z_1\ z_2$ will be generated and bound, where z_1 and z_2 now identify unbound logical variables. Subsequent backtracking will bind z_2 to lists which grow each time.

This example demonstrates that the machine defined from specification 3.2-1 to specification 3.4-2 implements narrowing with call-by-need semantics. Narrowing with call-by-value semantics (innermost narrowing) is easily achieved by using strictness annotations for argument expressions which causes that their evaluation precedes the application.

3.5 Recapitulation

Having reached the top of our triangle let us recall the stations we passed on our way.

- The starting point of our investigation was a graph reduction machine which performs normal order evaluation. This machine was subsequently refined by adding new concepts which were identified as being basic concepts since they are inevitable either to support single language features, or to achieve a reasonable efficiency.

- Code can be used to replace graphs when the code performs the same actions as the interpretation of the graphs. This important concept was called compiled graph reduction. A compiled graph reduction machine (CGRM) with argument stack ($\mathcal{A}$), environment ($\mathcal{E}$), and dump stack ($\mathcal{D}$) was taken as a fundament for further developments. The basic concepts $\mathcal{A}$, $\mathcal{E}$ and $\mathcal{D}$ support currying, the propagation of bindings along with the code that accesses them, and applicative order evaluation, respectively.

- The closure technique is a basic concept which supports call-by-need, pattern matching and unification, partial application, and in connection with tripwires the realization of sharing. It was shown that closures provide a uniform representation of functional and logical data objects which facilitates their integration as well as the interface between normal control flow and closure evaluation.

- The CGRM-$\mathcal{AED}$ machine type with closures supports higher order functional languages with both lazy and strict evaluation strategies.

- The choice point technique ($\mathcal{CP}$) is a basic concept which involves a choice point stack and a trail stack and which supports backtracking. We have shown that a (lazy) narrowing machine is obtained when the CGRM-$\mathcal{AED}$ with closures is extended by $\mathcal{CP}$. In particular the integration of $\mathcal{CP}$ and the closure technique provides the means to realize a backtrackable finite state automaton which selects a defining rule whose head unifies a given function application. This is the fundamental mechanism needed to implement any kind of declarative operational model such as narrowing, SLD-resolution, rewriting and reduction.

4 Classifying Existing Approaches

This section gives a classification of a selection of existing abstract machines in terms of basic concepts and by the way of their combination. As a particular point, we will discuss the relation between the conventional stack based machine and the compiled graph reduction machine.

4.1 The conventional core

The main feature of the conventional abstract machine is its single stack which stores for each function call an activation record. This activation record contains the actual arguments of a call, parts of the calling context, and the values of local variables (registers) which need to be saved across subcalls. The machine supports first order evaluation and is used in many variants for implementing imperative programming languages (see, for instance, [ASU86]).

According to our design space, the conventional machine is a compiled graph reduction machine without *environments* and *closures* whose *argument and dump stack* are merged, and whose *store* is partially located on the dump. This is of extreme importance since it gives us immediately at hand the whole wealth of code generation and optimizations techniques which have been developed for the conventional machine.

This conventional core is integral part of the WAM, of several functional machines such as FPM/2 [Per88], the STGM [PS88], ABC [KEN+90], and of the narrowing machines JUMP [CL91] and LANM [Loo91].

4.2 The WAM

The WAM [War83] can be classified as a conventional core extended by *term closures* and a *choice point technique*. The control stack and the choice point stack are merged such that a choice point protects all activation records below it. The control stack is only deallocated during backtracking, but never by a return operation since this would collide with protection. Therefore, giving the answer to an earlier remark, it is not necessary to copy the whole machine state in order to create a choice point. The control component performs an innermost evaluation strategy which is well suited for the implementation of SLD-resolution. The tagged representation of terms, logical variable and indirection nodes in the WAM is an optimized variation of the closure technique presented here.

4.3 Functional machines

The SECD-machine designed by Landin [Lan64] was the first functional machine at all, and it is based on interpretation and call-by-value semantics. It uses the basic concepts *argument stack* (called S), *environments* (E), *dump stack* (D), and *closures*. The control stack (C) is used to translate expressions to graphs which consist of closures (see [FH88]).

If one separates the translation and execution phase the concepts of the SECD can lead to a very efficient machine design. This has been demonstrated by Perry with FPM/2 [Per88]. An important idea is that the integration of (S,E,D) in a single control stack yields a conventional machine design which can be mapped with traditional code generation methods to stock hardware.

TIM [FW87] is a CGRM with *environments*, *argument stack*, and *closures* which executes lazy supercombinators[2]. Its main idea is to move all arguments of a supercombinator into an environment which then can be used directly to create closures. The idea of updating a closure by its result by placing a *tripwire* on the argument stack is due to Meijer [Mei85] and has been incorporated in the TIM and the STGM [PS88]. The simple and elegant design of TIM has inspired many authors since and, in particular, the development of the STGM [PS88]. However, the STGM uses a dump stack which is merged with the argument stack. Furthermore, a block-structured intermediate code and the concept of registers were introduced. Both authors of the STGM and Meijer [Mei88] have independently emphasized the importance of conventional compiler technology for implementing functional languages. A relative of TIM and STGM has been proposed by Meijer and Paterson which makes λ-lifting superfluous [MP90].

4.4 Narrowing machines

Compiled narrowing machines can be divided in two groups: extensions of the WAM, e.g. K-WAM [BCM89] and A-WAM [Han90], and extensions of graph reduction machines, e.g.

---

[2]Functional programs are transformed to supercombinator programs by means of a technique called λ-lifting, see [Pey87]. The idea of a supercombinator is that it neither contains lambda abstractions nor free variables.

LBAM [MKLR90], LANM [Loo91], and JUMP [CL91].

The K-WAM adds a *closure concept* to the WAM in order to support call-by-need semantics. Since the A-WAM executes general term rewriting systems the selection of the next redex is more general than in functional application graphs. Therefore, it introduces a new concept, the occurrence stack, in order to manage positions in the graph which need to be evaluated. However, we have shown recently [Loc91] that the general redex selection can be implemented by means of the *dump stack*, and hence, the occurrence stack is not strictly necessary.

The LBAM is a machine whose code creates *graphs* which then become interpreted. Graphs nodes are also used to store the backtracking information. LBAM is a combination of a *stackless graph reduction machine* with a *stackless choice point technique*. The LANM is a descendent of the SECD, the FPM [FH88] and the WAM. Its design involves a *frame stack, closures*, and a *choice point technique*. The frame stack integrates a *dump stack*, an *environment stack, registers* and a *choice point stack*. Thus, the LANM contains an extented conventional core such as the WAM does. Environments and closures are realized as in the SECD: environments reside on the stack and closures are large suspension nodes which contain a copy of an environment on the stack.

Finally, the JUMP machine is a systematic extensions of a conventional core which integrates all basic features presented in this paper in some optimized form. Its design can be seen as an extension of the STGM and of [MP90]; at least its code was directly inspired by their code conception.

5 Conclusions

The essence of this work is a relation between the operational concepts of functional logic languages and machine concepts. This relation establishes not only a design space, but also the systematic construction of a narrowing machine. We have further shown that the conventional stack-based machine relates to the compiled graph reduction machine. This core can be extended in two directions: such that (lazy) functional languages become supported, and such that an implementation for logic progamming languages is provided. It was demonstrated that the stack based model and a closure technique are the key concepts for integrating functional and logical features. This integration establishes an abstract narrowing machine.

6 Acknowledgments

This work was funded by the EC, BRA 3147 (PHOENIX). The author is indebted to Erik Meijer for sharing his ideas, intellectual support and cooperative criticism, and to Manuel Chakravarty for many fruitful discussions. Ross Paterson advice was taken to revise the intermediate language $\mathcal{L}_0$. Nick Graham and Gabi Keller helped to improve this paper.

References

[AK90]   Hassan Ait-Kaci. The WAM: a real tutorial. Technical report, DEC research center, Paris, 1990.

[ASU86] Alfred V. Aho, Ravi Sethi, and Jeffrey D. Ullman. *Compilers – Principles, Techniques and Tools*. Addison-Wesley, 1986.

[BCM89] P.G. Bosco, C. Cecchi, and C. Moiso. An extension of WAM for K-LEAF: a WAM-based compilation of conditional narrowing. In *Poceedings of the 6th Int. Conf. on Logic Programming*, 1989.

[CL91]   Manuel M.T. Chakravarty and Hendrik C.R. Lock. The implementation of lazy narrowing. In *PLILP '91*, LNCS 528, pages 312–333, Aug 1991.

[Emd82]   M.H. van Emden. An interpreting algorithm for Prolog programs. In *proceedings of the First Int. Logic Progr. Conf.*, 1982.

[FH88]   Anthony J. Fields and Peter G. Harrison. *Functional Programming*. Int. Computer Science Series. Addison Wesley, 1988.

[FW87]   Jon Fairbairn and Stuart Wray. TIM - A Simple Machine to Execute Supercombinators. In *Conference on Functional Programming Languages and Computer Architecture*, LNCS 274, 1987.

[Han90]   Michael Hanus. Compiling logic programs with equality. In *PLILP*, LNCS 348, Springer Verlag, pages 387–401, 1990.

[KEN+90]   P. Koopman, M. van Eekelen, E. Nocker, J. Smetsers, and M. Plasmeijer. The ABC-machine: A sequential stack-based abstract machine for graph rewriting. Technical Report 90-22, University of Nijmegen, Toernooiveld 1, Nijmegen, The Netherlands, Dec. 1990.

[Lan64]   Peter J. Landin. The mechanical evaluation of expressions. *Computer Journal*, 6:308–320, 1964.

[LM91]   Hendrik C.R. Lock and Anamaria Martins. Issues in the implementation of Prolog, and their optimization. In *Microprocessing and Microprogramming*, volume 32, pages 505–514. North Holland, Sept 1991.

[Loc91]   Hendrik C.R. Lock. The implementation of functional logic programming languages, 1991. forthcoming dissertation.

[Loo91]   Rita Loogen. From reduction machines to narrowing machines. In *CCPSD, TAPSOFT*, LNCS 494, pages 438–454, 1991.

[Mei85]   Erik Meijer. unbuplished notes, 1985.

[Mei88]   Erik Meijer. A taxonomy of function evaluating machines. In *Proceedings of a Workshop on Implementations of Lazy Functional Languages*, Aspenas, Sept. 1988. Report 53, PMG, Univ. of Göteborg, Sweden.

[Mei92]   Erik Meijer. *Calculating Compilers*. PhD thesis, University of Nijmegen, Toernooiveld, Nijmegen, The Netherlands, 1992.

[MKLR90]   Juan J. Moreno-Navarro, Herbert Kuchen, Rita Loogen, and Mario Rodriguez-Artalejo. Lazy narrowing in a graph machine. In *Conf. on Algebraic and Logic Programming*, LNCS 463, 1990. also appeared as report N° 90-11 at RWTH Aachen.

[MP90]   Erik Meijer and Ross Paterson. Down with λ-lifting. University of Nijmegen and Imperial College, London, Sept. 1990. unpublished manuscript.

[Osb91]   Hugh Osborne. Update plans. In Susan L. Graham and Robert Giegerich, editors, *Proceedings of Code '91*, 1991. to appear.

[Pat90]   Ross Paterson. A non-deterministic λ-calculus. Imperial College, London, Sept. 1990. manuscript.

[Per88]   Nigel Perry. FPM2. In *Workshop on Implementations of Lazy Functional Languages*, Aspenas,Sweden, Sept. 1988.

[Pey87]   Simon L. Peyton-Jones. *The Implementation of Functional Programming Languages*. Series in Computer Science. Prentice-Hall, 1987.

[PS88]   Simon L. Peyton-Jones and J. Salkild. The Spineless Tagless G-Machine. In *Workshop on Implementations of Lazy Functional Languages*, Aspenas,Sweden, Sept. 1988. appeared also in 1989 ACM Conf. on Functional Progr. Languages and Computer Architecture.

[War83]   D.H.D Warren. An abstract Prolog instruction set. Techn. Note 309, SRI International,Menlo Park,Calif., October 1983.

Some Algorithms for Fast and Complete Execution of Logic Programs

Roland Olsson

Department of Computer Science
Molde Distriktshøgskole
Postboks 308
6401 Molde
Norway

Abstract

SLD-tree search algorithms that are complete, i.e. guaranteed to find an SLD-resolution proof if one exists, are described and analyzed both theoretically and experimentally. In addition to new variants of depth-first iterative-deepening, a novel complete strategy, random iterative-probing, is introduced. The best algorithm in the article combines deep and shallow search and has in comparison with Prolog a much greater class of programs and queries that can be executed with reasonable efficiency. The price to be paid is an increase of 2 to 3 times in the no of inferences done for the best cases, e.g. deterministic computations.

1 Introduction

A logic program can be viewed as consisting of the 2 components knowledge and control, but should ideally only need the former in order to be easy to write and to modify. Ease of writing and ease of modification is particularly important for

1. Executing programs produced by inductive inference systems like the one in [10].

2. Rapid prototyping.

3. Novice programmers.

A complete logic programming language needs the control component only to improve efficiency and not, as opposed to for example Prolog, to also ensure termination. Many programs written without concern for clause or literal ordering or without cuts do not terminate when executed by Prolog but can easily be run with the interpreters presented here.

Complete logic programming languages are sparsely treated in the literature on logic programming, which by and large ignores the issue of completeness, and the literature on theorem proving, which neglects the programming language aspect.

Some attempts to obtain a "more complete" logic programming language are the so called delay mechanism of Nu-Prolog [8] and the use of tight derivations in [12]. Both of these trade a small performance penalty for a comparatively minute increase in language expressiveness.

The methods presented below are more related to theorem provers such as PTTP [11], which was specifically designed to have a low overhead per inference. PTTP is however by its author not considered to be an interpreter for a programming language and is for some of the typical programs in section 4 hundreds or thousands of times slower than the best of the interpreters that follow. The work to be described shortly is unique in the respect that completeness and thereby also substantially increased expressiveness is obtained with a much lower performance penalty than what is common for theorem provers.

Since the interpreters primarily are intended to execute logic programs and not to prove theorems, a design criterion for the heuristic rules employed was that each rule should increase the time required for an inference by no more than a small constant. Rules that for some theorem proving applications diminish the search space, but are computationally expensive, were in other words omitted.

New methods presented include random iterative-probing (RIP) SLD-tree search, using extrapolation in conjunction with depth-first iterative-deepening (DFID), loop detection with penalization and combining deep and shallow SLD-tree search.

2 The Interpreters

Each interpreter has as input a logic program and a resolvent, i.e. a query, and as output an answer substitution or 'Finite failure'. All experimental interpreters handle negation-as-failure with depth-first (DF) search. The SLD-tree search algorithms, that will be presented, are:

1. DFID.

2. DFID with extrapolation (DFIDE).

3. DFIDE with repeated call penalization (DFIDER).

4. DFIDE with unit clause instance cut (DFIDERU).

5. RIP.

6. DFIDERU-RP

2.1 DFID

Standard DFID as described in [4] sets a depth bound d, searches the tree depth-first and backtracks when the depth bound is exceeded. A standard DFID iteration thus produces all nodes at a depth $\leq d$ if a solution is not found. DFID iterates with depth bounds $1, 2, 3, 4, \ldots$ till a goal node is discovered.

The variant of DFID used here considers the depth difference between a node and its parent to be the number of literals in the body of the clause used to infer the node from its parent. This gives preference to clauses with few literals in their bodies. An inference with a unit clause thus leaves the depth unchanged, which is akin to the so called unit preference strategy commonly used in resolution theorem proving. The variant can alternatively be characterized as a form of iterative-deepening A^*, where the total number of literals in the resolvent is the admissible estimator of remaining depth to solution. It is as complete as standard DFID, but with earlier and more cutoff.

The problem with DFID is that the increase in the number of nodes expanded from one iteration to the next can be very small if many nodes in the SLD-tree only have 1 child. With standard DFID, the increase for deterministic computations is as a case in point just 1 node. If a deterministic computation has depth d, breadth-first and depth-first both expand d nodes whereas standard DFID expands $1 + 2 + \ldots + d = d(d + 1)/2$ nodes.

2.2 DFIDE

DFIDE decides in advance how many nodes that ought to be expanded if an answer is not found during an iteration and then computes a suitable depth-bound using a quadratic extrapolation polynomial.

Let n_i be the number of nodes that was expanded during the ith iteration, d_i be the depth bound for the ith iteration and αn_i be the number of nodes that ought to be expanded during iteration number i+1. The depth bound d_{i+1} is computed by first finding coefficients a_2, a_1 and a_0 such that $n_j = a_2 d_j^2 + a_1 d_j + a_0$ for all $j \in \{i - 2, i - 1, i\}$ and then solving $\alpha n_i = a_2 d_{i+1}^2 + a_1 d_{i+1} + a_0$.

The experimental DFIDE interpreter has $\alpha = 2$. The depth bounds d_1, d_2 and d_3 used to produce initial values for extrapolation were rather arbitrarily chosen to 3,6 and 9 respectively.

Extrapolation is actually not quite as simple as outlined above since there are some special cases that need to be considered. For DFIDER, it can for example happen that $n_{i-2} = n_{i-1} = n_i$ even though $d_{i-2} < d_{i-1} < d_i$. These rare cases are handled by resorting to DFID until extrapolation can be used.

It is in practice very unusual that extrapolation returns a depth-bound that is much too big. All depth-bounds observed experimentally with $\alpha = 2$ make $n_{i+1} \leq 10\alpha n_i$. The experimental DFIDE interpreter employs the following "emergency break" to so to speak play it safe: If the number of nodes expanded so far during iteration number $i + 1$ exceeds $10\alpha n_i$ then set $d_{i+1} := (d_{i+1} + d_i)/2$ and restart the iteration.

2.3   DFIDER

DFIDER is an improvement of DFIDE that detects and to a certain extent avoids repeated calls. The only difference between DFIDER and DFIDE is that the former iteratively deepens the penalized depth, which is defined below.

Definition: 2 literals L and L' are alphabetic variants iff the only difference between L and L' is the choice of variable names i.e. iff the most general unifier of L and L' is a renaming substitution.

Let L be a literal and Ls a literal sequence. Assume that a path in the SLD-tree has nodes and corresponding resolvents as shown in the table below.

Node	Resolvent
N_i	$\leftarrow L, Ls.$
N_{i+1}	$\leftarrow L_1, L_2, \ldots, Ls.$
$\vdots$	$\vdots$
N_{i+k}	$\leftarrow Ls.$

Definition: L is under evaluation for a node N_l iff $i < l < i + k$.

Let $N_0, N_1, \ldots, N_l$ be a path from the root N_0 to a node N_l in the SLD-tree. Assume that the resolvent corresponding to N_j for $0 \leq j \leq l$ is $\leftarrow M_j, \ldots$.

Infinite branches in the SLD-tree can be partially avoided by requiring that proofs are tight, which means that there is no pair (l, j) such that M_l and M_j are identical and such that M_j is under evaluation for N_l. Note that a non-tight proof contains a redundant loop. In [12], tightness is used to improve the termination properties of negation-as-failure. Tightness is in [11] employed to reduce the size of the search space.

There are unfortunately many loops that are not detected by tightness checking. An example is the loop that can arise with the program and query

```
p([a|Xs]) <- p(Xs).
p([]).
```

```
<- p(Ys).
```

DFIDER therefore uses a modification of tightness that checks if M_l and M_j are alphabetic variants instead of checking identity. This modification detects more loops, but some of these loops may not be redundant and therefore have to be allowed. This is the reason why DFIDER penalizes instead of simply fails when a loop is detected.

The penalized depth d_p is defined by:

function $d_p(N_l)$
begin
    if $l = 0$ **then**
        return 0;
    Let n_B be the number of literals in the body of the clause used to produce N_l from N_{l-1};
    if there is no j such that the literals M_l and M_j are alphabetic variants and such that M_j is under evaluation for N_l **then**
        return $d_p(N_{l-1}) + n_B$
    else
        return $d_p(N_{l-1}) + \beta(d_p(N_{l-1}) + n_B - d_p(N_j))$ where
            j is the maximum node index such that M_l and M_j are
            alphabetic variants and such that M_j is under evaluation for N_l
end

Note that this only is a definition and that d_p in a practical algorithm can be much more efficiently computed. The experimental DFIDER interpreter has $\beta = 20$.

Checking if a literal is an alphabetic variant of any literal in a given set can be done efficiently by using a combination of hashing and a probabilistic technique that I will call fingerprinting, which is akin to a method with the same name described in [3]. A fingerprinting function f, returning bit strings of fixed length b, is a kind of hash-function such that for any two literals L_x and L_y it is the case that $P(f(L_x) = f(L_y)) \approx 2^{-b}$ if L_x and L_y are not identical. By choosing b to say 64 bits, this probability can be made negligibly small.

The following 2 steps are performed for every new literal L :

1. Convert L to a canonical form L' by applying a renaming substitution to L. The canonical forms of any 2 literals are identical iff the literals are alphabetic variants.

2. Store $f(L')$ in a hash table entry with index $h(f(L'))$ where h is an ordinary hashing function.

2.4 DFIDERU

DFIDERU adds the following rule to DFIDER: If the left-most literal L in the resolvent, i.e. the selected literal, is an instance of a unit clause, then do not use any other clause to prove L i.e. unify L with the unit clause and cut. This rule is as indicated by the experimental results in section 4 primarily useful for theorem proving applications. The reduction in the number of inferences performed might therefore for other applications not be big enough to compensate for the time it takes to do the unit clause instance checking.

An alternative that has less cutoff but also less overhead is to order the clauses so that units are selected first and then use them sequentially as usual, unifying them with L, and cutting off if examination of the unifier reveals that L was an instance of a unit. Extra work will have been done in the case of earlier unifying unit clauses, but there does not need to be a separate instance-checking phase.

2.5 RIP

DF as used in Prolog visits the children of a node in the SLD-tree in left to right order which corresponds to selecting clauses in the order they appear in the program text. DF has a small termination class i.e. an answer substitution is guaranteed to be found for relatively few programs and queries. The termination class can be altered by randomly choosing the order in which the children of a node are visited. This variant of DF will be called Random Probing (RP). The program and query

```
p(X) <- p(X).
p(a).

<- p(a).
```

is for instance in the termination (in the limit) class of RP but not in the termination class of DF.

Notice that RP's termination class is not a superset of DF's. DF does for instance terminate for the program and query

```
p([]).
p(Xs) :- p([a|Xs]).

<- p([]).
```

RP might on the other hand choose the second clause and thereby be trapped in an infinite branch.

Random Iterative-Probing is a modification of RP that sets a bound on the number of nodes n allowed to be expanded and repeats random probes with greater and greater n till a solution is found. If n_i is the maximum number of nodes that RIP allows to be expanded during the ith iteration, then $n_1 = 1$ and $n_i = \alpha n_{i-1}$ for $i \geq 2$. The experimental RIP interpreter has $\alpha = 2$. RIP's termination (in the limit) class is a superset of DF's and is in fact equal to the class of programs and queries for which an SLD-resolution proof exists i.e. as proven in section 3, RIP is complete in the limit.

2.6 DFIDERU-RP

For some goal literals, DFIDERU is much better than RP and the other way around. DFIDERU-RP is an amalgamation of DFIDERU and RP that attempts to provide the best of both. The search carried out by DFIDERU-RP has one shallow component, i.e. DFIDERU, and one deep component, i.e. RP. For each predicate, either DFIDERU or RP is chosen as the strategy to be used.

DFIDERU-RP alternates between DFIDERU and RP runs as follows. Assume that $\leftarrow$ q($\ldots$),$\ldots$ is a child of $\leftarrow$ p($\ldots$),$\ldots$ in the SLD-tree. Let s_p and s_q be the strategies chosen for p and q respectively. If $s_q \neq s_p$, the run in progress is suspended, the literal q($\ldots$) is evaluated with strategy s_q and the suspended run resumed. A problem with this approach is that a run can be suspended, another run started and suspended, then yet another run started and so on. A restriction which ensures that this nesting problem does not arise is given below.

Cases that can be handled by RIP but neither RP nor DFIDERU are in practice extremely rare. DFIDERU-RP was therefore chosen instead of DFIDERU-RIP since it suffers less from the nesting problem.

A predicate q is said to be single-strategy iff no other strategy than s_q is ever used during the evaluation of any literal q(...). Predicate definitions and strategy choices are primarily intended to be such that for every predicate q occurring in the definition of a predicate p, $s_q \neq s_p$ implies that q is single-strategy. No more than 1 run will ever be suspended at a given point in time if all predicate definitions satisfy this restriction and if all predicates in the resolvent at the root of the SLD-tree have the same chosen strategy. This almost always holds in practice without the programmer needing to care about it.

If all predicates are single-strategy and all predicates in the root resolvent have the same chosen strategy, the same strategy will of course be used in the entire SLD-tree and no run will ever be suspended.

The main problem with DFIDERU-RP is how to determine which strategy to use for each predicate. One way of choosing strategies is to make a choice for one or just a few predicates at a time.

Let S be the set of predicates for which strategies have been chosen so far. Let I be the set of predicates for which strategy is to be chosen next. I should usually be either a singleton or a set of mutually recursive predicates.

begin
    $S := \{\}$;
    repeat
        Input I and a set of queries only containing predicates in $I \cup S$;
        I must be such that no definition for a predicate in I contains
        a call to a predicate that is not in $I \cup S$.
        Run DFIDERU and RP in pseudo-parallel on the queries and select
        the strategy that performs best on the entire set of queries to be
        the chosen strategy for every predicate in I;
        $S := S \cup I$
    until $S =$ The set of all predicates in the program
end

RP is preferred to DFIDERU iff $T_{RP} < 2T_{DFIDERU}$ since a DFIDERU-inference is more time consuming than an RP-inference due to the extra heuristic rules used by DFIDERU.

It is the responsibility of the programmer to provide training examples so that strategies can be chosen incrementally as above. This does not seem to be a heavy burden since such examples usually are constructed anyhow during the debugging and testing of a program.

DFIDERU-RP in practice often carries out about double the number of inferences performed by the best of DFIDERU and RP since DFIDERU and RP are run in pseudo-parallel for queries containing predicates for which strategy has not been chosen. The experimental DFIDERU-RP interpreter first runs RP for 100 inferences, then DFIDERU for 100, then RP for another 100 and so on till an answer has been found.

3   Theoretical Results

Let T_{BF} and T_{DFIDE} be the total number of nodes expanded by breadth-first (BF) and DFIDE respectively.

PROPOSITION: $T_{\mathrm{DFIDE}}/T_{\mathrm{BF}} < l/(l-1) + u$ if $l \leq n_i/n_{i-1} \leq u$ for each DFIDE iteration number i.

Proof: Let k be the number of the last iteration. Note that no completed iteration can expand T_{BF} or more nodes without finding the goal node found by BF, which means that $n_{k-1} < T_{\mathrm{BF}}$. An upper bound on T_{DFIDE} is obtained with $n_k = un_{k-1}, n_{k-1} = T_{\mathrm{BF}} - 1, n_{k-2} = n_{k-1}/l, n_{k-3} = n_{k-2}/l, n_{k-4} = n_{k-3}/l$, which implies $n_i = n_1 l^{i-1}$ for $1 \leq i \leq k-1$. We thus have $T_{\mathrm{DFIDE}} = n_1 + n_2 + \ldots + n_k = n_1(l^0 + l^1 + \ldots + l^{k-2}) + un_1 l^{k-2} = n_1((l^{k-1}-1)/(l-1) + ul^{k-2})$ and $T_{\mathrm{BF}} = n_{k-1} + 1 = n_1 l^{k-2} + 1$ which gives

$$T_{\mathrm{DFIDE}}/T_{\mathrm{BF}} < \frac{n_1(l^{k-1}/(l-1) + ul^{k-2})}{n_1 l^{k-2}} = l/(l-1) + u.$$

If the SLD-tree has such a structure that extrapolation is highly accurate, one can assume $\alpha = l = u$, which gives $T_{\mathrm{DFIDE}}/T_{\mathrm{BF}} < \alpha^2/(\alpha - 1)$. Minimizing $\alpha^2/(\alpha - 1)$ under the constraint $\alpha > 1$ shows that the lowest upper bound in this case is for $\alpha = 2$.

Extrapolation accuracy varies from program to program. It was found empirically that $l = 1.4$ and $u = 4.8$ holds for all examples in section 4.

Let T_{DF} and T_{RIP} be the total number of nodes expanded by DF and RIP respectively.

PROPOSITION: The expected value of $T_{\mathrm{RIP}}/T_{\mathrm{DF}}$ is approximately $1 + (\alpha \ln \alpha)/(\alpha - 1)^2$ and $T_{\mathrm{RIP}}/T_{\mathrm{DF}} < 1 + \alpha/(\alpha - 1)$ for a successful deterministic computation if $\alpha > 1$.

Proof: An SLD-tree for a deterministic computation is a linear graph i.e. no node has more than 1 child. Let k be the number of the last iteration, i.e. $n_{k-1} < T_{DF} \leq n_k$. Since $T_{RIP} = n_1+n_2+\ldots+n_{k-1}+T_{DF} = \alpha^0+\alpha^1+\ldots+\alpha^{k-2}+T_{DF} = (\alpha^{k-1}-1)/(\alpha-1)+T_{DF}$, it is the case that

$$T_{RIP}/T_{DF} = 1 + \frac{\alpha^{k-1}-1}{(\alpha-1)T_{DF}}.$$

T_{RIP}/T_{DF} is maximized for $T_{DF} = n_{k-1}+1 = \alpha^{k-2}+1$ which shows that

$$T_{RIP}/T_{DF} < 1 + \frac{\alpha^{k-1}}{(\alpha-1)\alpha^{k-2}} = 1 + \frac{\alpha}{\alpha-1}.$$

T_{DF} can be assumed to have a uniform distribution on

$$\{n_{k-1}+1, n_{k-1}+2, \ldots, \alpha n_{k-1}\}.$$

The expected value $E(T_{RIP}/T_{DF})$ is

$$\sum_x x P(T_{RIP}/T_{DF} = x)$$

for all values x that T_{RIP}/T_{DF} can have i.e.

$$E(T_{RIP}/T_{DF}) = \frac{1}{\alpha^{k-1}-\alpha^{k-2}} \sum_{T_{DF}=\alpha^{k-2}+1}^{\alpha^{k-1}} (1 + \frac{\alpha^{k-1}-1}{(\alpha-1)T_{DF}}).$$

The sum

$$\frac{1}{\alpha^{k-2}+1} + \frac{1}{\alpha^{k-2}+2} + \ldots + \frac{1}{\alpha^{k-1}}$$

is for large values of $\alpha^{k-1} - \alpha^{k-2}$ closely approximated by

$$\int_{\alpha^{k-2}+1/2}^{\alpha^{k-1}+1/2} \frac{1}{x} dx = \ln \frac{\alpha^{k-1}+1/2}{\alpha^{k-2}+1/2} \approx \ln \alpha$$

which implies

$$E(T_{RIP}/T_{DF}) \approx 1 + \frac{(\alpha^{k-1}-1)\ln\alpha}{(\alpha-1)(\alpha^{k-1}-\alpha^{k-2})} \approx 1 + \frac{\alpha\ln\alpha}{(\alpha-1)^2}.$$

PROPOSITION: DFID, DFIDE, DFIDER and DFIDERU are complete.
Proof: Straightforward.

PROPOSITION: RIP is complete in the limit if α is finite and > 1.
Proof: Assume that there is a goal node at a finite depth d. Let the kth iteration be the first with $n_k \geq d$. Let p_i be the probability of finding a goal node during the ith iteration. It is then the case that

$$0 < p_k \leq p_{k+1} \leq p_{k+2} \leq \ldots \leq p_{k+m}.$$

The probability of not finding a goal node during iterations $k, k+1, \ldots, m$ is

$$\le (1 - p_k)(1 - p_{k+1}) \ldots (1 - p_{k+m}) \le (1 - p_k)^m.$$

Since

$$\lim_{m \to \infty} (1 - p_k)^m = 0,$$

RIP is complete in the limit.

There are unfortunately some programs for which RIP's completeness in the limit only is of theoretical interest as shown by the following analysis.

Assume for instance that RIP for each iteration with an order number $\ge i$ either finds a goal node or gets trapped in an infinite branch. Furthermore, let the ith iteration be the first one for which n_i is so big that a goal node can be found. Notice that i decreases when α increases and vice versa.

For iterations number $i, i+1, \ldots$, assume that the probability of finding a goal node is a constant p and that the probability of getting trapped in an infinite branch is $1 - p$.

Example: Let the SLD-tree below have a single goal node A and 3 infinite branches.

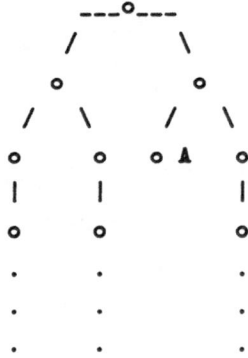

For this tree, α equal to for example 4 implies $i = 2$. Obviously, $p = 1/4$ and $1 - p = 3/4$.

Study iterations $i, i+1, \ldots, i+\xi$ where iteration number $i+\xi$ is the first that finds a goal node.

The probability that the $(i + x)$th iteration is the first during which a goal node is found is $P(\xi = x) = (1 - p)^x p$.

The probability that $i + x$ or fewer iterations are needed is

$$P(\xi \le x) = p \cdot (1 + (1 - p) + (1 - p)^2 + \ldots + (1 - p)^x) = 1 - (1 - p)^{x+1}$$

which implies $x = \log(1 - P(\xi \leq x))/\log(1 - p) - 1$.

Choose $P(\xi \leq x)$ to 0.95.

Since $T_{RIP} \leq \alpha^0 + \alpha^1 + \ldots + \alpha^{i-1} + \ldots + \alpha^{i+x-1} = (\alpha^{i+x} - 1)/(\alpha - 1)$ $\approx \alpha^i \alpha^x/(\alpha - 1)$ with a probability of at least 0.95, an indication of the bad case time complexity of RIP can be obtained by studying $\alpha^x/(\alpha - 1)$.

The table below for example shows that with $\alpha = 2$, RIP's completeness in the limit has little practical significance if $p \leq 0.1$. For sample programs 4 and 7 given below, the p-values are so small that RIP is extremely inefficient.

x and $\alpha^x/(\alpha - 1)$ values are given with 2 significant digits.

α	p	x	$\alpha^x/(\alpha - 1)$
1.01	0.01	$3.0 \cdot 10^2$	$1.9 \cdot 10^3$
	0.1	27	$1.3 \cdot 10^2$
1.1	0.01	$3.0 \cdot 10^2$	$2.0 \cdot 10^{13}$
	0.1	27	$1.4 \cdot 10^2$
2	0.01	$3.0 \cdot 10^2$	$2.7 \cdot 10^{89}$
	0.1	27	$1.8 \cdot 10^8$
	0.2	12	$5.5 \cdot 10^3$

4 Experimental Results

The sample programs were written to be as simple as possible. Even though it would be easy for an experienced programmer to rewrite sample programs 4, 5 and 6 so that they can be efficiently executed using DF, a novice programmer or an inductive inference system might find it difficult to do so.

Ex. 1. Naive list reversal.

nrev(Is,Ys) was called with Is instantiated to lists of length 3,9,27 and 81.

```
nrev(□,□).
nrev( [X|Is] ,Ys ) <- nrev(Is,Zs), append(Zs,[X],Ys).

append(□,Is,Is).
append( [X|Is] ,Ys ,[X|Zs] ) <- append(Is,Ys,Zs).
```

Ex. 2. The N Queens Problem.
The problem was solved for 4,6,8 and 10 queens.

```
Predicate: q(N+, Queens-).
Queens is a possible configuration with N queens.

q(N,Qs) <- q(N,N,Qs).

q(Ntot,0,[]).
q(Ntot,N,[Q|Qs]) <- N>0, N1 is N-1, q(Ntot,N1,Qs), for(Q,1,Ntot),
                    ok(Q,1,Qs).

ok(Q,D,[]).
ok(Q,D,[Q1|Qs]) <- Q=\=Q1, Q-D=\=Q1, Q+D=\=Q1, D1 is D+1, ok(Q,D1,Qs).

for(N,N,U).
for(N,L,U) <- L<U, L1 is L+1, for(N,L1,U).
```

Ex. 3. Right recursive context-free grammar for arithmetic expressions.

Let e, f and t be nonterminals in the grammar:

```
e -> t | t+e
t -> f | f*t
f -> x | (e)
```

The expression (x+x+x+x)*(x+x)*x+x*(x+x) was parsed with the following
program:

```
e(E-E0) <- t(E-E0).
e(E-E0) <- t(E-['+'|E1]), e(E1-E0).

t(T-T0) <- f(T-T0).
t(T-T0) <- f(T-['*'|T1]), t(T1-T0).

f([x|Is]-Is).
f(['('|F]-F0) <- e(F-[')'|F0]).
```

Ex. 4. Left recursive variant of ex. 3.

```
e -> t | e+t
t -> f | t*f
f -> x | (e)
```

The same expression as in ex. 3 was parsed with the program below.

```
e(E-E0) <- t(E-E0).
e(E-E0) <- e(E-['+'|E1]), t(E1-E0).
```

```
t(T-T0) <- f(T-T0).
t(T-T0) <- t(T-['*'|T1]), f(T1-T0).

f([x|Xs]-Xs).
f(['('|F]-F0) <- e(F-[')'|F0]).
```

Ex. 5. The Cannibals and Missionaries Problem.

```
Predicate: mc( ( Bank_x+, Persons_on_x+ ),
               ( Bank_y+, Persons_on_y+ ),
               Trips-).
```

A bank is either left_bank or right_bank.
A person is either a cannibal (c) or a missionary (m).
A trip is one person or a pair of persons.

```
mc( (Bx,Psx), (By,Psy), [P|Trips] ) <-
    ok(Psx), ok(Psy),
    del(P,Psx,Ps),
    mc( (By,[P|Psy]), (Bx,Ps), Trips ).

mc( (Bx,Psx), (By,Psy), [(P1,P2)|Trips] ) <-
    ok(Psx), ok(Psy),
    del(P1,Psx,Ps1), del(P2,Ps1,Ps2),
    mc( (By,[P1,P2|Psy]), (Bx,Ps2), Trips ).

mc( _, (left_bank,[]), [] ).

ok(B) <-
        count(m,B,Nm),
        ifthen( Nm>0, (
                count(c,B,Nc),
                Nm>=Nc
                )
            ).

count(P,[],0).
count(P,[P|Ps],N) <-  count(P,Ps,N1), N is N1+1.
count(P,[P1|Ps],N) <- P\=P1 , count(P,Ps,N).

del(I,[I|Xs],Xs).
del(I,[Y|Xs],[Y|Zs]) <- del(I,Xs,Zs).
```

The goal evaluated was

```
<- mc( (left_bank,[c,c,c,m,m,m]), (right_bank,[]), Trips).
```

Ex. 6. Path Finding. Inspired by [2].

A polygon is a list of points [P_1, P_2,..., P_n, P_1].
A world is a list of polygons.
A sequence of moves is a list of points.

A path from point A to point B was found in the world shown in
the figure below.

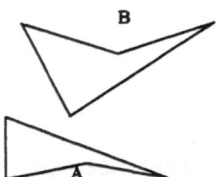

The goal evaluated was:

```
<- move( (5,1),
 (8,11),
 [ [(1,1),(6,2),(11,1),(1,5),(1,1)],
   [(5,5),(14,11),(8,9),(2,11),(5,5)]
 ],
 Moves).
```

CP = Current Point
TP = Target Point
NP = Next Point

Predicate: move(CP+, TP+, World+, Moves-). Moves represent a path from
          CP to TP.

```
move(CP,TP,W,[TP]) <-
        not ( mem(Pol,W), intersect(CP,TP,Pol) ).

move(CP,TP,W,[NP|Ms]) <-
        mem(Pol,W),
        edge(CP,NP,Pol),
        move(NP,TP,W,Ms).

move(CP,TP,W,[NP|Ms]) <-
        mem(Pol,W),
        not edge(CP,_,Pol),
        mem(NP,Pol),
        not ( mem(Pol1,W), intersect(CP,NP,Pol1) ),
        move(NP,TP,W,Ms).

edge(Px,Py,[Px,Py|_]).
```

```
edge(Px,Py,[Py,Px|_]).
edge(Px,Py,[_|Pol]) <- edge(Px,Py,Pol).

mem(X,[X|_]).
mem(X,[_|Xs]) <- mem(X,Xs).

intersect( (X1,Y1), (X2,Y2), [(X1p,Y1p),(X2p,Y2p)|Pol] ) <-
        (X1,Y1)\=(X1p,Y1p), (X1,Y1)\=(X2p,Y2p),
        (X2,Y2)\=(X1p,Y1p), (X2,Y2)\=(X2p,Y2p),
        D is (X2-X1)*(Y2p-Y1p)+(X1p-X2p)*(Y2-Y1),
        D\=0,
        K is (Y1*X2p-Y1*X1p-X1*Y2p+X1*Y1p-Y1p*X2p+Y2p*X1p)/D,
        0=<K, K=<1,
        Kp is -(Y2*X1-Y2*X1p-X2*Y1+Y1*X1p+X2*Y1p-X1*Y1p)/D,
        0=<Kp, Kp=<1.

intersect(CP,NP,[_|Pol]) <-
        intersect(CP,NP,Pol).
```

Ex. 7. Proving that a group is commutative if the square of every element is the identity element [11].

X * Y = Z is equivalent to p(X,Y,Z).

```
p(X,e,X).
p(e,X,X).
p(X,X,e).
p(a,b,c).
p(U,Z,W) <- p(X,Y,U), p(Y,Z,V), p(X,V,W).
p(X,V,W) <- p(X,Y,U), p(Y,Z,V), p(U,Z,W).
```

The goal evaluated was <- p(b,a,c).

The tables at the end of this article show the number of nodes expanded i.e. the number of logical inferences. RIP and DFIDERU-RP were run 10 times for each resolvent.

5   Future Work and Conclusions

Some possible improvements of the SLD-tree search algorithms presented above are to add Repeated Call Penalization to RIP, to a higher degree automate DFIDERU-RP's strategy selection and to develop an abstract machine based compiler.

The interpreters in this article are intended to be used for executing logic programs and not for proving theorems. They do therefore not use the same plethora of heuristic pruning rules often employed by theorem provers, since these rules are almost exclusively useful for theorem proving applications. For theorem proving problems, such rules can however drastically reduce the search space. The full first-order logic prover PTTP [11], that uses fewer pruning rules than most other provers, does for instance solve example 7 using 1589 logical inferences, which is much better than the 13279 inferences used by DFID, but not much of an improvement compared with the 1792 inferences needed by DFIDERU. PTTP would unfortunately for examples 1, 2 and 3 perform about the same number of inferences as DFID and more inferences than DFIDER on all examples except number 7 and therefore be extremely inefficient if used as a logic programming language interpreter.

It is difficult to find one single SLD-tree search algorithm that performs well on all examples. For every algorithm in this article, it is relatively easy to contrive a program for which its performance is poor. The choice of an algorithm should be strongly influenced by "real life" programs and not by purely academic ones. Loosely speaking, DFID, DFIDE, DFIDER and DFIDERU are bad for deep and bushy SLD-trees with very many goal nodes. Examples 2 and 5 have such trees. RIP performs poorly on bushy trees with many infinite branches and only one or a few goal nodes. Examples 4 and 7 have such trees. The experimental data gathered so far indicate that DFIDERU-RP is a good SLD-tree search algorithm if a very big decrease in bad case execution time is desired and an increase of 2 to 3 times for the best case does not matter. DFIDERU-RP has good all-round performance and can easily execute all 7 of the examples in the preceding section, whereas Prolog, even if augmented with a delay mechanism as in [8] and loop detection as in [12], only terminates for 3 examples.

References

1. Fribourg, L., SLOG: A Logic Programming Language Interpreter Based on Clausal Superposition and Rewriting, in Proceedings of the 1985 Symposium on Logic Programming, IEEE Computer Society Press, 1985, pp. 172–184.

2. Jorgensen, C., Hamel, W. and Weisbin, C., Autonomous Robot Navigation, Byte, January 1986, pp. 223–235.

3. Karp, R.M. and Rabin, M.O., Efficient Randomized Pattern-Matching Algorithms, Technical Report TR-31-81, Harvard University, 1981.

4. Korf, R.E., Depth-First Iterative-Deepening: An Optimal Admissible Tree Search, Artificial Intelligence, vol. 27, 1985, pp. 97–109.

5. Lloyd, J.W., Foundations of Logic Programming, Second Edition, Springer-Verlag, 1987.

6. Loveland, D.W., Near-Horn Prolog, in: Proceedings of the 4th International Conference on Logic Programming, Melbourne, 1987, pp. 163–190.

7. Mukai, K. and Furukawa, K., An Ordered Linear Resolution Theorem Proving Program in Prolog, ICOT TM-0027, Inst. for New Generation Computer Technology, Tokyo, 1984.

8. Naish, L., Automating Control for Logic Programs, J. Logic Programming, no. 3, 1985, pp. 167–183

9. Naish, L., Negation and Control in Prolog, Technical Report 85/12, Dept. of Computer Science, University of Melbourne, 1985.

10. Shapiro, E.Y., Algorithmic Program Debugging, MIT Press, 1983.

11. Stickel, M.E., A Prolog Technology Theorem Prover: Implementation by an Extended Prolog Compiler, in Proceedings of the 8th International Conference on Automated Deduction, Oxford, 1986, pp. 583–587.

12. van Gelder, A., Negation as Failure Using Tight Derivations for General Logic Programs, J. Logic Programming, no. 6, 1989, pp. 109-133.

Input Size	DF	DFID	DFIDE	DFIDER	DFIDERU
Ex. 1.					
3	10	45	24	24	24
9	55	1375	145	145	145
27	406	78967	932	932	932
81	3403	5700025	7132	7132	7132
Ex. 2.					
4	201	12383	963	963	963
6	1790	498450	17180	17180	17180
8	12021	19859437	430771	430771	430771
10	15991	$> 10^8$	10282130	10282130	10282130
Ex. 3.					
	189	4488	563	563	563
Ex. 4.					
	∞	170817	47563	3079	3079
Ex. 5.					
	∞	$> 10^8$	$> 10^8$	$> 10^8$	$> 10^8$
Ex. 6.					
	∞	3431	1433	1332	1332
Ex. 7.					
	∞	13279	12005	5041	1792

Input Size	RIP	DFIDERU-RP

Ex. 1.

3	25 25 25 25 25	10 10 10 10 10
	25 25 25 25 25	10 10 10 10 10
9	118 118 118 118 118	55 55 55 55 55
	118 118 118 118 118	55 55 55 55 55
27	917 917 917 917 917	806 806 806 806 806
	917 917 917 917 917	806 806 806 806 806
81	7498 7498 7498 7498 7498	6803 6803 6803 6803 6803
	7498 7498 7498 7498 7498	6803 6803 6803 6803 6803

Ex. 2.

4	368 216 486 472 478	405 209 439 95 257
	347 466 217 356 481	427 293 403 429 97
6	983 3992 3961 3629 3711	3814 3082 872 3264 3058
	3260 415 5653 2414 2413	260 667 872 663 2413
8	3659 22043 3401 5872 5529	3212 11260 2654 3477 2834
	2536 6563 9830 11454 12592	22041 4868 3239 6463 8801
10	2753 44001 7035 7491 30394	28071 5214 8638 29178 2615
	3362 30961 12529 6709 30454	6696 5840 22434 28614 28011

Ex. 3.

	428 359 376 432 125	273 221 204 227 162
	223 416 231 434 113	96 50 279 209 261

Ex. 4.

	$> 10^8 > 10^8 > 10^8 > 10^8 > 10^8$	6179 6179 6179 6179 6179
	$> 10^8 > 10^8 > 10^8 > 10^8 > 10^8$	6179 6179 6179 6179 6179

Ex. 5.

	25285 51919 28489 25321 7499	13468 35654 48200 76484 35418
	13038 21583 12498 29638 24187	17802 38252 24206 17838 6804

Ex. 6.

	1784 1281 694 1879 2872	408 1003 694 482 277
	1200 798 1117 1526 463	1461 858 2283 1656 1625

Ex. 7.

	$> 10^8 > 10^8 > 10^8 > 10^8 > 10^8$	3592 3592 3592 3592 3592
	$> 10^8 > 10^8 > 10^8 > 10^8 > 10^8$	3592 3592 3592 3592 3592

A Common Graphical Form

David Parrott *

Department of Computer Science, University College London

London, England.

Chris Clack

Department of Computer Science, University College London

London, England.

30th April 1991

Abstract

We present the Common Graphical Form, a low level, abstract machine independent structure which provides a basis for implementing graph reduction on distributed processors. A key feature of the structure is its ability to model disparate abstract machines in a uniform manner; this enables us to experiment with different abstract machines without having to recode major parts of the run-time system for each additional machine. Because we are dealing with a uniform data structure it is possible to build a suite of performance measurement tools to examine interprocessor data-flow and to apply these tools to different abstract machines in order to make relative comparisons between them at run-time. As a bonus to our design brief we exploit the unifying characteristics of the Common Graphical Form by using it as an intermediate language at compile-time.

1 Introduction

Graph reduction is a well established method for executing lazy, higher order, functional programs on sequential architectures and a number of abstract machines have been designed to execute programs using this technique (e.g. [1]). Recent research has been directed towards graph reduction on parallel architectures, adapting existing abstract machines to cope with the added complexities (e.g. [2]) and building new computational models with parallelism as a primary design factor ([3]).

Some study has been made towards theoretically comparing abstract machine designs [4, 5]. The research concentrates on the mathematical equivalence of abstract reduction mechanisms but does not encompass the wider environmental issues such as suspending and resuming tasks and the effects due to the way program state is represented in different machines. Our research programme includes the *practical* comparison of the behaviour of parallel abstract machines and, in this paper, we present the development of a data structure which greatly simplifies the experimental process. Much of the overhead experienced by distributed parallel architectures is due to interprocessor communication, hence the structure is designed to standardise the mechanisms for performing and measuring run-time communication, irrespective of the abstract machine employed.

Parallel architectures are amazingly diverse, ranging from tightly coupled, shared memory systems (e.g. the BBN Butterfly) to loosely coupled, distributed memory systems (e.g. the Intel iPSC). Understanding why abstract machines behave as they do in given circumstances should be an important factor influencing the choice or design of an abstract machine

---

*Supported by a SERC research studentship

for a particular environment. We shall be concentrating on distributed memory architectures which rely on message passing for interprocessor communications but the techniques described will also be applicable to those shared memory architectures which use some form of message passing. The data structure is based on the lambda calculus, common to most modern abstract reduction mechanisms, and is a graphical expression of functional programs, hence it is called the Common Graphical Form (or $\mathcal{CGF}$).

The *primary* use for $\mathcal{CGF}$ is to encapsulate programs at run-time in an abstract machine independent manner. However, because it identifies the common ground between various classes of abstract machine, we can also use the structure at other stages of implementation where there is a need for low level functional program description. For example, $\mathcal{CGF}$ can be used as a low-level intermediate language at compile-time. We shall discuss this secondary issue in the latter sections of the paper but it is worth noting at this point the existence of the dual modes of operation and to realise that they are distinct.

1.1 Machine Comparisons

It is possible to compare the raw performance statistics of abstract machines and to state which takes the least amount of time to execute a particular program [6, 7]. Unfortunately, this does not provide sufficient information to say *why* one machine runs faster than another. Also, distributed processing systems often communicate over data networks and so a degree of non-determinism is introduced due to network loadings, bottlenecks, and the reliability of the communications hardware. Non-determinism reduces the consistency of real-time measurements and makes it difficult to glean useful information. It is therefore more informative to monitor directly the internal workings of the abstract machines in order to investigate the effects of the host environment on the machines' efficiency. This provides a rationale for a machine's performance statistics and so helps to make predictions about how the machine would fare if the environment were altered.

Comparing the internal operations of different abstract machines is difficult because each machine uses its own, unique, data structures to denote programs. If the number of *reductions* is used as the performance metric then we have to account for the fact that there may be significant variation in the amount of work done by a single reduction (this can also be dependent on the way a program is compiled [6]). Moreover, the relationship between similar instructions on different machines may not be linear (e.g. instructions to select the next redex, and those to build graph structures).

We turn to parallel processing in order to speed up program execution, thence success depends heavily on the ability of a number of processing elements to cooperate efficiently. We believe, therefore, that interprocessor communication is an important factor when measuring distributed abstract machine behaviour and we use it as a basis for our study. A method of standardising interprocessor communications is required; $\mathcal{CGF}$ fulfils this requirement, making it possible to construct a monitoring and measurement package that can cope with all of the abstract machines likely to be studied. If $\mathcal{CGF}$ is properly designed then it will not be necessary to rebuild the mechanisms for each new abstract machine.

The peripheral advantages gained by using $\mathcal{CGF}$ are also applicable to *shared* memory systems. For instance, it is possible to build a standard set of tools to manipulate the data structure without committing the techniques to any specific abstract machine. The unification of communication measurement facilities made possible by the data structure is also relevant to a shared memory architecture, although it is of greatest utility when the primary method of interprocessor communications is message passing.

1.2 Organisation of the Paper

The remaining sections of this paper are organised as follows. Section 2 examines the depiction of functional programs at the lowest, abstract machine level. Using this as a starting point, we consider what is desired of a Common Graphical Form. Section 3 contains a complete description of $\mathcal{CGF}$ for use at run-time, giving justifications for the design decisions taken. Section 4 deals with the secondary use of $\mathcal{CGF}$ as a compile-time intermediate language, examining higher level characterisations of functional programs and presenting a full textual representation for the structure. Section 5 gives examples of uses for $\mathcal{CGF}$ and, finally, section 6 concludes with $\mathcal{CGF}$'s achievements.

2 Representing Functional Programs

$\mathcal{CGF}$'s primary goal is to describe lazy, higher order, functional programs at run-time in a manner that is not dependent on any one abstract machine so that interprocessor communications can be normalised.[1] To achieve this it is necessary to discover (*a*) the fundamental properties that are common to the many abstract models and (*b*) what information needs to be passed between remote processors. We shall examine both low and high level structures to obtain a complete picture. In this section we concentrate on the low level structures employed by some well documented abstract machines.

Graphs, Code, and Stacks

Implementations of lazy, higher order, functional languages typically have three distinct uses of memory:

heap space in which to build graphical structures,

code memory in which to place (abstract) machine code sequences, and

stacks on which evaluation is controlled (or, given that the result is not to be shared, the stack may be used by some compiled abstract machines to perform evaluation without having to access the heap).

Higher order functions and laziness call for a mechanism to implement *suspensions*; laziness also implies the ability to share the results of computations. The suspension mechanism is usually expressed using a *closure* which is described by a pair: ⟨function, environment⟩. This is precisely what every abstract machine needs to build. Both closures and shared values demand a more flexible storage medium than a stack, so a *heap* is required. The type of information stored in the heap is of consequence to $\mathcal{CGF}$'s design so a detailed study is made in the following sections.

2.1 Graphs

Table 1 lists a number of abstract machines, showing the *tuples* which make up the graphical run-time information on which each machine operates. The table contains a fairly small sample of abstract machines but it should be apparent that a trend is becoming established. The terminology varies from tuple to tuple (it is based on the sources referenced in the second column of the table), hence some explanation is necessary before we continue.

Function, code, and codeptr all reference some (abstract) machine code whilst $Field_1$ and head reference a graphical (i.e. interpretive) function definition. $Field_2$, tail, item, and arg are either unboxed data items or pointers, and Lal George's env is simply a collection of arguments (equivalent to arg*). Tim's frameptr is also a pointer to an environment but with a subtle difference: a Tim *frame* contains ⟨codeptr, frameptr⟩ pairs instead of single values or pointers. This is isomorphic to the ⟨code, arg*⟩ arrangement [15], as demonstrated in

---

[1]Note that $\mathcal{CGF}$ does not preclude the use of efficient, internal abstract machine representations (see section 5.1).

Machine	Reference	Node Description
Spineless G-Machine	[8]	⟨function, arg*, tag⟩
Spineless Tagless G-Machine	[9]	⟨function, arg*⟩
Tim	[10]	⟨⟨codeptr, frameptr⟩*⟩
⟨ν, G⟩-machine	[2]	⟨tag, code, link, arg*, tempspace⟩
Lal George Abstract Machine	[11]	⟨tag, code, waitcount, notechain, env⟩
Flagship	[12] [13]	⟨tag, item*⟩
G-machine	[1]	⟨tag, field$_1$, field$_2$⟩
Four-stroke Reduction Engine	[14]	⟨tag, head, tail⟩

* indicates zero or more

Table 1: Some examples of graphical data.

figure 1 (just *slide* each function reference, f_n, from the head of a *vector application node*, backwards along the arrow pointing to the node, and pair it with the pointer), so no special data structure is required to build Tim's heap.

The other items in the tuples in table 1 are house-keeping information of one sort or another and these will be dealt with in due course. (There will be yet further house-keeping overheads depending upon specific implementation details; again, this will be dealt with later.)

The reason for the similarities between the abstract machines' data structures is that all are realisations of closures, thus if CGF is to be abstract machine independent then a general purpose closure mechanism must be defined. A closure is a function and a set of arguments which form an environment. Conveniently, a *vector application* node satisfies the basic format of a function applied to a variable number of arguments, which just leaves the problem of describing a (possibly hierarchical) environment. This issue is tackled in section 3.2.1.

Any remaining data such as further tags and dynamic links (see section 5.1.2) can be packaged as *extra* information with respect to the minimal closure definition. The *extras* do not effect the semantics of the graph but merely carry state information as required by the abstract machine. Separating semantically relevant data from overheads in this way allows a more accurate interpretation of the interprocessor communications to be made.

2.2 Code

A naïve scheme for program loading may dictate that every compiled function definition is loaded onto every processing element before execution commences (e.g. see [16]). This is clearly undesirable for large programs because a great deal of time and memory is wasted by duplicating code that will never be executed. An intelligent program loader, however, might partition the program code so that it is divided amongst the processing elements in the same manner that a graph is divided between the processors of an interpretive graph reduction engine. In this scenario, code sequences must be transferred between remote processing elements when tasks are migrated and hence a special addressing mode is required to uniquely name the sequences. By exploiting this addressing mode further, CGF can be used

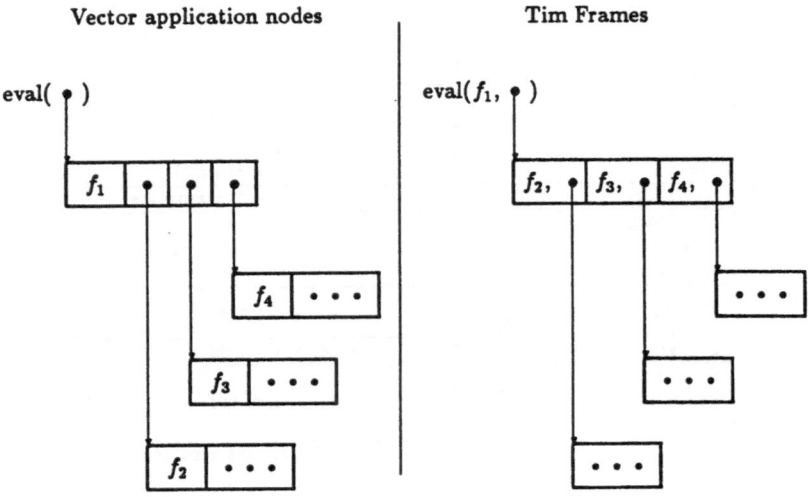

Figure 1: Tim's frames and vector applications are isomorphic.

by the loader itself for initial program distribution, again saving effort when experimenting with new abstract machines because the loader remains essentially unchanged from machine to machine.

Apart from insisting that separate code sequences are distinguishable, no structure is imposed on the code and no meaning is attributed to it. Each sequence may contain native machine code destined for a specific piece of hardware, abstract machine code that will be interpreted by an abstract machine, or some hybrid, depending upon the experimental whims of the implementer.

2.3 Stacks

Stacks are used extensively by abstract machines when evaluating programs. A stack is an efficient tool for expression evaluation and is an efficient medium for evaluating local, unshared, temporary values which do not incur heap updates [8, 9]. The terms *local* and *temporary* may give the misleading impression that it will not be necessary to move stacked information between non-local processors. There are cases, however, when stack based information will need to be moved—for example, state information required to resume a suspended task may reside on the stack; if the task is migrated then the stacked data must also be migrated. Passing arguments to a remote function may also benefit from the ability to transmit a segment of local stack. Therefore the tools for interprocessor communication are designed to cater for the transference of stacked data but, because stacks are an abstract machine mechanism and not a natural part of a program graph, no references are made to stacked items from the graph and hence no extension to the $\mathcal{CGF}$ addressing modes is necessary.

3 A Description of $\mathcal{CGF}$ for use at Run-Time

In this section we describe the Common Graphical Form as a mechanism for encapsulating functional programs at run-time. A program is represented in Common Graphical Form

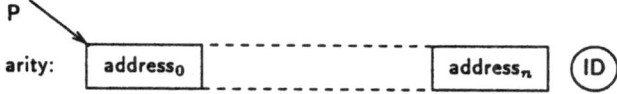

Figure 2: A node in Common Graphical Form.

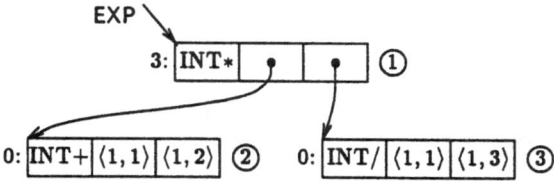

Figure 3: $\mathcal{CGF}$ structure for EXP $= \lambda x\, y\, z.\,(x + y) \times (x/z)$

by a collection of vector application nodes. Figure 2 presents an illustration of a node; the arity coefficient indicates the number of variables bound by the node, P is a *label*, ID is a unique *identifier* depicting the abstract address of the node, and address is one of the addressing modes described in section 3.2 below—the addressing modes are the singularly most important feature of $\mathcal{CGF}$.

Identifiers and labels serve two distinct diagrammatic purposes: identifiers are fixed to their respective nodes, but labels may move from one node to another. This will be useful when we perform transformations on $\mathcal{CGF}$ (e.g. note the label movement in figure 6).

3.1 $\mathcal{CGF}$'s Relation to the Lambda Calculus

$\mathcal{CGF}$ is based on the typed lambda calculus, augmented with a number of primitive functions and constants. Mechanisms for bound variable abstraction, function application, and beta reduction are provided and thus $\mathcal{CGF}$ is computationally complete. $\mathcal{CGF}$ also provides for explicit expression-sharing (which can be used to implement named functions) and for the definition of recursive functions by the use of cyclic graph structures.

User functions are defined by assigning an arity to an expression node, the expression can then be applied to some arguments in the usual way. Nodes with zero arity are employed to portray bracketed sub-expressions. For example, the lambda expression $\lambda x\, y\, z.\,(x + y) \times (x/z)$ requires three nodes (see figure 3), each containing an operator applied to two arguments. The top node applies the multiplication operator to each of the two (zero arity) sub-expressions.

3.2 Addressing Modes

We provide a fixed number of addressing modes to describe various entities. It is a straight-forward exercise to perform case analysis (or pattern matching) over the addressing modes in order to process the information within a node. The following sections describe the addressing modes in detail.

3.2.1 Bound variables

In [17] de Bruijn shows that variables bound within lambda expressions can be fully described by a pair of integers which provide access to *environments*. We use a modified version of his scheme, written $\langle d, i \rangle$, to reference the ith bound variable belonging to the node which occurs d bindings beyond the reference. (Binding levels are illustrated by following pointers backwards, counting the number of non-zero arity nodes visited.) We refer to the $\langle d, i \rangle$ construction as a *de Bruijn* address (Cousineau et al use a similar technique to overcome naming problems in their Categorical Abstract Machine [18]).

Note that all de Bruijn addresses in a lambda lifted program are of the form $\langle 1, i \rangle$ because variables must be bound by the innermost, non-zero arity node. There is no reason to suppose that all abstract machines will use lambda lifting however (e.g. [4]), so the full power of de Bruijn addressing is retained.

3.2.2   Inter-node references

To build a graph structure using $\mathcal{CGF}$ we must be able to make arbitrary references to nodes. Three addressing modes are provided for this purpose:

Abstract addresses are borrowed from [19] where graphs are described textually: each line of text symbolizes a unique node in the graph so that line numbers can be used to address the nodes. This abstracts away from machine level addressing and is ideal when graph segments are packaged up for interprocessor communication.

Real addresses are machine level pointers that identify memory locations within the concrete address space of the local processing element. (When graphs are migrated from one processor to another, some real addresses will be translated into remote addresses and others will become abstract addresses.)

Remote addresses refer to memory locations in remote address spaces. Hughes notes that remote pointers are rare in comparison to local pointers [20] and so by separating local and remote addressing into two distinct modes it is possible to build local indirections to remote addresses. Under non-strict evaluation, an indirection is followed only when a normal form is required, hence remote addresses are only ever encountered when a value *must* be obtained from a remote processing element.

Diagrammatically, a reference to a node may be shown (a) by an arrow physically pointing to the node, (b) by an identifier (which may be numeric), or (c) by a label. The graph to which a label, P, or an identifier, I, refers may be written $\vec{P}$ or $\vec{I}$, respectively.

3.2.3   Data objects

A single addressing mode is used to describe all data objects so that case analysis is not unduly slow. Structured data is built using boxed nodes and in the unevaluated state it is represented by the application of a constructor function to the requisite number of arguments. No constraints are placed on the range of structured data types available because new structures can be introduced by adding extra constructor primitives.

Data objects may or may not need to carry further information to distinguish different data types—this is dependent upon the underlying implementation. $\mathcal{CGF}$ possesses an explicit type mechanism for those implementations which need to perform type checking at run-time (a description of this mechanism is given in section 4.4) but it is not mandatory and need not be used when types are implied by context such as in strongly typed systems. Primitive functions are considered to be data, and may either be distinguished by context (i.e. by function application) or may be given a special tag. The choice of which primitive functions to employ is left to the discretion of the implementer.

4   A Description of $\mathcal{CGF}$ for use at Compile-Time

In this section we look at one way in which we can extend the compass of $\mathcal{CGF}$ beyond its use at run-time by demonstrating that, in order to satisfy those abstract machines which require

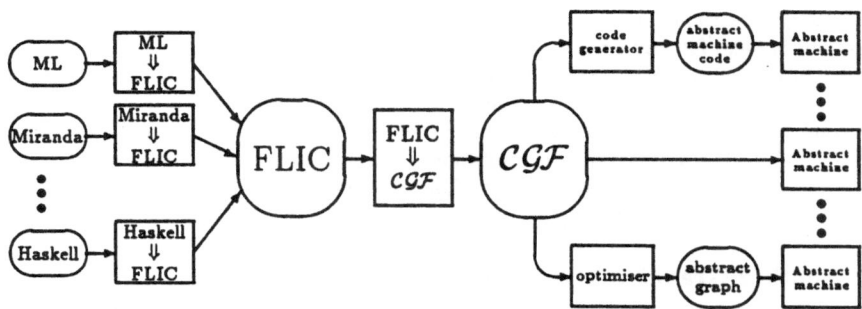

Figure 4: $\mathcal{CGF}$ can be used for compilation in conjunction with FLIC to provide a route from many high level languages to many abstract machines.

tagged data items at run-time, we have inadvertently developed a low level mechanism that can be used to implement FLIC at compile-time. $\mathcal{CGF}$ is thus promoted to the status of an intermediate language. Firstly, we consider $\mathcal{CGF}$'s relationship with FLIC and other intermediate languages to get an idea of where $\mathcal{CGF}$ fits into the overall framework. Then we present a *textual* description of $\mathcal{CGF}$ which is amenable to transmission using electronic mail, that can be used to inspect intermediate stages of compilation, and which is easily interpreted by parts of the compiler built using a functional programming language.

4.1 The Functional Language Intermediate Code

FLIC [21] was designed to sit one level below the high level programming languages to provide a reference point for compilers, allowing standardised mechanisms such as source to source compilation modules. Modularity implies that techniques can be freely exchanged and new languages can be easily accommodated. FLIC's design incorporates a powerful set of primitive functions which are capable of expressing many functional constructions, including complex data structures.

$\mathcal{CGF}$ is a low level tool, designed primarily to cope with run-time and communications demands. Nevertheless, FLIC's family of primitives are a powerful compile-time asset and so we have adopted them as our primitive function set for compilation purposes. Therefore, $\mathcal{CGF}$ can provide a compile-time facility similar to FLIC but at a lower level.

FLIC programs retain much of the flavour of the lambda calculus; they are textually concise, are human readable, and are amenable to straightforward *pretty-print* formatting. $\mathcal{CGF}$ programs are less readable than the equivalent FLIC versions and textually less concise (see, for example, section 4.4) but, just as FLIC removes syntactic sugaring such as list comprehensions, $\mathcal{CGF}$ does much the same with syntax such as arbitrarily nested let and letrec definitions which complicate parsing and concrete representation. $\mathcal{CGF}$'s low level structure is well suited to rapid compilation because, in addition to maintaining a level of abstraction above the underlying abstract machine, it imposes little or no parsing overhead. This may be significant when there are many stages of compilation (for example, approximately 25 passes are claimed for the LML compiler [22]).

$\mathcal{CGF}$ is designed with efficient machine readability in mind and so does not necessarily replace FLIC; it is, however, complementary. Just as FLIC provides a focal point for high level languages, $\mathcal{CGF}$ is able to provide a similar focus for compiler backends. Figure 4 demonstrates how $\mathcal{CGF}$ fits into the compilation scheme—note that source to source transformations can occur at either the FLIC or $\mathcal{CGF}$ stages.

An important feature of FLIC is its ability to annotate programs in order to influence the compiler's decisions (although not influencing the semantics of the program). $\mathcal{CGF}$'s *extras* field is ideal for implementing FLIC annotations because, like the annotations, it is designed to hold information which is not directly related to program semantics. Program transformations performed at the $\mathcal{CGF}$ level can then either take annotations into account given code to interpret the fields correctly, or they can simply ignore them, naïvly carrying them through to the next stage of compilation. (Some further work may be needed in this area to decide how best to maintain annotations when non-trivial transformations cause the program to be altered significantly.)

4.2   Another Graphical Language: GCODE

The functional language project at Birmingham and Warwick universities found it necessary to create a standard, printable format for representing graphs which they called GCODE [19]. The underlying mechanism is a binary graph but the representation is reasonably high level—for example, the original variable names are retained from the source as an aid to debugging. The standard is very tightly defined as it is intended for a specific environment and, more importantly, it does not attempt to address the problems of distributing graphs across separate address spaces.

This differs from $\mathcal{CGF}$'s design brief which requires a more general purpose mechanism. $\mathcal{CGF}$ is consequently more flexible at compile-time (i.e. conversion from GCODE to $\mathcal{CGF}$ is simple, but not vice versa) and is more powerful at run-time, catering for interprocessor communications and providing low level access to function parameters. $\mathcal{CGF}$'s abstract addressing mode (section 3.2.2) was inspired by one of the techniques described in [19].

4.3   DACTL

$\mathcal{CGF}$ differs from the DACTL intermediate language [23] because the latter is designed to encompass a range of declarative programming styles and so describes programs at a higher level of abstraction; low level issues are ignored. Our objective was to develop an intermediate language that could be used to describe programs at the abstract machine level, i.e. in terms of memory cells. For example, DACTL utilises local naming to describe sharing whereas $\mathcal{CGF}$ describes a graph exactly, using its abstract addressing mode to build shared nodes and cycles.

It is clear then that the objectives of the two formats are quite different. DACTL provides a metric for reasoning about different programming styles while, by limiting its scope to the applicative programming style, $\mathcal{CGF}$ provides the facility to measure and reason about the low level functionality of different abstract machines.

4.4   Representing $\mathcal{CGF}$ Textually

$\mathcal{CGF}$ is ideally suited to internal low level representations within a run-time system or a compiler but it is sometimes necessary to build a textual version so that the code may be inspected manually and so that it can be read in a straightforward manner by compiler modules written in a functional language. The following textual representation is simple and efficient to parse.

Each vector application node is represented by a single line of text terminated with a newline character. The first entry specifies the number of cells and is followed by a textual description for each cell. The arity of the node is given next, followed lastly by any (implementation specific) *extra* information. Addressing modes are specified by a two character code and data types by a three character code as follows:

Code	Addressing mode	Code	Data type
NO	no address (NULL)	INT	integer
AB	abstract	FLP	floating point
RE	real	PRM	primitive function
DA	data	STR	string data
DB	de Bruijn	CHR	character data
RT	remote	BLN	boolean data

Qualifiers, GN and SC, specify whether abstract addresses refer to graph nodes, or super-combinators. The textual representation for addresses is unambiguous and so no special delimiters are needed to separate cell definitions. Numeric and character constants are written in ascii format and are distinguished by context. Primitive functions are given in uppercase, e.g. CONS, TRUE, INT+, IS-NIL. The following is an example specification (equivalent to EXP in figure 3):

Abstract address (line number)	cells	Textual description function	arguments		arity	extras
1	3	DA PRM INT*	AB GN 2	AB GN 3	3	
2	3	DA PRM INT+	DB 1 1	DB 1 2	0	
3	3	DA PRM INT/	DB 1 1	DB 1 3	0	

5 Examples of Use

This section demonstrates some of the ways that $\mathcal{CGF}$ can be used both at run-time, as was originally intended, and during compilation. The given examples currently form part of an active programme of research in distributed implementations for functional programming at UCL.

5.1 Implementing Run-Time Systems

The primary design aim of $\mathcal{CGF}$ is to simplify the creation and maintenance of a run-time environment and to support a range of different abstract machines and system configurations. The abstract machines will be of many types, including compiled and interpreted machines, and loading and reduction strategies will demand varying degrees of interprocessor communication with assorted levels of granularity.

$\mathcal{CGF}$'s structures can be optimised for run-time use and tailored for compatibility with specific abstract machines—the specification is sufficiently flexible to enable special versions to be constructed and still take advantage of the library of tools. Our library contains routines to manipulate $\mathcal{CGF}$'s addressing modes, utilities to measure the data-flow between remote processing elements, programs to flatten graphs into a form suitable for transmission between processing elements and to reconstruct them at the other end, and so on. The library utilities are expressed in terms of $\mathcal{CGF}$ addressing modes and require minimal interfaces to accommodate the implementation details of the individual abstract machines.

Much careful consideration has been given to the design and we have avoided imposing overheads that could bias measurements in favour of one abstract machine over another; this is important because $\mathcal{CGF}$ will be used to make relative comparisons between machines. Many options are left available to the implementer to make the most efficient possible use of $\mathcal{CGF}$.

5.1.1 $\mathcal{CGF}$ graph reduction engine

An interpretive graph reduction engine has been built which uses binary $\mathcal{CGF}$ nodes (i.e. every node has two cells) as the basis for building graphs. The interpretive engine has the

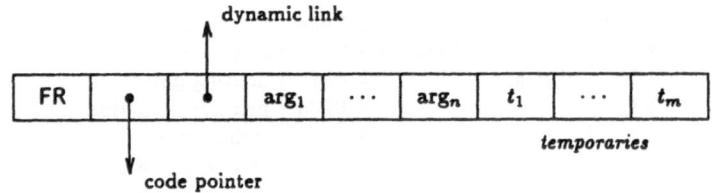

Figure 5: A $\langle \nu, G \rangle$-machine frame node.

advantage of simplicity, enabling experiments to be made with loading and task management strategies without the added complications resulting from compiled graph reduction. The simplicity of the machine allows new ideas to be rapidly prototyped and thus encourages experimentation—measurements can be taken from compiled abstract machines once the techniques are properly understood.

5.1.2 The $\langle \nu, G \rangle$-machine

The $\langle \nu, G \rangle$-machine [2] is a compiled abstract machine in which heap allocated graph nodes are treated as stack frames, thereby simplifying task suspension and removing the overhead of copying data between the heap and the stack. To emphasize their superior status the nodes are referred to as *frame nodes*. A frame node (shown in figure 5) consists of five parts:

1. A **tag** which distinguishes between *reducible* frame nodes (those which contain a function applied to the correct number of arguments), constant applications (a function applied to too few arguments), and constructor values (complex data items).

2. A **code pointer** identifying the compiled function that is to be applied to the arguments.

3. A **dynamic link** pointing backwards to the calling frame node (and hence to the preceding stack frame).

4. A list of **arguments**, $\arg_1 \ldots \arg_n$, to which the function is applied.

5. Cells, $t_1 \ldots t_m$, for **temporary** calculations. The stack frame grows and shrinks at run-time as items are effectively pushed onto and popped from the stack. This space can either be allocated dynamically or, where it is possible to calculate an upper bound on its size, can be fixed.

It is a straightforward exercise to build frame nodes in $\mathcal{CGF}$: the tag and the dynamic link are included as *extra* information because they are implementation details whilst the function, arguments, and temporaries are naturally represented by a standard $\mathcal{CGF}$ vector application. If the implementation uses a fixed size temporary space then another *extra* item is required to specify the size of the currently active part of the stack.

The purely interpretive facets of $\mathcal{CGF}$ such as de Bruijn addressing are, of course, not required by the $\langle \nu, G \rangle$-machine run-time environment but all other aspects of the format are employed by a distributed implementation.

5.1.3 Partitioning and loading

Partitioning and loading programs onto distributed processors is a non-trivial task which has inspired a large amount of interest (e.g. [24]) and will continue to do so as parallel and distributed processing become ever more common. Using $\mathcal{CGF}$ as the underlying structure for

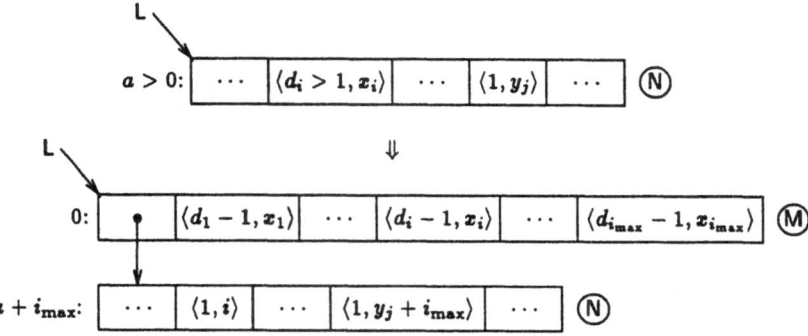

Figure 6: Lambda lifting a sub-graph, N, which contains i_{max} distinct free variables.

this activity allows the production of a single, generic program partitioner/loader that can be interfaced with a number of abstract machines. The advantages are three fold: firstly the algorithms do not have to be re-coded when the target abstract machine is changed and hence the corollary that improvements to the algorithms are automatically available to every abstract machine. The third advantage is that with the data already in CGF format, it is ready for transmission to the distributed processing elements without further transformation.

5.2 Modular Compilation

CGF is intended to highlight and exploit the common ground in disparate abstract machines so that we can experiment with run-time strategies and compare the effects across the spectrum of abstract machines under test. As a consequence of being a low level common core representation, CGF proves to be an ideal medium for source to source compilation. The format is very close to the underlying graph structures that will be used at run-time and as such can be manipulated with efficiency and ease.

5.2.1 Program transformation

Three types of program transformation have been implemented as CGF to CGF modules; these are lambda lifting, sharing analysis, and time-complexity analysis. Figure 6 illustrates how neatly the lambda lifting algorithm [25] translates to CGF's graph structure[2] with an arbitrary number ($= i_{max}$) of distinct free variables (this is the most general case). The code to lambda lift the whole graph consists of two nested depth-first graph traversals, the outer traversal to locate free expressions and the inner traversal to transform the whole subgraph including subsidiary nodes. Locating free variables is trivial because of the nature of de Bruijn addresses: an address $\langle d > 1, x \rangle$ depicts a free variable and is lifted by moving it outside the current binding, decrementing d to compensate for the reduced depth (a new node, M, is inserted into the graph to hold the lifted variables). Existing bound variables, $\langle 1, y \rangle$, are adjusted to account for the increased number of arguments. References which are buried many levels deep are simply *bubbled* upwards incrementally by the action of the outermost depth-first search. The algorithm requires the storage overhead of just a single marker which is used by both the inner and outer depth-first searches.

---

[2]full-laziness is achieved by modifying the algorithm slightly or by applying a second pass which recovers full-laziness upon completion of any other graph transformations.

236

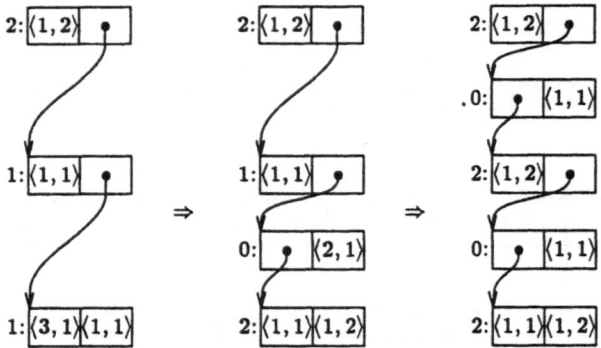

Figure 7: Lambda lifting $\lambda f\, g.g\,(\lambda h.h\,(\lambda x.f\,x))$ to give $\lambda f\, g.g\,((\lambda q\, h.h\,((\lambda p\, x.p\, x)\, q))\, f)$

Figure 7 provides a concrete example of lambda lifting using the algorithm given above. The lambda expression $\lambda f\, g.g\,(\lambda h.h\,(\lambda x.f\,x))$ contains three nested abstractions; the function variable f, which is applied at the innermost level, is free with respect to the two inner abstractions and is bound by the outermost abstraction. Two successive lift operations are needed to bubble the variable upwards, adding two extra nodes to the graph in the process.

5.2.2 Abstract machine backend

It is common for abstract machines to be specified by a set of transition rules and by a set of compilation rules (e.g. see [2, 10]) where the latter is usually defined over a small, convenient input language. $\mathcal{CGF}$ is ideal for use as input to a backend because the format so closely resembles the small languages employed in the specifications; the task of building a backend reduces to a simple implementation of the rules. As an example, we shall consider some of the compilation rules given in [2] for the $\langle \nu, G \rangle$-machine.

The $\langle \nu, G \rangle$-machine uses supercombinators and so all de Bruijn addresses will be of the form $\langle 1, i \rangle$. Advantage can therefore be taken of the constant *depth* by introducing a compiler pass which converts all de Bruijns into the form $\langle a, i \rangle$ where a is the *arity* of the enclosing user function; this gives the backend direct access to arity information without having to search the graph. The rule for compiling a parametric value, x, given an environment, ρ, and a current environment depth, n, is:

$$C[\![\, x\,]\!]\rho\, n = \mathsf{PUSH}(n - \rho(x))$$

which becomes just:

$$C'[\![\, \langle a, i \rangle\,]\!]n = \mathsf{PUSH}(n - a + i - 1)$$

thus reducing the environment function, ρ, to a closed form expression with respect to the values given by the de Bruijn address.

Consider the compilation scheme given for compiling function definitions:

$$\mathcal{F}[\![\, f\, x_1 \ldots x_n = e\,]\!] = \mathcal{R}[\![\, e\,]\!][x_1 = n, \cdots, x_n = 1]\, n$$

which maps to:

$$\mathcal{F}'[\![\, n > 0 : \boxed{\, e_0\, |\, \cdots\, |\, e_m\, }\,]\!] = \mathcal{R}'[\![\, \boxed{\, e_0\, |\, \cdots\, |\, e_m\, }\,]\!]n$$

The body of the function, e, is given by the application of e_0 to arguments $e_1 \ldots e_m$. The $\mathcal{R}$ scheme is responsible for compiling the application of a user function or primitive function (which may be a constructor) to a list of arguments. This is precisely what the $\mathcal{CGF}$ vector application node describes—we have just to examine the addressing mode of the function cell, e_0, to determine which $\mathcal{R}$ scheme case to invoke.

The other compilation schemes map just as easily onto $\mathcal{CGF}$'s structures and a compiler backend has been constructed for the $\langle \nu, G \rangle$-machine in a functional language. The functional code to manipulate the $\mathcal{CGF}$ bears a very close resemblance to the original set of compilation rules.

6 Conclusion

In this paper we have discussed two major advantages of using the Common Graphical Form: firstly, that it has encouraged the construction of shared libraries of utilities to manipulate functional data and, secondly, that it has provided a standard method to describe ideas in a low level, abstract machine independent manner. At UCL, $\mathcal{CGF}$ is employed as part of a distributed processing environment. It is helping to bind together various areas of our research including the development and performance measurement of distributed runtime strategies, the experimental comparison of abstract machines, and the construction of compilers for executing functional languages on distributed architectures.

$\mathcal{CGF}$ has been an invaluable tool for rapid prototyping at many stages of our system implementation, especially in constructing the compiler and its associated backends. Practice has shown that it is far more straightforward to manipulate the low level structure of $\mathcal{CGF}$ at compile time than to struggle with high level source languages, or intermediate forms such as FLIC. The format is simple to manipulate using both imperative and functional programming languages and so has provided the flexibility to choose whichever is most appropriate for each prototyping exercise. We have imperative and functional language library functions to translate efficiently between textual $\mathcal{CGF}$ and its internal representations and these form a simple interface between the otherwise incompatible programming styles.

As a mechanism for implementing run-time systems $\mathcal{CGF}$ has been extremely successful. During our continued research we expect it to save us a great deal of time and effort and to provide useful results when measuring abstract machine behaviour.

References

[1] T. Johnsson. Efficient compilation of lazy evaluation. In *Conf. on Compiler Construction*, pages 58–69. ACM, June 1984.

[2] L. Augustsson and T. Johnsson. Parallel graph reduction with the $\langle \nu, G \rangle$-machine. In *FPCA Conf.*, pages 202–213. ACM, 1989.

[3] G. Burn. Implementing lazy functional langauges on parallel architectures. In P. Trealeven, editor, *Parallel Computers (Object-Oriented, Functional, Logic)*, Series in Parallel Computing, chapter 7, pages 101–139. Wiley, 1990.

[4] E. Meijer. Cleaning up the design space of function evaluating machines. Tech. report, Univ. of Nejmegen, Dept. of Informatics, Mar. 1989.

[5] E. Meijer. A taxonomy of lazy function evaluating machines. Technical report, Univ. of Nejmegen, Dept. of Informatics, June 1989.

[6] I. Robertson. Hope+ on Flagship. In K. Davis and J. Hughes, editors, *Functional Programming, Glasgow 1989*, pages 296–307. Springer Verlag: Workshops in Computing, Aug. 1989.

[7] B. Goldberg and P. Hudak. *Alfalfa: distributed graph reduction on a hypercube multiprocessor*, volume 279 of *LNCS*, pages 94–113. Springer Verlag, Nov. 1986.

[8] G. Burn, S. Peyton Jones, and J. Robson. The Spineless G-Machine. In *Lisp and Functional Programming Conf.*, pages 244–258. Snowbird, July 1988.

[9] S. Peyton Jones and J. Salkild. The Spineless Tagless G-Machine. In *FPCA Conf.*, pages 184–201, 1989.

[10] J. Fairbairn and S. Wray. Tim: A simple, lazy abstract machine to execute supercombinators. In *FPCA Conf.*. ACM, Springer Verlag, Sept. 1987. LNCS 274.

[11] L. George. An abstract machine for parallel graph reduction. In *FPCA Conf.*, pages 214–228, 1989.

[12] P. Watson and I. Watson. Evaluating functional programs on the Flagship machine. In *FPCA Conf.*, pages 80–97. ACM, Springer Verlag, Sept. 1987. LNCS 274.

[13] I. Watson, V. Woods, P. Watson, R. Banach, M. Greenberg, and J. Sargeant. Flagship: A parallel architecture for declarative programming. T.R. FS/MU/IW/017-88, Manchester Univ., Dept. of Comp. Sci., Mar. 1988.

[14] C. Clack and S. Peyton Jones. The four-stroke reduction engine. In *Lisp and Functional Programming Conf.*, pages 220–232. ACM, Aug. 1986.

[15] S. Peyton Jones. The tag is dead—long live the packet. posting on fp electronic mailing list, Oct. 1987.

[16] P. Hudak and B. Goldberg. Experiments in diffused combinator reduction. In *Symposium on Lisp and Functional Programming*, pages 167–176. ACM, Aug. 1984.

[17] N. de Bruijn. Lambda calculus notation with nameless dummies, a tool for automatic formula manipulation, with application to the church-rosser theorem. *Indagationes Mathematicae*, 34:381–392, 1972.

[18] G. Cousineau, P. Curien, and M. Mauny. The categorical abstract machine. In *FPCA Conf.*, pages 50–64. ACM, Springer Verlag, Sept. 1985. LNCS 201.

[19] M. Joy and T. Axford. A standard for a graph representation for functional programs. In *Sigplan Notices 23(1)*, pages 75–82. ACM, 1988. Univ. of Birmingham I.R. CSR-87-1.

[20] J. Hughes. A distributed garbage collection algorithm. In *FPCA Conf.*, pages 256–272. ACM, Springer Verlag, Sept. 1985. LNCS 201.

[21] S. Peyton Jones and M. Joy. FLIC – a Functional Language Intermediate Code. I.N. 2048, University College London, Dept. of Comp. Sci., Aug. 1989.

[22] L. Augustsson and T. Johnsson. The Chalmers Lazy ML compiler. *The Computer Journal*, 32(2):127–141, 1989.

[23] J. Gluert, J. Kennaway, and M. Sleep. DACTL: A computational model and compiler target language based on graph reduction. *ICL Technical Journal*, 5(3), 1987.

[24] B. Goldberg. *Multiprocessor Execution of Functional Programs*. PhD thesis, Graduate School of Yale Univ., Apr. 1988. Research Report: YALEU/DCS/RR-618.

[25] S. Peyton Jones. *The Implementation of Functional Programming Languages*. Prentice Hall, 1987.

Generating Efficient Portable Code
for a Strict Applicative Language

Wolfram Schulte and Wolfgang Grieskamp
Institut für Angewandte Informatik, Technische Universität Berlin
E-mail: wolfram@opal.cs.tu-berlin.de wg@opal.cs.tu-berlin.de

Abstract

We discuss the overall style of code generation for the strict applicative language OPAL. It differs in two respects from the usual declarative language implementations. Firstly, instead of compiling to an abstract machine, we use C as the target language, inheriting many of the machine-dependent low-level optimizations nowadays performed by C compilers. Secondly, instead of using a copying or scanning garbage collector, we use an optimized variant of the classical reference counting scheme, resulting in a residual garbage collector and the capability to perform run-time-detected selective update on recursive data structures.

1 INTRODUCTION

Applicative languages are known primarily for their semantic simplicity and expressive power. Clarity and expressiveness result from the use of higher-order functions, recursive data structures, and referential transparency. Unfortunately, these aspects are the main reason for their inefficient implementations on present-day computer hardware, which continues to be built along the lines of the von Neumann architecture.

The usual implementations of applicative languages are based on abstract machines, which are implemented by assembler macros [1][2]. Whereas the abstract machines are designed to support recursion optimizations and higher-order functions, the target code generation via macros neglects machine-dependent optimizations, such as register cacheing and parameter passing. Moreover, the generated code usually assumes "infinite memory", leaving the problem of recovering unused memory to a general garbage collector [3]. It has been claimed that, if the amount of memory available were be big enough, there would seldom be any necessity to start the garbage collector [4]. However, knowledge of the *physical* memory limit is required to make this true – but this limit is not available to user processes in most modern multi-user, multi-tasking operating systems like UNIX and, even if it were, it would change dramatically from time to time.

To cope with these problems we made the following design decisions. Firstly, we *translate the applicative source language into a subset of the imperative target language C* [5]. This way, the compiler is portable to any environment supporting C, and it inherits many of the benefits of optimizing C compilers, especially machine-dependent ones. Although there are some inherent problems with this approach (cf. section 3.2 and 6) the performance results are surprising. Secondly, the *reference counting* (RC) *scheme is used for garbage collection,* since it uses memory resources economically without making assumptions about the environment [3]. To minimize the RC effort, we optimize RC instruction generation at compile time. At run time, the RC information is exploited to enable selective update on recursive data structures.

The testbed for our experiments is the OPAL programming language and environment that are currently being developed at the Technical University of Berlin. OPAL [6] is a strongly typed, strict, purely functional language whith a core in the tradition of ML [7] or HOPE [8]. But, unlike these, it does not support Hindley/Milner-style polymorphism – instead it supplies parameterized structures such as are known from algebraic specification languages like CIP-L [9], also called functors in Standard ML.

The aim of this paper is not to describe techniques, and hence we will not present compilation schemes or dataflow frameworks. Our objective is to illustrate by means of examples the overall style of code generation. Before embarking on a description of this subject in section 3 and 4, we will briefly introduce the code generator's source and target language in the following section. In section 5 we present performance results. Section 6 concludes the discussion.

2   SOURCE AND TARGET LANGUAGE

The code generator translates the analyzed source language, the applicative code, into the imperative target language, the imperative code.

2.1 The Applicative Code

The applicative code (AC) is, in principle, a normal form of OPAL or any other strict applicative language. It typically results from source-level transformations, such as the translation of pattern matching into case-statements, λ-lifting, the introduction of primitives for data creation and access, common-subexpression elimination and unfolding.

For example, a type declaration in OPAL may read

```
TYPE seq ≡   nil                      -- sum
             cons(hd: data, tl: seq)  -- ... of products
```

On the basis of this type, we may then define the sequence concatenation operation in OPAL as follows:

```
DEF conc(nil,y)        ≡ y
DEF conc(cons(h,t),y)  ≡ cons(h,conc(t,y))
```

This is transfomed into the AC normal form (the notation is explained below):

```
DEF conc(s1,s2) ≡
    SWITCH s1 OF
    1 ⇒ s2
    2 ⇒ LET h ≡ SEL[1](s1)  t ≡ SEL[2](s1)  IN
        LET s ≡ conc(t,s2)  IN
        CONS[1](h,s)
```

AC programs generally consist of a set of first- and higher-order combinators. Their bodies are built up from values, tuples, flat applications, abstractions, and switches. We write:

- $(v_1,...,v_n)$ for tuples consisting of values only. Values – denoted by v in the sequel – are either variables or combinators.
- $u(v_{11},...,v_{1n_1})...(v_{m1},...,v_{mn_m})$ for function applications which are built up from values applied to a sequence of (argument-) tuples.
- $CONS[t](v_1,...,v_n)$ or $SEL[i](v)$ for the construction of and selection from sum-of-product objects, where t is the tag encoding the injected variant, and i is the number of the projected component.
- $LET (x_{11},...,x_{1n_1}) \equiv U_1 ... (x_{m1},...,x_{mn_m}) \equiv U_m\ IN\ S$ for (parallel) abstraction, with x_{ij} fresh variables. Here, U must be an application or type primitive, and S is an expression. None of the variables x_{ij} may be applied in the right-hand side of the equations.
- $SWITCH\ v\ OF\ t_1 \Rightarrow S_1 ... t_n \Rightarrow S_n$. Switches are used for discriminating sum-of-products based on the tag encodings. Since booleans are treated as a sum of the constructors false and true, all conditionals can be represented by switches.
- $DEF\ f(x_{11},...,x_{1n_1})...(x_{m1},...,x_{mn_m}) \equiv S$ for combinator definitions, with x_{ij} disjoint variables.

Note that an AC expression immediately leads to a classical control-flow graph (actually a tree, according to the simplified normal form used in this paper), which nevertheless preserves freedom of evaluation order if we treat the equations in an abstraction as a single node.

2.2 The Imperative Code

The imperative code (IC) is, in principle, a subset of C enriched with object management primitives. The primitives will be introduced in the form of ANSI-C prototypes in the course of the paper. Here we discuss only the object representations.

Objects are either *values*, e.g. numbers or *references* to cells. *Cells* are continuous storage areas on the heap consisting of indexed *fields* which, again, contain objects. IC is dynamically typed: every data object carries its type information and may be passed and stored regardless of its type. We use the conventional bit-tagging scheme for byte-addressable machines to encode the type information: the low-order bit is zero for references and one for values [10].

Let the type *UNIT* be the platform-dependent machine word for representing objects. For documentation purposes, we introduce the following type declarations:

```
typedef UNIT ANY ;        /* value or reference */
typedef UNIT REF;         /* reference */
typedef UNIT VAL;         /* value */
```

Our first primitive *ISREF*

```
int   ISREF(ANY obj);     /* test if an object is a reference */
```

tests whether the object *obj* is a reference or a value. Other primitives to support code generation for recursive data structures and higher-order functions will be introduced in sections 3.1 and 3.3, respectively. In sections 4.1 and 4.2, the storage allocation primitives will be defined.

3   BASIC CODE GENERATION

In this section, we describe the basic compilation of applicative code to imperative code. Although the garbage collector is an integral part of the generated code, we postpone discussion of it until section 4, first concentrating on recursion handling (section 3.2) and the treatment of higher-order functions (section 3.3).

3.1   First-order Compilation

The compilation of first-order combinators is straightforward:

–   Combinators are implemented by procedures. Call-by-value and call-by-reference are used for passing multi-arguments and multi-results, respectively.
–   Abstractions are implemented by blocks introducing local variables.
–   Tuples are mapped on to a sequence of assignments.
–   Constructors and selectors are realized with the IC primitives:

```
VAL     CVAL(int tag);            /* create a value embedding a tag */
REF     CELL(int tag, int size);  /* create cell with tag & return its reference */
ANY*    FIELD(REF cell, int no);  /* address of no'th field of cell */
```

A 0-ary constructor is mapped to the *CVAL* primitive, which generates a value embedding the variant tag. A *n*-ary constructor is mapped to the *CELL* primitive, which creates a cell with a variant tag and returns a reference to it. The fields are assigned and selected with the *FIELD* primitive.
–   Switches are mapped on to their imperative counterpart using the *TAG* primitive for variant tag access.

```
int    TAG(ANY obj);              /* variant tag of value or referenced cell */
```

According to this scheme, the code for our introductory example, the concatenation of two sequences, will look like this:

```
void conc(s1,s2,r) ANY s1,s2; ANY *r;
{    switch(TAG(s1)){
     case 1: *r=s2; break;
     case 2:{ANY h,t;
             h=*FIELD(s1,1); t=*FIELD(s1,2);
             {ANY s;
             conc(t,s2,&s);
             *r=CELL(2,2); *FIELD(*r,1)=h; *FIELD(*r,2)=s; break; }}}}
```

3.2   Dealing with Recursion

Mapping recursion onto goto (or iterative) systems is an important issue in the translation of applicative to imperative code. It has been known for quite some time that systems of mutual *tail-recursive* functions are equivalent to goto systems. Hence, the problem reduces to the source-level transformation of general recursion to tail-recursion [9].

Nevertheless, there are still transformations that can only be performed on the imperative level, such as tail-recursive-modulo-cons simplification. A function is called *tail-recursive-modulo-cons* if the outermost operations consist solely of constructors and embed a recursive call; *conc* is a typical example of a situation of this sort. In such cases, we simply reorder the computation to establish a tail-recursive form. Consider the piece of code for *conc*

```
...    { ANY s;
         conc(t,s2,&s);
         *r=CELL(2,2);  *FIELD(*r,1)=h; *FIELD(*r,2)=s; break; }}}}
```

where *r* is the result parameter name of *conc*. The call to *conc* can be moved to the end of this statement sequence, taking advantage of call-by-reference parameter passing:

```
...    { ANY s;
         *r=CELL(2,2); *FIELD(*r,1)=h; conc(t,s2,FIELD(*r,2)); break; }}}}
```

This transformation has high payoff and can be applied, for example, to functions like filtering or splitting a list, and also to functions working on non-linear data structures like tree insertion.

Once tail recursion has been established, a machine-dependent technical problem remains: actually performing the mapping of general tail-calls to gotos. As a matter of fact, most decent compilers for applicative languages which generate native code realize this mapping. Unfortunately, most C compilers do not. It appears that the only way of achieving support of tail-calls in C is to use a uniform parameter-passing strategy and a non-portable small piece of assembler code, which contradicts our code generation principles.

We therefore transform only *tail-recursion to iteration,* and are not able to treat general tail calls. As experiments have shown, this is usually sufficient with regard to time efficiency. However, there remains some waste of stack space, especially in continuation-based algorithms. (Fortunately, this does not hold for the continuation-based IO system, which can be portably implemented to reset the stack after each IO operation with the *setjmp()* mechanism [5].)

3.3 Higher-order Compilation

A curried function can be partially applied resulting in a new function. However, we are not able (and not willing) to generate code at run time. Hence a partial application is represented by a data structure, usually called *closure*, consisting of the code address of the *uncurried* version of a combinator (coded as described in section 3.1) and the partially instantiated parameters. When all missing arguments are applied to the closure, which we call full application, the code address is selected, an argument list is constructed – retrieving the already instantiated arguments and adding the missing ones – and the combinator is called indirectly. In case a closure itself is partially applied, it is copied and enriched by the additional arguments.

Passing partially applied functions to higher-order functions boils down to passing closures. Passing combinators fits well in this scheme: here, a closure is constructed holding the code address and *zero* instantiated parameters. Hence, for a combinator accepting n argument tuples, we have to consider 0 to $n-1$ stages of partial application represented by a closure.

At the caller's site, the number of additional arguments of a full application is statically known, whereas the number of already instantiated parameters in a closure is unknown. In our compilation scheme, this poses a serious problem because calling the uncurried version of the combinator requires a fixed number of parameters. Thus, we refine the scheme as follows: for each stage of partial application of a combinator (i.e. 0 to $n-1$), we generate a specific entry for full application; this entry takes the closure and all missing arguments, constructing the full argument list and calling the uncurried version. This is possible because, unlike the caller's site, the callee site knows the number of parameters in the closure through typing information.

But now we have to keep track of which entry to call at the caller's site. This is realized by introducing a *table* of entry addresses. A pointer to this table is stored in the closure instead of the address of one single entry. The invariant holds that (1) by selecting the entry address to which the table pointer refers, the appropriate entry for the closure's stage is obtained; and (2) when partially applying the closure to n argument tuples, incrementing the table pointer by n results in the correct table pointer for the copied closure.

We introduce the following primitives to implement this scheme:

```
typedef void (*) CODE;                    /* type of code entries */
REF     CLOS(CODE tab[], int size, int n); /* create a closure */
REF     COPY(REF clos, int n);            /* copy a closure */
CODE    ENTRY(REF clos);                   /* return current code entry */
ANY *   ARG(REF clos, int i);              /* addr. of i'th field of closure*/
```

CLOS takes the maximal number of arguments the resulting closure may hold and the number of argument tuples the combinator associated with *tab* is applied to initially. *COPY* takes the number of argument tuples to which *clos* is partially applied, and increments the code entry table pointer appropriately. *ARG* stores and selects closure arguments: the j'th argument is stored in field $i =_{def} m-j+1$, where m is the total number of arguments excluding the last argument tuple.

For example, the compilation of the function composition operator defined in AC by

$$DEF\ comp(f,g)(x) \equiv LET\ y \equiv g(x)\ IN\ f(y)$$

results in the code:

```
void comp(f,g,x,r) ANY f,g,x; ANY *r;
/* The uncurried entry */
{    ANY y;
     (*ENTRY(g))(g,x,&y); (*ENTRY(f))(f,y,&*r);
}
void comp0(c,f,g,x,r) REF c; ANY f,g,x; ANY *r;
/* The entry where c is instantiated with 0 argument tuples */
{    comp(f,g,x,r);
```

```
void comp1(c,x,r) REF c; ANY x; ANY *r;
/* The entry where c is instantiated with 1 argument tuple */
{    comp(*ARG(c,2),*ARG(c,1),x,r);
}
CODE tab_comp = { comp0, comp1 };
```

The following example deals with the compilation of partial applications. Suppose there is a context where a variable *f* binds a function accepting two argument tuples, *a* is some value, and *F* and *P* represent combinators accepting two and one argument tuples, respectively.

```
...
LET      g ≡f(a)             -- apply f yielding g
         h ≡F(P)             -- apply F yielding h
IN LET   c ≡comp(g,h) IN ...
```

We obtain the code:

```
...{     ANY g,h;
         g=COPY(f,1); *ARG(g,1)=x;
         h=CLOS(tab_F,1,1); *ARG(h,1)=CLOS(tab_P,0,0);
         c=CLOS(tab_comp,2,1); *ARG(c,2)=g; *ARG(c,1)=h;
         ...
```

4   GARBAGE COLLECTION

Garbage collection, "a charming term for the recovery of unused space" [11], is concerned with determining the lifetime of an object and, in case it has expired, with recycling the storage resources used by it.

In the sequel, we present our version of the reference counting (RC) approach to garbage collection. We optimize the RC effort at compile time (section 4.1) and take advantage of RC information for run time-detected reusage and selective update (section 4.2). The principles of the run time storage manager are described in section 4.3.

In practice, to gather the necessary information for RC generation, we use non-iterative data flow analysis frameworks [12]. A formal description of these frameworks would be cumbersome and, we feel, not really of interest to the reader.

4.1 Reference Count Instruction Generation

The storage for references and values, represented by local variables, is implicitly recycled by the IC language, but *cells* – created by the *CELL, CLOS* and *COPY* primitives – need to be collected. RC demands the inclusion of an extra field – called *refcount*– to these cells, which records the numbers of references to the cell. If the counter drops to zero, no references to the cell exist and its storage can be reused. Freelists are supplied with a RC garbage collector to hold the reusable cells (see section 4.3).

The incrementation and decrementation of the *refcount* field is managed by the following RC primitives:

```
void INC(REF o, int n);      /* incr. refcount of cell by n */
void DEC(REF o, int n);      /* decr. refcount of cell by n */
```

The decrement operation will lead to a reclamation of the allocated storage if the RC reaches zero. The increment and decrement primitives have to be guarded by run time type tests (the *ISREF* primitive).

A given program should use *as little memory as possible*. This can be achieved if all arguments of a function are "destructive", i.e., if a function "owns" the references passed to it and is responsible for reclaiming them as soon as possible. Reclamation is done either by explicitly calling the decrement primitive or by inheriting the references to other functions – these functions then being responsible for them. In principle, if an argument is supplied n times to other functions, the reference count has to be incremented by $n-1$, and in case it is not supplied, the reference count has to be decremented by 1. The generalization from function arguments to variables introduced by abstractions is straightforward.

The task of the *refcount distribution analysis* is to calculate the optimal enrichment of the code by RC operations according to these principles. Here, optimality is concerned with generating the minimal number of increment and decrement operations and reclaiming references as soon as possible.

Only references require reference counting, and the run time test as to whether or not an object is a reference is time-consuming. Hence, the *type constraint analysis* calculates evaluation-path-relative type information of objects. The results of this analysis may lead to the elimination of RC at all (for values), or to the elimination of the type test (for references).

Combining the constraint and distribution analysis, our introductory example *conc* (cf. section 3.1) yields the following code:

```
void conc(s1,s2,r) ANY s1,s2; ANY *r;
{    switch(TAG(s1)){
     case 1: *r=s2; break;
     case 2: {ANY h,t;
              h=*FIELD(s1,1); if(ISREF(h)) INC(h,1);
              t=*FIELD(s1,2); if(ISREF(t)) INC(t,1);
              DEC(s1,1);
              {ANY s;
              conc(t,s2,&s);
              *r=CELL(2,2); *FIELD(*r,1)=h; *FIELD(*r,2)=s; break;}}}}
```

We like to draw attention to the following points: (1) Selections by *FIELD* generate references, and this necessarily enforces the generation of the increment operations. (2) The *FIELD* and *TAG* primitives are "non-destructive", and thus, for example, passing *s1* to *FIELD* requires no incrementation of *s1*'s refcount. On the other hand, this enforces the call to the *DEC* primitive after the last usage of *s1*. (3) The type constraint analysis prevents RC from being performed on *s1* in the case of an empty list and allows the elimination of the type test in the opposite case.

4.2 Reusage and Selective Update

Having once established RC, we are able to determine at run time whether a cell is shared (refcount>1), or whether it is exclusive (refcount=1). We can exploit this information to reuse cells immediately in a wide variety of algorithms. For example, let us consider *conc*. Here, a list is traversed as well as constructed. Assuming the reference count of the inspected cell to be exclusive for some function incarnation, it may be *reused* to construct the result cell. Since the data component remains unchanged in this case, there is no need to touch this component at all. This is called *selective update*.

We introduce the additional primitive EXCL that tests whether a cell is exclusive:

int EXCL(REF cell); /* test if cell is exclusive, i.e.refcount=1 */

In order to take advantage of the reuse and selective update potential, we compile the following code: whenever a cell, say A, is to be constructed at some program point p, and a cell B, whose size matches the size of A, is to be discarded at an earlier program point, the lifetime of B is virtually increased until p. Furthermore, if selections on B at index i are used only to define component i of A, then those selections can be suspended until p. At point p, code is generated to check if B is exclusive and, if so, to reuse it, or if not, to perform the suspended selections.

Now, *conc* will be coded as follows:

```
void conc(s1,s2,r) ANY s1,s2; ANY *r;
{     switch(TAG(s1)){
      case 1: *r=s2; break;
      case 2: {ANY h,t;
              t=*FIELD(s1,2); if(ISREF(t)) INC(t,1);
              /* selection of h suspended */
              {ANY s;
              conc(t,s2,&s);
              if (EXCL(s1)) {
                *r = s1;                        /* reuse s1 but ... */
                if(ISREF(t)) DEC(t,1);          /* don't forget to free this one */
                *FIELD(*r,2)=s;                 /* since it is overwritten here */
                /* h is already at its place */
                break;
              }else{
                /* bring up selection of h */
                h=*FIELD(s1,1); if(ISREF(h)) INC(h,1);
                DEC(s1,1);
                *r=CELL(2,2);*FIELD(*r,1)=h;*FIELD(*r,2)=s;
                break;  }}}}}
```

Unfortunately, the cell referred to by *s1* will never be exclusive for subsequent calls of *conc*. Since we have increased the lifetime of *s1* virtually, unnecessary sharing was introduced: the *t* object, passed as actual for *s1* to the next recursive incarnation of *conc*, is bounded by the "zombie" cell referred to by *s1* in the last incarnation of *conc*.

How do we cope with this problem? To illustrate the strategy we perform a safe code motion on the generated code. We move the call to *conc* and the selection of *t* inside the exclusive test:

```
case 2: {ANY h,t;
        {ANY s;
        if (EXCL(s1)) {
            t=*FIELD(s1,2); if(ISREF(t)) INC(t,1);
            conc(t,s2,&s);
            *r = s1;                /* reuse s1 but ... */
            if (ISREF(t)) DEC(t,1);  /* don't forget to free this one */
            *FIELD(*r,2)=s;          /* since it is overwritten here */
            /* h is already at its place */
            break;
        } else {
            t=*FIELD(s1,2); if(ISREF(t)) INC(t,1);
            conc(t,s2,&s);
            ...
```

Now, since *s1* is exclusive in the reuse case and the second component of *s1* which bounds *t* will be overwritten, the reference (count) of *t* can be *borrowed* by the call to *conc*. The increment and decrement instructions on *t* can be *eliminated*. This, of course, is only possible if *t* is not used after the call to *conc*.

The introduction of run time-checked selective update is performed by a *reuse and borrow dataflow analysis*. Both are based on the constraint and distribution analysis. The borrow analysis calculates the borrowable and suspendable selection candidates. The reuse analysis tries to find the "optimal" candidates for reuse and fixes the borrowed and suspended selections. Here, our optimality criterion is determining the maximum number of suspendable selections, i.e., the maximal degree of selective update.

We have arrived at a situation where, with a minimal RC effort, reusage and selective updating are performed on recursive data structures. Some details like handling the reusage of objects from which only parts are selected have been left out but can be integrated orthogonally. We present the final code for the example *conc*, combining recursion simplification and selective update (see below).

For-loops are used to map direct tail-recursion to iteration. The procedure parameters are used as the iteration variables. Note that, in case the first argument sequence is isolated (i.e., all cells have exclusive access), reference counting does not take place – only the exclusive test has to be performed for each sequence cell.

The resulting code is appropriate for the typical optimizations performed by C compilers. For example, in the exclusive case, copy propagation will eliminate the use of the local variable *t*.

```
void conc(s1,s2,r) ANY s1,s2; ANY *r;
{    for(;;){
     switch(TAG(s1)){
     case 1: *r=s2; break;
     case 2: {ANY h,t;
             {ANY s;
              if (EXCL(s1)) {
                t=*FIELD(s1,2);
                *r = s1;
                s1=t; s2=s2; r=FIELD(*r,2);
                continue;
              } else {
                h=*FIELD(s1,1); if(ISREF(h)) INC(h,1);
                t=*FIELD(s1,2); if(ISREF(t)) INC(t,1);
                DEC(s1,1);
                *r=CELL(2,2);
                *FIELD(*r,1)=h;
                s1=t; s2=s2; r=FIELD(*r,2);
                continue; }}}}
     break; }}
```

4.3 Run time Storage Allocation

We use a combination of a *quick-fit* [13] and *lazy-reference counting* [14] storage allocation strategy. The idea of quick-fit storage allocation is simple: size-specific freelists and a continuous storage area are distinguished. Allocation of a cell is performed by unlinking it from the freelist of the required size, and in case the freelist is empty, allocating it from the continuous storage area.

Deallocation of a cell is realized by discarding the references it may hold and linking it to the freelist associated with its size. Discarding the sub references may lead again to the deallocation of cells. To achieve a *constant-time behavior* of cell deallocation, we use the *lazy* method: the disposal of subreferences is delayed until a new object is actually required. The allocation scheme is modified, so as to force the (again lazy) disposal of the subreferences.

Actually, there are two freelists for cells of each size: one for cells (possibly) containing references, the lazy list; and one for cells which do not, the eager list. The eager list, to which access is significantly faster, is preferred by the compiler for allocation and deallocation based on type and borrow information.

5 PERFORMANCE

Evaluation of software systems must be based on a number of different criteria: correctness, reliability, ease of use, portability, adaptability, performance, etc.

5.1 Evaluation of the Compiler

After some initial prototyping, a *first* version of the language was successfully bootstrapped. The compiler, written *entirely* in OPAL, is stable and compiles itself using the strategy outlined in this paper. It translates a typical compilation unit, i.e., about 300 lines, in about 30 seconds on a Sun4. Having about 15 imported modules, it uses approximately 2 megabytes of heap space for this compilation task.

Tracing the reference counts, we observed that about two out of three cells could be reused (cf. [15]). Fragmentation poses no problems because, in general, the requested blocks of the OPAL compiler come only in a small range of sizes (2-6 components) evenly distributed over time. On the other hand, lazy reference counting sometimes destroys the possibility of selective update because objects bound indirectly by some freelist may still reference the – theoretically – updatable object.

The optimizations performed by the GNU C compiler speed up the OPAL compiler by about 15%. Furthermore, the substitution of handwritten C routines for compiler-generated ones is easy and may also have a considerable impact, e.g., implementing bitsets by the C primitives results in a compiler that is about 5% faster.

The compiler was successfully ported from Sun3 to Sun4 using the same run time system for both machines. It runs about 3 times faster on a Sun4/75 than on a Sun3/260.

5.2 Efficiency

We present five small characteristic benchmark programs; the first three of them were taken from the benchmark suite of [16]:

Tak, Fib: The Tak and Fib benchmarks are used for assessing recursion management performance. (Tak was called with (28,14,7); the 20'th Fibonacci number was computed.)

Tree: Tree forms a complete binary tree and flattens it. The resulting list of 2^{10} (2^{13}, 2^{16}) elements is reversed four times. "We selected this benchmark because it is typical of the kind of tree and list manipulation found in small ML programs."[16]

Histo: "Computing a histogram (frequency table) efficiently is considered a problem in functional programming. It is probably the simplest functional programm where efficient arrays can have a radical effect on time complexity."[17] (The histogram was calculated from numbers in the range 1..200, each of them occurring 200 times; the timing includes data generation.)

Double: The Double benchmark "shows how well functional values (e.g. partially defined functions) are handled"[18]. (We used a variant without an intermediate list generating 310000 closure evaluations.)

We ran the benchmarks on a Sun-3/260 (16 MB) and Sun-4/75 (32MB) using the following systems:

OPAL-0: The OPAL compiler described in this paper
HOPE[1]: HOPE plus Continuations, Release 3.2.2, Imperial College
ML[2]: Standard ML of New Jersey, Version 0.65 (Sun4), 0.56 (Sun3)
C[3]: GNU C Compiler, Version 1.4

---

[1] Hope data structures are lazy but have been constructed from evaluated elements only. HOPE does not support built-in arrays suitable for update operations; arrays have been implemented for the Histo benchmark as complete trees.

[2] ML arrays are not referentially transparent. The garbage collection parameters have been: ratio=16, softmax=20000000.

[3] The library function *malloc* has been used for the benchmarks. No garbage collection took place.

The next table summarizes the results. The suffix 3 is used for Sun3 and 4 for Sun4, respectively. The garbage collection times of the ML system are given in brackets, and are included in the total timing.

	HOPE/3	ML/3		OPAL/3	C/4	ML/4		OPAL/4
Tak	16.02	113.40	(0.4)	28.61	3.900	35.910	(0.04)	4.415
Fib	0.04	0.10	(0)	0.10	0.013	0.036	(0)	0.016
Tree[10]	0.13	0.13	(0)	0.07	0.031	0.048	(0)	0.015
Tree[13]	1.71	1.65	(0.6)	0.55	0.256	0.490	(0.12)	0.143
Tree[16]	27.17	17.20	(8.9)	4.73	2.045	6.110	(3.11)	1.228
Histo	9.66	2.73	(1.0)	0.57	0.061	0.524	(0.27)	0.151
Double	2.58	3.60	(0)	2.80		1.417	(0)	1.000

It is interesting to measure the improvement of the RC optimizations. It turns out, that they reduce the run time of Tree with respect to unoptimized RC to less than 25%.

	Standard RC	Optimized RC
Tree[10]	0.053	0.015
Tree[13]	0.565	0.143
Tree[16]	5.548	1.228

6 CONCLUSION

We believe we have "proved by experiment" that the compilation of applicative to imperative languages is a reasonable approach – at least for prototyping a new compilation scheme. Although we gain a lot from the optimizations performed by C compilers, the compilation scheme is still far from exploiting the real optimization potential. For example, the C compiler discards most register caches when a procedure is called, since it expects side-effects. And we were not able to exploit the built-in bit-tagging scheme of the SPARC architecture.

We also claim that the reference counting approach to garbage collection is more appropriate than general garbage collectors in operating system environments like UNIX. Although simple RC has the inherent disadvantage, that it accesses every cell ever in use several times, it has the advantage of supporting referential transparent arrays and using memory resources very economically. In addition, our static optimizations reduce the RC overhead to a minimum, thereby exploiting the reusage and selective update potential. Again, it is far from perfect. The following aspects have not been considered: Sharing analysis, code versions for destructive and non-destructive arguments, code versions for list of values only and list of references only, etc.

To sum up, the outlined compilation scheme is fully portable and efficient both in terms of time (see the benchmarks above) and space (only the minimal amount of memory is used).

Acknowledgement

The ideas and results presented in this paper were strongly influenced by our colleagues Gottfried Egger, Andreas Fett, Michael Jatzeck and Peter Pepper. Michael Jatzeck and Andreas Fett are also the authors of the excellent new frontend.

REFERENCES

[1]   Field, A.J., Harrison, P.G.: Functional Programming. Addison–Wesley (1988).

[2]   Peyton Jones, S.L.: The Implementation of Functional Programming Languages. Prentice–Hall (1987).

[3]   Cohen, J.: Garbage Collection of Linked Data Structures. Computing Surveys 13, 341–367 (1981).

[4]   Appel, A.W.: Garbage collection can be faster than stack allocation. Inform. Proc. Letters 25, 275-279 (1978).

[5]   Kernighan, B., Ritchie D.M.: The C Programming Language. 2nd. Ed. Prentice Hall (1988).

[6]   Pepper, P. (ed.): The Programming Language OPAL-1. Technical Report May-91, TU-Berlin (1991).

[7]   Milner, R., Tofte, M., Harper, R.: The Definition of Standard ML. MIT Press (1990).

[8]   Perry, N.: Hope+. Dept. of Computing, Imperial College London Internal Report IC/FPR/LANG /2.5.1/7 (1988).

[9]   Bauer, F.L., Wössner, H.: Algorithmic Language and Program Development. Springer (1981).

[10] Appel, A.W., MacQueen, D.B.: A Standard ML Compiler. In: Functional Programming Languages and Computer Architecture, (ed.) Kahn G, LNCS 274, 301-324 (1987).

[11] Aho, A.V., Hopcraft, J.E., Ullman, J.D.: Data Structures and Algorithms. Addison–Wesley (1983).

[12] Hecht, M.S.: Flow Analysis of Computer Programs. Elsevier North-Holland (1981).

[13] Weinstock, C.B., Wulf, W.A.: Quick Fit: An Efficient Algorithm for Heap Storage Allocation. SIGPLAN Notices 23, 141-148, (1988).

[14] Weizenbaum, J.: Symmetric List Processor. Communications of the ACM 6, 524-544 (1963).

[15] Clark, D.W., Green, C.C.: A Note on Shared List Structure in Lisp. Inform. Proc. Letters 7, 312-314 (1978).

[16] Stansifer, R.: Imperative versus Functional. SIGPLAN Notices 25, 69-72 (1990).

[17] Aasa, A., Holmström, S., Nilsson, C.: An Efficiency Comparison of Purely Functional Arrays. BIT 28, 490-503 (1988).

[18] Leroy, X.: The ZINC Experiment: An Economical Implementation of the ML Language. INRIA, Rapports Techniques No. 117 (1990).

Bird-Meertens Formalism (Squiggol)

More Advice on Proving a Compiler Correct: Improve a Correct Compiler

Erik Meijer
University of Nijmegen
Informatics Department
Toernooiveld
NL-6525 ED Nijmegen
email: erik@cs.kun.nl

1   Introduction

One of the objectives of denotational semantics is to give a precise description of pro-gramming languages that can serve as a standard against which implementations can be verified, or preferably, from which correct compilers can be derived. We want to use a *calculational* approach to derive correct and efficient implementations for program-ming languages from their denotational descriptions. Experience [12] has shown that it is not a good idea to validate an implementation a posteriori, rather development and proof should proceed hand in hand. Besides the correctness aspect, a transfor-mational approach can help to understand the relationships that may or may not exist between various implementations, or even suggest alternative methods. This paper pro-vides a leisurely exposition on the development of a calculational approach to semantics directed compiler generation.

2   The Compiler Correctness Problem

Many people [13, 3, 2, 22, 15, 7, 4] have suggested to use algebraic means to tackle the compiler correctness problem. Given a source language L, a target language T, their respective semantics $m \in L \rightarrow M$, $a \in T \rightarrow U$ and a compiler c from L to T, one seeks an encoding e of the source semantics into the target semantics such that the following diagram commutes.

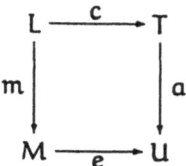

By enforcing an algebraic structure on the different domains and defining the respective functions as homomorphisms, initiality of L ensures commutativity. A sufficient condition to prevent trivial solutions resulting from taking U as a final algebra, is to require e to be injective, i.e. U must be a true implementation of M.

An F-algebra is a pair $(A, \varphi \in AF \rightarrow A)$ consisting of the *carrier* set A and the operations φ of *signature* F, for some suitable functor F. A *homomorphism* h between F-algebras (A, φ) and (B, ψ) is a structure preserving map $h \in A \rightarrow B$ that replaces the operations φ by ψ, formally, $h \circ \varphi = \psi \circ hF$. From the *initial* F-algebra (L, in) there is a unique homomorphism to any other F-algebra (A, φ). To stress the importance of this unique morphism it is called by the name "catamorphism" and written using so called banana-brackets $(\![in := \varphi]\!)$.

The abstract syntax of a programming language L is the initial F-algebra (L, in) where in is the set of constructors of the abstract syntax. Therefore we can define a denotational semantics $m \in L \rightarrow M$ for L as the catamorphism $(\![in := \varphi]\!)$ by imposing an F-algebraic structure (M, φ) on the semantic domain M. In a traditional, oxford-style, denotational description this is achieved by encoding φ using λ-abstraction and application. As argued by Mosses, Watt and others [14, 23, 8], such language descriptions have rather poor pragmatic qualities. It is hard to identify essential semantic concepts of the language being described, and the (automatic) generation of compilers is virtually impossible. Partial evaluation [19] is no solution; reducing a mess does not yield order. Careful engineering is required to obtain good results from partial evaluation [5]. Besides this critique of traditional denotational semantics, it must be said that on the other hand compiler writers seem to ignore the existence of formal semantics completely, probably because they don't like greek letters. This behavior is inexcusable as it undermines any attempt to implement software that has been proven correct.

Action Semantics as developed by Mosses and Watt [23, 14] is an attempt to improve the readability and modularity of formal descriptions of programming languages. The semantic domain M is cast into a G-algebra (M, α) where the set of *actions* α corresponds to the run-time concepts of the programming language in question. For an imperative language an action algebra includes primitive actions such as assignment and action combinators such as sequencing, looping and conditionals. The essence of writing a semantics now lies in extracting from the action algebra (M, α), a compile-time algebra (M, φ) of the same signature as the abstract syntax. In terms of the ADJ-group [22], the compile-time operations φ are *derived* from the run-time actions α.

Classical Initial Algebra Semantics has not been concerned with calculational issues, it only provided a framework to prove the correctness of a given compiler. We want to derive a new compiler by calculation not to prove a given one correct. Any semantics $m \in L \rightarrow M$ derived from an action G-algebra (M, α) can be factored into a static *compiler* $d \in L \rightarrow S$ and a dynamic or run-time component $a \in S \rightarrow M$ such that the following diagram commutes

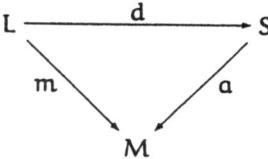

by simply letting d map a program into a textual representation of its denotation. Hence S is the initial G-algebra of the semantic algebra underlying M. Sethi [20] dubbs this representation 'concrete semantics'.

Usually the compiler generated as described above will not produce very efficient code as too little work can be done statically. The remedy is to *improve* the already correct compiler d. Improving a compiler derived from $m \in L \to M$ means finding an (injective) implementation $e \in M \to U$ such that

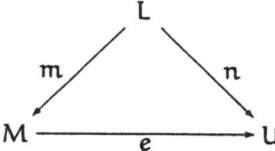

commutes. Ideally, the new semantics n is calculated from the composition of the old semantics m and the improving transformation e. If m is the catamorphism $(\![in := \varphi]\!)$ we may try to find a F-algebra (U, ψ) (and its underlying action algebra (U, β) of some signature H) such that the refinement e is a homomorphism between (M, φ) and (U, ψ), i.e. some β and a derived operation ψ such that $e \circ \varphi = \psi \circ eF$. In that case we have (by initiality of L) that the new semantics n is given by the catamorphism $(\![in := \psi]\!)$. No induction is needed. In many cases, unfortunately, the above method does not yield a satisfying result. Instead we want to determine a ξ such that $e \circ (\![\varphi]\!) l = (\![\xi]\!) l \circ e$. Now a full structural induction proof on l seems unavoidable (for a more thorough discussion see [10]). For our convenience we will therefore use structural induction for all our proofs, even if it is, technically speaking, redundant.

A useful heuristic to obtain a implementation function e is to add an extra argument to the semantics m, much akin to ever popular accumulating argument strategy, such that this argument is available at compile-time. Shifting work from run-time to compile-time is essential to generate realistic code. A low-level implementation results when the run-time operations are transformed into an easily and efficiently implementable form exploiting structural properties of the domains. This process is called *defunctionalization* [17]. Typical examples are converting stores into actual memory and continuations into concrete machine code or linked lists. Arguments of operations can become global variables provided at any moment there is at most one 'active' copy of that argument around. This is the case when the argument is passed sequentially between operations, i.e., the semantics is single-threading [18]. Otherwise the argument should be explicitly copied to maintain referential transparency.

Based on the improved semantics n we can again generate a compiler $c \in L \to T$ that solves the original compiler correctness diagram.

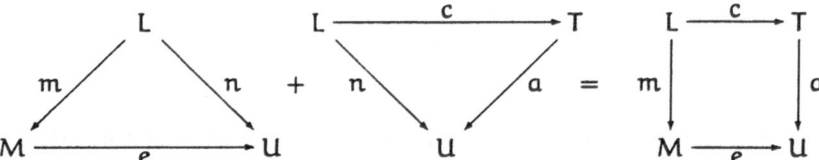

High-Level Semantics

An approach that is very close the one proposed here is *High-Level Semantics* as developed by Lee [8]. A High-Level semantic description consists of two levels. The *macro* semantics[1] $L \to (I \to S \| POT)$ maps a program into a function that given compile-time objects from I yields a pair consisting of the those values S that could be computed statically, for example type correctness, and a term of the run-time action algebra POT. The *micro* semantics $POT \to M$ provides an interpretation specifying the dynamic semantics of a program. For a single POT several interpretations may be given. Lee makes no attempt to to prove the correctness of a desired model (e.g. machine code) against an intended model (e.g. direct semantics).

Although it is good to make an explicit *distinction* between compile-time and run-time, it is a bad thing to make an explicit and fixed *separation* between the two. The key strategy to generate good code is to transfer as much work as possible from run-time to compile-time. Fixing the borderline between the two a priori make this impossible. Only when we have found an action algebra close enough to be implemented directly, the semantics may be changed into a compiler that yields a concrete representation of its dynamic semantics.

3   A simple imperative language $\mathcal{W}$

As a starting point for our derivations we take a simple imperative language whose most complicated construct is the **while**-loop. In §7 the language $\mathcal{W}$ will be extended with non-nested procedures to yield $\mathcal{C}$. The abstract syntax of $\mathcal{W}$ is given by the following grammar.

$$
\begin{aligned}
P \in program &::= \textbf{prog } statement \\
S, T \in statement &::= \textbf{skip} \\
&\mid var := expression \\
&\mid statement \, ; \, statement \\
&\mid \textbf{if } expression \textbf{ then } statement \textbf{ else } statement \textbf{ fi} \\
&\mid \textbf{while } expression \textbf{ do } statement \textbf{ od}
\end{aligned}
$$

---

[1]POT abbreviates "prefix-form operator term"

The classes of arithmetic and boolean expressions are defined by the single grammar expression. Type correctness could be enforced by defining an appropriate static semantics.

$$A, B, E, F \in \text{expression} \quad ::= \quad \textbf{var } var$$
$$| \quad \textbf{num } num$$
$$| \quad \textbf{true} \mid \textbf{false}$$
$$| \quad \text{expression} \textcircled{2} \text{expression}$$

The set of binary operators $\textcircled{2}$ includes boolean operators $\textcircled{\wedge}$ like **and** and **or**, arithmetic operators $\textcircled{+}$ like $+$ and $\times$, and relational operators $\textcircled{=}$ such as $=$ and $\geq$.

Diacritical Convention When making proofs about two semantic definitions we are frequently required to consider and to compare pairs of values, one from each definition, which are both called the same. The diacritical convention as proposed by [21] is a convenient and systematic way of distinguishing such values. All names from the one definition are given *acute* accents (´) while the names belonging to the other get *grave* accents (`). By convention acute accents are used for decorating the more 'abstract' semantics, while concrete, more to the 'ground' semantics get grave accents.

4 Semantics of $\mathcal{W}$

In order to define $\mathcal{W}$ completely, a *static semantics* and a *dynamic semantics* for each of the syntactic constructs program, statement and expression must be supplied. The static semantic part should describe all computations that can be done statically, for example type checking. Though some aspects of static semantics can be realized by refining the abstract syntax of the language, this is not always the case. Context dependent properties, such as whether identifiers have been defined twice, can not be imposed by a context free grammar. Usual practice in denotational semantics is to consider context conditions as 'syntactic', and assume only syntactically correct programs. This gives the undesirable situation that context dependency falls between two stools; it cannot be described by the (context free) syntax, while it is ignored in the semantics. In our opinion static semantics form an essential part of a language definition and thus should be treated as a first class citizen. Because of space limitations we refrain from giving a static semantics for $\mathcal{W}$. An interesting approach to the problem of static semantics is taken by Doh and Schmidt [6]. Their action combinators are defined in such a way that strong typing rules can be extracted automatically from language descriptions in terms of these actions.

Our initial dynamic semantics will be a standard direct semantics [18], hence the following definitions should pose no particular problems.

$$\mathcal{M}[\![\_]\!] \quad \in \quad \text{program} \rightarrow env$$
$$\mathcal{M}[\![\textbf{prog } S]\!] \quad = \quad \mathcal{S}[\![S]\!] \, \eta_0$$
$$\mathcal{S}[\![\_]\!] \quad \in \quad \text{statement} \rightarrow (env \rightarrow env)$$
$$\mathcal{S}[\![\textbf{skip}]\!] \quad = \quad \text{SKIP}$$

$$S[\![x := E]\!] \;=\; x := \mathcal{E}[\![E]\!]$$
$$S[\![S \,; T]\!] \;=\; S[\![S]\!]; S[\![T]\!]$$
$$S[\![\text{if } B \text{ then } S \text{ else } T \text{ fi}]\!] \;=\; \mathcal{E}[\![B]\!] \rightarrow S[\![S]\!] \;[\!]\; S[\![T]\!]$$
$$S[\![\text{while } B \text{ do } S \text{ od}]\!] \;=\; \mu(\lambda loop.\mathcal{E}[\![B]\!] \rightarrow (S[\![S]\!] \,; loop) \;[\!]\; \text{SKIP})$$
$$\mathcal{E}[\![\_]\!] \;\in\; expression \rightarrow (env \rightarrow \mathbb{N})$$
$$\mathcal{E}[\![\text{var } x]\!] \;=\; \text{LOOKUP } x$$
$$\mathcal{E}[\![\text{num } n]\!] \;=\; \text{LITERAL } n$$
$$\mathcal{E}[\![\text{true}]\!] \;=\; \text{LITERAL } 1$$
$$\mathcal{E}[\![\text{false}]\!] \;=\; \text{LITERAL } 0$$
$$\mathcal{E}[\![E \;\textcircled{2}\; F]\!] \;=\; \mathcal{E}[\![E]\!] \;\widehat{\textcircled{2}}\; \mathcal{E}[\![F]\!]$$

In the sequel we use TRUE resp FALSE as abbreviations for LITERAL 1 and LITERAL 0. It is assumed that in the clause $\mathcal{M}[\![\text{prog } S]\!] = S[\![S]\!]\, \eta_0$, the initial environment η_0 is a run-time object.

An *environment* $\eta \in env == var \rightarrow \mathbb{N}$, carries the dynamic values of type $\mathbb{N} = \{0, 1, \ldots\} \cup \{\perp\}$ of variables occurring in an expression. Updating the environment is strict; an assignment statement $x := E$ updates x with the *value* of E, thus if $\mathcal{E}[\![E]\!] = \perp$ the meaning of the statement $\mathcal{E}[\![x := E]\!]$ should be $\perp$ as well. The initial environment η_0 maps very variable to $\perp$.

$$\eta_0\, x \;=\; \perp$$
$$\eta[x := \perp]\, y \;=\; \perp$$
$$\eta[x := v]\, y \;=\; v, \quad x = y$$
$$\;=\; \eta\, y, \;\; x \neq y$$

Evaluating an expression should yield a value of type $\mathbb{N}$. Since expressions can contain variables, their values must be provided at run-time. Hence the denotation of an expression is of type $env \rightarrow \mathbb{N}$.

$$\text{LOOKUP } x\, \eta \;=\; \eta\, x$$
$$\text{LITERAL } v\, \eta \;=\; v$$
$$(e \;\widehat{\textcircled{2}}\; f)\, \eta \;=\; e\, \eta \;\textcircled{2}\; f\, \eta$$

When no confusion may arise we will just write $\textcircled{2}$ instead of $\widehat{\textcircled{2}}$.

Executing a statement modifies a given environment by updating variables with the values assigned to them in that statement; statement denotations s, t, u have type $env \rightarrow env$.

$$\text{SKIP } \eta \;=\; \eta$$
$$(x := e)\, \eta \;=\; \eta[x := e\, \eta]$$
$$(s \,; t)\, \eta \;=\; \text{strict } t\, (s\, \eta)$$
$$(b \rightarrow s\, [\!]\, t)\, \eta \;=\; \perp, \quad b\, \eta = \perp$$
$$\;=\; s\, \eta, \quad b\, \eta = 1$$
$$\;=\; t\, \eta, \quad b\, \eta = 0$$

where strict $f \perp = \perp$ and strict $f\, x = f\, x$ if $x \neq \perp$. Sequential composition ; is defined by strict composition as we want $\perp \,; t = \perp$ regardless of the value of t.

Example As an example take a program for computing the factorial for $n \geq 1$ and its denotation.

<table>
<tr>
<td>

fac := **num** 1 ;
while (**var** $n \geq$ **num** 1)
do
   fac := (**var** $n \times$ **var** fac) ;
   n := (**var** n − **num** 1)
od

</td>
<td>

fac := (LITERAL 1) ;
$\mu(\lambda$do.(LOOKUP $n \geq$ LITERAL 1) →
   (fac := (LOOKUP $n \times$ LOOKUP fac) ;
   n := (LOOKUP n − LITERAL 1) ; do)
⟦ SKIP)

</td>
</tr>
</table>

5 Continuation Semantics

Explicit manipulation of control, i.e. the evaluation order of a program's constructs, in the form of continuations will play a central rôle in our work. Invariably every efficiency improving transformation is aimed at making an otherwise implicit evaluation order explicit by the introduction of an additional continuation.

The first such continuation introduction makes the control-flow in sequencing of statements $\acute{s}; \acute{t}$ explicit. We would like to implement a statement denotation $\acute{s} \in env \rightarrow env$ as a function $\grave{s} = C \, \acute{s} \in (env \rightarrow env) \rightarrow (env \rightarrow env)$ such that $C \, \acute{s}$ takes its continuation as an explicit argument. Type considerations strongly suggest to define C as

$$C \, \acute{s} \, \acute{t} \;=\; \acute{s}; \acute{t}$$

The left-inverse A of C takes a concrete $\grave{s}$ that expects a continuation back into an abstract one $A \, \grave{s}$ that does not: $\grave{s} = C \, \acute{a} \Rightarrow \acute{s} = A \, \grave{s}$. A suitable choice is $A \, \grave{s} = \grave{s} \, id$. Using the fact that $A \circ C = id$ we will try to improve the previous direct semantics by turning it into a continuation semantics without changing the meaning of programs.

$$\grave{\mathcal{M}}\llbracket \textbf{prog } S \rrbracket$$
$$= \quad \text{demand}$$
$$\grave{\mathcal{M}}\llbracket \textbf{prog } S \rrbracket$$
$$= \quad A \circ C = id$$
$$(A \circ C) \, \grave{\mathcal{M}}\llbracket \textbf{prog } S \rrbracket$$
$$= \quad \text{unfold}$$
$$C\acute{s}\llbracket S \rrbracket \; id \; \eta_0$$
$$= \quad \text{assume} : C \, \acute{s}\llbracket S \rrbracket \, s = \grave{s}\llbracket S \rrbracket \, s$$
$$\grave{s}\llbracket S \rrbracket \; id \; \eta_0$$

The postulate $C \, \acute{s}\llbracket S \rrbracket \, s = \grave{s}\llbracket S \rrbracket \, s$ is proved by structural induction on $statement$, thereby calculating the new semantics $\grave{s}\llbracket \_ \rrbracket$ and new run-time actions.

In giving hints in the course of a calculation, we shall use "fold" and "unfold" when compile-time values are manipulated and "evaluate" in case run-time expressions are simplified. New run-time operations are "synthesized", while new compile-time operations are "derived".

skip Under the assumption that s is a compile-time object, we calculate C $\acute{S}$[**skip**] s to determine $\grave{S}$[**skip**] s.

$$C \; \acute{S}[\textbf{skip}] \; s$$
$$= \quad \text{unfold}$$
$$(\text{SK\'IP} \; ; \; s)$$
$$= \quad \text{evaluate}$$
$$s$$
$$= \quad \text{derive}$$
$$\grave{S}[\textbf{skip}] \; s$$

Note that all occurrences of SKIP are compiled away. If s was not available at compile-time we could only have synthesized a new run-time operation SK$\grave{I}$P s η = s η.

Assignments give rise to a new run-time operation (x :$\doteq$ e) s = s η[x := e η]. We cannot determine :$\doteq$ without using the run-time environment.

$$C \; \acute{S}[x := E] \; s$$
$$= \quad \text{unfold}$$
$$(x :\doteq \mathcal{E}[E] \; ; \; s)$$
$$= \quad \text{abutting calculation}$$
$$(x :\doteq \mathcal{E}[E]) \; s$$
$$= \quad \text{derive}$$
$$\grave{S}[x := E] \; s$$

$$(x :\doteq e \; ; \; s) \; η$$
$$= \quad \text{evaluate}$$
$$s \; (η[x := e \; η])$$
$$= \quad \text{synthesize}$$
$$(x :\doteq e) \; s \; η$$

sequential composition and conditionals are nearly as easy as **skip** and assignments and therefore are omited.

while-loops The most interesting case is the **while**-loop where recursion is involved. The following lemma,

$$μ(\lambda \text{loop}.b \to (s \; ; \; \text{loop}) \; [\!] \; t) \; ; \; u \; = \; μ(\lambda \text{loop}.b \to (s \; ; \; \text{loop}) \; [\!] \; (t \; ; \; u)) \quad (1)$$

intuitively says that loops are tail-recursive, and hence can be realized by a flow-chart program. Lemma (1) is easily proved by fixed-point induction. With (1) we can calculate

$$C \; \acute{S}[\textbf{while} \; B \; \textbf{do} \; S \; \textbf{od}] \; t$$
$$= \quad \text{unfold}$$

$$\mu(\lambda loop.\mathcal{E}[\![B]\!] \rightarrow (\acute{\mathcal{S}}[\![S]\!] \; ; loop) \; [\!] \; SKIP) \; ; t$$

=   (1) and evaluate

$$\mu(\lambda loop.\mathcal{E}[\![B]\!] \rightarrow (\acute{\mathcal{S}}[\![S]\!] \; ; loop) \; [\!] \; t)$$

=   fold

$$\mu(\lambda loop.\mathcal{E}[\![B]\!] \rightarrow (C \; \acute{\mathcal{S}}[\![S]\!] \; loop) \; [\!] \; t)$$

=   IH

$$\mu(\lambda loop.\mathcal{E}[\![B]\!] \rightarrow (\grave{\mathcal{S}}[\![S]\!] \; loop) \; [\!] \; t)$$

=   derive

$$\grave{\mathcal{S}}[\![\textbf{while } B \textbf{ do } S \textbf{ od}]\!] \; t$$

This completes the induction proof that $C \; \acute{\mathcal{S}}[\![S]\!] \; s = \grave{\mathcal{S}}[\![S]\!] \; s$, and yields the following set of new valuation functions.

$$\mathcal{M}[\![\textbf{prog } S]\!] \; = \; \mathcal{S}[\![S]\!] \; id \; \eta_0$$

$$\mathcal{S}[\![\textbf{skip}]\!] \; s \; = \; s$$
$$\mathcal{S}[\![x := E]\!] \; s \; = \; x := \mathcal{E}[\![E]\!] \; s$$
$$\mathcal{S}[\![S \; ; T]\!] \; u \; = \; \mathcal{S}[\![S]\!] \; (\mathcal{S}[\![T]\!] \; u)$$
$$\mathcal{S}[\![\textbf{if } B \textbf{ then } S \textbf{ else } T \textbf{ fi}]\!] \; u \; = \; \mathcal{E}[\![B]\!] \rightarrow (\mathcal{S}[\![S]\!] \; u) \; [\!] \; (\mathcal{S}[\![T]\!] \; u)$$
$$\mathcal{S}[\![\textbf{while } B \textbf{ do } S \textbf{ od}]\!] \; t \; = \; \mu(\lambda loop.\mathcal{E}[\![B]\!] \rightarrow (\mathcal{S}[\![S]\!] \; loop) \; [\!] \; t)$$

$$\mathcal{E}[\![\textbf{var } x]\!] \; = \; LOOKUP \; x$$
$$\mathcal{E}[\![\textbf{num } n]\!] \; = \; LITERAL \; n$$
$$\mathcal{E}[\![\textbf{true}]\!] \; = \; TRUE$$
$$\mathcal{E}[\![\textbf{false}]\!] \; = \; FALSE$$
$$\mathcal{E}[\![E \; \textcircled{2} \; F]\!] \; = \; \mathcal{E}[\![E]\!] \; \widehat{\textcircled{2}} \; \mathcal{E}[\![F]\!]$$

The clauses for expressions remain yet unchanged.

example The current semantics translates programs into flow-charts [20]. The well known idea of cutting loops and associating recursive equations with a flow-chart [9] can be applied here as well. Cut-points become 'labels' and all but one of the arcs pointing at such labels become GOTO's.

$$GOTO \; label \; t \; = \; label$$
$$IF_{false} \; b \; s \; t \; = \; b \rightarrow t \; [\!] \; s$$
$$EXIT \; s \; \eta \; = \; \eta$$

Using these extra instructions we can rewrite the denotation for the factorial program as:

$$factorial \; = \; (fac := (LITERAL \; 1)) \; loop$$
$$loop \; = \; (IF_{false} \; (LOOKUP \; n \geq LITERAL \; 1) \; done \; \circ$$
$$fac := (LOOKUP \; n \times LOOKUP \; fac) \; \circ$$

$$n := (\text{LOOKUP } n - \text{LITERAL } 1) \circ$$
$$\text{GOTO loop}) \perp$$
$$done = \text{EXIT } \perp$$

The translation scheme for flow-of-control statements can be modified easily to produce code with labels and jumps.

6 Expression Continuations

The next goal is to make control-flow in the evaluation of expressions explicit. Looking at $\mathcal{E}[\![E \ ⓧ\ F]\!]\,\eta = \mathcal{E}[\![E]\!]\,\eta \ ⓧ\ \mathcal{E}[\![F]\!]\,\eta$, we see that the order of evaluating the arguments of $ⓧ$ is not specified. For an actual implementation some order must be chosen, and subsequently intermediate values have to be stored. Usually a stack is introduced for this purpose. Explicit naming of intermediate values is not only easier to derive, it also gives better code for modern load-store RISC architectures such as the *Motorola 88.000* [16].

Explicit control-flow can be introduced into the evaluation of expressions by lifting the order of evaluating subexpressions to the level of statements.

$$\mathcal{S}[\![x := E \ ⓧ\ F]\!] = \mathcal{S}[\![y := E\,;\,z := F\,;\,x := \textbf{var } y \ ⓧ\ \textbf{var } z]\!] \tag{2}$$

where y and z are fresh variables.

This suggest that expressions should be turned into statements $E \in expr \to (var\|stat) \to stat$; the type of E leaves little choice but taking

$$E\ e\ (x, s) = (x := e)\ s \tag{3}$$

Although E may generate unnecessary assignments such as in $E\ \mathcal{E}[\![\textbf{var } x + \textbf{var } y]\!]\ (z, s)$, it is often simpler to eliminate these in subsequent compilation phases than to complicate the transformation to deal with these special cases. If we use for example graph coloring [1] to map identifiers into machine registers, redundant moves $x := \text{LOOKUP } y$ are eliminated for free.

The new semantics is determined by proving

$$\acute{\mathcal{S}}[\![S]\!]\ s = \grave{\mathcal{S}}[\![S]\!]\ s\ \wedge\ E\ \acute{\mathcal{E}}[\![F]\!]\ (x, t) = \grave{\mathcal{E}}[\![F]\!]\ (x, t)$$

using simultaneous structural induction on statement and expression. At first sight the clause $\acute{\mathcal{S}}[\![S]\!]\ s = \grave{\mathcal{S}}[\![S]\!]\ s$ may look somewhat odd. The semantic functions $\mathcal{E}[\![\_]\!]$ and $\mathcal{S}[\![\_]\!]$ are defined by mutual recursion, the equation $\acute{\mathcal{S}}[\![S]\!]\ s = \grave{\mathcal{S}}[\![S]\!]\ s$ expresses that we want a concrete semantics for statements that is equivalent to the abstract semantics for statements, but that is defined in terms of the concrete semantics of expressions.

binary operators The goal of transformation E is improving the compilation of binary operators. Observation (2) is the main driving force towards the induction step.

$$E \; \acute{\mathcal{E}}[\![E \oslash F]\!] \, (x, s)$$

$=$ unfold

$$x := (\acute{\mathcal{E}}[\![E]\!] \; \widehat{\oslash} \; \acute{\mathcal{E}}[\![F]\!]) \; s$$

$=$ observation, y and z fresh variables

$$y \stackrel{.}{:=} \acute{\mathcal{E}}[\![E]\!] \; (z \stackrel{.}{:=} \acute{\mathcal{E}}[\![F]\!] \; (x \stackrel{.}{:=} (\text{LOOKUP} \; y \; \widehat{\oslash} \; \text{LOOKUP} \; z) \; s))$$

$=$ fold twice

$$E \; \acute{\mathcal{E}}[\![E]\!] \; (y, E \; \acute{\mathcal{E}}[\![F]\!] \; (z, x \stackrel{.}{:=} (\text{LOOKUP} \; y \; \widehat{\oslash} \; \text{LOOKUP} \; z) \; s))$$

$=$ synthesize

$$E \; \acute{\mathcal{E}}[\![E]\!] \; (y, E \; \acute{\mathcal{E}}[\![F]\!] \; (z, x \stackrel{.}{:=} (y \oslash z) \; s))$$

$=$ IH twice

$$\grave{\mathcal{E}}[\![E]\!] \; (y, \grave{\mathcal{E}}[\![F]\!] \; (z, x \stackrel{.}{:=} (y \oslash z) \; s))$$

$=$ derive

$$\grave{\mathcal{E}}[\![E \oslash F]\!] \, (x, s)$$

This yields a new run-time operation $x \stackrel{.}{:=} (y \oslash z) \; s \; \eta = s \; \eta[x := \eta \, y \oslash \eta \, z]$.

6.1   Embedding the transformation into the semantics of statements

In order to derive a new semantics using expression continuations, we must show how E can be embedded into the meaning of statements. That is, we seek a new semantic function $\acute{\mathcal{S}}[\![S]\!]$ that uses the just determined semantic function for expressions $\grave{\mathcal{E}}[\![E]\!]$.

$$\acute{\mathcal{S}}[\![\textbf{if } B \textbf{ then } S \textbf{ else } T \textbf{ fi}]\!] \; u$$

$=$ unfold

$$\acute{\mathcal{E}}[\![B]\!] \to (\acute{\mathcal{S}}[\![S]\!] \; u) \; [\!] \; (\acute{\mathcal{S}}[\![T]\!] \; u)$$

$=$ eureka, x a fresh variable

$$x := \acute{\mathcal{E}}[\![B]\!] \; (\text{LOOKUP} \; x \to (\acute{\mathcal{S}}[\![S]\!] \; u) \; [\!] \; (\acute{\mathcal{S}}[\![T]\!] \; u))$$

$=$ fold

$$E \; \acute{\mathcal{E}}[\![B]\!] \; (x, (\text{LOOKUP} \; x \to (\acute{\mathcal{S}}[\![S]\!] \; u) \; [\!] \; (\acute{\mathcal{S}}[\![T]\!] \; u)))$$

$=$ IH three times

$$\grave{\mathcal{E}}[\![B]\!] \; (x, (\text{LOOKUP} \; x \to (\grave{\mathcal{S}}[\![S]\!] \; u) \; [\!] \; (\grave{\mathcal{S}}[\![T]\!] \; u)))$$

$=$ derive

$$\grave{\mathcal{S}}[\![\textbf{if } B \textbf{ then } S \textbf{ else } T \textbf{ fi}]\!] \; u$$

When the inductive proof is completed, we have derived the following semantics

$$\mathcal{M}[\![\textbf{prog } S]\!] \;\; = \;\; \mathcal{S}[\![S]\!] \; \text{id} \; \eta_0$$

$$\mathcal{S}[\![\textbf{skip}]\!] \; s \;\; = \;\; s$$

$$\mathcal{S}[\![x := E]\!]\, s \;=\; \mathcal{E}[\![E]\!]\,(x, s)$$
$$\mathcal{S}[\![\text{if } B \text{ then } S \text{ else } T \text{ fi}]\!]\, u \;=\; \mathcal{E}[\![B]\!]\,(x, \text{LOOKUP } x \to (\mathcal{S}[\![S]\!]\, u) \,[\!] \,(\mathcal{S}[\![S]\!]\, u))$$
$$\mathcal{S}[\![\text{while } B \text{ do } S \text{ od}]\!]\, t \;=\; \mu(\lambda \text{loop}.\mathcal{E}[\![B]\!]\,(x, \text{LOOKUP } x \to (\mathcal{S}[\![S]\!]\, \text{loop}) \,[\!] \,t))$$

$$\mathcal{E}[\![\text{var } y]\!]\,(x, s) \;=\; (x := \text{LOOKUP } y)\, s$$
$$\mathcal{E}[\![\text{num } n]\!]\,(x, s) \;=\; (x := \text{LITERAL } n)\, s$$
$$\mathcal{E}[\![\text{true}]\!]\,(x, s) \;=\; (x := \text{TRUE})\, s$$
$$\mathcal{E}[\![\text{false}]\!]\,(x, s) \;=\; (x := \text{FALSE})\, s$$
$$\mathcal{E}[\![E \,\textcircled{2}\, F]\!]\,(x, s) \;=\; \mathcal{E}[\![E]\!]\,(y, \mathcal{E}[\![F]\!]\,(z, x := (y \,\textcircled{2}\, z)\, s))$$

The new set of run-time operations is:

$$(x := \text{LOOKUP } y)\, s\, \eta \;=\; s\, \eta[x := \eta\, y]$$
$$(x := \text{LITERAL } n)\, s\, \eta \;=\; s\, \eta[x := n]$$
$$x := (y \,\textcircled{2}\, z)\, s\, \eta \;=\; s\, \eta[x := \eta\, y \,\textcircled{2}\, \eta\, z]$$

The full continuation version, using labels and GOTO's, of our example script looks like:

$$\begin{aligned}
\text{factorial} \;&=\; (r := \text{LITERAL } 1 \circ \text{fac} := r)\, \text{loop} \\
\text{loop} \;&=\; (r0 := \text{LITERAL } 1 \circ r1 := \text{LOOKUP } n \circ r2 := (r1 \geq r0) \circ \\
&\quad\; \text{IF}_{\text{false}}\, r2\, \text{done} \circ \\
&\quad\; r3 := \text{LOOKUP fac} \circ r4 := \text{LOOKUP } n \circ \text{fac} := r4 \times r3 \circ \\
&\quad\; r5 := \text{LITERAL } 1 \circ r6 := \text{LOOKUP } n \circ n := r6 - r5 \circ \\
&\quad\; \text{GOTO loop})\, \bot \\
\text{done} \;&=\; \text{EXIT } \bot
\end{aligned}$$

where $\text{IF}_{\text{false}}\, x\, s\, t = \text{LOOKUP } x \to t \,[\!]\, s$.

7 Adding Procedures: from $\mathcal{W}$ to $\mathcal{C}$

Procedures are added to $\mathcal{W}$ by extending the syntax with the following alternatives.

$$\begin{aligned}
\text{statement} \;&::=\; \ldots \,|\, \textbf{return } \text{expression} \\
\text{expression} \;&::=\; \ldots \,|\, \textbf{call } \text{procedure (expression)} \\
P \in \text{procedure} \;&::=\; \textbf{proc } (\text{var}) \textbf{ begin } \text{statement } \textbf{end}
\end{aligned}$$

Recursive procedures will be represented by *cyclic* programs. Usually programs are assumed to be finite and recursion is solved semantically by means of a recursive environment mapping procedure names into their denotations. Solving recursion on the syntax level as we do makes calculations a lot simpler, and the syntax as well. Procedures need not have names. One should consult Meyer [11] for examples where the use of environments makes derivations less elegant.

example An example recursive procedure is nfib

$$\mu(\lambda\text{nfib} \quad . \quad \textbf{proc}\ (n)$$
$$\textbf{begin}$$
$$\textbf{if}\ (n \leq 1)\ \textbf{then return}\ 1$$
$$\textbf{else return}\ (1 + \text{nfib}\ (n-1) + \text{nfib}\ (n-2))$$
$$\textbf{fi}$$
$$\textbf{end})$$

This function is a popular benchmark in the functional programming community. Our compiler has an nfib number of 1.200.000 on a *Data General AV300*. Formally derived compilers can be efficient.

7.1 Dynamic semantics of functions

We refrain, again, from giving a static semantics and continue by giving a dynamic semantics for $\mathcal{C}$. Denotations of statements will be of type $env \rightarrow \mathbb{N}$ instead of $env \rightarrow env$ because statements must return a value.

$$\begin{aligned}
\text{RETURN}\ x\ s\ \eta &= \eta\ x \\
x := \text{CALL}\ ((p, y), z)\ s\ \eta &= s\ \eta[x := v]\ where\ v = p\ (\eta_0[y := \eta\ z]) \\
\text{EXIT}\ s\ \eta &= \bot
\end{aligned}$$

The valuation functions for the new syntactic constructs are defined using these semantic actions. The meaning of complete programs must be redefined as well.

$$\begin{aligned}
\mathcal{M}[\![\textbf{prog}\ S]\!] &= \mathcal{S}[\![S]\!]\ (\text{EXIT}\ \bot)\ \eta_0 \\
\mathcal{S}[\![\textbf{return}\ E]\!]\ s &= \mathcal{E}[\![E]\!]\ (x, \text{RETURN}\ x\ s) \\
\mathcal{E}[\![\textbf{call}\ P(E)]\!]\ (x, s) &= \mathcal{E}[\![E]\!]\ (y, x := \text{CALL}\ (\mathcal{P}[\![P]\!], y)\ s) \\
\mathcal{P}[\![.]\!] &\in procedure \rightarrow stat\|var \\
\mathcal{P}[\![\textbf{proc}\ (x)\ \textbf{begin}\ S\ \textbf{end}]\!] &= (\mathcal{S}[\![S]\!]\ (\text{EXIT}\ \bot), x)
\end{aligned}$$

Function that do not RETURN explicitly, implicitly return $\bot$ by means of EXIT.

7.2 Introducing the Dump

The semantics of a procedure call

$$x := \text{CALL}\ ((p, y), z)\ s\ \eta \ = \ s\ \eta[x := v]\ where\ v = p\ (\eta_0[y := \eta\ z])$$

does not properly reflect the standard subroutine call, where evaluation on the caller's side is temporarily suspended and control is transferred from caller to callee which eventually returns its result to back to the caller. This implicit evaluation order will be explicated by introducing yet another continuation, the *dump*, which represents the suspended computation of the caller of the currently executing procedure. The dump continuation has type $\mathbb{N} \to \mathbb{N}$, and should be strict. Given the result of the callee, the caller may resume computing its result, but if the callee evaluates to $\perp$ the whole computation has to fail.

The injective function $C \in (env \to \mathbb{N}) \to (env \to dump \to \mathbb{N})$ maps an abstract continuation $\acute{s}$ that does not expect a dump, into a concrete one $\grave{s} = C\,\acute{s}$ that does expect a dump. Not surprisingly type considerations suggest

$$C\,\acute{s}\,\eta\,\delta\ =\ \delta\,(\acute{s}\,\eta)$$

The left-inverse $A \in (env \to dump \to \mathbb{N}) \to (env \to \mathbb{N})$ of C maps a concrete continuation $\grave{s} = C\,\acute{s}$ back into an abstract one $A\,\grave{s}\,\eta = \grave{s}\,\eta\,id$. The new semantics is derived using the fact that $A \circ C = id$.

$\qquad \acute{\mathcal{M}}[\![\textbf{prog } S]\!]$

$= \qquad$ demand

$\qquad \grave{\mathcal{M}}[\![\textbf{prog } S]\!]$

$= \qquad A \circ C = id$

$\qquad A \circ C \circ \grave{\mathcal{M}}[\![\textbf{prog } S]\!]$

$= \qquad$ unfold

$\qquad (A \circ C \circ \acute{S}[\![S]\!])\,(\text{EXIT } \perp)\,\eta_0$

$= \qquad$ assume $C\,\acute{S}[\![S]\!]\,s = \grave{S}[\![S]\!]\,(C\,s)$

$\qquad (A \circ \acute{S}[\![S]\!] \circ C)\,(\text{EXIT } \perp)\,\eta_0$

$= \qquad$ unfold A

$\qquad (\acute{S}[\![S]\!] \circ C)\,(\text{EXIT } \perp)\,\eta_0\,id$

The claim is resolved by a simultaneous induction proof of the propositions

$$C\,\acute{S}[\![S]\!] = \grave{S}[\![S]\!]\,(C\,s)\ \wedge\ C\,(\acute{\mathcal{E}}[\![E]\!]\,(x,s)) = \grave{\mathcal{E}}[\![E]\!]\,(x, C\,s)\ \wedge\ (C\|id)\,\acute{\mathcal{P}}[\![P]\!] = \grave{\mathcal{P}}[\![P]\!]$$

strictness Now that programs may be cyclic, we must check that C is strict. This is obvious, as we required dump continuations to be strict.

skip The meaning of **skip** statements remains unchanged when adding a dump.

$\qquad C\,(\acute{S}[\![\textbf{skip}]\!]\,s)$

$= \qquad$ unfold

$\qquad C\,s$

$= \qquad$ derive

$\qquad \grave{S}[\![\textbf{skip}]\!]\,(C\,s)$

If we use the perhaps more obvious statement $C\,(\acute{S}[\![\textbf{skip}]\!]\,s) = \grave{S}[\![\textbf{skip}]\!]\,s$ the result is an unsatisfying, but correct, semantics.

$$C \; (\acute{S}\llbracket \mathbf{skip} \rrbracket \; s) \; \eta \; \delta$$

$=$ unfold

$$C \; s \; \eta \; \delta$$

$=$ unfold

$$\delta \; (s \; \eta)$$

$=$ synthesize

$$SKIP \; s \; \eta \; \delta$$

$=$ derive

$$\grave{S}\llbracket \mathbf{skip} \rrbracket \; s \; \eta \; \delta$$

It forces the introduction of a weird run-time instruction $\widehat{SKIP}$.

The effect of C on RETURN-statements leads to the synthesis of a new and useful run-time instruction.

$$C \; (\acute{S}\llbracket \mathbf{return} \; E \rrbracket \; s)$$

$=$ unfold

$$C \; (\acute{E}\llbracket E \rrbracket \; (x, \text{RET}\acute{U}\text{RN} \; s))$$

$=$ IH

$$\grave{E}\llbracket E \rrbracket \; (x, C \; (\text{RET}\acute{U}\text{RN} \; s))$$

$=$ abutting calculation

$$\grave{E}\llbracket E \rrbracket \; (x, \text{RET}\grave{U}\text{RN} \; (C \; s))$$

$=$ derive

$$\grave{S}\llbracket \mathbf{return} \; E \rrbracket \; (C \; s)$$

$$C \; (\text{RET}\acute{U}\text{RN} \; x) \; s \; \eta \; \delta$$

$=$ unfold

$$\delta \; (\text{RET}\acute{U}\text{RN} \; x \; s \; \acute{\eta})$$

$=$ evaluate

$$\delta \; (\eta \; x)$$

$=$ synthesize

$$\text{RET}\grave{U}\text{RN} \; (C \; s) \; \eta \; \delta$$

This captures the intuition of the statement **return** E, namely return the value of E to the caller of the current function.

while-loops For **while**-loops the following lemma is needed,

$$g \; \mu(\lambda x.A[x]) = \mu(\lambda x.B[x]) \quad \Leftarrow \quad g \; A[x] = B[g \; x] \tag{4}$$

that can be proved by fixed-point induction. Lemma (4) takes care of the difficult work in the calculation of the new semantics for loops.

expressions Having shown that C promotes over $S\llbracket \_ \rrbracket$, we now must show that it promotes over $E\llbracket \_ \rrbracket$ as well.

$$C\ (\acute{\mathcal{E}}[\![E\ \textcircled{2}\ F]\!]\ (x, s))$$
$$=\quad \text{unfold}$$
$$C\ (\acute{\mathcal{E}}[\![E]\!]\ (y, \acute{\mathcal{E}}[\![F]\!]\ (z, x :\doteq (y\ \textcircled{2}\ z)\ s)))$$
$$=\quad \text{IH twice}$$
$$\grave{\mathcal{E}}[\![E]\!]\ (y, \grave{\mathcal{E}}[\![F]\!]\ (z, C\ (x :\doteq (y\ \textcircled{2}\ z)\ s)))$$
$$=\quad \text{abutting calculation}$$
$$\grave{\mathcal{E}}[\![E]\!]\ (y, \grave{\mathcal{E}}[\![F]\!]\ (z, x :\doteq (y\ \textcircled{2}\ z)\ (C\ s)))$$
$$=\quad \text{derive}$$
$$\grave{\mathcal{E}}[\![E\ \textcircled{2}\ F]\!]\ (x, C\ s)$$

$$C\ (x :\doteq (y\ \textcircled{2}\ z))\ s\ \eta\ \delta$$
$$=\quad \text{unfold}$$
$$\delta\ (x :\doteq (y\ \textcircled{2}\ z)\ s\ \eta)$$
$$=\quad \text{evaluate}$$
$$\delta\ (s\ \eta[x := \eta\ y\ \textcircled{2}\ \eta\ z])$$
$$=\quad \text{fold}$$
$$C\ s\ \eta[x := \eta\ y\ \textcircled{2}\ \eta\ z]\ \delta$$
$$=\quad \text{synthesize}$$
$$x :\doteq (y\ \textcircled{2}\ z)\ (C\ s)\ \eta\ \delta$$

For expressions compiled into LITERAL and LOOKUP we find new run-time actions:

$$(x := \text{LOOKUP}\ y)\ s\ \eta\ \delta\ =\ s\ \eta[x := \eta\ y]\ \delta$$
$$(x := \text{LITERAL}\ n)\ s\ \eta\ \delta\ =\ s\ \eta[x := n]\ \delta$$

procedure call The reason why doing the current derivation is to refine function calls. Synthesis of the concrete CALL-instruction is tedious.

$$C\ (\acute{\mathcal{E}}[\![\textbf{call}\ P(E)]\!]\ (x, s))$$
$$=\quad \text{unfold}$$
$$C\ (\acute{\mathcal{E}}[\![E]\!]\ (y, x :\doteq \text{CALL}\ (\acute{\mathcal{P}}[\![P]\!], y)\ s)$$
$$=\quad \text{IH}$$
$$\grave{\mathcal{E}}[\![E]\!]\ (y, C\ (x :\doteq \text{CALL}\ (\acute{\mathcal{P}}[\![P]\!], y)\ s))$$
$$=\quad \text{abutting calculation}$$
$$\grave{\mathcal{E}}[\![E]\!]\ (y, :\doteq \text{CALL}\ (C\|\text{id}\ \acute{\mathcal{P}}[\![P]\!], y)\ (C\ s))$$
$$=\quad \text{IH}$$
$$\grave{\mathcal{E}}[\![E]\!]\ (y, :\doteq \text{CALL}\ (\grave{\mathcal{P}}[\![P]\!], y)\ (C\ s))$$
$$=\quad \text{derive}$$
$$\acute{\mathcal{E}}[\![\textbf{call}\ P(E)]\!]\ (x, C\ s)$$

$$C\ (x :\doteq \text{CALL}\ ((p, y), z))\ s\ \eta\ \delta$$
$$=\quad \text{unfold}$$
$$\delta\ (x :\doteq \text{CALL}\ ((p, y), z)\ s\ \eta)$$
$$=\quad \text{evaluate}$$
$$(\delta \circ (\lambda v.s\ \eta[x := v]))\ (p\ (\eta_0[y := \eta\ z]))$$
$$=\quad \text{law for}\ \lambda$$
$$(\lambda v.\delta\ (s\ \eta[x := v]))\ (p\ (\eta_0[y := \eta\ z]))$$
$$=\quad \text{fold}$$
$$C\ p\ (\eta_0[y := \eta\ z])\ (\lambda v.C\ s\ \eta[x := v]\ \delta))$$
$$=\quad \text{synthesize}$$
$$x :\doteq \text{CALL}\ ((C\ p, y), z)\ (C\ s)\ \eta\ \delta$$

Function entrance The last case we have to tackle is $(C\|\text{id})\ \mathcal{P}[\![P]\!]$.

$$\begin{array}{ll}
& (C \| id) \; \acute{\mathcal{P}}[\![\textbf{proc}\ (x)\ \textbf{begin}\ S\ \textbf{end}]\!] \\
= & \quad \text{unfold} \\
& (C\ (\acute{\mathcal{S}}[\![S]\!]\ (\text{EX\'IT}\ \bot)), x) \\
= & \quad \text{IH} \\
& (\acute{\mathcal{S}}[\![S]\!]\ (C\ (\text{EX\'IT}\ \bot)), x) \\
= & \quad \text{abutting calculation} \\
& (\acute{\mathcal{S}}[\![S]\!]\ (\text{EX\`IT}\ \bot), x) \\
= & \quad \text{derive} \\
& \acute{\mathcal{P}}[\![\textbf{proc}\ (x)\ \textbf{begin}\ S\ \textbf{end}]\!]
\end{array}$$

$$\begin{array}{ll}
& C\ (\text{EX\'IT}\ s)\ \eta\ \delta \\
= & \quad \text{unfold} \\
& \delta\ (\text{EX\'IT}\ s\ \eta) \\
= & \quad \text{evaluate} \\
& \delta\ \bot \\
= & \quad \text{synthesize} \\
& \text{EX\`IT}\ (C\ s)\ \eta\ \delta
\end{array}$$

This completes our induction proof.

7.3 Final Semantics

The final semantics for $\mathcal{C}$ looks like

$$\mathcal{M}[\![\textbf{prog}\ P]\!] \;=\; \mathcal{S}[\![P]\!]\ (\text{EXIT}\ \bot)\ \eta_0\ id$$

$$\begin{array}{rcl}
\mathcal{S}[\![\textbf{skip}]\!]\ s &=& s \\
\mathcal{S}[\![x := E]\!]\ s &=& \mathcal{E}[\![E]\!]\ (x, s) \\
\mathcal{S}[\![S\ ;\ T]\!]\ u &=& \mathcal{S}[\![S]\!]\ (\mathcal{S}[\![T]\!]\ u) \\
\mathcal{S}[\![\textbf{return}\ E]\!]\ s &=& \mathcal{E}[\![E]\!]\ (x, \text{RETURN}\ x\ s) \\
\mathcal{S}[\![\textbf{if}\ B\ \textbf{then}\ S\ \textbf{else}\ T\ \textbf{fi}]\!]\ u &=& \mathcal{E}[\![B]\!]\ (x, \text{LOOKUP}\ x \to \mathcal{S}[\![S]\!]\ u\ [\!]\ \mathcal{S}[\![T]\!]\ u) \\
\mathcal{S}[\![\textbf{while}\ B\ \textbf{do}\ S\ \textbf{od}]\!]\ t &=& \mu(\lambda loop.\mathcal{E}[\![B]\!]\ (x, \text{LOOKUP}\ x \to (\mathcal{S}[\![S]\!]\ loop)\ [\!]\ t))
\end{array}$$

$$\begin{array}{rcl}
\mathcal{E}[\![\textbf{var}\ y]\!]\ (x, s) &=& x := \text{LOOKUP}\ y\ s \\
\mathcal{E}[\![\textbf{num}\ n]\!]\ (x, s) &=& x := \text{LITERAL}\ n\ s \\
\mathcal{E}[\![\textbf{true}]\!]\ (x, s) &=& x := \text{TRUE}\ s \\
\mathcal{E}[\![\textbf{false}]\!]\ (x, s) &=& x := \text{FALSE}\ s \\
\mathcal{E}[\![E\ \textcircled{2}\ F]\!]\ (x, s) &=& \mathcal{E}[\![E]\!]\ (y, \mathcal{E}[\![F]\!]\ (z, x := (y\ \textcircled{2}\ z)\ s)) \\
\mathcal{E}[\![\textbf{call}\ P(E)]\!]\ (x, s) &=& \mathcal{E}[\![E]\!]\ (y, x := \text{CALL}\ (\mathcal{P}[\![P]\!], y)\ s) \\
\mathcal{P}[\![\textbf{proc}\ (x)\ \textbf{begin}\ s\ \textbf{end}]\!] &=& (\mathcal{S}[\![s]\!]\ (\text{EXIT}\ \bot), x)
\end{array}$$

The run-time operations indeed are very close to concrete machine instructions

$$\begin{array}{rcl}
\text{EXIT}\ s\ \eta\ \delta &=& \delta\ \bot \\
\text{RETURN}\ x\ s\ \eta\ \delta &=& \delta\ (\eta\ x) \\
(x := \text{LOOKUP}\ y)\ s\ \eta\ \delta &=& s\ \eta[x := \eta\ y]\ \delta \\
(x := \text{LITERAL}\ n)\ s\ \eta\ \delta &=& s\ \eta[x := n]\ \delta \\
x := \text{CALL}\ ((p, y), z)\ s\ \eta\ \delta &=& p\ (\eta_0[y := \eta\ z])\ (\lambda v.s\ \eta[x := v]\ \delta) \\
x := (y\ \textcircled{2}\ z)\ s\ \eta\ \delta &=& s\ \eta[x := \eta\ y\ \textcircled{2}\ \eta\ z]\ \delta
\end{array}$$

8 Tail call elimination

Suppose the context condition holds that any variable appearing in a program is defined (occurs on the lhs of an assignment) before it is used (occurs on the rhs of an assignment), then we can redefine the CALL instruction as

$$x := \text{CALL} \, ((p,y),z) \, s \, \eta \, \delta \;=\; p \, (\eta[y := \eta \, z]) \, (\lambda v.s \, \eta[x := v] \, \delta)$$

Thus the current environment η may be passed to p instead of the empty environment η_0 because p does not use the values of the identifiers already bound in η. Using this modified CALL instruction we will show how certain recursive calls can be replaced by iteration. When a procedure returns by calling a procedure (either itself or another), that call is said to be a *tail call*. We can replace such a call by a jump; this not only saves time, but also space.

$$(x := \text{CALL} \, ((p,y),z) \circ \text{RETURN} \, x) \, s \, \eta \, \delta$$
$$=\quad \text{evaluate CALL}$$
$$p \, (\eta[y := \eta \, z]) \, (\lambda v.\text{RETURN} \, x \, s \, \eta[x := v] \, \delta)$$
$$=\quad \text{evaluate RETURN}$$
$$p \, (\eta[y := \eta \, z]) \, \delta$$
$$=\quad \text{devaluate LOOKUP and GOTO}$$
$$(y := \text{LOOKUP} \, z \circ \text{GOTO} \, p) \, s \, \eta \, \delta$$

Incorporating this into our translation scheme gives

$$\mathcal{S}[\![\textbf{return} \, (\textbf{call} \, P(E))]\!] \, s \;=\; \mathcal{E}[\![E]\!] \, (x, \text{GOTO} \, p \, s) \; \text{where} \, (p,x) = \mathcal{P}[\![P]\!]$$

Note that this definition is not homomorphic, but can be made so easily.

References

[1] Stijn Arts and Reijer Grimbergen. Taking a risc; implementing functional languages on a risc. Master's thesis, University of Nijmegen, 1990.

[2] R.M. Burstall and P.J. Landin. Programs and their proofs: an algebraic approach. *Machine Intelligence*, 4, 1969.

[3] J Mc Charthy and J Painter. Correctness of a compiler for arithmetic expressions. In *Symposium on Applied Mathematics 19*, 1967.

[4] L.M Chirica. *Contributions to Compiler Correctness*. PhD thesis, University of California at LA, USA, 1976.

[5] C. Consel and O. Danvy. Static and dynamic semantics processing. In *Proc. ACM POPL'91*, 1991.

[6] Kyung Doh and Dave Schmidt. Extracting strong typing laws from action semantics. Technical report, Kansas State University, 1991.

[7] Peter Dybjer. Using domain algebras to prove the correctness of a compiler. In *LNCS 182*. Springer.

[8] Peter Lee. *Realistic Compiler Generation*. MIT press, 1990.

[9] John McCarthy. Towards a mathematical science of computation. In *Information Processing 1962*. IFIP, North-Holland, 1962.

[10] Erik Meijer. *A Calculational Approach to Semantics Directed Compiler Generation*. PhD thesis, University of Nijmegen, Toernooiveld, Nijmegen, The Netherlands, To Appear.

[11] John-Jules Ch. Meyer. *Programming calculi based on fixed point transformations: semantics and applications*. PhD thesis, Vrije Universiteit, Amsterdam, 1985.

[12] R.E. Milne and C. Strachey. *A Theory of Programming Language Semantics*. Wiley, 1976. 2 volumes.

[13] F.L. Morris. Advice on structuring compilers and proving them correct. In *ACM POPL 3*, pages 144–152, 1973.

[14] P.D. Mosses. Abstract semantic algebras! In D. Bjørner, editor, *Formal Description of Programming Concepts II*, pages 63–88. North-Holland, 1983.

[15] Peter Mosses. A constructive approach to compiler correctness. In *LNCS 94: Workshop on Semantics Directed Compiler Generation*. Springer, 1980.

[16] Motorola Semiconductors. *m88100 Processor Manual*.

[17] John C. Reynolds. Definitional interpreters for higher order programming languages. In *25th ACM Anual Conference*, pages 717–740, 1972.

[18] David A. Schmidt. *Denotational Semantics*. Allyn and Bacon, 1986.

[19] Peter Sestoft and Harald Søndergaard. A bibliography on partial evaluation. *SIGPLAN Notices*, 23(2), 1988.

[20] Ravi Sethi. Circular expressions: Elimination of static environments. *Science of Computer Programming*, 1:203–222, 1982.

[21] Joseph E. Stoy. *Denotational Semantics, The Scott-Strachey Approach to Programming Language Theory*. The MIT press, 1977.

[22] J.W. Tatcher, E.C Wagner, and J.B Wright. More advice on structuring compilers and proving them correct. In *LNCS 94: Workshop on Semantics Directed Compiler Generation*. Springer, 1980.

[23] D.A. Watt. Executable semantic descriptions. *Software Practice and Experience*, 16(1):13–43, 1986.

Pers as Types, Inductive Types and Types with Laws

Ed Voermans

Department of Mathematics and Computing Science,
Eindhoven University of Technology,
Eindhoven, The Netherlands.

Abstract

This article develops a type system for based on partial equivalence relations for relational programming in the Bird-Meertens style .We introduce a general definition for an inductive type and show how inductive types with laws can be constructed in the type system. The usability of this theory is demonstrated on the Boom hierarchy (the class of types for the original Bird-Meertens formalism).

1 Introduction

The type theory of this article is intended for use with the relational style of programming that was introduced in [1][2][3]. It is a replacement for the "monotype-system" that is described there.

The relational programming method unifies specifications, programs, datatypes and type-judgements in the calculus of relations. All calculations are carried out using a small number of axioms and predicate calculus as a meta-language. The fact that the axioms (partially) model the set-theoretic relations is not used in the calculations.

We start out in section 2 by giving the axioms of the relational calculus and some of the the consequences of these axioms that are used in the proofs in this article.

In section 3 we describe how we can view partial equivalence relations as types and use them as domains.

Section 4 describes how disjoint sum and cartesian product can be introduced as type-constructors in the relational calculus.

In section 5 we generalize head-recursive relations to a more general class, define inductive types and document some of their properties.

Section 6 gives a method for constructing a new inductive type "with a law" from a given one as the least solution of an equation and considers types with laws as domains of recursive relations.

Section 7 shows how the method of section 6 can be applied for modelling the Boom hierarchy. This class of types (binary trees, lists, bags and sets) is created by imposing laws on a base type.

We do not give proofs in sections 2, 3 and 4 because they are trivial or can be found in the literature.

2   Some relational calculus

We use an axiomatic theory of relations, similar to that of [11] for our calculations. We call this calculus the SPEC calculus (from specification), to distinguish it from the the set-theoretic calculus of relations. Our axiomatization is not complete and. we even have a model for it (based on powersets of monoids) that is not isomorphic to the calculus of relations.

The specs (we use spec for relation) form a complete, completely distributive, complemented lattice. There is a bottom $\bot\!\bot$, a top $\top\!\top$ and glb and lub $\sqcap$ and $\sqcup$ for arbitrary sets of specs. The complement operator is denoted by prefix $\neg$. We denote the partial order of the lattice by $\sqsupseteq$.

These lattice-properties allow us to use the Knaster-Tarski fixpoint theorem. We use the following limited version for least fixpoints:

If function f from SPEC to SPEC is monotonic, i.e. $f.X \sqsupseteq f.Y \Leftarrow X \sqsupseteq Y$ then the equations

$$X :: X \sqsupseteq f.X \qquad\qquad\qquad X :: X = f.X$$

have the same least solution, that we denote by μf. μf is completely characterized by the following equations:

(0a) $\mu f = f.\mu f$ $\qquad\qquad$ (0b) $X \sqsupseteq \mu f \Leftarrow X \sqsupseteq f.X$

The first equation is called the calculation rule, the second the induction rule. We can apply Knaster-Tarski also to sets of equations. If f and g are monotonic then the equations

$$X :: X \sqsupseteq f.X \qquad\qquad\qquad X :: X \sqsupseteq g.X$$

combined have a unique least solution, because the equations are equivalent to

$$X :: X \sqsupseteq f.X \sqcup g.X$$

The induction rule becomes

(0c) $X \sqsupseteq \mu(f,g) \Leftarrow X \sqsupseteq f.X \wedge X \sqsupseteq g.X$

This is for two equations, but the same principle also applies to three or more equations. We have similar properties for the greatest fixpoint which is denoted by νf.

The next operator in our calculus is the reverse operator $\cup$, swapping pairs set-theoretically. This operator distributes over $\sqcup$ and $\sqcap$, so it is monotonic. We have

$$R\cup \sqsupseteq S \;\equiv\; R \sqsupseteq S\cup$$

for all specs R and S. From this follow the following often used properties:

(1) $X\cup\cup = X$ $\qquad\qquad$ (2) $I\cup = I$ $\qquad\qquad$ (3) $\top\!\top\cup = \top\!\top$

The last operator is the composition operator $\circ$. This operator is monotonic, associative, has a unit called I and distributes universally over $\sqcup$. We have the following distribution rule with $\cup$:

$$(R \circ S)\cup = S\cup \circ R\cup$$

We have two Galois correspondences because both $R\circ$ and $\circ R$ universally distribute over $\sqcup$. Their adjoint operators $R\backslash$ and $/R$ are called "under" and "over" and defined as follows:

Definition 4: $\qquad R\backslash S \sqsupseteq X \;\equiv\; S \sqsupseteq R \circ X \qquad\qquad\qquad S/R \sqsupseteq X \;\equiv\; S \sqsupseteq X \circ R$

for all specs R, S and X. Hoare and He [7] use the same symbols (they call them weakest pre-specifications) but swap them. We choose this notation because it makes it easier to spot the applicability of the following cancellation lemma's:

Lemma 5: $\qquad R \sqsupseteq R/S \circ S \qquad\qquad\qquad\qquad R \sqsupseteq S \circ S\backslash R$

Calculationally we reap great advantage by exploiting the Galois correspondence between factors and relational composition. There are two other axioms for the SPEC calculus,

$$\neg R \sqsupseteq S \circ \neg T \circ U \;\equiv\; T \sqsupseteq S\cup \circ R \circ U\cup$$
$$\top \circ X \circ \top = \top \;\equiv\; X \neq \bot\!\bot$$

but we will not use them in this article.

A lemma that we will use quite often is, for all specs R:

Lemma 6: $\qquad R \circ R\cup \circ R \sqsupseteq R$

Definition 7: A total function F that maps specs to specs is a relator iff for all specs X and Y:

(7a) $F.X \sqsupseteq F.Y \;\Leftarrow\; X \sqsupseteq Y$
(7b) $F.(X \circ Y) = F.X \circ F.Y$
(7c) $F.(X\cup) = (F.X)\cup$

The definition can be generalized to functions of arbitrary arity. For example a binary function $\otimes$ is a relator iff:

$$R \otimes S \sqsupseteq T \otimes U \;\Leftarrow\; R \sqsupseteq T \wedge S \sqsupseteq U$$
$$R\cup \otimes S\cup = (R \otimes S)\cup$$
$$R \otimes S \circ T \otimes U = (R \circ T) \otimes (S \circ U)$$

In our calculus the relators have the role of the functors in the categorical type-theory.

3 Pers as types

The SPEC calculus that we use models relations over a fixed universe. If we see types as sets then we could model a type by a subset of the universe and represent this subset in the spec calculus by the identity relation on that subset. This method leads to the monotype-system that is described in [2].

This is not a convenient method if we want to model a type like the quotients. We can define the quotients using a partial equivalence relation on pairs of integers:

(8) $(a, b) \, Q \, (c, d) \; \equiv \; ad = bc \wedge b \neq 0 \wedge d \neq 0$

It is easy to see that Q is symmetric and transitive. Q is partial because pairs with second component 0 are not related to anything. It is well-known that every partial equivalence relation induces equivalence classes on the domain of the relation. These equivalence classes can be seen as the elements of a type, in this case the quotients.

If we want to model this type in the monotype system then we have to choose an unique element of the universe for every equivalence class of the quotients. We don't have this problem if we accept Q as a model for the type. We have the partial equivalence relations in the SPEC calculus as pers:

Definition 9:   A spec A is called a per iff

(9a) $A^\cup = A$ $\qquad\qquad\qquad$ (9b) $A \sqsupseteq A \circ A$

The first condition is the symmetry, the second transitivity. We can replace (9b) in this definition by

(10) $A = A \circ A$

The proof that the combination of (9a) and (9b) is equivalent to the combination of (9a) and (10) is easy and left to the reader. Another property that is important is that relators preserve pers; a relator applied to a per has a per as result. Furthermore, μF and νF are pers for F a relator. From now on we will use A, B, etc. for pers.

Another advantage of using pers instead of monotypes is found when we want to impose a law on a type. A law specifies equalities on the elements of a type. For example, if we want to consider two quotients equal if their absolute values are equal then we can do this on Q by modifying the definition to

(11) $(a, b) \, Q^+ \, (c, d) \; \equiv \; abs(ad) = abs(bc) \wedge b \neq 0 \wedge d \neq 0$

If we examine the equivalence classes of Q^+ then we see that (except for the class $(0, ?)$) they are made by unioning two equivalence classes of Q together. We made an equivalence relation on the classes of Q: classes of Q are equivalent if they are contained in the same class of Q^+. Formalizing this notion in the SPEC calculus gives us the following definition for pers A and B:

Definition 12: A is an equivalence relation on B iff

$A \sqsupseteq B \wedge A \circ B = A$

The reader is urged to verify for himself that this indeeds means that the equivalence classes of A are made by unioning classes of B together.

Since we use the symbol for functional composition ∘ for relational composition we see specs as having their arguments on the rhs and their result on the lhs. A relation f is functional to A if the image of every element of the universe through f is empty or an equivalence class of A. This translates in the spec-calculus to

Definition 13: A spec f is functional to A to iff

$$A \sqsupseteq f \circ f^\cup \wedge A \circ f = f$$

Again the reader is urged to verify for himself that this indeeds formalizes the informal definition above. A consequence of this defintion is that every per A is functional to A. A is the identity function on A. We will sometimes use I_A for A if we are using it as the identity function.

We use pers to define the notion of a domain for specs. For $per.A$ we have:

Definition 14: A is a right-domain of R iff $R \circ A = R$

The notion of a left-domain can be defined similarly. An important operator is the >-operator defined by:

Definition 15: $R> \;\triangleq\; \top \circ R \sqcap I$

$R>$ is the least per that solves $X :: R \circ X = R$. So it is the least right-domain. We can define the least left-domain by $X< = X^{\cup}>$. Here follows a short list of properties that we use in this article:

Lemma 16: $R \circ R> \;=\; R$
Lemma 17: $R> \sqsupseteq S> \;\Leftarrow\; Q \circ R \sqsupseteq S$
Lemma 18: $A \sqsupseteq A> \;\Leftarrow\; per.A$
Lemma 19: $R^\cup \circ R \sqsupseteq R>$

4   Disjoint sum and cartesian product

Backhouse e.a. [1] gives a relational account of binary disjoint sum and binary cartesian product. This section generalizes the binary disjoint sum to finite disjoint sum and lists the properties of disjoint sum and cartesian product that we will use later on.

4.1   Finite disjoint sum

[1] gives two axioms for the injection functions ↪ and ↩, but we will only use one of them. The other is only necessary in a monotype-system.

Axiom 20:   For all specs R, S, T and U:

$$(R \circ \hookrightarrow_\cup \sqcup S \circ \hookleftarrow_\cup) \circ (\hookrightarrow \circ T \sqcup \hookleftarrow \circ U) \;=\; R \circ T \sqcup S \circ U$$

We introduce generalized injection functions with the following definition:

Definition 21: $\sigma.0 \triangleq \hookrightarrow$ $\sigma.(n+1) \triangleq \hookleftarrow \circ \sigma.n$

For R a family of N specs, indexed from 0 to $N-1$, we define the sum and its associated operator called "junc" in the following way:

Definition 22: $\triangledown(i : 0 \leq i < N : R.i) \triangleq \sqcup(i : 0 \leq i < N : R.i \circ (\sigma.i)_\cup)$
Definition 23: $\Sigma(i : 0 \leq i < N : R.i) \triangleq \sqcup(i : 0 \leq i < N : \sigma.i \circ R.i \circ (\sigma.i)_\cup)$

The junc can be considered as a case construction, depending on the injection function, one of the alternatives is chosen. We have the following properties: for $0 \leq n < N$,

Lemma 24: $\triangledown(i : 0 \leq i < N : R.i) \circ \sigma.n \;=\; R.n$
Lemma 25: $\Sigma(i : 0 \leq i < N : R.i) \circ \sigma.n \;=\; \sigma.n \circ R.n$
Lemma 26: Σ is a relator

We can also use an infix notation. Suppose $N = 3$, $R.0 = S$, $R.1 = T$ and $R.2 = U$. Then we write

$$S \triangledown T \triangledown U \quad \text{for} \quad \triangledown(i : 0 \leq i < N : R.i)$$
$$S + T + U \quad \text{for} \quad \Sigma(i : 0 \leq i < N : R.i).$$

If per A operates on a sum, i.e. $A \circ \Sigma(i : 0 \leq i < N : I) = A$, then we can write A the junc of a family of specs,

Lemma 27: $A = \triangledown(i : 0 \leq i < N : A \circ \sigma.i)$

We call this family of specs the constructors of A. For every component of the sum we define a constructor by

Definition 28: $\tau.i \triangleq A \circ \sigma.i$

The constructors are functional:

Lemma 29: $\tau.i$ is functional to A.

4.2   Binary cartesian product

We stick closer to the definition in [1] for binary cartesian products. We only omit the axiom for the monotypes.

There are two projection functions $\blacktriangleleft$ and $\blacktriangleright$ satisfying the following axioms:

Axiom 30: For all specs R, S, T and U:

(30a) $(R \circ \prec \sqcap S \circ \succ) \circ (\prec_\cup \circ T \sqcap \succ_\cup \circ U) = R \circ T \sqcap S \circ U$

(30b) $\pi \circ \prec = \pi \circ \succ$

We define the product and its associated operator "split" in the following way:

Definition 31: $R \vartriangle S \triangleq \prec_\cup \circ R \sqcap \succ_\cup \circ S$

Definition 32: $R \times S \triangleq \prec_\cup \circ R \circ \prec \sqcap \succ_\cup \circ S \circ \succ$

We will only use two properties of the cartesian product in this article:

Lemma 33: $\times$ is a relator

Lemma 34: $R \times S \circ T \vartriangle U = (R \circ T) \vartriangle (S \circ U)$

5 Recursive specs and inductive types

Inductive types and recursivily defined operations on these types are very important in the theory of datatypes. This section presents the start of a general theory about inductive pers and operations on them in the SPEC calculus.

A head-recursive operation consists of two parts, first the recursive operation is applied to the subcomponents of the argument, and the result of that is transformed to the endresult of the operation. In the SPEC calculus this formalizes for F a relator to

Definition 35: $F-right-recursive.X \triangleq \exists (R :: X = R \circ F.X)$

The $F.X$ is the application on the subcomponents, the R the postprocessing. The F comes from the shape of the induction. For example, if we have trees over A, then we have three constructors ε, τ and $+\!\!+$. ε is the constant function that returns an empty tree, τ produces a leaf of the tree from an element of A, $+\!\!+$ joins two trees together. Induction over the structure of trees has the following calculation rules for some specs S, T and U:

$$X \circ \varepsilon = S \circ \pi \qquad\qquad X \circ \tau = T \circ A \qquad\qquad X \circ +\!\!+ = U \circ X \times X$$

This leads to the following equation for X:

(36) $X \circ (\varepsilon \triangledown \tau \triangledown +\!\!+) = (S \triangledown T \triangledown U) \circ (\pi + A + X \times X)$

If we assume that X operates on trees, i.e. $X \circ (\varepsilon \triangledown \tau \triangledown +\!\!+) = X$ (Since the type is the junc of the constructors) then we see that X has the recursion scheme of definition 35 with relator $F.X = \pi + A + X \times X$ and $R = S \triangledown T \triangledown U$.

It is calculationaly not convenient to work with existential quantifications, but we have a way of eliminating this quantification. It is not difficult to prove, using the properties of factors, that the following definition is equivalent:

Definition 37: $F-right-recursive.X \triangleq X / F.X \circ F.X = X$

Here we see an important advantage of working in a relational system, because this formalization without the existential quantification is not possible in a functional setting.

We define inductive types as recursive pers with the following

Definition 38: $F-inductive.A \triangleq per.A \land F-right-recursive.A$

We can replace the rhs of this definition with the equivalent

(39) $per.A \land A \circ F.A = A$

Again, the proof of the equivalence is easy and left to the reader.

We have the following calculation rule for right-recursive operations: if F can be written as the sum of other relators, i.e. $F.X = \Sigma(i : 0 \le i < N : H.i.X)$ and $F-inductive.A$ and X satisfies

(40) $X = \triangledown(i : 0 \le i < N : R.i) \circ F.X \land X \circ A = X$

then we have the following

Lemma 41: $X \circ \tau.i = R.i \circ H.i.X$

Proof:

$$
\begin{array}{ll}
& X \circ \tau.i \\
= & \quad \{ \ (28) \ \} \\
& X \circ A \circ \sigma.i \\
= & \quad \{ \ \text{Assumption: } X \circ A = X \ \} \\
& X \circ \sigma.i \\
= & \quad \{ \ (40) \ \} \\
& \triangledown(i : 0 \le i < N : R.i) \circ F.X \circ \sigma.i \\
= & \quad \{ \ F \text{ is a sum, } (25) \ \} \\
& \triangledown(i : 0 \le i < N : R.i) \circ \sigma.i \circ H.i.X \\
= & \quad \{ \ (24) \ \} \\
& R.i \circ H.i.X
\end{array}
$$

If we instantiate this lemma with $X = A$ and $R.i = \tau.i$ then we get (using (27), (28) and (39)):

Lemma 42: $\tau.i \circ H.i.A = \tau.i$

6 Types with laws

The previous section introduced $F-inductive$ pers, but didn't show a construction method. Obvious $F-inductive$ pers are μF and νF. This section describes a method for the construction of inductive pers from other inductive per by imposing a law on the given base per.

Given is an $F-inductive$ per B and collections of specs $f.i$ and $g.i$ for $0 \le i < N$. We want to construct the least per C that satisfies the following

Specification 43:

(43a) C equivalence relation on B

(43b) $F-inductive.C$

(43c) $\forall(i : 0 \leq i < N : C \circ f.i = C \circ g.i)$

The first part specifies that B is the basetype of C, the second that our result is again $F - inductive$ and the third gives the laws that the new type has to satisfy. We want the least solution because we want to coalesce as few classes of B as possible.

Laws can often be expressed in the shape given above. For example, consider the type of natural numbers, this is isomorphic to the least fixpoint of the relator $F.X = \top + X$. We have two constructors for this type, $zero_{\mu F} = \mu F \circ \sigma.0$ and $succ_{\mu F} = \mu F \circ \sigma.1$. The per C that we want to construct has two classes, one for the even naturals and one for the odd naturals. We can achieve this by having the following property for the $succ$ constructor of C:

(44) $succ_C \circ succ_C = I_C$

Using $I_C = C$, (28) and (43a) this can be translated to

(45) $C \circ succ_{\mu F} \circ succ_{\mu F} = C \circ \mu F$

This specification of the law has the required shape. The existence of a least solution to the specification is in general not guaranteed, but the following conditions on B, f and g are sufficient:

Condition 46:

(46a) $B \sqsupseteq F.B$

(46b) $\forall(i : 0 \leq i < N : B \sqsupseteq f.i \circ f.i\cup \wedge B \sqsupseteq g.i \circ g.i\cup)$

(46c) $\forall(i : 0 \leq i < N : f.i> = g.i>)$

The example above with $B = \mu F$, $f.0 = succ_{\mu F} \circ succ_{\mu F}$ and $g.0 = \mu F$ satisfies the conditions

The equations in (43) are not monotonic, so we cannot guarantee the existence of a least solution using Knaster-Tarski. We will give another (this time monotonic) set of equations (47) and show that under conditions (46) every solution of the equations of the specification is a solution of the new set. Then we show that the least solution of (47) satisfies the specification , again using the conditions. The combination proves that the least solution of the specification (43) exists and is equal to the least solution of (47). We have the following

Equations 47:

(47a) $X \sqsupseteq X \circ X$

(47b) $X \sqsupseteq X\cup$

(47c) $X \sqsupseteq B$

(47d) $X \sqsupseteq F.X$

(47e) $X \sqsupseteq \sqcup(i : 0 \leq i < N : f.i \circ g.i\cup)$

This set of equations is monotonic, so the Knaster-Tarski fixpoint-theorem guarantees the existence of a least solution. We now prove the equivalence of the two definitions for types with laws.

First we show that every C satisfying (43) solves (47). For equations (47a) - (47c) this follows from C is a per and C is an equivalence relation on B. We prove the remaining two:

Proof C solves (47d):

$$
\begin{array}{ll}
& C \\
= & \{ \ F{-}inductive.C \ \} \\
& C \circ F.C \\
\sqsupseteq & \{ \ C \text{ equivalence relation on } B \ \} \\
& B \circ F.C \\
\sqsupseteq & \{ \ \text{Condition: } B \sqsupseteq F.B \ \} \\
& F.B \circ F.C \\
= & \{ \ \text{relators (7b)} \ \} \\
& F.(B \circ C) \\
= & \{ \ C \text{ equivalence relation on } B \ \} \\
& F.C
\end{array}
$$

Proof C solves (47e), $\forall(i : 0 \leq i < N : C \sqsupseteq f.i \circ g.i\cup)$:

$$
\begin{array}{ll}
& C \\
= & \{ \ C \text{ equivalence relation on } B \ \} \\
& C \circ B \\
\sqsupseteq & \{ \ \text{Condition: } B \sqsupseteq g.i \circ g.i\cup \ \} \\
& C \circ g.i \circ g.i\cup \\
= & \{ \ C \circ g.i = C \circ f.i \ \} \\
& C \circ f.i \circ g.i\cup \\
\sqsupseteq & \{ \ C \text{ equivalence relation on } B \ \} \\
& B \circ f.i \circ g.i\cup \\
\sqsupseteq & \{ \ \text{Condition: } B \sqsupseteq f.i \circ f.i\cup \ \} \\
& f.i \circ f.i\cup \circ f.i \circ g.i\cup \\
\sqsupseteq & \{ \ (6) \ \} \\
& f.i \circ g.i\cup
\end{array}
$$

Now we prove that the least solution of (47) satisfies the specification for the type with laws. From now on we will denote the least solution of (47) by L. We start by proving a useful lemma about the domain of L:

Lemma 48: $B{>} \sqsupseteq L{>}$

Proof:

$$
\begin{array}{ll}
& B{>} \sqsupseteq L{>} \\
\Leftarrow & \{ \ \text{domains (17)} \ \} \\
& B \circ \top\hspace{-0.3em}\top \circ B \sqsupseteq L \\
\Leftarrow & \{ \ L \text{ is the least solution of (47)} \ \} \\
& B \circ \top\hspace{-0.3em}\top \circ B \text{ solves (47)} \\
\equiv & \{ \ (i), (ii), (iii), (iv), (v), \text{ see below} \ \} \\
& true
\end{array}
$$

(i) $B \circ \pi \circ B \sqsupseteq B \circ \pi \circ B \circ B \circ \pi \circ B$

(ii) $B \circ \pi \circ B \sqsupseteq (B \circ \pi \circ B)\cup$

(iii) $B \circ \pi \circ B \sqsupseteq B$

(iv) $B \circ \pi \circ B \sqsupseteq F.(B \circ \pi \circ B)$

(v) $\forall (i : 0 \leq i < N : B \circ \pi \circ B \sqsupseteq f.i \circ g.i\cup)$

(i)-(iv) follow from $B = B\cup$ and $B \sqsupseteq F.B$.

Proof (v):

$$B \circ \pi \circ B$$
$\sqsupseteq$ { calculus. condition: $B \sqsupseteq f.i \circ f.i\cup$, $B \sqsupseteq g.i \circ g.i\cup$ }
$$f.i \circ f.i\cup \circ f.i \circ g.i\cup \circ g.i \circ g.i\cup$$
$\sqsupseteq$ { calculus (6) }
$$f.i \circ g.i\cup$$

L solves (47a) and (47b), so L is per. Now we prove the first part of the specification, L is an equivalence relation on B:

$$L \text{ equivalence relation on } B$$
$\equiv$ { definition equivalence relation on }
$$L \sqsupseteq B \land L \circ B = L$$
$\equiv$ { $L \sqsupseteq B$, $L \sqsupseteq L \circ L$ (L solves (47c) and (47a)) }
$$L \circ B \sqsupseteq L$$
$\Leftarrow$ { $per.B$, (18) }
$$L \circ B> \sqsupseteq L$$
$\Leftarrow$ { lemma (48) }
$$L \circ L> \sqsupseteq L$$
$\equiv$ { domains (16) }
$$true$$

The second part of the specification. L $F-inductive$ is proved by mutual inclusion below:

$$L \circ F.L$$
$\sqsupseteq$ { $L \sqsupseteq B$. relators monotonic }
$$L \circ F.B$$
$\sqsupseteq$ { $per.(F.B)$,(18) }
$$L \circ (F.B)>$$
$\sqsupseteq$ { $F-inductive.B \Rightarrow B \circ F.B = B$, (17) }
$$L \circ B>$$
$\sqsupseteq$ { lemma (48) }
$$L \circ L>$$
$=$ { domains (16) }
$$L$$
$=$ { $per.L$ }
$$L \circ L$$
$\sqsupseteq$ { $L \sqsupseteq F.L$ (L solves (47d) }
$$L \circ F.L$$

Finally we have the proof for the last part of the specification, $\forall(i : 0 \leq i < N : L \circ f.i = L \circ g.i)$. We only prove one inclusion, the proof for the other is similar.

$$
\begin{aligned}
& L \circ g.i \\
= \quad & \{ \ per.L \ \} \\
& L \circ L \circ g.i \\
\sqsupseteq \quad & \{ \ L \sqsupseteq f.i \circ g.i\upsilon \ \} \\
& L \circ f.i \circ g.i\upsilon \circ g.i \\
\sqsupseteq \quad & \{ \ \text{domains (19)} \ \} \\
& L \circ f.i \circ g.i> \\
= \quad & \{ \ g.i> = f.i> \ \} \\
& L \circ f.i \circ f.i> \\
= \quad & \{ \ \text{domains (16)} \ \} \\
& L \circ f.i
\end{aligned}
$$

The definition of L as the least solution of (47) only allows us to prove that a symmetric spec contains L because, from (47b), all solutions of (47) are symmetric. In the next section we have to prove that a not-neccesarily symmetric spec contains L. This can be done using the following lemma:

Lemma 49:

$$R \sqsupseteq L$$
$$\Leftarrow$$
$$R \sqsupseteq R \circ R \ \wedge \ R \sqsupseteq B \ \wedge \ R \sqsupseteq F.R \ \wedge$$
$$R \sqsupseteq \sqcup(i : 0 \leq i < N : f.i \circ g.i\upsilon \ \sqcup \ g.i \circ f.i\upsilon)$$

Proof:

$$
\begin{aligned}
& R \sqsupseteq L \\
\equiv \quad & \{ \ L = L\upsilon, \text{ calculus} \ \} \\
& R \sqsupseteq L \wedge R\upsilon \sqsupseteq L \\
\equiv \quad & \{ \ \text{calculus} \ \} \\
& R \sqcap R\upsilon \sqsupseteq L \\
\Leftarrow \quad & \{ \ L \text{ least solution of (47)} \ \} \\
& R \sqcap R\upsilon \text{ solves (47)} \\
\Leftarrow \quad & \{ \ (i). \ (ii), (iii), (iv), (v) \ \} \\
& R \sqsupseteq R \circ R \ \wedge \ R \sqsupseteq B \ \wedge \\
& R \sqsupseteq F.R \ \wedge \ R \sqsupseteq \sqcup(i : 0 \leq i < N : f.i \circ g.i\upsilon, \ \sqcup \ g.i \circ f.i\upsilon)
\end{aligned}
$$

(i) $R \sqcap R\upsilon \sqsupseteq (R \sqcap R\upsilon) \circ (R \sqcap R\upsilon) \ \Leftarrow \ R \sqsupseteq R \circ R$

(ii) $R \sqcap R\upsilon \sqsupseteq (R \sqcap R\upsilon)\upsilon$

(iii) $R \sqcap R\upsilon \sqsupseteq B \ \equiv \ R \sqsupseteq B$

(iv) $R \sqcap R\upsilon \sqsupseteq F.(R \sqcap R\upsilon) \ \Leftarrow \ R \sqsupseteq F.R$

(v) $R \sqcap R\upsilon \sqsupseteq f.i \circ g.i\upsilon \ \equiv \ R \sqsupseteq f.i \circ g.i\upsilon \sqcup g.i \circ f.i\upsilon$

6.1   Types with laws as domains

We have an important theorem about the condition under which a type with law is a right-domain of a right-recursive spec. If L, B, f and g are as in the previous sections, then we have:

Theorem 50: If $F - right - recursive.X$ then

$$X \circ L = X \quad \equiv \quad X \circ B = X \wedge \forall (i : 0 \leq i < N : X \circ f.i = X \circ g.i)$$

We first prove the $\Rightarrow$ direction:

$$
\begin{array}{ll}
& X \circ B \\
= & \{ \ X \circ L = X \ \} \\
& X \circ L \circ B \\
= & \{ \ L \ \text{equivalence relation on} \ B \ \} \\
& X \circ L \\
= & \{ \ X \circ L = X \ \} \\
& X
\end{array}
$$

$$
\begin{array}{ll}
& X \circ f.i \\
= & \{ \ X \circ L = X \ \} \\
& X \circ L \circ f.i \\
= & \{ \ L \circ f.i = L \circ g.i \ \} \\
& X \circ L \circ g.i \\
= & \{ \ X \circ L = X \ \} \\
& X \circ g.i
\end{array}
$$

Now the proof in the $\Leftarrow$ direction:

$$
\begin{array}{ll}
& X \circ L = X \\
\equiv & \{ \ X \circ L \sqsupseteq X \circ B = X \ \} \\
& X \sqsupseteq X \circ L \\
\equiv & \{ \ (4) \ \} \\
& X \setminus X \sqsupseteq L \\
\Leftarrow & \{ \ \text{lemma (49)} \ \} \\
& (i) \wedge (ii) \wedge (iii) \wedge (iv) \\
\equiv & \{ \ \text{see below} \ \} \\
& true
\end{array}
$$

(i) and (ii) are easy and left to the reader:

$$X \setminus X \sqsupseteq X \setminus X \circ X \setminus X \qquad\qquad X \setminus X \sqsupseteq B$$

We prove the other two, (iii):

$$
\begin{array}{ll}
& X \setminus X \sqsupseteq F.(X \setminus X) \\
\equiv & \{ \ (4) \ \} \\
& X \sqsupseteq X \circ F.(X \setminus X) \\
\equiv & \{ \ F - right - recursive.X \ \} \\
& X \sqsupseteq X \, / \, F.X \circ F.X \circ F.(X \setminus X) \\
\equiv & \{ \ \text{relators (7b)} \ \} \\
& X \sqsupseteq X \, / \, F.X \circ F.(X \circ X \setminus X) \\
\equiv & \{ \ \text{factors (5), relators (7a)} \ \} \\
& X \sqsupseteq X \, / \, F.X \circ F.X \\
\equiv & \{ \ \text{factors (5)} \ \} \\
& true
\end{array}
$$

(iv):
$$X \setminus X \sqsupseteq f.i \circ g.i \cup g.i \circ f.i \cup$$
$$\equiv \qquad \{ \ (4), \circ \text{ distributes over } \cup \ \}$$
$$X \sqsupseteq X \circ f, i \circ g, i \cup \cup X \circ g.i \circ f.i \cup$$
$$\equiv \qquad \{ \ X \circ f.i = X \circ g.i \ \}$$
$$X \sqsupseteq X \circ g.i \circ g.i \cup \cup X \circ f.i \circ f.i \cup$$
$$\Leftarrow \qquad \{ \ B \sqsupseteq f.i \circ f.i \cup, \ B \sqsupseteq g.i \circ g.i \cup \ \}$$
$$X \sqsupseteq X \circ B$$
$$\equiv \qquad \{ \ X = X \circ B \ \}$$
$$true$$

7 The Boom hierarchy

The Boom hierarchy is the group of types that was used in the original Bird-Meertens formalism [4][5][6][9]. Meertens [10] credits this class of types to H.J. Boom.

The base type is binary trees with values at the leafs of the tree. In our system this becomes the least fixpoint μF of the relator F defined by:

$$(51) \quad F.X \; \triangleq \; \mathrm{TT} + I + (X \times X)$$

The first summand gives the empty tree, the second gives the singleton trees (or leafs) and the third is responsible for the join operation. We denote the three corresponding constructors for an $F-inductive.A$ in the usual way:

$$(52) \ \varepsilon_A \triangleq A \circ \sigma.0 \qquad (53) \ \tau_A \triangleq A \circ \sigma.1 \qquad (54) \ \#_A \triangleq A \circ \sigma.2$$

The least solution of the equation $\quad X :: X \; = \; P \triangledown Q \triangledown R \circ F.X \quad$ is denoted by $(\!| P \triangledown Q \triangledown R |\!)$ and satisfies

$$(55) \quad (\!| P \triangledown Q \triangledown R |\!) \circ \mu F \; = \; (\!| P \triangledown Q \triangledown R |\!)$$

The $(\!|\_|\!)$ is called a catamorphism. [3] gives many other interesting properties of catamorphisms, (55) is also proved there.

We instantiate lemma 41 to get the calculation rules for composition with the constructors: if $(\!| P \triangledown Q \triangledown R |\!) \circ A = (\!| P \triangledown Q \triangledown R |\!)$ then

$$(56) \ (\!| P \triangledown Q \triangledown R |\!) \circ \varepsilon_A \; = \; P \circ \mathrm{TT}$$
$$(57) \ (\!| P \triangledown Q \triangledown R |\!) \circ \tau_A \; = \; Q$$
$$(58) \ (\!| P \triangledown Q \triangledown R |\!) \circ \#_A \; = \; R \circ (\!| P \triangledown Q \triangledown R |\!) \times (\!| P \triangledown Q \triangledown R |\!)$$

The type $Tree$ is constructed as an equivalence relation on μF by imposing laws such that ε is left- and right-unit of $\#$. The constructors for $Tree$ have to satisfy the following

Specification 59:

$$(59a) \ \#_{Tree} \circ \varepsilon_{Tree} \triangle I_{Tree} \; = \; I_{Tree}$$

$(59b)$ $+\!\!\!+_{Tree} \circ I_{Tree} \vartriangle \varepsilon_{Tree} = I_{Tree}$

Now we bring this specification in the shape that is required for the definition of a type with law:

$+\!\!\!+_{Tree} \circ \varepsilon_{Tree} \vartriangle I_{Tree} = I_{Tree}$

$\equiv$ { definition constructors, *Tree* equivalence relation on μF, (34) }

$+\!\!\!+_{Tree} \circ$ $Tree \times Tree \circ (\mu F \circ \sigma.0) \vartriangle \mu F = Tree \circ \mu F$

$\equiv$ { (42), definition constructors, *Tree* equivalence relation on μF }

$Tree \circ \mu F \circ \sigma.2 \circ (\mu F \circ \sigma.0) \vartriangle \mu F = Tree \circ \mu F$

$\equiv$ { definition constructors }

$Tree \circ +\!\!\!+_{\mu F} \circ \varepsilon_{\mu F} \vartriangle I_{\mu F} = Tree \circ I_{\mu F}$

This was for the left-unit. We can do a similar calculation for the right-unit. We conclude that we can specify the unit laws with f and g defined by:

Definition 60:

$$f.0 = +\!\!\!+_{\mu F} \circ \varepsilon_{\mu F} \vartriangle I_{\mu F} \qquad\qquad g.0 = I_{\mu F}$$
$$f.1 = +\!\!\!+_{\mu F} \circ I_{\mu F} \vartriangle \varepsilon_{\mu F} \qquad\qquad g.1 = I_{\mu F}$$

It is not difficult to prove that f and g satisfy condition (46). Instantiating theorem (50) with X the catamorphism, $B = \mu F$ and f, g as above gives:

$(\!(P \triangledown Q \triangledown R)\!) \circ Tree = (\!(P \triangledown Q \triangledown R)\!)$

$\equiv$ { (50), (55) }

$(\!(P \triangledown Q \triangledown R)\!) \circ f.0 = (\!(P \triangledown Q \triangledown R)\!) \circ g.0 \;\wedge$
$(\!(P \triangledown Q \triangledown R)\!) \circ f.1 = (\!(P \triangledown Q \triangledown R)\!) \circ g.1$

We try to find conditions on P, Q and R such that the condition above is satisfied. For the first conjunct we get:

$(\!(P \triangledown Q \triangledown R)\!) \circ f.0 = (\!(P \triangledown Q \triangledown R)\!) \circ g.0$

$\equiv$ { definition f,g }

$(\!(P \triangledown Q \triangledown R)\!) \circ +\!\!\!+_{\mu F} \circ \varepsilon_{\mu F} \vartriangle I_{\mu F} = (\!(P \triangledown Q \triangledown R)\!) \circ I_{\mu F}$

$\equiv$ { (58), (55) }

$R \circ (\!(P \triangledown Q \triangledown R)\!) \times (\!(P \triangledown Q \triangledown R)\!) \circ \varepsilon_{\mu F} \vartriangle I_{\mu F} = (\!(P \triangledown Q \triangledown R)\!)$

$\equiv$ { (34), (56), (55) }

$R \circ (P \circ \top) \vartriangle (\!(P \triangledown Q \triangledown R)\!) = (\!(P \triangledown Q \triangledown R)\!)$

$\Leftarrow$ { domains, calculus }

$R \circ (P \circ \top) \vartriangle (\!(P \triangledown Q \triangledown R)\!)< = (\!(P \triangledown Q \triangledown R)\!)<$

The last expression still contained the catamorphism, but we can remove it by using the following lemma: (proof omitted, can be found in [2],[3])

Lemma 61: $(P \sqcup Q \sqcup R)< \sqsupseteq (\!(P \triangledown Q \triangledown R)\!)<$

We will use the lhs of the previous expression several times, so we introduce the abbreviation D for that. Using lemma (61) we can give a condition on P, Q, and R such that *Tree* is a right-domain of the catamorphism:

Lemma 62: $(\!(P \triangledown Q \triangledown R)\!) \circ \mathit{Tree} = (\!(P \triangledown Q \triangledown R)\!) \Leftarrow$
$$R \circ (P \circ \pi) \vartriangle D = D \;\land\; R \circ D \vartriangle (P \circ \pi) = D$$

The second conjunct of the condition above comes from $\varepsilon_{\mathit{Tree}}$ being a right-unit of $+\!\!\!\!+_{\mathit{Tree}}$. The condition in the last lemma is true if P is a unit of R.

The next type in the Boom-hierarchy is the type *List*. We add the law that the $+\!\!\!\!+$ operator is associative. To express this law we need the spec β that satisfies for all specs R, S and T (for a definition in primitive operators see [2]):

$$R \times (S \times T) \circ \beta = \beta \circ (R \times S) \times T$$

We have the following specification for associativity of $+\!\!\!\!+_{\mathit{List}}$:

Specification 63: $+\!\!\!\!+_{\mathit{List}} \circ +\!\!\!\!+_{\mathit{List}} \times I_{\mathit{List}} = +\!\!\!\!+_{\mathit{List}} \circ I_{\mathit{List}} \times +\!\!\!\!+_{\mathit{List}} \circ \beta$

This leads, using similar calculations as for (60), to the following definition for $f.2$ and $g.2$ (We keep of course the laws for units):

Definition 64:
$$f.2 = +\!\!\!\!+_{\mu F} \circ +\!\!\!\!+_{\mu F} \times I_{\mu F} \qquad\qquad g.2 = +\!\!\!\!+_{\mu F} \circ I_{\mu F} \times +\!\!\!\!+_{\mu F} \circ \beta$$

The condition on P, Q and R such that *List* is a right-domain of the catamorphism is stated in:

Lemma 65: $(\!(P \triangledown Q \triangledown R)\!) \circ \mathit{List} = (\!(P \triangledown Q \triangledown R)\!) \;\Leftarrow\; R \circ R \times D = R \circ D \times R \circ \beta$

The condition in the last lemma is true if R is associative.

The next type in the hierarchy is the type *Bag*. This has the previous laws combined with the law that $+\!\!\!\!+_{\mathit{Bag}}$ is symmetric. We use the spec $\bowtie$ to expres this law. This spec satisfies for all specs R and S:

$$R \times S \circ \bowtie = \bowtie \circ S \times R$$

The specification for the symmetry of $+\!\!\!\!+_{\mathit{Bag}}$ is as follows:

Specification 66: $+\!\!\!\!+_{\mathit{Bag}} = +\!\!\!\!+_{\mathit{Bag}} \circ \bowtie$

This leads to the following definitions for $f.3$ and $g.3$:

Definition 67:
$$f.3 = +\!\!\!\!+_{\mu F} \qquad\qquad g.3 = +\!\!\!\!+_{\mu F} \circ \bowtie$$

The condition for *Bag* being a right-domain of the catamorphism is given in:

Lemma 68: $(\!(P \triangledown Q \triangledown R)\!) \circ \mathit{Bag} = (\!(P \triangledown Q \triangledown R)\!) \;\Leftarrow\; R = R \circ \bowtie$

The last condition is true if R is symmetric. The last type in the hierarchy is the type *Set*. Here we want all the previous laws together with the law that the $+\!\!\!\!+_{\mathit{Set}}$

operator is idempotent. The law is specified by :

Specification 69: $+\!\!\!+_{Set} \circ I \vartriangle I = I_{Set}$

The definition for $f.4$ and $g.4$ is

Definition 70:
$$f.4 = +\!\!\!+_{\mu F} \circ I \vartriangle I \qquad\qquad\qquad g.4 = \mu F$$

Here we have a problem for the condition. Composition doesn't distribute over $I \vartriangle I$ in general. The following lemma is valid if the catamorphism is functional to D:

Lemma 71: $(\!|P \triangledown Q \triangledown R|\!) \circ Set = (\!|P \triangledown Q \triangledown R|\!) \quad \Leftarrow \quad R \circ I \vartriangle I = D$

8   Conclusions

Working with partial equivalence relations is a calculationally convenient way of handling types. The fact that the equivalence relations induced by a law don't have to be divided out makes the relational calculus an appropriate tool for reasoning about and calculating with types with laws. We can construct types with laws as the least solutions of an equation and show that these types satisfy the desired algebraic properties. The Boom hierarchy is an example of an important class of types that can be modelled using the theory that is presented here.

9   Acknowledgements

We would like to thank the members of the Eindhoven relational type-theory club for their helpful comments on the theory that is presented here. Development and typesetting of the proofs were done using the proof editor developed by Paul Chisholm.

References

[1] R.C. Backhouse. Bruin P. de. P. Hoogendijk. G. Malcolm. Voermans T.S., and J. van der Woude. Polynomial relators. To appear: 2nd Conference on Algebraic Methodology and Software Technology, May 22-25, 1991.

[2] R.C. Backhouse. Bruin P. de. P. Hoogendijk. G. Malcolm, Voermans T.S., and J. van der Woude. A relational theory of datatypes. In preparation: copies of draft available on request, 1991.

[3] R.C. Backhouse, Bruin P. de. G. Malcolm, Voermans T.S., and J. van der Woude. Relational catamorphisms. In Möller B., editor, *Proceedings of the IFIP TC2/WG2.1 Working Conference on Constructing Programs.* Elsevier Science Publishers B.V.. 1991.

[4] R.S. Bird. An introduction to the theory of lists. In M. Broy, editor, *Logic of Programming and Calculi of Discrete Design*. Springer-Verlag, 1987. NATO ASI Series, vol. F36.

[5] R.S. Bird. A calculus of functions for program derivation. Technical report, Programming Research Group, Oxford University, 11, Keble Road, Oxford, OX1 3QD, U.K., 1988.

[6] R.S. Bird and L. Meertens. Two exercises found in a book on algorithmics. In L.G.L.T. Meertens, editor, *Program Specification and Transformations*, pages 451–457. Elsevier Science Publishers B.V., North Holland, 1987.

[7] C.A.R. Hoare and Jifeng He. The weakest prespecification. *Fundamenta Informaticae*, 9:51–84, 217–252, 1986.

[8] Ali Jaoua and Martin Beaudry. Difunctional relations: A formal tool for program design. Technical report, Université de Sherbrooke, Faculté des Sciences, Département de mathèmatiques et d'informatique, July 1989.

[9] G. Malcolm. *Algebraic data types and program transformation*. PhD thesis, Groningen University, 1990.

[10] L. Meertens. Algorithmics – towards programming as a mathematical activity. In *Proceedings of the CWI Symposium on Mathematics and Computer Science*, pages 289–334. North-Holland, 1986.

[11] A. Tarski. On the calculus of relations. *Journal of Symbolic Logic*, 6(3):73–89, 1941.

Program Analysis

Failure Analysis based on Abstract Interpretation

M-M. Corsini

LaBRI (URA 1304 du CNRS), Université Bordeaux II, France
e-mail: corsini@labri.greco-prog.fr

K. Musumbu

LaBRI (URA 1304 du C.N.R.S.), Université de Bordeaux I
33405 Talence Cedex, France *
e-mail: musumbu@geocub.greco-prog.fr

Abstract

This paper presents a study of correctness of pure Prolog programs, based on the technique of Abstract Interpretation for logic programs. The notion of (partial) correctness of a program relies on the type pre-analysis of call and success substitutions compared (dynamically) with concrete data-flow. It is possible to deduce, by the mean of a global static analysis, properties on variables of the analyzed program (groundness, type, sharing ...) but also general properties of the entire program such as: how look the solutions like, the number of these solutions, ... The technique we propose is based on a novel approach of type inference (see [18, 7]) which relies on a recent method of global analysis for logic programs formalized within the abstract interpretation framework (see [18]).

key-words: Logic Programming, Type Inference, Failure Analysis, Abstract Interpretation

1 Introduction

This paper presents a study of (partial) correctness of pure Prolog programs based on a new approach of type inference see [7]. Deriving detailed information such as sharing between variables or type information, allows improvements in performance as shown by Mülkers *et al.* in [17]. The abstract interpretation, first defined in [3], is a general framework in which it is possible to define techniques allowing the *"static"* computation of information about the run-time behavior of programs, this has been broadly studied in logic programming [1, 4, 8, 9, 10, 11, 12, 19]. Following [6], we call T-Abint any method based on abstract interpretation. A T-Abint specifies an abstract domain D, whose elements (called abstract states) approximate the substitutions. The task of any T-Abint is to analyze any logic program P with a goal (or set of goals) and associate to each clause c of P a set S of abstract states such that during the execution of P, whenever c is called with a substitution σ there exists a state in S that approximates σ. If so, we will say that the T-Abint is correct (or safe). The T-Abint developed here can be used in any top-down or bottom-up abstract interpretation [1, 6, 4, 10, 19, 20, 13]. We focus on the formal justification of an analysis of groundness and sharing information, and of the use of these information in the failure analysis of logic programs.

Roughly speaking, an abstract state β is defined as a 4-tuple (sv, tp, frm, Ps) where sv corresponds to the equality constraints between variables of the domain of substitution,

---

*This work was partially supported by the GRECO de programmation (METHEOL project)

tp is their type definition, *frm* restricts their forms pointing out the relation of inclusion between subterms, finally *Ps* (for possible sharing) restricts the sharing relation of variables. Each component is described with the *ad-hoc* properties, then we give the derived operation which abstract the unification of concrete terms. Finally we describe the failure analysis itself. The description is done in 3 steps, first the user has to describe his (her) type system which has to respect some (non restrictive) constraints, from this user_types_set we construct (automatically) a complete lattice, then we perform the type inference on the program. This step returns the allowed type(s) of each literal of the analyzed program; then the type checking of the program can be done wrt some initial query. One of the major interest of this method is that we do the type inference once for all, whilst the type checking is done dynamically at each step of the resolution. Notice that 1. a failure is detected before it really occurs (in fact the point of failure is just after the last point where the type checking was correct) 2. not all the failures can be detected since the type might be correct but the call might not match with the selected clauses. The rest of the paper is divided as follows: Section 2 describes the notations and definitions used throughout the paper. Section 3 specifies the abstract states for type inference, section 4 presents the derived algorithm of abstract unification and a shortcoming proof of its correctness. In section 5, we present the different parts of the failure analysis. Section 6 is a comparison with related works and section 7 summarizes our conclusions.

2 Preliminaries

2.1 Normalized logic programs

We assume the reader familiar with the principles of Logic programming (see for instance [14]). We only consider normalized Prolog programs, that is to say, the operations of unification are explicitly written. More formally a clause in normalized logic program contains only distinct variables in its head, while the literals in the body are either

- $x_i = x_j$
- $x_i = f(x_{i_1}, \ldots, x_{i_n})$
- $p(x_{i_1}, \ldots, x_{i_n})$

where $x_i, x_j, x_{i_1}, \ldots, x_{i_n}$ are distinct variables.

2.2 Substitutions

Let **Var** denote an enumerable set of variables, and **Term** be the set of valid Prolog terms. A substitution θ is a total function from **Var** to **Term**, such that the set $dom(\theta) = \{x \in$ **Var** $: x\theta \neq x\}$ is finite. A substitution σ can be depicted by a list of *variable/value* pairs $\{x/x\sigma : x \in dom(\sigma)\}$; codom$(\sigma)$ denotes the set of variables $\{y \in$ **Var** such that $y \in var(x\sigma)$ and $x \in dom(\sigma)\}$. The composition of two substitutions σ and ϕ is denoted $\sigma\phi$. In this paper we only consider idempotent substitutions i.e. $\sigma\sigma = \sigma$.

2.3 Most general unifier

A substitution θ is more general than a substitution σ, $\sigma \leq \theta$, if their exists a substitution ϕ such that $\sigma = \theta\phi$. A substitution σ is a unifier of two terms a and b if $a\sigma \equiv b\sigma$. We call σ most general unifier, *mgu*, if σ is more general than any other unifier of a and b.

2.4 Notations

- Csub_D denotes the set of substitutions θ such that $\text{dom}(\theta)=D$

- $\#$ S denotes the cardinality of set S.

- $\text{Var}(t)$ denotes the set of variables occuring in the term t.

- $F \nrightarrow G$ denotes a partial mapping from F to G.

2.5 Preliminary domain

Let $(T, \leq)$ be a given domain of types with:
– a monotonic function of concretization $\text{Cc}: T \longrightarrow P(\textbf{Term})$
– four primitives, which have to be monotonic and consistent, specified as follows:

- Cons (construction): it takes a functor of arity n and n types T_i and returns a new type T' such that $t_i \in \text{Cc}(T_i)$ $\forall i \Rightarrow f(t_1,\ldots, t_n) \in \text{Cc}(T')$.

- Extr (extraction): it takes a functor of arity n and a type T and returns a tuple $(T_1,\ldots,T_n)$ such that $f(t_1,\ldots, t_n) \in \text{Cc}(T) \Rightarrow t_i \in \text{Cc}(T_i)$

- UaT(abstract unification of types): it takes two types T_1 and T_2 and returns a new type T st. $t_i \in Cc(T_i)$, σ mgu(t_1,t_2) $\Rightarrow t_1\sigma, t_2\sigma \in \text{Cc}(T)$.

- IaT (abstract instantiation of type): it takes a type T and returns a new type T' st. $t \in \text{Cc}(T)$ and σ a substitution $\Rightarrow t\sigma \in \text{Cc}(T')$.

3 Abstract domain

3.1 Motivation

An abstract state represents a set of concrete substitutions. In our framework, the notion of abstract states $\beta = (sv, tp, frm, Ps)$ is based upon a set of indicies (consecutive positive integers) $[1..p]$ with each index corresponding to a subterm of a term bound to variable of some domain. The type of each subterm is defined by a function tp from $[1..p]$ to the types domain under interest. A partial function frm from $[1..p]$ to a set Frm_p, describes the inclusion between subterms, an element of Frm_p looks like $f(i_1,\ldots,i_n)$, where f is a functor and $1 \leq i_1,\ldots, i_n \leq p$. Whenever $frm(i) = f(i_1,\ldots,i_n)$, this means that the term t_i represented by the index i is something like $f(t_{i_1},\ldots, t_{i_n})$ where the concrete term t_{i_j} is represented by the index i_j. This approach is a powerful representation of relationship between terms and subterms, moreover one index may occur many times within a same form, or even within different forms. Possible sharing is described by a binary relation Ps on indicies having undefined forms. Finally, the relation between terms and variables is given by a function sv, notice that we associate the same index to 2 different variables whenever they are equal.

In the following parts, we will define precisely each component of an abstract state together with a concretization function Cc and finally the abstract domain itself.

3.2 Same value component

Let $\theta = \{\ldots, X_i/t_i,\ldots\} \in \text{Csub}_D$. The component sv on D is any onto mapping $D \rightarrow [1..m]$, where m$= \#\{t_i : \forall i,j \; i \neq j \; t_i \neq t_j\}$. Sv_m is the set of all sv and $Sv = \bigcup_m \text{Sv}_m$.

$$Cc : Sv \longrightarrow Csub_D$$
$$sv \mapsto \{\theta : dom\theta = D \text{ and} \forall x, x' \in D \text{ st. } sv(x) = sv(x') \Rightarrow x\theta = x'\theta\}$$

sv^{-1} splits D in equivalence classes of elements associated to equals terms.

3.3 Type component

Definition 3.1 Any mapping tp on $[1..p], p \in N$: $tp : [1..p] \longrightarrow T \cup \{\perp\}$ is called *type* component. Tp_p denotes the set of these mappings for some p and $Tp = \bigcup_p Tp_p$ the entire set of mappings, for any p.

For each $p \in N$, we define:
$$Cc : Tp_p \longrightarrow Term^p$$
$$tp \mapsto \{(t_1, \ldots, t_p) \forall i\, 1 \leq i \leq p : t_i \in tp(i)\}$$

3.4 Form component

A *form* is a term $f(i_1, \ldots, i_p)$ where f is a functor of arity p, $i_1, \ldots, i_p$ are strictly positive integers not necessary distinct. Frm_p is the set of forms such that $1 \leq i_1, \ldots, i_p \leq p$. Moreover, any constant is a form itself.

Definition 3.2 A form component is a partial mapping $frm : [1..p] \not\longrightarrow Frm_p$ such that $\forall i, 1 \leq i \leq p : frm(i) = f(i_1, \ldots, i_p)$. When $frm(i)$ is undefined we just write $frm(i)=\underline{ind}$.

For each $p \in N$, we define :
$$Cc : Frm_p \longrightarrow Term^p$$
$$frm \mapsto \{(t_1, \ldots, t_p) : \forall i\, 1 \leq i \leq p\, frm(i) = f(i_1, \ldots, i_p) \Rightarrow t_i = f(t_{i_1}, \ldots, t_{i_p})\}$$

3.5 Possible sharing component

Definition 3.3 Let $p \in N$, we call component Ps on $[1..p]$ any binary symetric relation on $[1..p]$. We denote Psh_p the set of these relations for some p and $Psh=\bigcup_p Psh_p$.
Let frm be a form component on $[1..p]$. Ps is said to be compatible with frm if:

$$\forall i, j : 1 \leq i, j \leq p : Ps(i,j) \Rightarrow frm(i) = \underline{ind} = frm(j).$$

For each Ps defined with frm, we consider the closure of Ps, denoted Ps^*, which is defined as the smallest Ps on $[1..p]$ such that $\forall i, j, k$ such that $1 \leq i, j, k \leq p$:

1. $Ps(i,j) \Rightarrow Ps^*(i,j)$

2. $frm(k)=f(\ldots, j, \ldots)$ and $Ps(i,j) \Rightarrow Ps^*(i,k)$.

In the sequel, we only consider possible sharing component compatible with the *form* component. For each $p \in N$ we define :
$$Cc: Psh \longrightarrow Term^p$$
$$Ps \mapsto \{(t_1, \ldots, t_p) : \forall i, j : 1 \leq i, j \leq p \text{ and } frm(i)=frm(j)=\underline{ind}$$
$$\text{such that } Var(t_i) \cap Var(t_j) \neq \emptyset \Rightarrow Ps(i,j)\}$$

This notion of possible sharing component compatible with the form component is fundamental to prevent abnormal information during the abstract computation. It has been proved in [18], that the abstract operations preserve this property. Notice that the closure of Ps contains all the information about sharing, because the form component contains all the relations between a term and its subterms, whilst Ps contains all the relations between uninstantiated variables.

3.6 Abstract Domain

We first define a "preliminary domain", denoted $Pasub_D$, and an order on its elements, then we restrict this domain to obtain the effective abstract domain.

Definition 3.4 Let θ be a substitution $\{x_1/t_1,\ldots, x_n/t_n\}$, and $D=\text{dom}(\theta)$. An abstract state β is a 4-tuple (sv, tp, frm, Ps) which, intuitively, gives information on θ.
The meaning of tp is, first, to define the type of the terms $t_1, \ldots, t_n$; tp is not defined as a mapping from D to T for two reasons. On one hand, the sv component specifies that some t_i's are equals; so it is sufficient to define tp on the co-domain $[1..m]$ of sv. In other words m is the number of distinct terms among $t_1,\ldots,t_n$ This choice restricts the domain of tp and, moreover, avoid problems of inconsistency. On the other hand, it is possible to extend the domain $[1..m]$ to $[1..p]$ (where m$\leq$p) to specify the type of some subterm of $t_1, \ldots, t_m$, that is to say to extend the "expressive power" of β. The meaning of the frm component is to point out these subterms within the t_i's, but also to give the principal functor of the t_i's. The Ps component, is used to indicate that some terms t_i, t_j, or even some subterms, might share variables; notice that "not $Ps(i,j)$" means that the terms associated with i and j, surely do not share variables.

The Concretization function Cc associated with $Pasub_D$ is defined as follows :

$$
\begin{aligned}
Cc : \quad Pasub_D &\longrightarrow Csub_D \\
\beta &\longmapsto \{\theta : \text{dom}\theta = D \text{ and } \exists t_1,\ldots, t_p \in Cc(tp)\cap Cc(frm)\cap Cc(Ps^*) \\
&\qquad st.\,\forall x \in D : x\theta = t_{sv(x)}\}
\end{aligned}
$$

We are now able to define a partial order, denoted $\leq$, among the elements of $Pasub_D$. Consider two abstract states β and β', we say that $\beta' \leq \beta$ whenever the information induced by β' are more restrictive than those induced by β. Intuitively this means that whenever a concrete substitution can be depicted by β', it can also be done by β. In other words the set of concretization of β' is smaller than that of β

Definition 3.5 Let $\beta, \beta' \in Pasub_D$. $\beta' \leq \beta$ if and only if there exists a function

$$ti : [1..p] \longrightarrow [1..p']$$

such that

1. $\forall x \in D : sv'(x) = ti(sv(x))$,

2. $\forall i, 1 \leq i \leq p, tp'(ti(i)) \leq tp(i)$,

3. $\forall i : 1 \leq i \leq p : frm(i) = f(i_1,\ldots,i_q) \Rightarrow frm'(ti(i)) = f(ti(i_1),\ldots, ti(i_q))$,

4. $\forall i,j : 1 \leq i,j \leq p : frm(i) = frm(j) = \underline{ind} : Ps'^*(ti(i), ti(j)) \Rightarrow Ps(i,j)$.

The relation $\leq$ defined on $Pasub_D$ is a preorder, *i.e.* there exists elements of $Pasub_D$ which are distinct but equivalent in the sense that:

$$\beta \neq \beta', \beta \leq \beta', \beta' \leq \beta \text{ and } Cc(\beta) = Cc(\beta')$$

In fact these elements are deducible from each other by a permutation of the indicies.

Definition 3.6 Let $\equiv$ be the equivalence of two elements of $Pasub_D$ which are distinct but equivalent in the sense above. The abstract domain $Asub_D$ is then defined as:

$$Asub_D = (Pasub_{D_{/\equiv}}) \cup \{\bot\}.$$

Let $\beta \in Pasub_D$, $\overline{\beta}$ denotes the class of β in $Asub_D$

The concretization function:
Cc: Asub$_D$ $\longrightarrow$ Csub$_D$ is defined as follows:

$$Cc(\perp)=\emptyset$$

$$Cc(\overline{\beta})=Cc(\beta)$$

We can now define an order on the elements of Asub$_D$

$$\perp \leq \overline{\beta}, \forall \overline{\beta} \in \text{Asub}_D$$

$$\overline{\beta} \leq \overline{\beta'} \text{ iff } \beta \leq \beta' \forall \beta, \beta' \in \text{Pasub}_D$$

Theorem 3.1 *There are no infinite increasing sequences in Asub$_D$.*

Proof: A formal version can be found in [18].

□

This theorem means that (Asub$_D$,$\leq$) is an inductive set and that the converse strict order relation of $\leq$ is well-founded. This result ensures that the algorithm of the abstract interpretation will terminate whenever the abstract operations are monotonic and consistent.

4   Abstract operations

In any framework of abstract interpretation [1, 6, 4, 10, 15, 12, 19, 20, 18], it is necessary to define processes which mimic the operations in the concrete domain. In fact, the extension called procedure-exit in [1] and the abstract interpretation of built-ins ($X = X'$ or $X = f(X_1,\ldots,X_n)$) can be easily deduced from a kind of "super-unification" (an abstract unification of a list of pairs of terms). The only remainding point is the definition of the LUB (least upper bound), which relies on the properties of monotonicity. Its consistency is deducible from the fact that any LUB is an upper bound, which is *de facto* consistent. The rest of the abstract operations are easy to define because they are exact.

Notation Let $\alpha=(tp, frm, Ps)$ a q-tuple of abstract terms i.e. tp $\in$ Tp$_q$, frm $\in$ Frm$_q$, Ps $\in$ Psh$_q$. We note Uact1(i,j,α)=α' with $1\leq$i, j$\leq$q.

This notation is only an other way to say that we consider an abstract state $\beta = (sv, tp, frm, Ps)$ such that the co-domain of sv is the set of indicies [1..q]. Moreover this allows us to focus on the crucial information (type and sharing of variables) rather than on the technical point (consistency of the indicies).

4.1   Abstract unification of pair of terms

Specification of Uact1: it takes two integers and a q-tuple α and returns a q-tuple α' st.

$$(t_1,\ldots, t_q) \in Cc(\alpha) \text{ and } \sigma = mgu(t_i, t_j) \Rightarrow (t_1,\ldots, t_q)\sigma \in Cc(\alpha')$$

Definition 4.1 The operation Uact1(i,j,α) is defined only if frm(i)=$\underline{ind}$=frm(j). Let $\alpha'=(tp',frm',Ps')$, the computation of each component of α' is as follows :

1. tp' ($1\leq$ k $\leq$ q)
   case of

(a) not Ps*(i,k) and not Ps*(j,k) then $tp'(k)=tp(k)$

(b) Ps*(i,k) or Ps*(j,k)

    i. i=k or j=k then $tp'(k)=UaT(tp(i),tp(j))$

    ii. $i{\neq}k{\neq}j$ and frm(k)=f($k_1, \ldots, k_n$) then $tp'(k)=UaT(tp(k),Cons(f,tp'(k_1), \ldots, tp'(k_n)))$

    iii. $i{\neq}k{\neq}j$ and frm(k)=$\underline{ind}$ then $tp'(k)=IaT(tp(k))$.

2. *frm'*=frm.

3. Let $Ps_1=\{(k,l)$ st. Ps(k,l) and ng($tp'(k)$) and ng($tp'(l)$)$\}$ and $Ps_2=\{(k,l)$ such that Ps(k,l) and $\exists k', l' \in \{i,j\} : $ Ps(k,k') and Ps(l,l') $\}$. We have that if ng($tp'(i)$) then $Ps'=Ps_1 \cup Ps_2$ else $Ps'=Ps_1$.

The previous (though hard to read) definition is easy to understand, we first compute the type of terms, which depends on their sharing. Obviously the form component has no change. Then we have to compute the new sharing relations (but some might have disappeared due to the instantiation to a ground term). So if the term i is ground (the function ng returns false) no new sharing has been created so the *Ps'* is *Ps* minus some terms (propagation of groundness) otherwise there might be new relations which are computed in Ps_2.

We now have to prove that Uact1 is monotonic, the property is established for each component of a q-tuple of abstract term.

Property 4.2 Let α_1 end α_2 be two q-tuples. Let *i* and *j* such that $1 \leq i,j \leq q$, then we have:
$$\alpha'_1 = Uact1(i,j,\alpha_1) \leq Uact1(i,j,\alpha_2) = \alpha'_2$$

proof We consider some *k* such that $1 \leq k \leq q$, and we compute the different components of α'_1 and α'_2 wrt *k*. The proof relies on the property of monotonicity of the four primitives UaT, IaT, Cons and Extr. See [18] for the details.

$\square$

4.2 Abstract specialization of a term

Specification of Specat: it takes two integers and a q-tuple α and returns a q-tuple α' such that
$$(t_1,\ldots,t_q) \in Cc(\alpha) \text{ and } \sigma = mgu(t_i, t_j) \Rightarrow (t_1,\ldots,t_q)\sigma \in Cc(\alpha')$$

The operation Specat(i,j,α) is defined only if frm(i)=$\underline{ind}$ and frm(j)=f($j_1, \ldots, j_n$). As the operation is straightforward, but the formal definition a bit tedious, we only describe the process.

To compute σ, the mgu of t_i and t_j, it is possible to compute first the mgu σ' of t_i and f($y_1, \ldots, y_n$) where the $y_k \notin Var(t_i)\forall k$, and then the mgu of $(y_1, \ldots, y_n)\sigma'$ and $(t_{j_1}, \ldots, t_{j_n})$. We illustrate the process by the following example

Example Let $\theta=\{X_1/g(Z), X_2/Z, X_3/f(a,b),X_4/Y\}$, let $\alpha=(tp,frm,Ps)$ describes properties about the value bound to X_i. For sake of simplicity we consider as type domain, the generalized modes one. Then we have :

tp=$\{<1,nvar>, <2,var>, <3,ground>, <4,var>, <5,ground>, <6,ground> \}$
frm=$\{<1,g(2)>, <3,f(5,6)>, <5,a>, <6,b> \}$
Ps=$\emptyset$

Suppose that we compute Specat(2,3,α)=(tp',frm',Ps') then
$tp'(1)$=IaT($tp(1),tp'(2)$)=ground
$tp'(2)$=UaT($tp(2)$,Cons(f,$tp(5),tp(6)$))=ground
$tp'(i)$=$tp(i)$ for i=3 .. 6
frm'=$frm \cup$ {<2,f(5,6)>}
Ps'=Ps

4.3 Abstract unification of a pair of terms

Specification of Uact : it takes two integers and a q-tuple α and returns a q-tuple α' st.

$$(t_1,\ldots,t_q) \in Cc(\alpha) \text{ and } \sigma = mgu(t_i,t_j) \Rightarrow \exists(t'_1,\ldots,t'_q) \in Cc(\alpha')$$
$$\text{and } \exists\theta \text{ st.}(t_1,\ldots,t_q)\sigma\theta = (t'_1,\ldots,t'_q)$$

Definition 4.3 Uact(i,j,α)=α' is defined as follows :

a. i=j $\Rightarrow \alpha = \alpha'$

b. i$\neq$j and frm(i)=_ind_=frm(j) $\Rightarrow \alpha'$=Uact1(i,j,α)

c. i$\neq$j and frm(i)$\neq$_ind_ or frm(j)$\neq$_ind_ if frm(i)=_ind_ then α'=Specat(i,j,α)
   else α'=Specat(j,i,α)

d. otherwise it must exist a functor f such that frm(i)=f($i_1,\ldots,i_n$) and frm(j)=f($j_1, \ldots, j_n$), assume that α_k=Uact(i_k,j_k,α_{k-1}) with k=1,$\ldots$,n then α'=Fcta(i,j,α_n) where Fcta is some process which permits to merge two indicies i and j having the same property.

The definition of Uact is recursive, so we have to give some argument to justify its non circularity. Let h(i,α) the height of some index i in α defined below

Definition if frm(i)=_ind_ then h(i,α)=0 else h(i,α)=1+max(h(i_1,α),$\ldots$,h(i_n,α)) with frm(i) = f($i_1,\ldots,i_n$)

As Uact(i,j,α) does not modify the value of max(h(i,α),h(j,α)) it is possible to establish that: max(h(i_k,α_{k-1}),h(j_k,α_{k-1}))<max(h(i,α),h(j,α)).
We have now to establish that Uact is monotonic and consistent, as the proofs are really tedious and hard to read, we just sketch them.

Property 4.4 Uact is consistent in the sense of its specification

proof See [18] for the complete demonstration. We only focus on the point d. of the definition 4.3. Since there exists a unifier of t_i and t_j, the terms have the same functor with same arity n. There exists $\sigma_0,\ldots,\sigma_n,\sigma'_1,\ldots,\sigma'_n$ substitutions such that

- σ_0 is the empty substitution
- σ'_k=$mgu(t_{i_k}\sigma_{k-1}, t_{j_k}\sigma_{k-1})$,$\forall k, 1 \leq k \leq n$
- $\sigma_k = \sigma_{k-1}\sigma'_k$,$\forall k, 1 \leq k \leq n$

Let $\sigma = \sigma_n\tau$ where τ is a renaming substitution. We prove by induction on k that there exists a q-tuple of abstract terms s_k and a substitution θ_k such that s_k=$t\sigma_k\theta_k$ where $s_k \in Cc(\alpha_k)$.

$\square$

Property 4.5 Let α_1 and α_2 two q-tuples. Let i,j such that $1 \leq i,j \leq q$. We have

$$\text{Uact}(i,j,\alpha_1) \leq \text{Uact}(i,j,\alpha_2)$$

proof This proof is very lengthy. It is an induction on the structure of the definition of Uact.

□

4.4 Abstract unification for a list of pairs of terms

This operation, called Ualct, is a generalization terminal recursive of Uact. Let $l=((i_1,j_1),$ $\ldots, (i_r,j_r))$ such that $1 \leq i_1,j_1 \ldots, i_r,j_r \leq q$, let $u \in Cc(\alpha)$, and σ the mgu of $(u_{i_1}, \ldots, u_{i_r})$ and $(u_{j_1}, \ldots, u_{j_r})$:
specification of Ualct: it takes a list of pairs of terms and a q-tuple and returns a q-tuple such that

$$\text{Ualct}(l,\alpha)=\alpha' \Rightarrow \exists\ v \in Cc(\alpha')\ \text{and}\ \exists \theta\ \text{st.}\ u\sigma\theta=v$$

Theorem 4.1 *Let α, i, j st. $1 \leq i$, $j \leq q$ and l a list of pairs of indicies belonging to $[1..q]$ then we have :*

$$\text{Ualct}((i,j).l,\alpha)=\text{Ualct}(l,\text{Uact}(i,j,\alpha))$$

with the convention that $\text{Ualct}(l,\perp)=\perp$

Proof: Immediate, by induction on the structure of the definition of Uact

□

4.5 Least upper bound

In this section we define the notion of least upper bound in our abstract domain. This operation permits to represent a set of abstract states by a unique state.
Specification of LUB : Let β_1 and β_2 be abstract states on the same domain D. Then $\text{LUB}(\beta_1,\beta_2)=\beta'$ such that

$$\theta \in Cc(\beta_1)\ \text{or}\ \theta \in Cc(\beta_2) \Rightarrow \theta \in Cc(\beta')$$

$$\beta_1,\beta_2 \leq \beta'\ \text{and}\ \forall\beta,\ \text{such that}\ \beta_1,\beta_2 \leq \beta\ \text{we have}\ \beta' \leq \beta$$

Definition 4.6 Let D be the domain of the abstract states β_1,β_2. As the index associated to a variable can be different in β_1 and in β_2, we have to define two sets:
$E=\{(i,j) : \exists X \in D\ \text{st.}\ i=sv_1(X)\ \text{and}\ j=sv_2(X)\}$
$F=\{(i,j) : (i,j) \in E, \text{or}$
$\qquad\qquad \exists i',j',k\ \text{such that}$
$\qquad\qquad (i',j') \in F \qquad \text{and}\ frm_1(i') = f(i_1,\ldots,i_n)\ \text{and}$
$\qquad\qquad (i,j) = (i_k,j_k) \qquad \text{and}\ frm_2(j') = f(j_1,\ldots,j_n)\}$
where $p'=\#\ F$ and fc is a 1-to-1 mapping from $F \rightarrow [1..p']$. Each component of β' is computed as follows :

- $tp'(k)=\text{Lub}(tp_1(i),tp_2(j))$ where $k=fc(i,j)$ and Lub is a least upper bound defined on the given type domain.

- $frm'(k)=f(k_1,\ldots,k_n)$ where $k=fc(i,j)$ and $frm_1(i)=f(i_1,\ldots,i_n)$ and $frm_2(j)=f(j_1,\ldots,j_n)$ and $k_s=fc(i_s,j_s)$.

- $Ps'=\{(k,k')$ such that $frm'(k)=frm'(k')=\underline{ind}$ and $\exists\ i, j, i', j', fc(i,j)=k\ fc(i',j')=k'$ and $Ps_1^*(i,i')$ or $Ps_2^*(j,j')\ \}$.

- $sv'(X)=fc(sv_1(X),sv_2(X)), \forall X \in D$.

Example Let $\beta_1=(sv_1,\ldots,Ps_1)$ and $\beta_2=(sv_2,\ldots,Ps_2)$ where $sv_1=\{< X_1,1 >, < X_2,2 >, < X_3,2 >, \ldots\}$ and $sv_2=\{< X_1,2 >, < X_2,1 >, < X_3,1 >, \ldots\}$. We leave the type and the possible sharing components undescribed. Let $frm_1 = \{< 2, f(4,5) >\}$ and $frm_2 = \{< 1, f(4,6) >\}$ then we have :
$E=\{(1,2),(2,1),\ldots\}$ and $F=\{(1,2),(2,1),\ldots,(4,4),(5,6),\ldots\}$
Moreover let $fc : F \rightarrow [1..p']$ st. $fc(1,2)=1, fc(2,1)=2, fc(4,4)=7, fc(5,6)=8$; it is then possible to compute the different components as, for example :
$tp'(1)=Lub(tp_1(1),tp_2(2)),\ldots$
$frm'(2)=f(7,8),\ldots$

5 Failure analysis

As an application of our abstract domain, we propose a useful tool for debugging Prolog programs. Our failure analysis is described in 3 steps. The user has to define, first, his own type system which is in fact the definition of the types under interest, from these definitions we construct automatically $(T,\leq)$. The 2nd step consists to perform type inference on the program, the query is not used in this step since we want to do it once for all. As result, this step returns the type (or set of types) allowed for each clause of the program. The 3rd step is the type checking, which is performed dynamically at each step of the resolution.

5.1 User types domain

In our technique, the user can freely choose his/her own type system provided the respect of some (non restrictive) constraints given below. Assume that $T_1, \ldots, T_n$ are the user types names, then we need the following requirements :

1. $Cc(T_i)=\{$ terms t such that t is of type $T_i \}$

2. $\forall i,j\ i \neq j \Rightarrow Cc(T_i) \cap Cc(T_j)=\emptyset$

An easy way to respect the point 2. is to forbid the overloading of type constructors (this is also present in language such as ML [16]). Let us call User_Types the set $\{ T_1, \ldots, T_n \}$, from this set we construct the complete lattice T, with $\emptyset$ as bottom element and **Term** as top element; where do appear each element of the poset of User_Types. The partial order relation $\leq$, associated is the straightforward inclusion order. Notice that types are not restricted to ground object, *i.e.* variables are allowed; as an example the user can define the type List (given with BNF syntax) :
List ::= [] | .(**Term**, List).
The UaT (recall section 2.5) is then defined as the intersection relation. Assume S and S' are elements of T then $UaT(S,S')=S \cap S'$. The next step can now be depicted.

5.2 Type inference

For this step any abstract interpretation algorithm with memorization can be performed see for instance [6, 10, 12, 13]. None of them will be described. The only interesting point is that we perform the analysis for each modules, with an initial query wherein all the arguments are unbound variables. As the abstract states contain information such as possible sharing, form description, equality constraint (the *sv* component) and type description, the abstract state associated with each clause is very accurate as illustrated in the following example.

Example Let us consider the well-known append, the program looks like :

```
<1> app(X,Y,Z):- X=[] , Y=Z.
<2> app(X,Y,Z):- X=[A|B], Z=[A|C], app(B,Y,C).
```

Assume User_Types={List} as defined above, then the analysis returns the following abstract states :

```
<1> ({<X,1>, <Y,2>, <Z,2>}, {<1,List>, <2,var>}, {<1,[]>})
<2> ({<X,1>, <Y,2>, <Z,3>, <A,4>, <B,5>, <C,6>}, {<1,List>, <2,List>,
      <3,List>, <4,var>, <5,List>, <6,List>}, {<1,.(4,5)>, <3,.(4,6)>})
```

Notice that these states correspond to success patterns. Moreover, whenever the type of some variable is **var**, which stands for unbound variable, any value of this parameter is acceptable in any query. It is well known that the call app([],9,X) succeeds (unfortunately) and bind X to 9.

It is possible to decrease the complexity of this step by ordering the different predicates of the program P, and first analyze the predicate(s) which do not call any others, whenever there is some cycle select one of the predicate in the cycle and perform the ordering on the rest of the predicates.

Example visit merge two lists, these predicates are used in a simulation of intelligent backtracking based on abstract interpretation

```
visit(J,[],L,[[J,L]]):-!.
visit(J,[[I,Li]|Ls],L,[[I,Li]|Ln]):-ote(I,L,L1),!,ordo(Li,L1,Li1),
                                    visit(J,Ls,Li1,Ln).
visit(J,[Y|Ls],L,[Y|Ln]):-!,visit(J,Ls,L,Ln).

ordo([],L,L):-!.
ordo(L,[],L):-!.
ordo([X|L1],[X|L2],L):-!,ordo(L1,L2,L).
ordo([X|L],[Y|L1],[Z|L2]):-sup(X,Y),!,X=Z,ordo(L,[Y|L1],L2).
ordo([X|L],[Y|L1],[Z|L2]):-Z=Y,ordo([X|L],L1,L2).

ote(X,[X|L],L):-!.
ote(X,[Y|L],[Y|Lx]):-ote(X,L,Lx).

sup(s(X),0).
sup(s(X),s(Y)):-sup(X,Y).
```

On this example, the ordering gives sup, (ordo, ote), visit. And the static analysis can be performed by :
1. analyze sup.
2. analyze ordo (use the states computed at step 1.)

3. analyze ote.
4. analyze visit (use the states computed at steps 3. & 2.)

Assume User_Types is { Nat, List }, the abstract interpretation find that the arguments of predicate sup have type Nat, those of predicate ote are `<X,var>`, `<L,List>` and `<X,var>`, `<Y,var>`, `<L,List>`, `<Lx,List>`. The analysis of ordo raises to the following states (only the *sv* and *tp* components are given)

```
<1>  ({<A,1>,<L,2>}, {<1,List>, <2,var>} ...)
<2>  ({<L,1>,<A,2>}, {<1,var>, <2,List>} ...)
<3>  ({<A,1>,<B,2>,<L,3>,<X,4>,<L1,5>,<L2,6>}, {1, 2, 3, 5, 6 are List
     and <4,var>} ...)
<4>  ({<A,1>,<B,2>,<C,3>,<X,4>,<L,5>,<Y,6>,<L1,7>,<Z,4>,<L2,8>},
     {4, 6 are Nat, the rest of variables are List} ...)
<5> same as <4> except that X, Y and Z are var
```

The variables A, B, C which have appeared in the abstract states have been created by the normalization of the program.

5.3 Failure diagnostic

Notice first that the type inference is correct, since all the abstract operations respect the usual conditions of monotonicity and consistency. The correctness means that whenever a goal succeeds, the value of the arguments have one of the types inferred by the abstract interpretation. The interesting point is that $\sigma_{call} \leq \sigma_{success}$ ie. whenever the goal succeeds, the values in the initial query are compatible with the value computed; from this obvious remark we make the following definition and claim:

Definition A query is type compatible wrt a program P iff the type of each argument in the query belongs to the type inferred for the corresponding parameter of the predicate during the type inference step.

claim Assume P be a program and G the initial query. It is easy to prove that P∪{G} cannot succeed if G is not type compatible wrt P.

For example app(4,_,_) is not type compatible wrt the classical append program since 4∉List. The query app(_,4,a) is neither type compatible since the 2nd and 3rd parameters have to be either of the same value (clause `<1>`, this information is provided by the *sv* component of the corresponding abstract state) either of type List (clause `<2>`). As examplify above, the pertinent information for the failure analysis are the types allowed and the same value component. The failure detection algorithm looks like:

Algorithm:
begin
consider the current goal
select the candidate clauses (with same predicate in the head)
check if some abstract states correspond to the call
if none then
return the current goal and the allowed abstract states
else
perform a resolution step
fi
end.

At each step this algorithm terminate since the number of abstract states associated to each clause is finite (see [18]). This algorithm must be performed at each step of the resolution. Notice that only finite failure can be detected, and moreover not all failure can be detected since the cause can be a mismatch error.

6 Related works

First of all we mention that the type inference approach of De Boeck *et al.* [2] independently developed is very closed to ours. The differences reside in two points:
it is possible for us to find (deduce) the type of a term which has a known form, and moreover, we believe that our presentation provides easier proofs of correction and monotonicity.

In [12] Kanamori *et al.* present a framework for analyzing prolog programs based on OLDT Resolution [21], a top-down prolog interpreter with memo-ization. They consider a type definition as set of definite clauses satisfying the two conditions:

1. The head of each clause is a unary predicate p called type predicate. The argument of p is either a constant b called bottom element of p, or a term t of the form $c(X_1, \ldots, X_n)$ where c is a constructor of p.

2. The body of each clause consists of literals whose predicate is a type one and whose arguments X_j are in the head. The type of a type predicate p is the set of terms t such that $p(t)$ succeeds without instantiating variables of t.

Our framework is as efficient as theirs is. For example, if we consider disjoint types:
- *any* is the set of all terms,
- p_i is the set of terms of type p_i, and
- $\emptyset$ is the empty set

1. The UaT can be defined as follows :
   Let A and B be literals, ν the type substitution associated with A, and τ the type substitution associated with B. First, unify the two literals, and let η (if it exists) be the mgu. The information types (ν and τ) is then propagated in two steps: an inward propagation from terms to subterms and an outward propagation from subterms to terms. See [12] for the formal definitions.

2. The IaT is only the outward propagation.

In their paper [22], Yardeni and Shapiro present a theoretical model for typing logic programs. As ours, it contains three parts : type declaration, type inference and type checking. We shall only consider the first and last parts .

Type declaration
Types are recursively enumerate sets of *ground* atoms which are tuple-distributive. They are defined by regular unary logic predicates, which are a subset of the pure prolog predicates with one argument. With each variable X, is associated a type τ, X:$\{\tau\}$, with each predicate of arity k, is associated a k-tuple of types $(\tau_1, \ldots, \tau_k)$ where the ith component is associated to the ith argument of p, finally with each function symbol f of arity k is associated a type τ of the form $cons(f, \tau_1, \ldots, \tau_k)$. Their primitive types correspond to our User_Types. Their derived types are build from the BNF syntax for RUL programs, while ours are classes of the poset of User_Types. Moreover, we do not type all the syntactical objects, but only the arguments of the program's predicates. Roughtly speaking, one clause specifies all terms whose type has the predicate as principal functor.

Type checking

Type checking determines whether a program is well-typed wrt some type declaration. They describe an algorithm that type-checks programs defined with regular type declaration. Assume P be a program and S a regular type. To check if P is well typed by S, the algorithm seek, for each clause of P the maximal set of atoms that can be inferred relatively to S. Then, it takes the union of all these sets and check whether or not it is equal to S. This method is purely static.

In our framework, we check dynamically if the current goal satisfy the type of the selected clause, *i.e.* if the type of each parameter of the current query belongs to the set of types statically computed during the static analysis. Moreover the efficiency of our failure detection is highly improved by the accuracy of our abstract domain.

7 Conclusion

We have presented an abstract domain which deals with type inference and derivation of accurate sharing information. The novelty of our approach is in a "meta"-type inference framework. That is to say that on the contrary of [11, 12, 22], our framework is independent of the type domain. The application we have proposed, uses types to detect if variables are used consistently in an untyped prolog program, with the aim to detect goals that cannot succeed. The detection is made and some helpful diagnostic is delivered.

References

[1] M. Bruynooghe *A practical framework for the abstract interpretation of logic programs*; 5th ICLP–SLP 88;tutorial N°2.

[2] P. De Boeck, B. Le Charlier *Static analysis of prolog procedures for ensuring correctness*; Proc. 2nd workshop on Programming Language Implementation and Logic Programming, Linköping university, Sweden, Aug 1990.

[3] P. Cousot, R. Cousot *Abstract Interpretation: A Unified Lattice Model for Static Analysis of Programs by Construction of Approximation of Fixpoints*;POPL 1977;Sigact Sigplan;pp 238–252.

[4] M. Codish, D. Dams, E. Yardeni *Bottom-up abstract interpretation of logic programs*; technical report CS90-24 Weizmann institute.

[5] M. Codish, D. Dams, E. Yardeni *Derivation and safety of an abstract unification algorithm for groundness and aliasing analysis*; draft oct. 90 Weizmann Institute.

[6] M-M. Corsini, G. Filè *A complete framework for the abstract interpretation of logic programs: theory and application*; research report Università di Padova.

[7] M-M Corsini, K. Musumbu *Type inference in Prolog: a new approach*; to appear in proc. of Informatika91.

[8] S. Debray *Static Inference of Modes and Data Dependencies in Logic Programs*; Rep.87-15, Univ. of Arizona 1987.

[9] S. Debray, D. Warren *Automatic Mode Inference for Logic Programs*; J. Logic Programming 1988 vol. 5;pp 207–229.

[10] **G. Filé, A. Cortesi** *Abstract interpretation of logic programs: an abstract domain for groundness, sharing, freeness and compoundness analysis*; ACM Sigplan symposium on partial evaluation 91.

[11] **G. Janssens, M. Bruynooghe** *Deriving descriptions of possible values of program variables by means of abstract interpretation*; draft revised version for Journal of Logic programming.

[12] **T. Kanamori, T. Kawamura** *Abstract interpretation based on OLDT resolution*; ICOT research report 1990.

[13] **B. Le Charlier, K. Musumbu, P. Van Hentenryck** *A general abstract interpretation algorithm and its complexity analysis*; ICLP 91; pp 64–78.

[14] **J. Lloyd** *Foundations of logic programming*;Springer Verlag;series in symbolic of computation 1987.

[15] **C. Mellish** *Abstract Interpretation of Prolog Programs*; ICLP 86;LNCS 225;pp 463–474.

[16] **R. Milner** *A theory of type polymorphism in programming*; Edinburgh internal report CSR 9–77.

[17] **A. Mariën, G. Janssens, A. Mulkers, M. Bruynooghe** *The impact of abstract interpretation on code generation : an experiment in efficiency*; ICLP 89;pp 33–47.

[18] **K. Musumbu** *Abstract interpretation of prolog programs*;PHD thesis (in french); sept. 90.

[19] **K. Marriott, H. Sondergaard** *Bottom up abstract interpretation of logic programs*; ICLP/SLP 88.

[20] **K. Marriott, H. Sondergaard** *Abstract interpretation of logic programs : the denotaional approach*; GULP90.

[21] **T. Sato, H. Tamaki** *OLD resolution with tabulation* ICLP 86;LNCS 225;pp 84–98.

[22] **E. Yardeni, E. Shapiro** *A type system for logic programs*; Research report CS87–05 Weizmann Institute.

Sequentializing Parallel Programs

Mark Korsloot

Dept. of Electrical Engineering, Delft University of Technology
Delft, the Netherlands

Evan Tick

Dept. of Computer Science, University of Oregon
Eugene, OR 97403, USA

Abstract

A compile-time technique is presented for determining if a set of procedures within a parallel program can be executed sequentially without causing deadlock. The analysis and methods are described for committed-choice parallel logic programming languages; however, the concepts are general enough for any concurrent languages with fine-grain communicating processes. We derive methods for ensuring that sequential evaluation of a program module cannot result in producer-consumer suspension within the module itself, thereby resulting in deadlock. The advantages of sequentializing fine-grain languages include the use of all "traditional" compiler optimizations, such as global register allocation, and continuation-stacking procedure invocation.

1   Introduction

Traditional parallel procedural languages evolved from sequential programming languages. In the evolution of these languages, the quest to uncover more parallelism, in more efficient ways, is paramount. Alternatively, concurrent languages, such as committed-choice parallel logic programming languages, have a great deal of inherent parallelism. The evolution of these languages has been to exploit the parallelism efficiently, with increasingly sophisticated interpreters and emulators, in both software, firmware, and hardware. Little research has been done concerning the efficient compilation of these concurrent languages. It is often the case that by sequentializing portions of a fine-grain parallel program, execution time decreases and processor utilization increases. The trick is to determine which sets of procedures should be serialized for overall benefit, and if they can be serialized safely, i.e., without chance of deadlock.

In this paper, we introduce a method to safely sequentialize pieces of concurrent programs, with the intention of increasing execution speed. Specifically, we describe our method with respect to the family of flat committed-choice parallel logic programming languages, such as FCP, FGHC, and Parlog [9]. Sequential execution can be beneficial because it increases granularity. An often-mentioned problem of committed-choice languages is their small average granularity, causing a high overhead for process management and an abundance of light-weight processes.

To achieve serialization, we combine a general mode-analysis algorithm [13] with a goal-ordering algorithm described here. We fully describe the conditions under which the analysis can successfully sequentialize a program, and indicate practical uses of the technique, such as global register allocation and continuation-based goal management [1]. For now, we envision the programmer defining the modules and their import/export procedures. By judicious modularization of a program, overall efficiency of committed-choice programs will improve significantly with relatively simple analysis. Algorithms for selecting sequential modules and basic blocks (i.e., their composite procedures and appropriate size) are an ongoing research topic of great importance, closely related to granularity analysis (e.g., [4,11]). However, this is beyond the scope of this paper.

2 Background and Terminology

In this section we define the terminology used in this paper and its background. In the literature, most notions are somewhat overloaded in their meaning, through sloppy usage and intuitive bias. We hope to clarify the intended meanings. We limit ourselves to the family of flat committed-choice languages [9], with Horn clauses of the form "$H :- G_1, G_2, ..., G_m \mid B_1, B_2, ..., B_n$." for $m \geq 0$ and $n \geq 0$. H is the clause head, G_i is a guard goal, and B_i is a body goal. A *conjunction* of a goals is simply a set of goals (normally only body goals), appearing within the same clause. The commit operator '$\mid$' divides the clause into a passive part (the *guard*) and active part (the *body*). For flat languages, the guard goals can only be built-in predicates, such as `functor(X,F,A)`, or simple test goals, such as `X>0`.

An important concept is the notion of *modes*. Mode declarations can be either explicit or implicit. A mode can be either *input* or *output*. In Parlog, the user must explicitly declare the modes for each "top-level" argument of a predicate. A top-level argument is the outermost term passed to a procedure, distinct from any subterms that it may be composed of. The following definitions are due to Gregory [5] and others.

> *Definition*: An *input argument* of a goal, denoted here by mode '?', is an argument which is either instantiated when the goal is called, or it is a variable. However, during head matching or guard evaluation, when the input argument is a variable, it can never be instantiated by the head-matching process. Basically, only input matching is performed. □

> *Definition*: An *output argument*, denoted here by mode '^', is an argument which is always unbound in the caller, and whose value is bound by the called goal. □

In the following, arguments of a predicate which have been declared as input or output will be named *input positions* or *output positions*, respectively. Furthermore, the goal(s) which instantiate a variable are called the *producer(s)* of this variable, while the goal(s) which use, but not instantiate, a variable are called the *consumer(s)* of that variable.

There are some flaws, however, in the simple mode system. Primarily, the modes concern only top-level functors. For example, consider the following program:

```
mode f(?,^).
f([X|Xs], Z) :- true | g(X),h(Xs,Z).
```

The mode declaration of the first argument does not convey anything about the value of X when f/2 is called: it only specifies that the first argument of the caller must be a (non-empty) list. Furthermore, specifying an argument as input does not prohibit that the argument is bound to a non-variable term in the body, as shown below:

```
mode f(?).
f(X) :- true | X=[].
```

The above is a legal Parlog program, and when called with the query "?- f(X)," X will be bound to [], which contradicts the intuitive notion of input argument.

The notions of input and output modes, as introduced by Ueda [13], are somewhat more consistent in this regard. Instead of simply specifying the top-level arguments, Ueda's method attempts to infer the modes of *all* variables and structures occurring in the clause. Ueda distinguishes terms by specifying the *path* which must be taken to get to a specific term, e.g., the path to get to variable X in predicate f/2 above is specified as $<f,1><.,1>$,[1] i.e., the head of the first argument of f/2.

The *value* of a path is then defined as the first (principal) functor following this path when the term at the end of the path is instantiated. In our previous example, if X is instantiated to a(0,0), then the value of the path $<f,1><.,1>$ is a/2. We now give definitions of input and output path modes due to Ueda [12].

> *Definition*: If a path is defined as *input*, the value of this path *may* (but need not) be bound by the caller, and *will never* be bound by the callee.
> ☐

> *Definition*: If a path is defined as *output*, the value of this path *will never* be bound by the caller, and *may* (but need not) be bound by the callee. ☐

Intuitively, this implies that an input path will not be (further) instantiated, while an output path implies that a process can never suspend on the value of the path.

We now define the notions of a *sequential module* and a *sequential basic block*. In this paper we use the term *module* to describe a set of self-contained predicates, which is entered (called) through a single entry-point (the *module entry-point*). In this context, "self-contained" means that no predicate inside the module calls any predicates outside the module, nor does any predicate outside the module call any predicate inside the module, apart from the visible module entry-point. Extending this notion, a complete program can be viewed as a module with the top-level query as the module entry-point. If the goals inside a module are executed sequentially, the module is called a *sequential module*, for obvious reasons.

A *basic block* is defined simply as a conjunction of body goals. Note that this definition is more general than the standard definition for machine instructions [1],

---

[1]For lists, the functor ./2 is used, so $<.,1>$ is the head of a list, while $<.,2>$ is the tail of a list.

although the intention is similar. If these body goals are executed sequentially, the block is called a *sequential basic block*. Grouping together these body goals can be done in several ways. First, the goals can be folded together (either by the user or as a source-level transformation by the compiler) into another goal, which is specifically marked as "sequential." A second possibility for grouping a set of body goals is using an operator such as the sequential conjunction operator '&' from Parlog. In the third option for marking a sequential basic block, no explicit transformations or annotations are made, but rather the compiler detects the presence of a sequential basic block, and implicitly transforms the block into an internal representation.

Another important notion to be defined in this context is that of *suspension*. The execution of a committed-choice goal will *suspend* whenever an input variable is not sufficiently instantiated for the goal to commit. This situation changes when another process further instantiates the variable, allowing the suspended process to resume. If the variable is never instantiated, *deadlock* will arise, which is defined as a situation where one or more suspended processes exist, but no runnable processes exist. It is important to define suspension with respect to both modules and basic blocks:

> *Definition*: A process (or a set of processes) is suspended *externally*, when the cause of the suspension lies outside the suspended module. □

Intuitively, external suspension means that a process, external to the module, which produces data for the module, has run of out of data, and the module must wait for this producer to produce more data. When a process is suspended on more than one variable, with at least one of the causes of suspension outside the module, this is also called external suspension.

> *Definition*: A process (or a set of processes) is suspended *internally*, when the cause of the suspension lies inside the suspended module. □

Intuitively, internal suspension means that some variable which is local to the module or basic block is not sufficiently instantiated to allow the process to continue. If a process is suspended on more than one variable, suspension is called internal if and only if all causes are inside the suspended module. With these definitions, the following theorem is easy to derive:

> **Theorem 1** *If the goals inside a module or basic block are executed sequentially, then internal suspension will always cause deadlock for the top-level call of the module entry-point.* □

The proof is simple: if suspension occurs, the module has to wait for some other process to produce more data. However, this process is located inside the module, and will never be executed because the goals inside the module are executed sequentially. Therefore the call to this module deadlocks. Although this theorem may be obvious, its importance is that it clearly shows that internal suspension must be prevented for sequential basic blocks and modules. In the next section we begin to develop conditions under which this is true.

3   Directional Programs

One of the first attempts towards a parallel logic language which could be implemented efficiently on a distributed, loosely-coupled architecture was the Relational Language [2], the direct precursor of Parlog [5]. Apart from the mode system, which is also present in Parlog, the Relational Language featured *strong* arguments.

> *Definition*:   A *strong argument* of a procedure invocation, if it is in an output position, is a term that is completely constructed by a single body goal in that procedure's definition, without any contribution from other goals in this conjunction. The constructing goal is often called the *producer*. If a strong argument is in an input position, it is completely constructed by external goal(s), and no bindings are made through this occurrence.   □

Thus there can never be an output substitution for any variable occurring in a strong input argument position. This does not preclude the construction of terms containing unbound variables, but these variables can *never* be instantiated within the conjunction by a goal other than the producer. As an example, consider the following code segment:

```
f1(X)  :- X = g(0).
f2(X)  :- X = g(Y).
f3(X)  :- X = g(Y), Y = 0.
```

The arguments in both f1/1 and f2/1 are strong, as their values are completely constructed by a single body goal. Note that Y is not instantiated by another body goal in f2/1. The implication of strong variables is far reaching: no "back communication," i.e., the use of incomplete messages, is possible. In general, the full power of the logical variable is lost.

To retain the full power of the logical variable, *weak input arguments* are necessary. For example, argument X in f3/1 is *weak*, because its value is constructed by two body goals within the same clause. For output arguments, the distinction between weak and strong is irrelevant.

> *Definition*:   A *weak input argument* of a goal is one in which variables might be instantiated by the evaluation of the goal.   □

Weak input arguments were introduced in Parlog (and implicitly used in other committed-choice languages), because Parlog programs only specify the modes for top-level arguments, without considering subterms of these top-level arguments. Consider, for example, the following correct Parlog program:

```
mode f(?).
f(g(X)) :- X=[].
```

Although the weak argument of f/1 is (correctly) defined as input, because it is a structured term g/1, the variable X inside this argument will be instantiated when f/1 is called. Using the definition of strong arguments, a *directional program* can be defined [5]:

> *Definition*:   A *directional logic program* is a program in which all arguments (of all clauses of all procedures) are strong.   □

In a directional program, the mode declarations indicate which body goal constructs the value of a variable: the goal in which the variable appears in an output argument position. Gregory [5] uses directionality only to check for the compile-time safety of guards, something which we do not discuss here. However, the directionality mechanism is more powerful — we show, in Theorem 2, that it can be used to significantly lower the number of suspensions:

> **Theorem 2** *If a program is directional, and given a correct ordering of the body goals, no deadlock will occur, and the program can only suspend externally, i.e., on variables whose producer is the top-level query.*   □

It may be the case that more than one ordering exists satisfying this theorem; however, it is also possible that no such ordering exists, thus leading to internal suspension of a directional program. For example, consider the body goals f(A, B) and g(A, B), where f/2 is producer for A and g/2 is producer for B. In this case, the program is still directional, but there is no ordering of f/2 and g/2 satisfying Theorem 2. When body goals are executed in the "correct order," the number of suspensions is reduced because a producer of a variable is always executed before its consumer(s). As Section 3.2 illustrates, the requirement for a program to be directional (i.e., for all arguments to be strong), however, is too restrictive, and in the remainder of this paper we will describe an approach to ease this requirement, while retaining the full use of Theorem 2.

3.1 Program Directionality Check

A program is directional if all arguments are strong, i.e., for each variable there is no more than one goal that is able to instantiate this variable at any time. For Parlog, some programs are directional, whereas others, which use programming techniques such as incomplete messages, are not directional. To check for directionality, the entire program must be checked, including the query.

In a query, variables in output argument positions must be *distinct* variables, i.e., each variable may occur in no more than one output argument of a goal; this goal will then be the producer of this variable. To test whether a given program is directional, all clauses must be tested for the validity of the following rules due to Gregory [5]:

R1. A variable occurring in a head input position must not occur in output positions of goals in the body.

R2. Variables not occurring in head input positions must not occur in the output positions of more than one body goal.[2]

As is clear from these rules, the number of occurrences in input positions in body goals is of no relevance for program directionality.

To avoid internal suspension, we extend these rules with:

R3. For a variable occurring more than once in the body, the first "executed" occurrence[3] must be in an output position, thus later occurrences can only be in input positions.

---

[2]Note that such a variable may occur in one or more output positions in the head!

[3]Normally, assuming a left-to-right execution order, this is also the textually first occurring body goal.

```
:- sequential module qsort.          :- export q/2.
:- export q/3.
                                     mode q(?,?).
mode q(?,^,?).                       q([],R0-R) :- R0=R.
q([],R,R).                           q([X|L],R0-R) :-
q([X|L],R0,R) :-                         s(L,X,L1,L2),
    s(L,X,L1,L2),                        q(L1,R0-[X|R1]),
    q(L1,R0,[X|R1]),                     q(L2,R1-R).
    q(L2,R1,R).

mode s(?,?,^,^).
s([],_,[],[]).
s([X|Xs],A,S,[X|L1]) :- A>X | s(Xs,A,S,L1).
s([X|Xs],A,[X|S1],L) :- A=<X | s(Xs,A,S1,L).
            (a)                                  (b)
```

Figure 1: Quicksort Program in Parlog (a) with split D-list (b) with explicit D-list.

Now, by extending Theorem 2 to cover only modules, and defining "correct ordering" to be that ordering of body goals which adheres to rule R3 for directionality, the following theorem follows:

Theorem 3 *If, at compile-time, a sequential module can be proved to be directional, then only external suspension can occur with respect to that module.* □

In the rest of the program, other forms of suspension can occur, but the important point is that there can never be internal suspension in that module. If directionality can be forced or proved, the module can be compiled efficiently, as will be discussed in Section 6. Otherwise, compilation of the sequential module defaults to standard committed-choice compilation techniques (e.g., [3,6,7,10]).

3.2 Example of Directionality Check

In this section we gives two examples of the directionality check to show why the requirement of strong arguments is too restrictive. Consider the sequential module qsort, containing the quicksort function, in Figure 1a. In this program we use a split difference list: the second and third arguments of q/3 are the two parts of the difference list. A typical query to this program is: "?- q([4,2,1,3],Sorted,[])." with the answer binding: Sorted=[4,3,2,1].

With the modes given in Figure 1a and applying rules R1 and R2, it is easy to determine that the module is directional. As Gregory [5] points out, we can determine this because the input arguments are "strong." Consider, however, the version of the qsort module with a difference list of the form X-Y in Figure 1b, with the same definition of s/4. Here the query appears as: "?- q([4,2,1,3],Sorted-[])." with the same answer binding. The first clause of q/2 violates R1, so the directionality algorithm will qualify this program as non-directional, although in fact both programs function in the exact same manner. To overcome problems like this, making it possible to use the full power of sequential modules, another form of mode analysis is necessary.

4   Mode Analysis

A viable alternative to avoid the previously discussed pitfalls is the mode analysis described by Ueda, which automatically infers the modes of all arguments at the top-level *and* those inside structured top-level arguments [13]. Other options, which we do not consider in this paper, are available, such as abstract interpretation [8]).

4.1   Simplified Rules

The mode analysis described in this section reviews Ueda's technique. The mode analysis uses the notion of a *path* to denote a specific (textual) occurrence of a term, as described in Section 2. The mode of a path p, which is denoted as $m(p)$, is defined as either input or output (see Section 2). If possible, the modes of all paths must be inferred to find a safe goal ordering, which avoids internal suspension. The mode of a path can be found with the rules given in Figure 2 [12,13].

To better understand the modes, we now give the intuition for these rules. If a path leads to a non-variable in the clause, then the value of the path is already known, and it will not be instantiated by the callee, thus its mode is 'in.' If a variable occurs more than once in the head, it can be only used for equality checking before commitment. No bindings are allowed, thus again its mode is 'in'. Similarly, if a variable in the guard is used for checking (i.e, its mode is 'in'), then it is clear that value of the path to that variable is provided by the caller, so its mode is 'in.'

Because of the nature of unification, one of the arguments of =/2 will function as producer for a specific path, while the other argument functions as consumer. Note, however, that §2 does not require that for all possible paths p, the mode of an argument is the same. For example, given the unification $[1,X]=[Y,2]$, $m(<=,1><.,1>)=$in, while $m(<=,1><.,2>)=$out.

When a variable occurs more than once, with at least one occurrence in the body, the situation gets more complicated. Because paths to variables occurring more than once in the head all have the same mode (see §1b), it is correct (and simpler) to count only one occurrence of a variable in the head in rules §3 and §4.

The inversion in §3 can be intuitively explained by looking at an input path in a clause head. For that clause, the variable acts as a consumer of data (therefore its mode is input). However, within the clause the variable in the head acts as a producer for the body of the clause, thus inverting its mode within the clause. The opposite of this holds for an output path in the head.

The complexity of §4 can be explained intuitively by looking at the inversion of the modes discussed previously, combined with the fact that only one occurrence of a variable can be its actual producer. The problem with this last rule is that it causes non-binary constraints to occur.

§1. For some path p in a clause, $m(p)$ = in, if either

    (a) p leads to a non-variable in the head or body, or

    (b) p leads to a variable which occurs more than once in the head, or

    (c) p leads to a variable which also occurs in the guard at path p_h and $m(p_h)$ = in

§2. Two arguments of a unification body goal have opposite modes, for all possible p, or more formally: $\{\forall p \; m(<=, 1 > p) \neq m(<=, 2 > p)\}$.

§3. If there are exactly two "occurrences," we have two possibilities:

    (a) If both occurrences are in the body, the modes of their paths are inverted.

    (b) If there is one (or more) occurrence in the head and one in the body, the modes of their paths are the same.

§4. If there are more than two "occurrences" of a shared variable (i.e., at least two occurrences in the body), the situation is even more complex:

    (a) If the body contains more than two occurrences of the shared variable and the head has no occurrences, then one of the modes is 'out,' and the others are 'in.'[a]

    (b) If the head contains one (or more) occurrences of the shared variable (so the body has two or more occurrences), then the modes are as follows:

        i. If the mode of the head occurrence is 'in,' the modes of all body occurrences are 'in' as well.

        ii. If the mode of the head occurrence is 'out,' then *one* of the body occurrences is 'out,' and the other body occurrences are 'in.'

[a]This means that one of the occurrences is designated as the producer of this variable.

Figure 2: Proof Rules in Ueda's Mode Analysis

```
q([], R0,R) :- R0 =₁ R.
q([X|L],R0,R) :- s(L,X,L1,L2),q(L1,R0,[X|R1]),q(L2,R1,R).
```

1. q1(ε) = in   §1a

2. q3(ε) = in   §1a, 2nd body goal

3. q2(ε) = out
    a. ∀p q2(p) = m(<=₁,1>p)   §3b
    b. ∀p q3(p) = m(<=₁,2>p)   §3b
    c. ∀p q2(p) ≠ q3(p)   §2
    d. q2(ε) = out   "2"+c: sub p=ε

4. ∀p q1(<.,2>p) = s1(p)   §3b (on L)

5. ∀p q3(p) = q3(<.,2>p)
    a. ∀p q3(<.,2>p) ≠ q2(p)   §3a (on R1)
    b. ∀p q3(p) = q3(<.,2>p)   "3.c" + a

6. Three possibilities: §4b
    a. q1(<.,1>p) = in, s2(p) = in, q3(<.,1>p) = in
    b. q1(<.,1>p) = out, s2(p) = out, q3(<.,1>p) = in
    c. q1(<.,1>p) = out, s2(p) = in, q3(<.,1>p) = out

7. s3(ε) = out
    a. ∀p q1(p) ≠ s3(p)   §3a (on L1)
    b. s3(ε) = out   "1" + a

8. s4(ε) = out   see "7"

Figure 3: Mode Analysis Proof for Quicksort: q/3.

4.2 An Example of Mode Analysis

To explain the concept of modes and paths, and to understand the rules given above, it is best to start with an example. Figures 3 and 4 give the mode analysis for quicksort, shown in Figure 1. In these proofs, let $q_i(p) \equiv m(<q,i>p)$, and $s_i(p) \equiv m(<s,i>p)$, while '$=_k$' represents the kth instance of $=/2$ and 'ϵ' represents an empty path. Furthermore, each step in the proof is annotated with the rule used. Each mode relationship proved is called an *axiom*, e.g., there are eight axioms comprising the full mode definition for q/2. These axioms together give an idea how the flow of data within this procedure is, i.e., which arguments (and which variables within structures) are input, and which are output. This information is then useful for a compiler to make optimal use of its resources, such as memory and registers.

The most interesting point about this analysis is the sixth axiom in Figure 3. The analysis shows that three distinct modes of execution are possible for q/3, hinging on the use of shared variable X. Since X appears twice in the body of the second clause, the proof uses rule §4b. The three distinct modes depend on whether X is input by the clause head (first choice) or bound by a body goal (latter two choices). Given the mode analysis of s/4 in Figure 4, the second choice (b) is contradicted, since s2(ε)=in. Therefore only two choices remain.

The problem is that these two choices are both valid: essentially Ueda's analysis indicates that without further information (e.g., modes of the query), X may be generated by the third argument of q/3 and output through the first argument (c), or vice versa (a). To the programmer, whose intent may have been the standard use of quicksort (a), this result may seem odd. However, choice (c) is valid — the query "?- q([X],[3,2,1],[2,1])." will succeed with X=3. Although unlikely to appear in most programs, this query is valid, and should execute successfully!

This example shows that to safely execute this module sequentially, more information is needed about the mode of the first argument. One way of finding this mode is by looking at the context information: at the place(s) where the module is called. A second method is having the user explicitly specify modes to disambiguate such cases. For example, to indicate that an argument will be input throughout, i.e., for all subterms, the user can specify a *strong input argument mode*. However, mode analysis can fail as well, for example, when contradictory modes are derived. This implies that this piece of code cannot safely be considered as a sequential module, and standard compilation techniques must be used.

5 Goal Ordering

In this section we discuss how the mode information is used to order body goals within a clause to ensure safe sequential execution. Recall that in Section 3.1 we gave a directionality rule, R3, which ensured that internal suspension was impossible in a sequential module. The rule states that for a variable occurring more than once in the body, the first executed occurrence must be in an output position, thus later occurrences can be in input positions only. The basic idea is to find an ordering that does not contradict this rule, using the axioms derived by the mode analysis. We now present an algorithm for doing this.

The first point to consider is that not all the mode axioms that fully describe a procedure are needed here, nor do we need the axioms in their full generality. Certain axioms, which we call *recursive axioms*, have a general form similar to axiom 5 of q/3: $\forall p\ q3(p)=q3(<.,2>p)$. The meaning is that the mode of any third argument path is the same as the mode of the tail of that path. Intuitively, the procedure is recursing on the third argument, which is a list.

For the purposes of goal ordering, only the modes of variables appearing (syntactically) in the procedure definition are needed. Therefore all general paths p in recursive axioms can be instantiated to ϵ. For example, in the previous axiom, $q3(\epsilon) = q3(<.,2>)$. Combining this with axiom 2 in Figure 3 allows us to derive that $q3(<.,2>)=in$. We call this process of instantiating general mode axioms into less general axioms, *recursive grounding*. As another example, combining axiom 4 in Figure 3 with axiom 1 in Figure 4 gives $q1(<.,2>)=in$.

After recursive grounding, we are left with two possible sets of modes for procedure

```
s([], _,S,L) :- S =₁ [], L =₂ [].
s([X|Xs],A,S,L) :- A>X | L =₃ [X|L1], s(Xs,A,S,L1).
s([X|Xs],A,S,L) :- A=<X | S =₄ [X|S1], s(Xs,A,S1,L).
```

1.	s1(ε) = in	§1a
2.	s1(<.,1>) = in	§1c
3.	s2(ε) = in	§1c
4.	s3(ε) = out	
	a. m(<=₁,2>) = in	§1a
	b. m(<=₁,1>) = out	§2
	c. ∀p m(=₁,1>p) = s3(p)	§3b
	d. s3(ε) = out	c: sub p=ε
5.	s4(ε) = out	see "4"
6.	∀p s1(p) = s1(<.,2>p)	§3b
7.	∀p s4(p) = s4(<.,2>p)	
	a. ∀p s4(p) ≠ m(<=₃,2><.,2>p)	§3a (on L1)
	b. ∀p s4(p) = m(<=₃,1>p)	§3b (on L)
	c. ∀p s4(<.,2>p) = m(<=₃,1><.,2>p)	b: sub p=<.,2>
	d. m(<=₃,1>p) ≠ m(<=₃,2>p)	§2
	e. ∀p s4(p) = s4(<.,2>p)	a+c+d
8.	∀p s3(p) = s3(<.,2>p)	see "7"
9.	s4(<.,1>) = out	
	a. s1(<.,1>) = in	"2"
	b. ∀p s1(<.,1>p) = m(<=₃,2><.,1>p)	§3b
	c. m(<=₃,2><.,1>) = in	b: sub p=ε
	d. m(<=₃,1><.,1>) = out	§2
	e. s4(<.,1>) = out	"7.b"
10.	s3(<.,1>) = out	see "9"

Figure 4: Mode Analysis Proof for Quicksort: s/4.

q/3. The next step is to attempt to order the body goals in the second clause[4] so that the constraints implied by both sets of axioms (with respect to rule R3) are satisfied. The two sets of modes can be illustrated as follows:

```
q([X|L],R0,R)  :- s(L,X,L1,L2),  q(L1,R0,[X|R1]),  q(L2,R1,R).
q([?|?],  ^,?) :- s(?,?,  ^,  ^), q( ?,  ^,[?|  ?]), q( ?,  ^,?).
q([^|?],  ^,?) :- s(?,?,  ^,  ^), q( ?,  ^,[^|  ?]), q( ?,  ^,?).
```

For each set of modes, the ordering algorithm iterates through each variable occurring more than once in the body: X, L1, L2, and R1. For each, constraint(s) are created relating the goals containing that variable. For example, for the first set of modes, X induces no constraints (since both the first and second goals use X for input). Examination of L1, however, induces the constraint: $G1 < G2$. Each new constraint is checked for consistency with previously generated constraints. A contradiction is fatal: the clause cannot be ordered for sequential execution.

Continuing with this example, L2 induces $G1 < G3$ and R1 induces $G3 < G2$. So far, all these constraints are consistent. However, analyzing the second set of modes, we find that X induces $G2 < G1$. This alone causes the analysis to fail (and subsequent examination of L1 causes contradictions within the second set of modes itself). If we can derive, from the context information, that the mode of the head of the first argument is 'in' (as discussed in the previous section), then there is only one set of modes, and the algorithm terminates successfully with the order:

```
q([X|L],R0,R)  :- s(L,X,L1,L2),  q(L2,R1,R),  q(L1,R0,[X|R1]).
q([?|?],  ^,?) :- s(?,?,  ^,  ^), q( ?,  ^,?), q( ?,  ^,[?|  ?]).
```

6 Conclusions and Future Research

This paper presents a compile-time technique for determining if a set of procedures within a parallel program can be executed sequentially without causing deadlock. More specifically, the analysis and methods are described in the context of committed-choice parallel logic programming languages, such as FCP, FGHC, and Parlog. These concurrent languages have inherent fine-grain parallelism, so the task at hand is to throttle high-overhead parallelism, rather than to uncover more parallelism. We present a framework of sequential program modules and basic blocks that can be derived and guaranteed to be deadlock-free at compile time. This paper outlines a source-to-source code optimization that ensures that sequential execution can proceed smoothly. Thus "traditional" procedural language optimizations that have previously been discarded by those implementing committed-choice languages (e.g., [3,6,7,10]) can now be considered, such as continuation-based goal management and interprocedural register allocation.

Future research in this area includes two major targets. First, algorithms must be designed for the selection of sequential modules and basic blocks. Selection walks a fine line between making modules too large, thereby throttling too much parallelism, and making modules too small, thereby not increasing granularity enough to be effective. The second target of future research is to gain experience with the techniques by

---

[4] The first clause has only one goal, so it does not require ordering.

automating the mode analysis algorithm, and characterizing some benchmark programs. Automation of Ueda's method is an open research area, as is the characterization of what percentage of code within real programs can be successfully sequentialized.

Acknowledgements

M. Korsloot was supported by a grant from the Delft University of Technology. E. Tick was supported by an NSF Presidential Young Investigator Award. We are indebted to Kazunori Ueda for helping us understand the mode analysis.

References

[1] A. Aho, R. Sethi, and J. Ullman. *Compilers, Principles, Techniques, and Tools.* Addison-Wesley, Reading MA, 1985.

[2] K. L. Clark and S. Gregory. A Relational Language for Parallel Programming. In *Conference on Functional Programming Languages and Computer Architecture*, pages 171–178. ACM, Portsmouth NH, October 1981.

[3] J. A. Crammond. *Implementation of Committed-Choice Logic Languages on Shared-Memory Multiprocessors.* PhD thesis, Heriot-Watt University, Endinburgh, May 1988.

[4] S. K. Debray, N.-W. Lin, and M. Hermenegildo. Task Granularity Analysis in Logic Programs. In *SIGPLAN '90 Conference on Programming Language Design and Implementation*, pages 174–188, June 1990.

[5] S. Gregory. *Parallel Logic Programming in PARLOG: The Language and its Implementation.* Addison-Wesley Ltd., Wokingham, England, 1987.

[6] A. Harsat and R. Ginosar. CARMEL-2: A Second Generation VLSI Architecture for Flat Concurrent Prolog. In *International Conference on Fifth Generation Computer Systems*, pages 962–969, Tokyo, November 1988. ICOT.

[7] Y. Kimura and T. Chikayama. An Abstract KL1 Machine and its Instruction Set. In *International Symposium on Logic Programming*, pages 468–477. San Francisco, August 1987.

[8] C. S. Mellish. Abstract Interpretation of Prolog Programs. In *International Conference on Logic Programming*, number 225 in Lecture Notes in Computer Science, pages 463–475. Imperial College, Springer-Verlag, July 1986.

[9] E.Y. Shapiro, editor. *Concurrent Prolog: Collected Papers*, volume 1,2. MIT Press, Cambridge MA, 1987.

[10] S. Taylor. *Parallel Logic Programming Techniques.* Prentice Hall, Englewood Cliffs, NJ, 1989.

[11] E. Tick. Compile-Time Granularity Analysis of Parallel Logic Programming Languages. *New Generation Computing*, 7(2):325–337, January 1990.

[12] K. Ueda. personal communication, November 1990.

[13] K. Ueda and M. Morita. A New Implementation Technique for Flat GHC. In *International Conference on Logic Programming*, pages 3–17. Jerusalem, MIT Press, June 1990.

Author Index